Jakarta Struts Cookbook™

Bill Siggelkow

O'REILLY®

Beijing · Cambridge · Farnham · Köln · Paris · Sebastopol · Taipei · Tokyo

Jakarta Struts Cookbook™
by Bill Siggelkow

Published by O'Reilly Media, Inc., 1005 Gravenstein Highway North, Sebastopol, CA 95472.

O'Reilly books may be purchased for educational, business, or sales promotional use. Online editions are also available for most titles (*safari.oreilly.com*). For more information, contact our corporate/institutional sales department: (800) 998-9938 or *corporate@oreilly.com*.

Editor:	Brett McLaughlin
Production Editor:	Matt Hutchinson
Production Services:	GEX, Inc.
Cover Designer:	Ellie Volckhausen
Interior Designer:	David Futato

Printing History:

February 2005:   First Edition.

 This book uses RepKover,™ a durable and flexible lay-flat binding.

ISBN: 0-596-00771-X
[M]

Table of Contents

Preface

In just a few short years, Struts (now officially called *Apache* Struts) has grown from a simple idea hatched in Craig McClanahan's head into the most popular framework for building Java™-based web applications. There are other excellent Java-based web application frameworks available; many are newer than Struts, and most have benefited from lessons learned by the Struts users and developers. However, none of these frameworks offer the broad-range of features and functionality for which Struts is known.

Just as important, the Struts community—one of the largest in the world of open source development—actively supports fellow Struts users and drives Struts development. The *struts-user* mailing list often receives upwards of one hundred messages a day. Struts novices, experienced Struts users, and Struts committers are all active on this list. It has become an open, tolerant community in which the precept of knowledge sharing thrives in a congenial and refreshingly humorous environment. It's with that attitude that I have written this book.

As developers, we latch onto tools, patterns, and software that works for us. Once we find a certain way of solving a problem, we tend to stick with that solution. We are naturally wary of new approaches to the same problem. It goes back to the old saying, "If it ain't broke, don't fix it."

For a Struts developer, staying with the comfortable and familiar techniques will get you by, but you'll be missing out on many innovative, creative, and entertaining ways of working with Struts. My aim with this book is to take away some of that anxiety when it comes to trying a new way of solving what may be an old problem.

The topics covered in these pages include:

- Tools and techniques for developing a Struts application
- Configuring your Struts application
- Creating your user interface with the tag libraries
- Working with Struts actions and action forms

- Validating input and handling errors
- Integrating Struts with your business model
- Applying security to your application
- Internationalization
- Testing and debugging
- Using Tiles and other presentation approaches

Audience

You will find this book most useful if you have some experience with Struts. If this isn't the case, then you should first read *Programming Jakarta Struts* by Chuck Cavaness (O'Reilly).

Even if you consider yourself an advanced Struts user, you will find a great deal of useful information within these pages. This book covers the new features of Struts 1.2, as well as new ways of integrating Struts with emerging technologies, such as Java Server Faces and the Spring Framework. You will find that many of the solutions leverage Struts extensibility in ways that you may not have used or considered.

Knowledge of Java and JavaServer Pages technology is a prerequisite for any reader of this book. You will find it beneficial, though not required, to be familiar with the JSP (JavaServer Pages) Standard Tag Library (JSTL). JSTL allows you to write cleaner, more functional JSP pages than ever before.

Scope and Organization

Shortly after I started on the real meat of the recipes I ran into a dilemma. Do I focus on only those issues related directly to Struts? More importantly, should the Solutions only use technology available with Struts? I quickly realized that considering solutions that used Struts exclusively would be a disservice to the developer. Struts overlays and intersects with many other technologies from HTML to JSP to XML. I wanted the recipes to reflect this synergy as well.

Within the pages of this book you will find solutions that use tools and technologies not provided by Struts, such as the use of the JSTL. This ability to plug-and-play using external software tools and libraries demonstrates Struts's flexibility and robustness. If you prefer to use JSTL over the Struts tags, then do it! Struts integrates just fine with JSTL, and I present many recipes that help you along. If you need to display tabular data with sorting and paging, you can roll your own solution or use a third-party library. This book will show you how to use both approaches.

Almost all of the solutions, which use third-party libraries, leverage open source software. Open source software has really come of age in the last few years. Though open source solutions are traditionally linked with bleeding-edge dot-com'ers, it's been my experience that corporate IT shops are now seriously considering and using open source technology alongside traditional vendor offerings.

This environment empowers all developers. Through these freely available tools and libraries, you can easily set up—on your desktop computer no less—an environment capable of developing and testing enterprise-caliber J2EE applications. With the proliferation of high-speed Internet access, developing Java-based web applications has never been easier.

Sounds easy, right? If you're like me, you are overwhelmed with so many choices. It's hard to choose the right solution for the problem at hand. The recipes in this book help with this problem. I give you solutions that let you judge whether a particular tool or technique is well-suited to your situation. Instead of spending hours researching possible solutions, in 10 minutes you can solve your problem. Here's the breakdown, chapter by chapter:

Chapter 1, Getting Started: Enabling Struts Development

> This first chapter describes how to download Struts and deploy the sample applications. I'll show you what's involved in upgrading your application to the latest Struts Version. I will cover some advanced topics, presenting ways you can be more productive as a developer using tools like Ant and XDoclet.

Chapter 2, Configuring Struts Applications

> Chapter 2 presents recipes illustrating the myriad of ways you can configure, organize, initialize, and architect your Struts application to suit your needs. I will show you how to separate your development into manageable groups using multiple configuration files. You will see how to set up Struts plug-ins, modules, and message resources.

Chapter 3, User Interface

> Figuring out how to present data can be just as important as how to acquire data in the first place. This chapter delves into the world of the Struts tag libraries and focuses on creating robust pages that can adapt as the underlying model changes. Topics in this chapter include using indexed properties, incorporating the JSTL, working with date fields, and taking advantage of dynamically generated JavaScript.

Chapter 4, Tables, Sorting, and Grouping

> This chapter is fairly straightforward and focuses primarily on using HTML tables for display of tabular data.

Chapter 5, Processing Forms

> Struts uses action forms to move data from the view to the controller and back. Chapter 5 shows you how to be productive with action forms including the use of dynamic action forms. I'll look at some different ways of mapping action forms to business objects.

Chapter 6, Leveraging Actions

Struts actions represent the integration point between the view and the model. Actions hook into your applications business logic and drive functionality. In Chapter 6, you'll see how to get the most out of your actions. You'll learn how to take advantage of Struts pre-defined actions, simplifying and improving your application.

Chapter 7, Execution Control

This chapter addresses problems related to managing your application's life cycle and handling different navigation requirements. The solutions show you how to use Struts plug-ins, servlet context, and session listeners. The chapter covers creating wizard-style interfaces, preventing double-form submission, and handling file uploads.

Chapter 8, Input Validation

A good web application verifies that entered data is valid before it sends that data to the business layer. Chapter 8 shows you how you can build validation into your application using the Struts Validator. Even when your data is valid, your application may still need to handle unexpected errors.

Chapter 9, Exception and Error Handling

Chapter 9 shows you how you can handle errors and exceptional conditions in a predictable manner.

Chapter 10, Connecting to the Data

Struts doesn't provide the model for your application; rather, it provides hooks that allow you to integrate your model with the controller. I show you a number of popular ways that you can integrate Struts to the model in this chapter. In particular, I'll explore integrating Struts with the persistent frameworks like iBATIS and Hibernate. I'll show you some useful patterns for abstracting data access behind service interfaces. I'll show you how you can integrate Struts with the Spring inversion-of-control (IOC) framework.

Chapter 11, Security

Most web applications have some requirements for security. These can vary widely from simple password authentication to complex integration with back-end directory services. In this chapter, I consider those security issues that are particularly applicable at the web tier. I'll show you various techniques for securing your application from simple base Actions to container-managed security and beyond.

Chapter 12, Internationalization

From the outset, the ability to localize a web application for a particular spoken language and geographic region has been a core feature of Struts. In Chapter 12, I'll show you how to maximize those features to address problems related to supporting multiple languages.

Chapter 13, Testing and Debugging

If you can't test your application, you are bound to become overwhelmed with defects when you release your application to production. This chapter shows you a number of techniques for solving the tricky issues of testing and debugging J2EE applications. With the recipes in this chapter, you will be well-equipped to find defects before your application gets to production or the QA team.

Chapter 14, Tiles and Other Presentation Approaches

Struts was designed from the beginning with extensibility and customization as first-class features. This final chapter shows how you can leverage this ability with the presentation side of your application. This chapter shows you how to get started using Tiles. I'll investigate an alternative approach to layout-management using SiteMesh. This chapter closes with recipes that show you how to integrate Struts with alternative presentation approaches such as JavaServer Faces, Velocity, and XSLT.

It's not possible to cover every problem that you may encounter in development of a Struts application. Keep in mind that the solution is not necessarily meant to be taken in isolation. In fact, you may find that your problem is solved by combining several solutions together. If you still can't resolve your problem, please let me know. More importantly, take your problem to the *struts-user* mailing; the Struts community is always willing to help.

Assumptions This Book Makes

This book assumes that you have some experience with Struts. It's expected that you know how to build and deploy a J2EE web application. A servlet container like Tomcat or Resin is required to run the sample web applications. Full-blown J2EE application server like JBoss, Weblogic, and WebSphere will work fine though they are not required as none of the solutions utilize Enterprise JavaBeans™.

The majority of the sample applications were built and tested on a Windows XP machine running Tomcat 5.0.29. I primarily used Firefox (Version 1.0) as my browser.

Conventions Used in This Book

In addition to the normal typographical conventions of an O'Reilly book, Struts has a large number of confusing terms. I've reduced that confusion by adopting some programming conventions throughout the book.

Programming Conventions

Throughout the book, I use the following conventions regarding Struts actions:

action
> Refers to the concept of an action

Action
> Refers to the Java class

`action`
> Refers to the `<action>` element in an XML file

Java classes and interfaces are always written in constant width with the first character in upper case. When I refer to a particular method of a class, I use the convention of `ClassName.methodName( )`. This does not mean that the method is *static*; instead, it is just a convenient means of reference.

When XML, HTML, and JSP elements and tags are referenced in text, the angle braces are omitted and appear like `forward`, `td`, and `bean:write`. When I refer to a Struts configuration file, I use the canonical name, *struts-config.xml*, though you can give these files any name that you prefer. Similarly, the Validator and Tiles configuration files are referred the *validation.xml* and *tiles-defs.xml* canonical names.

Typographical Conventions

The following typographical conventions are used in this book:

Plain text
> Indicates menu titles, menu options, menu buttons, and keyboard accelerators (such as Alt and Ctrl).

Italic
> Indicates new terms, URLs, email addresses, filenames, file extensions, pathnames, directories, and Unix utilities.

`Constant width`
> Indicates commands, options, switches, variables, attributes, keys, functions, types, classes, namespaces, methods, modules, properties, parameters, values, objects, events, event handlers, XML tags, HTML tags, macros, the contents of files, and the output from commands.

`Constant width bold`
> Shows commands or other text that should be typed literally by the user.

`Constant width italic`
> Shows text that should be replaced with user-supplied values.

This icon signifies a tip, suggestion, or general note.

 This icon indicates a warning or caution.

Using Code Examples

This book is here to help you get your job done. In general, you may use the code in this book in your programs and documentation. You do not need to contact us for permission unless you're reproducing a significant portion of the code. For example, writing a program that uses several chunks of code from this book does not require permission. Selling or distributing a CD-ROM of examples from O'Reilly books *does* require permission. Answering a question by citing this book and quoting example code does not require permission. Incorporating a significant amount of example code from this book into your product's documentation *does* require permission.

We appreciate, but do not require, attribution. An attribution usually includes the title, author, publisher, and ISBN. For example: "*Jakarta Struts Cookbook* by Bill Siggelkow. Copyright 2005 O'Reilly Media, Inc., 0-596-00771-X."

If you feel your use of code examples falls outside fair use or the permission given above, feel free to contact us at *permissions@oreilly.com*.

Comments and Questions

Please address comments and questions concerning this book to the publisher:

O'Reilly Media, Inc.
1005 Gravenstein Highway North
Sebastopol, CA 95472
(800) 998-9938 (in the United States or Canada)
(707) 829-0515 (international or local)
(707) 829-0104 (fax)

O'Reilly maintains a web page for this book that lists errata, examples, and any additional information. You can access this page at:

http://www.oreilly.com/catalog/jakartastrutsckbk

To comment or ask technical questions about this book, send email to:

bookquestions@oreilly.com

For more information about O'Reilly books, conferences, Resource Centers, and the O'Reilly Network, see O'Reilly's web site at:

http://www.oreilly.com

Safari Enabled

 When you see a Safari® Enabled icon on the cover of your favorite technology book, that means the book is available online through the O'Reilly Network Safari Bookshelf.

Safari offers a solution that's better than e-books. It's a virtual library that lets you easily search thousands of top tech books, cut and paste code samples, download chapters, and find quick answers when you need the most accurate, current information. Try it for free at *http://safari.oreilly.com*.

Acknowledgments

Writing this book has been a demanding and rewarding experience. I have learned a great deal in the process and I am thankful to many of my friends, family, and peers. First, I want to thank the folks at O'Reilly and especially my editor, Brett McLaughlin. His patience and encouragement helped me make it through some worrisome times. Most of all, Brett emphasized quality above anything else.

I would like to thank my family, as well. As a part-time writer, finding time to write, research, and code was not always easy. I sincerely appreciate the sacrifices that my wife, Debbie, and my boys, Kyle and Cameron, made while I worked on the book. Their encouragement and patience was a blessing. I want to thank my brother, Ed, and my Mom and Dad. Mom, I know you may not know exactly what a "Strut" is, but thanks for always being interested.

This book would not have been possible without the prior work of Chuck Cavaness and Brian Keeton. Chuck's book *Programming Jakarta Struts* (O'Reilly), a staple of Struts literature, laid the groundwork for this book. Chuck and Brian also wrote the preliminary set of recipes for this book which really helped me get started.

Finally, big thanks go out to my technical editors: Ted Husted, James Mitchell, and James Holmes. Ted can rightly be called a Struts legend and I was honored to have him as a reviewer. He provided a historical perspective which helped me explain and understand the evolution of Struts. As far as James and James go, these fellows are not just my respected colleagues; they are my good friends. I appreciate their time, effort, and encouragement throughout the entire process. In particular, I want to thank James Mitchell for recommending me as a writer and helping out with the initial chapter outlines. I want to thank James Holmes for allowing me to contribute to his book, *Struts: The Complete Reference* (McGraw-Hill/Osborne).

Finally, this book would not have been possible without the Struts community of developers. Many of the recipes in this book are based on the common—and not so common—questions, answers, and discussions from the *struts-user* mailing list. I did my best to give credit where a particular solution was provided by a specific developer. However, I may have missed giving credit where it is due. Please accept my apologies where this has occurred, and let me know of any gross omissions.

I would like to thank Craig McClanahan for developing Struts and helping me with the Struts-Faces recipe. Jonathan Freeman and Stephanie Peretti supplanted my lack of graphic and Spanish-speaking skills. Niall Pemberton and Hubert Rabago provided excellent feedback on a number of recipes. I would like to thank Rick Reumann for the excellent tutorials on his "Struttin' with Struts" web site. Finally, thanks to my good friend, Anuj Soni, whose friendship, advice, and encouragement has been a blessing over the years.

Getting Started: Enabling Struts Development

1.0   Introduction

The popularity of the Struts framework has grown tremendously in the last year. Since the release of Struts 1.1 in June 2003, Struts has become one of the most popular frameworks for developing complex JSP-based web applications. Traffic on the Strut's user's mailing list is heavy, typically 70 messages a day.

Despite its popularity, figuring out how to get started developing with Struts is still a common topic of conversation. The recipes in this first chapter should help you jump-start your development with Struts.

Good commercial tools have been built around Struts, the primary focus here is on tools and frameworks that are open source and free (as in "free beer"). By focusing on freely available tools, developers should be more encouraged to experiment with these tools than if they had to pay to use them.

1.1   Downloading Struts

Problem

You want to start developing applications using Struts.

Solution

Download the Struts binary and source distributions from *http://struts.apache.org/ acquiring.html* and deploy the example applications to your web container.

Discussion

A common question among developers new to Struts is which release to use. Without question, any new Struts project should use the latest best available release. At the time this was written, Struts 1.2.4 (referred to in this book as Struts 1.2) had just gone GA (General Availability).

 For developers looking to gain experience with the latest and greatest Struts features, the Struts Nightly Build will provide a peek into Struts 1.3.

You will find it useful to have the binary and source distributions available. The binary distribution includes the Struts JARs and associated dependent JARs. The source distribution, on the other hand, contains the source code for the Struts framework itself, as well as the Java source for the Struts tag libraries. Just as important, the source distribution contains the Java source, deployment descriptors, HTML pages, and JSP pages for all of the supplied sample applications.

 The exact content of these distributions varies depending on whether you are getting the latest Release Build or the Struts Nightly Build.

The Struts 1.2 Release Build binary distribution includes a basic *README* file, an installation document, and release notes. The *lib* folder contains the Struts JAR file, as well as the dependent JAR files from the Jakarta Commons project. The *contrib* folder contains contributions to the Struts distribution that aren't considered part of the Struts core. In particular, this folder contains the JAR files and sample web applications for Struts-EL. Struts-EL allows you to use JSTL (JSP Standard Tag Library) style expression language in the Struts tags. It includes, by necessity, the JSTL tag libraries.

The Struts 1.2 Release Build source distribution contains the source code for the Struts framework, and the source and web resources for the sample applications. In addition, the *contrib* folder contains the source code for contributions made by the Struts community that are not, but may later become, part of the Struts core. Some contributions of particular interest include the following:

Struts-EL
  JSTL Expression language support for Struts tags

Struts-Faces
  A framework layer that supports integration between Struts application and Java Server Faces technology.

Scaffold
  A set of base and helper classes that assist in integrating your data layer (Model) with Struts.

Once you have downloaded the source and binary distributions, you will want to deploy the example applications included with Struts, as described in Recipe 1.2.

See Also

Recipe 1.2 describes how to deploy the Struts example applications included in the Struts distribution.

If you are completely new to Struts, you will want to first check out *Programming Jakarta Struts* by Chuck Cavaness (O'Reilly). Additional resources can be directly from the Struts home page at *http://struts.apache.org*.

1.2   Deploying the Struts Example Application

Problem

You want to deploy the Struts MailReader example application to Tomcat.

Solution

If you don't already have the Tomcat running on your box, you can download it from *http://jakarta.apache.org/tomcat*. This recipe assumes that you are using Tomcat 5. Set environment variables for Struts and Tomcat, copy the Struts example WAR file to Tomcat, and start Tomcat.

 If you are using Struts 1.2, the WAR file for the Struts example application has been changed from *struts-example.war* to *struts-mailreader.war*.

The commands for a Windows machine are shown here:

```
C:\>set STRUTS_HOME=c:\jakarta-struts-1.1

C:\>set CATALINA_HOME=c:\tomcat5

C:\>copy %STRUTS_HOME%\webapps\struts-example.war %CATALINA_HOME%\webapps
        1 file(s) copied.

C:\>%CATALINA_HOME%\bin\startup
Using CATALINA_BASE:   c:\tomcat5
Using CATALINA_HOME:   c:\tomcat5
Using CATALINA_TMPDIR: c:\tomcat5\temp
Using JAVA_HOME:       c:\j2sdk1.4.2
```

The last command shown, %CATALINA_HOME%\bin\startup, starts Tomcat. On Windows, you will see Tomcat startup in a separate terminal window. The output in this terminal window displays information about the applications deployed and the state of Tomcat:

```
Jun 22, 2004 12:23:34 AM org.apache.catalina.core.StandardHostDeployer install
INFO: Installing web application at context path /struts-example from URL file:c
```

```
:/tomcat5/webapps/struts-example
Jun 22, 2004 12:23:38 AM org.apache.struts.util.PropertyMessageResources <init>
INFO: Initializing, config='org.apache.struts.util.LocalStrings', returnNull=tru
e
Jun 22, 2004 12:23:38 AM org.apache.struts.util.PropertyMessageResources <init>
INFO: Initializing, config='org.apache.struts.action.ActionResources', returnNul
l=true
Jun 22, 2004 12:23:40 AM org.apache.struts.util.PropertyMessageResources <init>
INFO: Initializing, config='org.apache.struts.webapp.example.AlternateApplicatio
nResources', returnNull=true
Jun 22, 2004 12:23:40 AM org.apache.struts.util.PropertyMessageResources <init>
INFO: Initializing, config='org.apache.struts.webapp.example.ApplicationResource
s', returnNull=true
Jun 22, 2004 12:23:40 AM org.apache.struts.webapp.example.memory.MemoryDatabaseP
lugIn init
INFO: Initializing memory database plug in from '/WEB-INF/database.xml'
Jun 22, 2004 12:23:40 AM org.apache.struts.validator.ValidatorPlugIn initResourc
es
INFO: Loading validation rules file from '/WEB-INF/validator-rules.xml'
Jun 22, 2004 12:23:41 AM org.apache.struts.validator.ValidatorPlugIn initResourc
es
INFO: Loading validation rules file from '/WEB-INF/validation.xml'
...
Jun 22, 2004 12:23:44 AM org.apache.coyote.http11.Http11Protocol start
INFO: Starting Coyote HTTP/1.1 on port 80
Jun 22, 2004 12:23:45 AM org.apache.jk.common.ChannelSocket init
INFO: JK2: ajp13 listening on /0.0.0.0:8009
Jun 22, 2004 12:23:45 AM org.apache.jk.server.JkMain start
INFO: Jk running ID=0 time=20/50  config=c:\tomcat5\conf\jk2.properties
Jun 22, 2004 12:23:45 AM org.apache.catalina.startup.Catalina start
INFO: Server startup in 49852 ms
```

You can use this output to verify that the application deployed and that Tomcat successfully started and is running. In the output shown above, you can see that Tomcat deployed the *struts-example.war* file. In addition, the last line indicates that Tomcat is running and the length of time it took to start up.

On Unix/Linux, you would use similar commands:

```
$ export STRUTS_HOME=/usr/local/jakarta-struts-1.1

$ export CATALINA_HOME=/usr/local/tomcat5

$ cp $STRUTS_HOME/webapps/struts-example.war $CATALINA_HOME/webapps

$ $CATALINA_HOME/bin/startup.sh
Using CATALINA_BASE:   /usr/local/tomcat5
Using CATALINA_HOME:   /usr/local/tomcat5
Using CATALINA_TMPDIR: /usr/local/tomcat5/temp
Using JAVA_HOME:       /usr/local/j2sdk1.4.2
```

Tomcat starts up as a background process. You can monitor the output from Tomcat using the following:

```
$ tail -f $CATALINA_HOME/logs/catalina.out
```

Other than the different operating system file paths, the output will be identical to the output on Windows shown previously.

Navigate your browser to *http://localhost:8080/struts-example*. You should see the page shown in Figure 1-1.

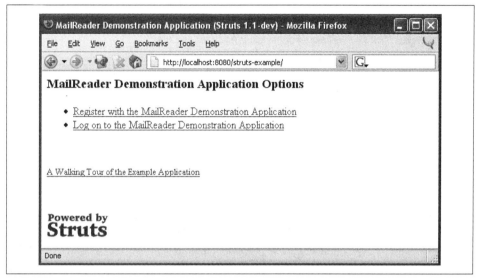

Figure 1-1. Struts example application

Discussion

Using and examining the *struts-example* web application is an excellent learning aid for Struts. Before you write your first Struts application, you should understand how the *struts-example* application works. The best way to do this is to deploy the application. Experiment with the interface and take the walking tour. You will want to follow along in the walking tour by using your text editor or IDE to view the source code.

You will need to download the Struts binary and source distributions to deploy the *struts-example*. The WAR files are included in the binary distribution. The source code is supplied in the source distribution.

In addition to the *struts-example* application, additional web applications demonstrate other Struts features as shown in Table 1-1.

Table 1-1. Struts 1.1 example applications

WAR file to deploy	Description
struts-blank.war	A boilerplate Struts application.
struts-documentation.war	Struts User's Guide and tag library reference documents.

Table 1-1. Struts 1.1 example applications (continued)

WAR file to deploy	Description
struts-example.war	The seminal Struts Mail Reader example. Demonstrates most of the basic core features and functions provided by Struts.
struts-exercise-taglib.war	An application that exercises the functionality of the Struts tag libraries.
struts-upload.war	Shows how to use Struts support for file uploads.
struts-validator.war	Demonstrates the use of the Validator with Struts.
tiles-documentation.war	Includes Tiles documentation, sample layouts and tutorials.

Struts 1.2 reorganized the example applications. Table 1-2 lists the web applications contained in the Struts 1.2 */webapps* directory.

Table 1-2. Struts 1.2 example applications

WAR file to deploy	Description
struts-blank.war	A boilerplate Struts application.
struts-documentation.war	Struts User's Guide and tag library reference documents.
struts-examples.war	Replaces the *struts-exercise-taglib.war*, *struts-upload.war*, and *struts-validator.war*. Combines the tag library, upload, and Validator examples into one application.
struts-mailreader.war	The seminal Struts Mail Reader example. Demonstrates most of the basic core features and functions provided by Struts.
tiles-documentation.war	Includes Tiles documentation, sample layouts and tutorials.

See Also

Recipe 1.1 discusses how to download Struts and the details different distributions that are available.

1.3   Migrating from Struts 1.0 to Struts 1.1

Problem

You need to migrate a Struts 1.0-based application to Struts 1.1.

Solution

Replace the Struts 1.0 JAR files, tag library descriptor (TLD) files, and XML DTD files with the corresponding files from Struts 1.1. If you have JSP pages that use the absolute URI from the Struts tag libraries, you'll need to change these. Recompile your application using the new libraries and address any compilation errors.

Finally, you'll want to modify your code that is using deprecated APIs to use the new Struts 1.1 APIs.

Discussion

While Struts 1.1 was a significant change to Struts 1.0, functionally speaking, applications based on Struts 1.0 can be migrated without much difficulty by replacing the Struts 1.0 JARs and TLDs with the corresponding files for Struts 1.1. You will need to change your use of the tag library URIs, as they have changed in Struts 1.1; this generally means changing your *web.xml* deployment descriptor. If you use the absolute URIs in your JSP pages, these values will need to be changed as well. Table 1-3 shows the changes to the tab library URIs.

Table 1-3. Struts tag library URIs

Struts 1.0.2 Taglib URI	Struts 1.1 Taglib URI
http://jakarta.apache.org/struts/tags-bean-1.0.2	*http://jakarta.apache.org/struts/tags-bean*
http://jakarta.apache.org/struts/tags-html-1.0.2	*http://jakarta.apache.org/struts/tags-html*
http://jakarta.apache.org/struts/tags-logic-1.0.2	*http://jakarta.apache.org/struts/tags-logic*
http://jakarta.apache.org/struts/tags-template-1.0.2	*http://jakarta.apache.org/struts/tags-template*
Not Available with Struts 1.0.2	*http://jakarta.apache.org/struts/tags-tiles*
Not Available with Struts 1.0.2	*http://jakarta.apache.org/struts/tags-nested*

The most significant changes in Struts 1.1 were the Struts ActionServlet (org.apache.action.ActionServlet) and the Struts Action class (org.apache.struts.Action). Struts 1.1 introduced the concept of the RequestProcessor (org.apache.struts.action.RequestProcessor) as well. The ActionServlet delegates request handling to the request processor. With Struts 1.1, you no longer have to extend the ActionServlet for customization; instead, you subclass the RequestProcessor. If a Struts 1.0–based application did not extend the ActionServlet, then no changes are required to use the RequestProcessor. If ActionServlet was subclassed, you should extend the RequestProcessor instead.

The other primary enhancement, as mentioned, is in the Struts Action. Struts 1.1 introduced a new method, execute( ), that subclasses should implement instead of the perform( ) method. Example 1-1 shows a simple Action that implements the perform( ) method.

Example 1-1. Struts 1.0 Action

```
package org.apache.struts.webapp.example;

import java.io.IOException;
import javax.servlet.*;
import javax.servlet.http.*;
import org.apache.struts.action.*;

public final class ExampleAction extends Action {
    public ActionForward perform(ActionMapping mapping,
                ActionForm form,
```

Example 1-1. Struts 1.0 Action (continued)

```
                HttpServletRequest request,
                HttpServletResponse response)
            throws IOException, ServletException {

        try {
            ExampleService service = new ExampleService( );
            Service.doService( );
        }
        catch (ServiceException ex) {
            throw new ServletException( ex );
        }
        return (mapping.findForward("success"));
    }
}
```

Example 1-2 is the same Action using Struts 1.1.

Example 1-2. Struts 1.1 Action

```
package org.apache.struts.webapp.example;

import java.io.IOException;
import javax.servlet.*;
import javax.servlet.http.*;
import org.apache.struts.action.*;

public final class ExampleAction extends Action {
    public ActionForward execute (ActionMapping mapping,
                ActionForm form,
                HttpServletRequest request,
                HttpServletResponse response)
            throws Exception {

            ExampleService service = new ExampleService( );
            Service.doService( );

            return (mapping.findForward("success"));
    }
}
```

As you can see, with the Struts 1.1–based Action, the exception handling no longer needs to be performed in the method. Struts 1.1 now supports exception handling as part of the framework as will be shown in Recipe 9.1.

You aren't required to change your Actions to use the execute( ) method, as Struts 1.1 still supports the perform( ) method; however, the method is deprecated.

 If you are migrating directly from Struts 1.0 to Struts 1.2, Struts 1.1 deprecations, such as the perform( ) method, have been formally removed from the Struts 1.2 API.

Though it will continue to function as is, I recommend convert your code to use the execute( ) method as soon as you can. Doing so will reduce the work to convert to Struts 1.2. More significantly, it will allow to you take advantage of the Struts 1.1 exception-handling capability.

See Also

Recipe 9.1 details exception processing with Struts 1.1.

1.4   Upgrading from Struts 1.1 to Struts 1.2

Problem

You want to upgrade an application based on Struts 1.1 to Struts 1.2.

Solution

1. Download the Struts 1.2 binary distribution from *http://struts.apache.org/ acquiring.html*.
2. Copy the JAR files and Tag Library Descriptor (TLD) files from the Struts *lib* folder to your application's *WEB-INF/lib* folder.
3. If you use absolute URIs for the `taglib` directives in your JSP pages, change these to use the new URIs shown in Table 1-4.

Table 1-4. Struts 1.1 and 1.2 Taglib URIs

Struts 1.1 Taglib URI	Struts 1.2.4 Taglib URI
http://jakarta.apache.org/struts/tags-bean	*http://struts.apache.org/tags-bean*
http://jakarta.apache.org/struts/tags-html	*http://struts.apache.org/tags-html*
http://jakarta.apache.org/struts/tags-logic	*http://struts.apache.org/tags-logic*
http://jakarta.apache.org/struts/tags-template	*http://struts.apache.org/tags-template*
http://jakarta.apache.org/struts/tags-tiles	*http://struts.apache.org/tags-tiles*
http://jakarta.apache.org/struts/tags-nested	*http://struts.apache.org/tags-nested*

4. Change the DOCTYPE declaration at the beginning of your *validation.xml* file(s) to the following:

```
<!DOCTYPE form-validation PUBLIC
"-//Apache Software Foundation//DTD Commons Validator Rules Configuration 1.1.3//
EN" "http://jakarta.apache.org/commons/dtds/validator_1_1_3.dtd">
```

5. Change the DOCTYPE declaration at the beginning of your *struts-config.xml* file(s) to the following:

```
<!DOCTYPE struts-config PUBLIC
"-//Apache Software Foundation//DTD Struts Configuration 1.2//EN" "http://struts.
apache.org/dtds/struts-config_1_2.dtd">
```

6. Replace your use of the `ActionError` class with the `ActionMessage` class.

7. Replace your use of the `ActionErrors` class with the `ActionMessages` class except within the `validate( )` method of any custom `ActionForms`.

8. Remove reliance on any `init-param` elements on the `ActionServlet` other than the `config` parameters. These parameters were deprecated in Struts 1.1 and are no longer supported in Struts 1.2. Instead, move these parameter values to your *struts-config.xml* file. Most of these parameters are replaced by attributes of the controller element.

9. Remove reliance on the `name`, `scope`, and `type` attributes of the `html:form` tag. These attributes were deprecated in Struts 1.1 and are no longer supported in Struts 1.2.

Discussion

The formal goal of Struts 1.2 was to remove deprecated methods and complete support for modules. Though Struts 1.2 doesn't make sweeping changes to the Struts core as Struts 1.1 did, it includes new features and enhancements that are worth the effort of upgrading. Many of these features are discussed throughout this book. Here are some of the most significant enhancements:

- New validwhen Validator rule for complex cross-field validations (Recipe 8.4)
- Wildcard action mappings that allow you to reuse action elements for multiple related URLs (Recipe 7.8)
- New prebuilt actions including a new `MappingDispatchAction` class and a locale-switching `LocaleAction` (Recipes 6.10 and 12.4)

For a new application, you should use Struts 1.2. If you have an existing Struts 1.1 application, you will find that Struts 1.2 introduces a number of new and useful features. In comparison to migrating from Struts 1.0 to Struts 1.1, upgrading to Struts 1.2 is less intrusive and requires less code changes.

See Also

The Struts wiki has additional details on this upgrade. The relevant wiki page can be found at *http://wiki.apache.org/struts/StrutsUpgradeNotes11to124*.

1.5   Converting JSP Applications to Struts

Problem

You want to convert an existing JSP-based web application to a Struts application.

Solution

Take a refactoring-style approach by applying Struts as you add new features to your application. As you increase your Struts knowledge, you can re-architect the existing code to use Struts. If no new development is planned for the application, refactor the existing JSPs a page at a time.

Discussion

The level of difficulty to migrate an existing JSP application depends greatly on the complexity and architectural soundness of the application. If the application uses a Model 1 architecture—that is, all logic is contained in the JSP page—it could be quite a challenge. You may find that you need to redesign the application from scratch to separate out the business logic from the presentation before you begin.

If you are new to Struts, then learn Struts on development of a new application instead of attempting to retrofit Struts to an application well into development. Struts is not a technology that can easily be "bolted on" late in the development process. However, some projects have altered their architectural underpinnings in midstream. If you are in this situation, steer the project plan so Struts is applied to new development first and preferably to features not on the critical path. Once you increase your Struts knowledge, it will be easier to convert existing code.

To make this more concrete, consider a simple example consisting of three JSP pages. The first page is the main welcome page that displays a link to the second page. The second page displays two form input fields. When the user submits the form, the result of adding the values is displayed on the third JSP page.

First, Example 1-3 shows the *index.jsp* page that provides a link to the input page.

Example 1-3. Linking to an input page

```
<%@ page contentType="text/html;charset=UTF-8" language="java" %>
<html>
    <head>
       <title>Simple Calculator</title>
    </head>
    <body>
       <a href="get_input.jsp">Calculator</a>
    </body>
</html>
```

Example 1-4 shows the *get_input.jsp* page that submits the entered values.

Example 1-4. Submitting data

```
<%@ page contentType="text/html;charset=UTF-8" language="java" %>
<html>
    <head>
```

Example 1-4. Submitting data (continued)

```
      <title>Add Two Numbers</title>
   </head>
   <body>
      <form action="display_result.jsp">
         Value 1: <input name="value1" type="text"/><br/>
         Value 2: <input name="value2" type="text"/>
         <p>
            <input type="submit"/>
         </p>
      </form>
   </body>
</html>
```

The page in Example 1-4 submits the form to a JSP page for displaying results. This target page (shown in Example 1-6) utilizes a JavaBean to hold the values received in the request from the form. Before looking at the target JSP, Example 1-5 shows the code for the JavaBean that will store this data.

Example 1-5. Simple JavaBean

```java
package com.oreilly.strutsckbk;

public class ValueHolder {
    private int value1;
    private int value2;

    public int getValue1() {
        return value1;
    }

    public void setValue1(int value1) {
        this.value1 = value1;
    }

    public int getValue2() {
        return value2;
    }

    public void setValue2(int value2) {
        this.value2 = value2;
    }
}
```

The *display_result.jsp* page, shown in Example 1-6, uses the JSP setProperty tag to populate the bean with the request values. The values are outputted using request-time expressions, and the sum is calculated using a scriptlet. Finally, this calculated sum is displayed.

Example 1-6. Displaying results

```
<%@ page contentType="text/html;charset=UTF-8" language="java" %>
<html>
   <head>
      <title>Add Two Numbers</title>
   </head>
   <body>
      <jsp:useBean
           id="valueHolder"
           class="com.oreilly.strutsckbk.ValueHolder">
         <jsp:setProperty name="valueHolder" property="*"/>
      </jsp:useBean>
      The sum of <%= valueHolder.getValue1() %> plus
      <%= valueHolder.getValue2() %> is:<p>
      <% int sum = valueHolder.getValue1() + valueHolder.getValue2(); %>
      <%= sum %>.<p>
      <a href="get_input.jsp">Perform another calculation</a>
   </body>
</html>
```

This application demonstrates some of the more undesirable approaches to using JSP. While the use of the JavaBean is laudable, the calculation is performed within the JSP using scriptlet. This results in a mixing of business logic with presentation, and scriptlets (embedded Java code) can lead to maintainability problems for JSP applications.

Formulating a strategy for converting this application to Struts is simple. Though this example may be trivial, the strategy followed will be applicable to more complex applications. Remove as much embedded Java code as possible from the JSP pages. Start with the scriptlet (<% %>); if possible, remove the request-time expressions (<%= %>). To accomplish this with the JSP, in Example 1-6, move the sum calculation into the JavaBean (from Example 1-5) by adding a method that calculates and returns the sum:

```
public int getSum() {
   return value1 + value2;
}
```

Now change the JSP to use the bean:write tag:

```
<%@ page contentType="text/html;charset=UTF-8" language="java" %>
<html>
   <head>
      <title>Add Two Numbers</title>
   </head>
   <body>
      <jsp:useBean
           id="valueHolder"
           class="com.oreilly.strutsckbk.ValueHolder">
         <jsp:setProperty name="valueHolder" property="*"/>
      </jsp:useBean>
      The sum of <bean:write name="valueHolder" property="value1"/> plus
```

```
        <bean:write name="valueHolder" property="value2"/> is:<p>
        <bean:write name="valueHolder" property="sum"/>.<p>
      <a href="get_input.jsp">Perform another calculation</a>
    </body>
  </html>
```

This is a significant improvement over the earlier version of this mini-application.

 Before continuing with more changes, now would be a good time to rebuild and redeploy the application to ensure it still works.

The next step, integrating the Struts controller into the mix, requires more work. First, create a Struts Action, like the one in Example 1-7, that is responsible for receiving the values from the form on the *get_input.jsp* page. The values are retrieved as request parameters which the Action marshals into a JavaBean. The bean instance is set as a servlet request attribute. The Action then forwards to the *display_result.jsp* page.

Example 1-7. Adding a Struts action

```
package com.oreilly.strutsckbk;

import javax.servlet.http.HttpServletRequest;
import javax.servlet.http.HttpServletResponse;

import org.apache.struts.action.Action;
import org.apache.struts.action.ActionForm;
import org.apache.struts.action.ActionForward;
import org.apache.struts.action.ActionMapping;

public final class ProcessInputAction extends Action {
    public ActionForward execute(ActionMapping mapping,
                ActionForm form,
                HttpServletRequest request,
                HttpServletResponse response)
            throws Exception {
        ValueHolder bean = new ValueHolder( );
        bean.setValue1( Integer.parseInt(
            request.getParameter("value1")) );
        bean.setValue2( Integer.parseInt(
            request.getParameter("value2")) );
        request.setAttribute( "valueHolder", bean );
        return (mapping.findForward("success"));
    }
}
```

Create an ActionMapping in your *struts-config.xml* file for the Action:

```
<!-- Process input data -->
<action    path="/processInput"
            type="com.oreilly.strutsckbk.ProcessInputAction">
  <forward name="success" path="/display_results.jsp"/>
</action>
```

To use this `Action`, change the target action for the form on the *get_input.jsp* page:

```
<form action="ProcessInput.do">
  Value 1: <input name="value1" type="text"/><br/>
  Value 2: <input name="value2" type="text"/>
  <p>
    <input type="submit"/>
  </p>
</form>
```

Once you have developed a new feature like this, linking to the new action from existing JSP pages is simple using the specified `ActionServlet` mapping (e.g., **.do*). You can link back from the Struts-based pages to your existing JSPs using the JSPs' URLs.

See Also

Recipe 6.1 describes how to create a base action for additional common behavior to all of your actions. Recipe 9.1 details how to leverage the declarative exception handling of Struts. Recipe 5.6 discusses ways of integrating existing JavaBeans with Struts action forms.

1.6 Managing Struts Configuration Files

Problem

You want to avoid typographical errors in the various Struts configuration files and make editing and maintenance of these files easier.

Solution

Use a tool like Struts Console for viewing and editing the Struts configuration files.

Discussion

One of the most common causes of errors in web applications is typographical mistakes. In general, most modern software applications—Struts included—rely on configuration files and deployment descriptors in some form of ASCII text, typically XML. Using a validating XML editor can help alleviate mistakes; however, it does not eliminate the mistyped path, form-bean name, or class name.

The Struts Console, available for download at *http://www.jamesholmes.com*, provides a graphical editor for the Struts (*struts-config.xml*), Validator (*validation.xml* and *validator-rules.xml*), and Tiles (*tiles-defs.xml*) configuration files. Instead of hand-editing these files, you use the Swing-based editor provided by Struts Console. In addition to reducing the typos, Struts Console gives you a birds-eye view of these files for easier browsing. You will find this feature invaluable when your configuration files start to get large.

Struts Console provides "smart" graphical editors for the XML-based configuration files used in Struts development. Figure 1-2 is the view of the *struts-config.xml* file for the `struts-example` application.

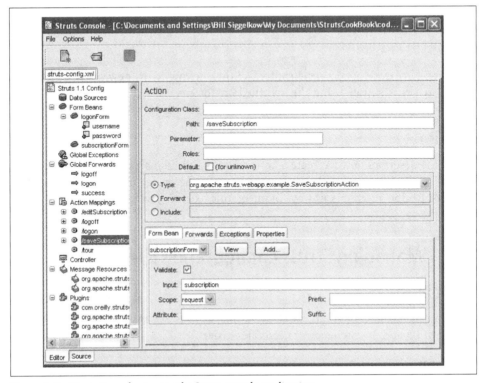

Figure 1-2. Struts Console viewing the Struts sample application

The Editor tab presents two panes. The left pane contains a tree view of the elements that make up the configuration file. The right pane contains a graphical editor window. Different editors are shown depending on the element selected in the tree view. In Figure 1-2, the */saveSubscription* action mapping is selected in the tree view and the Action editor displays all the details.

In a read-only window, the Source tab displays the XML source of the configuration file. As you make changes using the graphical editors, the source is updated as well. However, changes are not committed to disk until you save the file.

 Because the Struts Console parses and manages actual XML data, when the file is resaved, it won't contain any custom formatting or comments in the original file.

One aspect that sets Struts Console apart from a conventional XML editor is that the Struts console understands how the elements interrelate. For example, in Figure 1-2, a drop-down list of the available Form Beans can be displayed. Clicking the View button to the right of the Form Bean drop-down will display the selected Forms definition. The Form Bean editor will be displayed and the selected element in the left pane tree view will be updated to reflect the form bean being viewed.

As of this writing, Struts Console Version 4.4.1 supported creation and editing of the following files:

- Struts Configuration (for Struts 1.2, 1.1, and 1.0); e.g., *struts-config.xml*
- Tiles Configuration; e.g., *tiles-defs.xml*
- Validator Configuration (for Struts 1.1, and 1.0); e.g., *validator-rules.xml*, *validation.xml*
- JSP Tag Library Descriptor (TLD) (JSP Version 1.2, 1.1); e.g., *struts-html.tld*

In addition to its use as a standalone application, Struts Console can be plugged into most Java IDEs such as Eclipse, NetBeans, and IntelliJ IDEA.

The best recommendation before using any graphical editing tool is to become familiar with the structure and meaning of the elements with the Struts configuration files. Only then do you want to rely on using a tool that hides this structure from you. It's similar to when you learn a new programming language—before you start relying on an IDE to do the heavy lifting, you must learn how to use the language using simple text editors and the command line. Though graphical tools are useful and will save you debugging effort in the long run, you need to understand the basics of these files so you can diagnose configuration issues when they occur.

New Developers, New Console

One scenario in which a tool such as Struts Console shines is when a new developer is brought into a project where these configuration files are large. Using a tool like Struts Console will make the developer's life easier when digesting the interrelationships of the web application when compared to performing the same task using a simple text editor.

See Also

James Holmes's web site is where you get the Struts Console. His excellent site provides additional detail on the Struts Console. James is working on other tools, so visit him at *http://www.jamesholmes.com*.

Struts 1.2 includes a plug-in, the `ModuleConfigVerifier`, that is designed to catch errors in your Struts configuration file when your application initializes. For details on this plug-in, see *http://struts.apache.org/api/org/apache/struts/plugins/ModuleConfigVerifier.html*.

MyEclipse is a customized version of the Eclipse IDE. This excellent IDE provides an environment tailored to developing J2EE applications. At the time of this writing, the latest MyEclipse version was based on Eclipse 3.0, so it is quite up to date. MyEclipse is not free; however, the annual subscriptions are under $50 and well worth it if you are looking for a one-stop-shop IDE. Check it out at *http://www.myeclipse.com*.

Struts Studio is an ambitious undertaking bringing a commercial-grade graphical development to Struts developers. It's located at *http://www.exadel.com/products_strutsstudio.htm*.

1.7 Using Ant to Build and Deploy

Problem

You want to be able to build and deploy your Struts web application in a repeatable and portable manner.

Solution

Create an Ant (*http://ant.apache.org*) build script and use Ant (or your IDE's Ant integration) to compile, test, package, and deploy your application. Example 1-8 is a boilerplate Ant build file that can compile, build, and deploy a Struts application.

Example 1-8. Boilerplate Ant build file

```
<project name="jsc-ch01-r02" default="dist" basedir=".">
  <description>
      Jakarta Struts Cookbook - Ant Template
  </description>

  <!-- Enable access to environment variables -->
  <property environment="env"/>

  <!-- Set to use JDK 1.4 -->
  <property name="build.compiler" value="javac1.4"/>

  <!-- set global properties for this build -->
  <property name="src.dir" location="src"/>
  <property name="build.dir" location="build"/>
  <property name="dist.dir"  location="dist"/>
  <property name="server.dir" location="${env.CATALINA_HOME}"/>
  <property name="servlet.jar"
     location="${server.dir}/common/lib/servlet-api.jar"/>
  <property name="jsp.jar" location="${server.dir}/common/lib/jsp-api.jar"/>
  <property name="struts.dist.dir" location="c:/jakarta-struts-1.1/lib"/>

  <!-- Struts -->
  <fileset id="struts.lib.files" dir="${struts.dist.dir}">
      <include name="**/*.jar"/>
  </fileset>
```

Example 1-8. Boilerplate Ant build file (continued)

```
<path id="struts.classpath">
    <fileset refid="struts.lib.files"/>
</path>

<path id="project.class.path">
  <pathelement location="${servlet.jar}"/>
  <pathelement location="${jsp.jar}"/>
  <path refid="struts.classpath"/>
</path>

<!-- Deployment Properties -->
<property name="deploy.dir" location="${server.dir}/webapps"/>

<target name="clean"
      description="clean up" >
  <!-- Delete the ${build.dir} and ${dist.dir} directory trees -->
  <delete dir="${build.dir}"/>
  <delete dir="${dist.dir}"/>
</target>

<target name="init">
  <!-- Create the build directory structure used by compile -->
  <mkdir dir="${build.dir}"/>
</target>

<target name="compile" depends="init"
      description="compile the source " >
  <!-- Compile the java code from ${src.dir} into ${build.dir} -->
  <javac srcdir="${src.dir}" destdir="${build.dir}" debug="on">
    <classpath>
        <path refid="project.class.path"/>
    </classpath>
  </javac>

  <copy todir="${build.dir}">
    <fileset dir="${src.dir}">
      <include name="**/*.properties"/>
    </fileset>
  </copy>
</target>

<target name="dist" depends="compile"
      description="generate the distribution" >

  <!-- Create the distribution directory -->
  <mkdir dir="${dist.dir}"/>

  <!-- Copy the build dir to WEB-INF/classes -->
  <mkdir dir="web/WEB-INF/classes"/>

  <copy todir="web/WEB-INF/classes">
      <fileset dir="${build.dir}"/>
  </copy>
```

Example 1-8. Boilerplate Ant build file (continued)

```
  <!-- Put everything in ${build} into the war file -->
  <war destfile="${dist.dir}/${ant.project.name}.war"
      webxml="web/WEB-INF/web.xml">
    <fileset dir="web" excludes="**/web.xml"/>
      <webinf dir="web/WEB-INF">
        <include name="*.xml"/>
        <exclude name="web.xml"/>
      </webinf>
    <lib dir="web/WEB-INF/lib">
      <include name="${struts.dist.dir}/**/*.jar"/>
      <include name="${struts.dist.dir}/**/*.tld"/>
    </lib>
    <classes dir="build"/>
  </war>
</target>

<!-- Deploy the application by copying it to the deployment directory -->
<target name="deploy" depends="dist"
      description="deploy to server" >
    <unjar src="${dist.dir}/${ant.project.name}.war"
      dest="${deploy.dir}/${ant.project.name}"/>
</target>

</project>
```

Discussion

The build file displayed in the Solution can be used with minor modifications for most Struts-based web applications. You should change the value for the name attribute of the project element to the name of your application. This project name will be used as the name of the WAR file that's created, as well as the name of the folder to which the application will be deployed. In addition, you should set the struts.dist.dir property to the *lib* directory for your particular installation of the Struts distribution.

An Ant-based build will allow you to perform various development tasks:

- Retrieving your latest code from a source control system (e.g., CVS)
- Packaging your Struts application into a WAR file
- Running unit tests against your application
- Generating code and configuration files utilizing XDoclet from Ant
- Deploying your Struts application to your application server
- Precompiling your JSP files to detect translation errors

By using a build script to create the WAR file, you can structure the physical location of your code as well as the Struts distribution however you see fit. Then you can use the Ant script to pull it all together.

See Also

The main web site for Ant can be found at *http://ant.apache.org*. Also, *Ant: The Definitive Guide* by Jesse E. Tilly and Eric M. Burke (O'Reilly) is a great reference to use when working with Ant. Recipe 1.8 shows the use of the XDoclet tool for the generation of Struts-related files.

1.8 Generating Struts Configuration Files Using XDoclet

Problem

When you make changes to or create a new `Action` or `ActionForm`, you have to make the corresponding changes to Struts configuration files.

Solution

Use the XDoclet tool, in conjunction with Ant, to process annotations in your Java code for automatic generation of the *struts-config.xml* file.

Discussion

Modern software applications are commonly composed of executable code as well as text configuration files. This approach makes it easier to port your application between environments and reduces the amount of code you have to change for different deployments. However, it adds an additional burden: keeping the code and the configuration files consistent with each other.

The XDoclet tool, originally developed for use in Enterprise JavaBean development, addresses this problem. With XDoclet, the developer places annotations, similar to JavaDoc tags, in the code that describes configuration attributes related to the code. At build time, you employ custom Ant tasks that use XDoclet to process these tags and generate the corresponding XML configuration files.

For Struts, XDoclet can generate the following elements for the *struts-config.xml* file:

- `action` elements
- `form-bean` elements

In addition, XDoclet can create the field-level Struts Validator configuration, typically found in the *validation.xml* file. Finally, if you are mapping properties of EJB Entity Beans to Struts `ActionForms`, XDoclet can generate the `ActionForm` Java source code.

XDoclet can be downloaded from *http://xdoclet.sourceforge.net*. Follow the installation instructions provided to install it. You will need to have Ant installed as well.

First, you will need to add a task to your Ant build script to call the XDoclet tasks. Example 1-9 shows an Ant target that can generate the *struts-config.xml* file for the *struts-example* web application.

Example 1-9. Webdoclet Ant target

```
<target name="webdoclet" depends="init">
  <taskdef
      name="webdoclet"
      classname="xdoclet.modules.web.WebDocletTask"
      classpathref="project.class.path"/>
  <webdoclet
      mergedir="${merge.dir}"
      destdir="${generated.xml.dir}"
      excludedtags="@version,@author"
      force="${xdoclet.force}">
    <fileset dir="${src.dir}">
      <exclude name="**/*Registration*.java"/>
      <include name="**/*.java"/>
    </fileset>
    <strutsconfigxml
            version="1.1"/>
  </webdoclet>
</target>
```

This target calls the `webdoclet` custom Ant task, provided by XDoclet. This task can generate several web-related artifacts including the *web.xml* file, the *struts-config.xml* file, and the *validation.xml* file. For Struts applications, you probably won't need to generate the *web.xml* file; for Struts applications, this file doesn't change often. In Example 1-9, the `webdoclet` task is being used to generate the *struts-config.xml* file.

Not all elements of a *struts-config.xml* file can or should be based on annotated source code. Elements such as global forwards, global exception handlers, message resources, and plug-ins are not associated with a specific `Action` or `ActionForm` class. XDoclet handles this by letting you place this static configuration in files located in a special directory. At build time, XDoclet merges these files with elements generated in your source code. You use the `mergedir` attribute to specify the location of these static files. The `destdir` attribute specifies the directory where the generated files will be created. Generally, you want to create a separate directory for these files and copy the files into the appropriate directory for packaging and deployment after they are generated. The `excludedtags` attribute specifies JavaDoc tags that are to be excluded from processing by XDoclet.

It is common to exclude the @author and @version tags.

Finally, the force attribute forces XDoclet to generate new configuration files. If this attribute's value is false, new files are generated only if the corresponding annotated Java source files have changed.

The fileset element tells XDoclet which Java source files to process. You can use this element to indicate which source files contain XDoclet annotations. For example, the *struts-example* application uses two Struts configuration files: *struts-config.xml* and *struts-config-registration.xml*. As Example 1-9 shows, you can exclude the elements that go into the *struts-config-registration.xml* by setting the fileset element to exclude classes that contain the name "Registration".

The strutsconfigxml element instructs XDoclet to generate the *struts-config.xml* file. XDoclet generates a Struts Version 1.0–compliant file by default. Therefore, you must specify the version as "1.1" if you are using Struts 1.1. It is anticipated that XDoclet will provide support for Struts 1.2 via this attribute as well.

Once you have created this target in your build file, you can add annotations to your Action and ActionForm classes. For an ActionForm, XDoclet provides the @struts.form tag for generation of a form-bean element. The following code shows how this class-level tag is used in the SubscriptionForm of the *struts-example* application:

```
/**
 * Form bean for the user profile page...
 *
 * @struts.form
 *     name="subscriptionForm"
 */

public final class SubscriptionForm extends ActionForm  {
   ...
}
```

When the webdoclet target is executed, the following form-beans element will be created in the generated *struts-config.xml* file:

```
<!-- ========== Form Bean Definitions ================================= -->
<form-beans>
  <form-bean
    name="subscriptionForm"
    type="org.apache.struts.webapp.example.SubscriptionForm"
  />

  <!--
       If you have non XDoclet forms, define them in a file called
       struts-forms.xml and place it in your merge directory.
  -->
</form-beans>
```

XDoclet generates the form-bean element using the name you specified and creates the type attribute using the fully qualified class name of the ActionForm. This feature is one of the greatest benefits of XDoclet. Attributes of your classes, such as class names, packages, and method names are available to XDoclet just as they would be when you generate Javadocs for your application. XDoclet then uses these values where appropriate for the files being generated.

 If you change the class name or package of a class, XDoclet will generate the correct configuration element without any other intervention. While IDE refactoring tools can be used to handle these types of changes, using XDoclet yields a solution that can be integrated with your existing Ant build process.

You can use XDoclet to generate action elements from your Action classes. XDoclet uses the @struts.action custom tag to allow for specification of the action element. In addition, the @struts.action-forward tag can specify nested forward elements. Likewise, @struts.action-exception tag can be used to generate action-specific declarative exception handling. The *LoginAction.java* class of the *struts-example* application is shown below with the annotations required to generate the complete action element:

```
/**
 * Implementation of <strong>Action</strong> that validates a user logon.
 *
 * @struts.action
 *     path="/logon"
 *     name="logonForm"
 *     scope="session"
 *     input="logon"
 *
 * @struts.action-exception
 *     key="expired.password"
 *     type="org.apache.struts.webapp.example.ExpiredPasswordException"
 *     path="/changePassword.jsp"
 */
public final class LogonAction extends Action {
    ...
}
```

The syntax of the custom tags closely matches the syntax of the corresponding XML elements. If you have your *struts-config.xml* defined, a good approach for using XDoclet is to cut and paste the XML elements from the *struts-config.xml* file into the Action class. Make the changes necessary for XDoclet to recognize the tags. The following are the annotated class comments in the *LogoffAction.java* file that show how the @struts.action-forward tag is used:

```
/**
 * Implementation of <strong>Action</strong> that processes a
 * user logoff.
```

```
 *
 * @struts.action
 *    path="/logoff"
 *
 * @struts.action-forward
 *    name="success"
 *    path="/index.jsp"
 */

public final class LogoffAction extends Action {
    ...
}
```

Though XDoclet can go a long way to generating your *struts-config.xml* file, it can't do everything. Some action elements do not correspond to Action classes that you create. For example, the *struts-example* application includes the following action mapping:

```
<action path="/tour"
        forward="/tour.htm">
</action>
```

The *struts-config.xml* file may contain global forwards, global exceptions, a controller element, message resource elements, and plug-in elements. XDoclet doesn't generate these elements. However, it can merge files containing these elements with the generated file to produce a complete *struts-config.xml* file. Table 1-5 lists the files that XDoclet expects to find in the directory specified by the mergedir attribute when creating the *struts-config.xml* file.

Table 1-5. Files for merging into the generated struts-config.xml

Merge file	Used for
struts-data-sources.xml	An XML document containing the optional data-sources element
struts-forms.xml	An XML unparsed entity containing form-bean elements, for additional non-XDoclet forms
global-exceptions.xml	An XML document containing the optional global-exceptions element
global-forwards.xml	An XML document containing the optional global-forwards element
struts-actions.xml	An XML unparsed entity containing action elements, for additional non-XDoclet actions
struts-controller.xml	An XML document containing the optional controller element
struts-message-resources.xml	An XML unparsed entity containing any message-resources elements
struts-plugins.xml	An XML unparsed entity containing any plug-in elements

Most developers would agree that XDoclet doesn't do as much for Struts development as it does for EJB development. For example, if you are primarily using dynamic action forms declared in your *struts-config.xml*, then form-bean generation from ActionForm classes doesn't buy you anything. However, if you have a large application with lots of action elements and your application uses Ant, then XDoclet is certainly worth considering. XDoclet also supports generation of other types of configuration documents such as Hibernate mappings.

See Also

Recipe 1.7 provides a boilerplate Ant build script to which you can add the XDoclet targets.

Complete information for XDoclet can be found at *http://xdoclet.sourceforge.net*.

## CHAPTER 2

Configuring Struts Applications

2.0 Introduction

Struts provides a flexible framework. It can be used in many different ways and supports customizations and extensions at several levels. As a result of this flexibility, many developers have difficulty understanding how to configure Struts to suit their purposes. Struts can be configured using the web application's *web.xml* file as well as one or more Struts configuration files (*struts-config.xml*). In addition, the Struts Validator is configured through an additional set of XML files.

This chapter goes over some of the more common and not-so-common scenarios that utilize Struts configurability. The coverage includes creating plug-ins and is a simple, yet powerful mechanism that can be used to solve a number of problems. We will cover the use of multiple configuration files, for facilitating team development as well as structuring and partitioning the web application. Finally, we will review Struts' built-in support for extensibility and the use of custom configuration properties.

2.1 Using Plug-ins for Application Initialization

Problem

You want to load initial data into the application context when your application starts up.

Solution

Create a class that implements the org.apache.struts.action.PlugIn interface and specify the plug-in element in the *struts-config.xml*. The following XML fragment shows a plug-in declaration and a nested set-property element for setting a custom property:

```
<plug-in className="com.oreilly.strutsckbk.CustomPlugin" >
  <set-property property="customData"
```

```
                              value="Hello from the plugin"/>
    </plug-in>
```

Discussion

Struts provides a `PlugIn` interface you can use to create custom services that are initialized on application startup. The Java source for the `PlugIn` interface is shown in Example 2-1. (For clarity, the JavaDoc documentation has been removed from this listing.)

Example 2-1. The Struts PlugIn interface

```
package org.apache.struts.action;

import javax.servlet.ServletException;
import org.apache.struts.config.ModuleConfig;

public interface PlugIn {

    public void destroy();

    public void init(ActionServlet servlet, ModuleConfig config)
        throws ServletException;
}
```

To implement a plug-in, you only need to implement this interface and declare the plug-in implementation in the *struts-config.xml* file. The two methods that must be implemented, init( ) and destroy( ), are called during the lifecycle of the plug-in. Struts calls the init( ) method after it instantiates the plug-in on startup of the `ActionServlet`. Struts calls the destroy( ) method when the `ActionServlet` is destroyed, usually on shutdown of the application server. At first, this plug-in feature may seem simplistic and limited. However, by utilizing another feature of Struts, the set-property element, you can pass ad hoc information to the plug-in. This capability enhances the flexibility of these classes.

 The set-property element is supported by most all of the elements that define Struts entities such as form-bean, action-mapping, action, and plug-in. The set-property element takes two attributes: name and value. Struts calls the *setter* method for the property identified by the value of the name attribute, setting the property to the String value of the value attribute.

All set-property elements for a given plug-in will be processed prior to calling the plug-in's init( ) method. This allows the plug-in to use the value of the properties in the init( ) method.

If you are using multiple set-property elements for a plug-in, Struts can't guarantee the order in which they will be called. Each *setter* method should be independent of any other methods.

Struts passes references to the `ActionServlet` and the plug-in's `ModuleConfig` as arguments to the `init( )` method. The `ActionServlet` allows access to the `ServletContext` for storing application-scoped objects. The `ActionServlet` gives you access to more advanced container-managed J2EE components, such as data sources and message queues. The `ModuleConfig` gives you access to the Struts configuration of the module in which the plug-in is defined.

 Every Struts application has at least one module: the default module. If you are unfamiliar with modules, you can read more about them in Recipe 2.5.

To make this more concrete, consider a simple, yet relevant example. You want to define a plug-in that lets you to determine when your application was started, and how long it has been up and running. You can use the class shown in Example 2-2 to track and report on your application's uptime.

Example 2-2. Application uptime tracker object

```
package com.oreilly.strutsckbk;

import java.util.Date;

public class TimeTracker {

  private long startUpTimeMillis;
  private Date startedOn;

  public TimeTracker( ) {
    startUpTimeMillis = System.currentTimeMillis( );
    startedOn = new Date( );
  }

  public long getUptime( ) {
    return System.currentTimeMillis( ) - startUpTimeMillis;
  }

  public Date getStartedOn( ) {
    return startedOn;
  }
}
```

Create an implementation of the `PlugIn` interface, like the one shown in Example 2-3, that instantiates the `TimeTracker`. The plug-in stores the `TimeTracker` instance in the `ServletContext` using the value of a plug-in property. You can use this value to retrieve the `TimeTracker` instance from the servlet context. Though this value could have been hard-coded, using a property provides greater flexibility.

Example 2-3. Time tracker plugin

```java
package com.oreilly.strutsckbk;

import javax.servlet.ServletException;

import org.apache.struts.action.ActionServlet;
import org.apache.struts.action.PlugIn;
import org.apache.struts.config.ModuleConfig;

public class TimeTrackerPlugin implements PlugIn {

    private String contextKey;

    public void setContextKey(String key) {
        this.contextKey = key;
    }

    public void init(ActionServlet servlet, ModuleConfig conf)
            throws ServletException {
      servlet.getServletContext().setAttribute(contextKey, new TimeTracker());
    }

    public void destroy() {
    }
}
```

Now that you have the Java classes created for the plug-in, you can integrate them into your Struts application by adding the `plug-in` element to the *struts-config.xml* file:

```xml
<plug-in className="com.oreilly.strutsckbk.TimeTrackerPlugin">
    <set-property property="contextKey" value="timeTracker"/>
</plug-in>
```

The plug-in stores the time tracker object in the servlet context. You can access the `TimeTracker` to display information about your application's uptime as in the following JSP snippet:

```jsp
<h4>Continuously running since
    <bean:write name="timeTracker"
            property="startedOn"
              format="MM/dd/yyyy HH:mm"/> for
    <bean:write name="timeTracker"
            property="uptime"/> milliseconds!
</h4>
```

You can use a servlet to load initial data like a Struts plug-in. A servlet with the load-on-startup initialization parameter set to a low number, such as 1, will be loaded on application startup. The container will call the servlet's init( ) method after instantiating the servlet. But the Struts plug-in approach has several advantages. First, most

Struts applications don't require changes to the *web.xml* file once it's initially setup. Having to declare additional servlets in *web.xml* means an extra file to be maintained. Second, the `PlugIn` interface provides access to Struts-specific information if needed. Finally, since the lifecycle of the plug-in follows the lifecycle of the `ActionServlet`, you are guaranteed that the data will be available when needed by your Struts application.

See Also

Recipe 2.8 shows another usage of the set-property element. The Struts documentation on plug-ins can be found at *http://jakarta.apache.org/struts/userGuide/building_controller.html#plugin_classes*.

You can use a Servlet context listener to load initial data.

2.2   Eliminating Tag Library Declarations

Problem

You want to avoid having to add `taglib` elements to the *web.xml* file every time you want to use a new tag library.

Solution

Create a JSP file containing `taglib` directives that refer to the absolute URIs for the tag libraries you are using. Example 2-4 (*taglibs.inc.jsp*) shows a JSP file containing the `taglib` declarations for the Struts bean, `html`, and `logic` tag libraries as well as the JSTL core and formatting tag libraries.

Example 2-4. Common tag library declarations

```
<%@ page contentType="text/html;charset=UTF-8" language="java" %>
<%@ taglib uri="http://jakarta.apache.org/struts/tags-bean" prefix="bean" %>
<%@ taglib uri="http://jakarta.apache.org/struts/tags-html" prefix="html" %>
<%@ taglib uri="http://jakarta.apache.org/struts/tags-logic" prefix="logic" %>
<%@ taglib uri="http://java.sun.com/jstl/core" prefix="c" %>
<%@ taglib uri="http://java.sun.com/jstl/fmt" prefix="fmt" %>
```

Then include this file in all of your JSP pages using the `include` directive:

```
<!DOCTYPE HTML PUBLIC "-//W3C//DTD HTML 4.01 Transitional//EN">

<!-- start taglib -->
<%@ include file="/includes/taglibs.inc.jsp" %>
<!-- end taglib -->

<html:html>
  <body>
    ...
```

Since you are using the absolute URIs in the `taglib` directive, you aren't required to enter a corresponding `taglib` element in the application's *web.xml* file.

Discussion

If you are using a JSP 1.2/Servlet 2.3 compliant container, such as Tomcat 4.x or later, you can use an absolute URI in the `taglib` directive on the JSP page and you don't have to specify `taglib` elements in the *web.xml*.

Prior to the Servlet 2.3 specification, you were required to declare any JSP tag libraries you used in your applications *web.xml* deployment descriptor. The following snippet from a *web.xml* deployment descriptor shows the typical `taglib` descriptors used for a Struts application:

```
<!-- Struts Tag Library Descriptors -->
<taglib>
  <taglib-uri>/tags/struts-bean</taglib-uri>
  <taglib-location>/WEB-INF/struts-bean.tld</taglib-location>
</taglib>
<taglib>
  <taglib-uri>/tags/struts-html</taglib-uri>
  <taglib-location>/WEB-INF/struts-html.tld</taglib-location>
</taglib>
<taglib>
  <taglib-uri>/tags/struts-logic</taglib-uri>
  <taglib-location>/WEB-INF/struts-logic.tld</taglib-location>
</taglib>
<taglib>
  <taglib-uri>/tags/struts-nested</taglib-uri>
  <taglib-location>/WEB-INF/struts-nested.tld</taglib-location>
</taglib>
```

With the introduction of the Servlet 2.3 specification, a tag library's absolute URI is specified in that library's tag library descriptor (TLD) file. For example, here's this declaration from the *struts-bean.tld* file:

```
<?xml version="1.0" encoding="UTF-8"?>
<!DOCTYPE taglib PUBLIC "-//Sun Microsystems, Inc.//DTD JSP Tag Library 1.1//EN"
"http://java.sun.com/j2ee/dtds/web-jsptaglibrary_1_1.dtd">
<taglib>
  <tlibversion>1.0</tlibversion>
  <jspversion>1.1</jspversion>
  <shortname>bean</shortname>
  <uri>http://jakarta.apache.org/struts/tags-bean</uri>
```

Any JSP page that needs to use this tag library can reference it with the following page-level directive. The tag library doesn't need to be referenced in the *web.xml* file:

```
<%@ taglib
      uri="http://jakarta.apache.org/struts/tags-bean"
      prefix="bean" %>
```

If you use the same tag libraries throughout your application, you can use the approach shown in the Solution, which is creating an include file that contains all your needed `taglib` directives. No significant performance hit occurs if you refer to tag libraries that aren't needed, so you can safely include this file on every JSP page. If a URI changes, you will only need to change the one include file instead of every JSP.

Table 2-1 shows the complete list of tag library absolute URIs for Versions 1.1 and 1.2 of Struts.

Table 2-1. Struts tag library URIs

Tag library	Struts 1.1 URI	Struts 1.2 URI
struts-bean	http://jakarta.apache.org/struts/tags-bean	http://struts.apache.org/tags-bean
struts-html	http://jakarta.apache.org/struts/tags-html	http://struts.apache.org/tags-html
struts-logic	http://jakarta.apache.org/struts/tags-logic	http://struts.apache.org/tags-logic
struts-nested	http://jakarta.apache.org/struts/tags-nested	http://struts.apache.org/tags-nested
struts-template	http://jakarta.apache.org/struts/tags-template	No longer included with Struts; replaced by Tiles
struts-tiles	http://jakarta.apache.org/struts/tags-tiles	http://struts.apache.org/tags-tiles
struts-bean-el	http://jakarta.apache.org/struts/tags-bean-el	http://struts.apache.org/tags-bean-el
struts-html-el	http://jakarta.apache.org/struts/tags-html-el	http://struts.apache.org/tags-html-el
struts-logic-el	http://jakarta.apache.org/struts/tags-logic-el	http://struts.apache.org/tags-logic-el

Some developers (like me) enjoy using the absolute URIs, others still prefer to make the declarations in the *web.xml*. They make the point that using the latter approach ensures that your application code is shielded from underlying changes to the tag libraries. If a URI changes, you only need to change the *web.xml* file which is a deployment descriptor. You don't have to make changes to any JSP pages, even included JSP fragments. This argument is valid and has merit. In the end, it primarily comes down to personal preference.

See Also

The JavaServer Pages specification has some fairly complicated rules that it follows to resolve tag library URIs. Complete details can be found in the JSP specifications which can be downloaded from *http://java.sun.com/jsp*. Recipe 3.1 shows how to use the JSP Standard Tag Library (JSTL) tags within your Struts application.

2.3   Using Constants on JSPs

Problem

Without resorting to scriptlets, you want to use application constants—public static fields defined in Java classes—on a JSP page.

Solution

Use the bind tag provided by the Jakarta Taglibs *unstandard* tag library to create a JSTL variable containing the value of the constant field:

```
<%@ taglib uri="http://jakarta.apache.org/taglibs/unstandard-1.0" prefix="un" %>
<un:bind var="constantValue"
         type="com.foo.MyClass"
         field="SOME_CONSTANT"/>
<bean:write name="constantValue"/>
```

Discussion

A lot of teams put hard work into avoiding hard-coded String literals in their Java classes by using public static fields (constants). Unfortunately, neither Struts nor JSP provide a means to access these constants from a JSP page without resorting to JSP scriptlet like the following:

```
<%= com.foo.MyClass.SOME_CONSTANT %>
```

However, many development teams ban, or at least frown on scriptlet use on JSP pages.

Scriptlets (<%...%>) and runtime expressions (<%=...%>) place Java code directly onto a JSP page. They are not inherently evil, but they can lead your development down a slippery slope by turning your JSP pages into a tangled brittle mass of intermixed HTML, JSP, and Java code. Find solutions that don't require you to use scriptlets. You'll find—particularly with the introduction of JSTL—that you can always find a way around the dreaded scriptlet.

The Solution provides a way around this quandary through the use of a custom JSP tag, the un:bind tag. This tag is part of the *unstandard* tag library, part of the Jakarta Taglibs distribution. The *unstandard* tag library contains custom JSP tags that have been or are being considered for use in the *standard* tab library. The *standard* tag library is the Jakarta Taglibs implementation of the JSTL specification.

The *unstandard* tag library can be downloaded from *http://cvs.apache.org/builds/ jakarta-taglibs-sandbox/nightly/projects/unstandard/*. To use the library, copy the *unstandard.jar* and *unstandard.tld* files into your web applications *WEB-INF/lib* directory.

The un:bind tag provides a means for creating a JSP page context variable, which references a field of any Java class. The fields can be instance variables or static variables. Most well-designed Java classes don't expose instance variables as public fields, yet many expose static variables as public fields.

You can put the Solution to work by creating a simple JSP page that uses some of the static fields provided by Struts. Since Struts 1.1, the constants used by Struts are kept in the class `org.apache.struts.Globals`. The values of these constants specify the key values under which various Struts-related entities are stored in the request, session, or application context. The JSP page in Example 2-5 uses the `un:bind` tag to show one of these values.

Example 2-5. Using bind to access Struts globals

```
<%@ page contentType="text/html;charset=UTF-8" language="java" %>
<%@ taglib uri="http://jakarta.apache.org/taglibs/unstandard-1.0" prefix="un" %>
<%@ taglib uri="http://jakarta.apache.org/struts/tags-bean" prefix="bean" %>
<%@ taglib uri="http://java.sun.com/jstl/core" prefix="c" %>
<html>
<head>
  <title>Struts Cookbook - Chapter 4 : Using Bind</title>
</head>
<body>
  <un:bind var="servletKey"
           type="org.apache.struts.Globals"
           field="SERVLET_KEY"/>
  <p>
  Field name: SERVLET_KEY<br />
  Field value: <bean:write name="servletKey"/>< br />
  Attribute Value: <c:out value="${applicationScope[servletKey]}"/>< br />
  </p>
</body>
</html>
```

This page uses `un:bind` to retrieve the value of the `SERVLET_KEY` field from the Struts Globals class. The value of the `SERVLET_KEY` field is used as the servlet context attributes key under which the mapping (e.g. */action/** or **.do*) defined for the Struts controller servlet is stored.

The `un:bind` tag is good to use when you need to access constants on an ad hoc basis. However, it is fairly verbose since you need to use the `un:bind` tag first to create the variable, and then the `bean:write` or `c:out` tag to render the value. Imagine the size of a JSP page showing all of the constants from the Globals class—there are 17 constants in all! Many applications rely heavily on constants and may have several classes, each containing dozens of these fields. Requiring the use of a separate tag for every single use of a constant can be cumbersome.

You can use an alternative solution, albeit one requiring some additional Java coding, by binding the constants into a `Map` property of a JavaBean. You store the bean in the servlet context. You can then access the values directly using the `bean:write` and `c:out` tags. The `Constants` class in Example 2-6 defines a JavaBean containing a map of the constants from the Struts Globals class. The `ConstantsPlugin` in Example 2-7 loads an instance of `Constants` into the servlet context.

Example 2-6. JavaBean holding constants from Struts Globals

```
package com.oreilly.strutsckbk.ch04;

import java.util.HashMap;
import java.util.Map;

import org.apache.struts.Globals;

public class Constants {
    private Map strutsGlobals;

    public Constants( ) {
        strutsGlobals = new HashMap( );
        strutsGlobals.put( "ACTION_SERVLET_KEY",
                        Globals.ACTION_SERVLET_KEY );
        strutsGlobals.put( "SERVLET_KEY", Globals.SERVLET_KEY );
    }

    public Map getStrutsGlobals( ) {
        return strutsGlobals;
    }
    public void setStrutsGlobals(Map strutsGlobals) {
        this.strutsGlobals = strutsGlobals;
    }
}
```

Example 2-7. Plug-in that loads Constants into the servlet context

```
package com.oreilly.strutsckbk.ch04;

import javax.servlet.ServletException;

import org.apache.struts.action.ActionServlet;
import org.apache.struts.action.PlugIn;
import org.apache.struts.config.ModuleConfig;

public class ConstantsPlugin implements PlugIn {
    public void destroy( ) {
    }
    public void init(ActionServlet servlet, ModuleConfig module)
            throws ServletException {
        Constants constants = new Constants( );
        servlet.getServletContext( ).setAttribute("Constants", constants);
    }
}
```

Example 2-8 (*globals_test.jsp*) shows a JSP page that accesses and displays values loaded by the ConstantsPlugin. The first constant is rendered using the Struts bean:write tag and the second using the JSTL c:out tag.

Example 2-8. Accessing constants using Struts and JSTL

```
<%@ page contentType="text/html;charset=UTF-8" language="java" %>
<%@ taglib uri="http://jakarta.apache.org/struts/tags-bean" prefix="bean" %>
<%@ taglib uri="http://java.sun.com/jstl/core" prefix="c" %>
<html>
<head>
  <title>Struts Cookbook - Chapter 4 : Accessing Constants</title>
</head>
<body>
  <p>
  Field name: ACTION_SERVLET_KEY<br />
  Field value: <bean:write name="Constants"
                    property="strutsGlobals(ACTION_SERVLET_KEY)"/><br />
  </p>
  <p>
  Field name: SERVLET_KEY<br />
  Field value: <c:out value="${Constants.strutsGlobals.SERVLET_KEY}"/><br />
  </p>
</body>
</html>
```

The greatest drawback to this approach is that you manually have to create the map to hold the values. If a new constant is added to a class, you will have to change the source for the Constants class to retrieve it.

See Also

All details on the Jakarta Taglibs project can be found at *http://jakarta.apache.org/ taglibs*. Recipe 5.4 provides details on accessing maps from Struts and JSTL. Struts plug-ins are discussed in Recipe 2.1.

Kris Schneider built a JavaBean similar to the Constants class of Example 2-6 that uses reflection to access the public static variables of any specified class. The source is available from the archived struts-user mailing list discussion at *http:// marc.theaimsgroup.com/?l=struts-user&m=108929374300664&w=2*.

2.4   Using Multiple Struts Configuration Files

Problem

You want to break apart a large *struts-config.xml* file into smaller files for improved organization and easier maintenance, particularly in a team environment.

Solution

Split your monolithic *struts-config.xml* into multiple configuration files. Each file must be well-formed and valid according to the *struts-config* XML DTD. Reference these files as the value for the config initialization parameter of the `ActionServlet` in the *web.xml* file as shown in Example 2-9.

Example 2-9. Multiple config files (single module)

```
<servlet>
  <servlet-name>action</servlet-name>
  <servlet-class>
    org.apache.struts.action.ActionServlet
  </servlet-class>
  <init-param>
    <param-name>config</param-name>
    <param-value>
      /WEB-INF/struts-config.xml,
      /WEB-INF/struts-config-2.xml
    </param-value>
  </init-param>
  <load-on-startup>1</load-on-startup>
</servlet>
```

When the `ActionServlet` is loaded, Struts will merge the results of the specified configuration files into a single in-memory configuration.

Discussion

For anything other than the most trivial applications, the *struts-config.xml* file tends to get large and unwieldy. Many applications may have `action` elements numbering in the hundreds. Combine this with the use of a locking source control system, and soon you will have developers in constant contention for the same file.

Struts 1.1 introduced support for multiple configuration files. Each configuration file must be a valid XML file and conform to the *struts-config* XML Document Type Definition (DTD). You declare the set of files as the parameter value for the config `ActionServlet` initialization parameter in your *web.xml* file. You specify the files as a comma-separated list of file paths. At runtime, the files are merged in memory into a single configuration set. If duplicate elements exist—for example, a form bean declaration with the same value for the `name` attribute—the value read from the last configuration file listed takes precedence.

Just because you are using multiple configuration files doesn't necessarily mean that you're using Struts modules. In fact, you can have multiple configuration files for one individual module. In the Solution above, the `param-name` element value of *config* dictates to the `ActionServlet` the path to the Struts configuration files for the default module. Additional modules are indicated by using a `param-name` value of `config/` *module-name*. Example 2-10 shows a Struts `ActionServlet` declaration from a *web.xml* file with a default module and two additional modules. The default module uses two configuration files: *module1* uses only one configuration file, and *module2* uses three configuration files.

Example 2-10. Multiple config files (multiple modules)

```
<servlet>
  <servlet-name>action</servlet-name>
  <servlet-class>
    org.apache.struts.action.ActionServlet
  </servlet-class>
  <init-param>
    <param-name>config</param-name>
    <param-value>
      /WEB-INF/struts-default-config.xml,
      /WEB-INF/struts-default-config-2.xml
    </param-value>
  </init-param>
  <init-param>
    <param-name>config/module1</param-name>
    <param-value>
      /WEB-INF/struts-module1-config.xml
    </param-value>
  </init-param>
  <init-param>
    <param-name>config/module2</param-name>
    <param-value>
      /WEB-INF/struts-module2-config.xml,
      /WEB-INF/struts-module2-config-2.xml,
      /WEB-INF/struts-module2-config-3.xml
    </param-value>
  </init-param>
  <load-on-startup>1</load-on-startup>
</servlet>
```

If you are doing team development, consider splitting your configuration files based on functional area, use cases, or user stories. Individual team members can focus on their areas of responsibility without bumping into the rest of the team.

See Also

Recipe 2.5 details the nuances of using Struts modules. Recipe 1.8 describes how to generate the struts configuration files automatically.

2.5   Factoring Your Application into Modules

Problem

You want to segregate portions of a web application into distinct subapplications, or *modules*, each with its own separate configuration.

Solution

Create a Struts configuration file for each module in addition to a Struts configuration file for the default module. Then declare each module using initialization parameters for the ActionServlet in the *web.xml*, as shown in Example 2-11.

Example 2-11. ActionServlet configuration for modules

```
<!-- Action Servlet Configuration -->
<servlet>
  <servlet-name>action</servlet-name>
  <servlet-class>org.apache.struts.action.ActionServlet</servlet-class>
  <init-param>
    <param-name>config</param-name>
    <param-value>/WEB-INF/struts-config.xml</param-value>
  </init-param>
  <init-param>
    <param-name>config/module1</param-name>
    <param-value>/WEB-INF/struts-config-module1.xml</param-value>
  </init-param>
  <init-param>
    <param-name>config/module2</param-name>
    <param-value>/WEB-INF/struts-config-module2.xml</param-value>
  </init-param>
  <load-on-startup>1</load-on-startup>
</servlet>
```

Discussion

Struts 1.1 introduced the ability to define separately configurable sub-applications known as *modules*. Modules were incorporated into Struts to address the need for subdividing a web application into distinct, manageable portions. Each module is defined with its own configuration file(s). Every Struts application implicitly has a default module. The default module has no module name.

> To provide backward compatibility with Struts 1.0 applications, the actual name of the default module is the empty string.

Additional modules are defined by specifying a module prefix. The prefix is the value following config/ in the initialization parameter for the Struts' ActionServlet. In Example 2-11, three modules are defined. The first init-param element defines the *default* module. The second and third init-param elements establish *module1* and *module2*, respectively.

Struts pre-pends the module prefix to every URL accessed through declarations in the *struts-config.xml* file for each module. This rule applies to path attributes used in global forwards, global exceptions, action mappings, local forwards, and local exceptions.

However, the module's Struts configuration file doesn't need to know and should not use the module prefix.

URLs that are generated using Struts tags, such as `html:link` and `html:rewrite`, will include the module name. This implicit inclusion of the module prefix can be a headache when you want to refer to globally shared web resources like images and cascading stylesheets. Web applications commonly place all images referenced throughout the site in a top-level */images* folder. If you are using modules and you use the `html:img` tag to display these images, you must create a separate */images* folder for each module or set the `module` attribute of the `html:img` tag to the empty string ("") to indicate the default module.

Suppose you wanted to create an administrative user interface for the *struts-example* MailReader application. The changes required to add the administrative module to the *web.xml* file are shown below, and the second `init-param` element defines the *admin* module:

```
<!-- Action Servlet Configuration -->
<servlet>
  <servlet-name>action</servlet-name>
  <servlet-class>org.apache.struts.action.ActionServlet</servlet-class>
  <init-param>
    <param-name>config</param-name>
    <param-value>
      /WEB-INF/struts-config.xml,
      /WEB-INF/struts-config-registration.xml
    </param-value>
  </init-param>
  <init-param>
    <param-name>config/admin</param-name>
    <param-value>/WEB-INF/struts-config-admin.xml</param-value>
  </init-param>
  <load-on-startup>1</load-on-startup>
</servlet>
```

A common mistake when working with modules is to assume that if you navigate to a URL containing the module prefix, Struts will know you are in that module. For example, you might provide a standard HTML link (i.e., `<a href...>`) to the administrative module's *index* page from the application's main page. If users select that link, they may see the correct page rendered. However, as far as Struts is concerned, *the user is still within the default module*. To switch between modules in a Struts 1.1 application, you must forward the user through a special action, called the `SwitchAction`. In Struts 1.2, the Struts `html` tags that generate links and URLs support the `module` attribute, allowing you to explicitly indicate the target module.

Using modules with Struts 1.1 can have its drawbacks. Not all of the tags in Struts 1.1 support modules; so, you may find that the JSP pages within a module can't be written completely irrespective of the module to which they belong. Many of these gaps in usability for modules have been filled in Struts 1.2. Therefore, I recommend you use modules only if you are using Struts 1.2. If you must use Struts 1.1 and your application is anything more than even slightly complex, you may want to avoid the inconsistencies with using modules and instead organize your application by into subfolders, using the technique shown in Recipe 2.4 to split apart your *struts-config.xml* file.

See Also

Recipe 2.4 describes a technique for splitting the *struts-config.xml* file into multiple files without using modules. Recipe 6.7 shows techniques to use when you need to switch between modules in a running Struts application.

2.6   Using Multiple Resource Bundles

Problem

You want to break apart your application resources properties file into multiple files for improved organization and easier maintenance, particularly in a team environment.

Solution

Create separate properties files and declare a `message-resources` element for each file in your *struts-config.xml* file:

```
<message-resources
  parameter="com.oreilly.strutsckbk.MessageResources"/>
<message-resources
  parameter="com.oreilly.strutsckbk.LabelResources"
  key="labels">
</message-resources>
<message-resources
  parameter="com.oreilly.strutsckbk.HeaderResources"
  key="headers">
</message-resources>
```

Discussion

Struts uses a concept known as *message resources* to provide a mechanism for storing error messages, field labels, and other static text. With the default Struts implementation, you store the messages as name/value pairs in a *.properties* file. A message resources set is basically the same as a Java `ResourceBundle`.

You make your message resources properties file available to Struts using the `message-resources` element. The `parameter` attribute identifies the classpath-relative name of the properties file. You derive the value for this attribute by replacing the path separator in the file's path with a dot (".") and removing the *.properties* extension from the filename. For example, if the properties file was located in */WEB-INF/*

classes/com/oreilly/strutsckbk/MessageResources.properties, you would set up the message resources element as follows:

```
<message-resources
    parameter="com.oreilly.strutsckbk.MessageResources"/>
```

On application startup, Struts creates a runtime representation of the message resources and stores it in the servlet context.

You are not limited to one set of message resources. However, unlike using multiple Struts configuration files, if you use multiple message resource files, they are not combined or merged. Instead, you define distinct sets of message resources. Each set is identified with a unique value specified using the key attribute. If this attribute isn't used, then that message resources set is created as the default set. Only one default set exists. Likewise, only one message resources set corresponds to each unique key within the same module. If you were to define multiple message resources bundles with the same key, the last one specified would be the one used.

The value of the key attribute serves as the name of the servlet context attribute under which the message resources bundle, created from the properties file, is stored. The key value is used in Struts tags, such as bean:message, to identify the message resources set, referred to as the *bundle*, from which to retrieve a property value. Here is how you would access a message from the labels message resources specified in the Solution:

```
<bean:message bundle="labels" key="label.url"/>
```

The value of the bundle attribute corresponds to the key attribute of the message-resources element in the *struts-config.xml* file. The bean:message tag has a key attribute that has a different meaning with of the message-resources element. It specifies the specify property to access from the message resources.

Unfortunately, this approach of using the same attribute for different purposes across XML elements and JSP tags is common in Struts. Make sure you keep the Struts taglib documentation (*http://jakarta.apache.org/struts/userGuide/index.html*) as well as the notes on configuring Struts (*http://jakarta.apache.org/struts/userGuide/configuration.html#struts-config*) bookmarked for handy reference to avoid confusion.

Struts doesn't care how you split your message resource property files. One approach is to split it by message type. For example, you could have separate message resource bundles for the following:

- Error messages
- Informational messages
- Field labels
- Table header cell text

While breaking up the message resources by these types is logical and reasonable, in a team environment it makes more sense to divide the resources by functional area. For example, consider a human resources application that has functional areas for payroll, benefits, and administration. You would create a message resources properties file for each of these areas. Each property file would have within it the error messages, field labels, and other message types specific to that area. If your development team has been divided around these business functional areas, breaking up configuration files in the same manner makes a lot of sense and reduces contention for these resources. The same approach can be used for splitting the Struts configuration file, as well.

If you are familiar with Struts modules, each of the functional areas mentioned above could be a good candidate for a Struts module. If you are using modules, the message resources you define in the *struts-config* file for a module only apply to that module. In fact, you can define `message-resource` elements in different modules that have the same key attribute. Recall from the discussion that Struts stores the `MessageResources` in the servlet context using the key value. More precisely, the actual value used is a concatenation of the module name, often referred to as the *module prefix*, with the message resources key attribute value.

See Also

Recipe 2.4 provides additional information on segregating application components. The Struts User Guide provides documentation on defining message resources that can be found at *http://jakarta.apache.org/struts/userGuide/configuration.html#resources_config*.

The JavaDoc API for the Struts MessageResources can be found at *http://jakarta.apache.org/struts/api/org/apache/struts/util/MessageResources.html*.

The Struts documentation on the `bean:message` tag can be found at *http://jakarta.apache.org/struts/userGuide/struts-bean.html#message*.

2.7 Accessing Message Resources from a Database

Problem

You want to store all labels, messages, and other static text in a database rather than a properties file, while still being able to access the values using the `bean:message` tag.

Solution

1. Download the OJBMessageResources distribution from *http:// prdownloads. sourceforge.net/struts/ojb-message-resources.zip?download*.
2. Extract the ZIP file into a directory on your computer.

---

3. Copy the *ojb-msg-res.jar* file from the *ojb-message-resources/dist* folder into your application's *WEB-INF/lib* folder.

4. Copy the properties, XML, and DTD files from the *ojb-message-resources/config* folder to your application's *src* folder. When you build your application, these files must be copied to the *WEB-INF/classes* folder.

5. Create the tables to hold the Objec Relational Bridge (OJB) metadata tables. OJB uses these tables to keep internal mapping information. Example 2-12 shows the data definition SQL that creates these tables for the MySQL database. These statements for other databases are included with the OJB distribution.

Example 2-12. OJB metadata DDL (MySQL)

```
CREATE TABLE ojb_dlist (
  ID int NOT NULL default '0',
  SIZE_ int default NULL,
  PRIMARY KEY  (ID)
) TYPE=MyISAM;

CREATE TABLE ojb_dlist_entries (
  ID int NOT NULL default '0',
  DLIST_ID int NOT NULL default '0',
  POSITION_ int default NULL,
  OID_ longblob,
  PRIMARY KEY  (ID)
) TYPE=MyISAM;

CREATE TABLE ojb_dmap (
  ID int NOT NULL default '0',
  SIZE_ int default NULL,
  PRIMARY KEY  (ID)
) TYPE=MyISAM;

CREATE TABLE ojb_dmap_entries (
  ID int NOT NULL default '0',
  DMAP_ID int NOT NULL default '0',
  KEY_OID longblob,
  VALUE_OID longblob,
  PRIMARY KEY  (ID)
) TYPE=MyISAM;

CREATE TABLE ojb_dset (
  ID int NOT NULL default '0',
  SIZE_ int default NULL,
  PRIMARY KEY  (ID)
) TYPE=MyISAM;

CREATE TABLE ojb_dset_entries (
  ID int NOT NULL default '0',
  DLIST_ID int NOT NULL default '0',
  POSITION_ int default NULL,
  OID_ longblob,
```

Example 2-12. OJB metadata DDL (MySQL) (continued)

```
  PRIMARY KEY  (ID)
) TYPE=MyISAM;

CREATE TABLE ojb_hl_seq (
  TABLENAME varchar(175) NOT NULL default '',
  FIELDNAME varchar(70) NOT NULL default '',
  MAX_KEY int default NULL,
  GRAB_SIZE int default NULL,
  PRIMARY KEY  (TABLENAME,FIELDNAME)
) TYPE=MyISAM;

CREATE TABLE ojb_lockentry (
  OID_ varchar(250) NOT NULL default '',
  TX_ID varchar(50) NOT NULL default '',
  TIMESTAMP_ decimal(10,0) default NULL,
  ISOLATIONLEVEL int default NULL,
  LOCKTYPE int default NULL,
  PRIMARY KEY  (OID_,TX_ID)
) TYPE=MyISAM;

CREATE TABLE ojb_nrm (
  NAME varchar(250) NOT NULL default '',
  OID_ longblob,
  PRIMARY KEY  (NAME)
) TYPE=MyISAM;

CREATE TABLE ojb_seq (
  TABLENAME varchar(175) NOT NULL default '',
  FIELDNAME varchar(70) NOT NULL default '',
  LAST_NUM int default NULL,
  PRIMARY KEY  (TABLENAME,FIELDNAME)
) TYPE=MyISAM;
```

6. Create the table to hold the message resources data using the SQL DDL shown in Example 2-13.

Example 2-13. MessageResources DDL

```
create table application_resources (
  subApp          varchar(100)     not null,
  bundleKey       varchar(100)     not null,
  locale          varchar(10)      not null,
  msgKey          varchar(255)     not null,
  val             varchar(255),
  Primary Key(
    subApp,
    bundleKey,
    locale,
    msgKey
  )
);
```

7. Populate the table with your message resources. Example 2-14 shows an easy means of loading the table using SQL.

Example 2-14. SQL to load message resources table

```
insert into application_resources (
    subApp, bundleKey, locale, msgKey, val )
  values ('', '', '', 'label.index.title',
        'Struts Cookbook');
insert into application_resources (
    subApp, bundleKey, locale, msgKey, val )
  values ('', '', 'fr', 'label.index.title',
        'Struts Livre de Cuisine');
```

8. Change the Struts configuration file to use the OJBMessageResources factory:

```
<message-resources
    factory="org.apache.struts.util.OJBMessageResourcesFactory"
    parameter="."
/>
```

9. Change the *repository.xml* in your *WEB-INF/classes* folder (copied over in step 4) to use the database connection properties specific to your database. Example 2-15 demonstrates a configuration for a MySQL database.

Example 2-15. OJB connection descriptor for MySQL

```
<jdbc-connection-descriptor
    platform="MySQL"
    jdbc-level="2.0"
    driver="com.mysql.jdbc.Driver"
    protocol="jdbc"
    subprotocol="mysql"
    dbalias="//localhost:3306/test"
    username="user"
    password="pass"
/>
```

Discussion

The Struts MessageResources facility manages static text such as error messages, field labels, table headers, and window titles. With this facility, the text is stored as name/value pairs in one or more *.properties* files known as resource bundles; the name is a logical key and the value is the text to display. If your application needs to be localized for a particular language and country, then you create a new properties file. You associate the file with the particular locale (language and country) by adding a suffix composed of a language and country code for the particular locale. For example, the *MessageResources.properties* file for French Canadian users would be *MessageResources_fr_CA.properties*. The properties in the localized file contain values specific to the locale. This approach of localizing resources is specified by Java itself.

More details, including a list of language and country codes, can be found at *http://java.sun.com/j2se/1.4.2/docs/guide/intl/locale.doc.html*.

This facility works well for most small to medium-sized applications. However, you may want to store the text using a more manageable persistent means such as a database. While Struts does not support this out-of-the-box, it does support it through extension. Behind the scenes, Struts uses an implementation of the `MessageResourcesFactory` to create the `MessageResources` object that is stored in the servlet context at runtime. You can provide a custom implementation of the Struts `MessageResourcesFactory` and then declare that implementation in your Struts configuration file:

```
<message-resources
  factory="com.foo.CustomMessageResourcesFactory"
  parameter="moduleName.bundleKey"
/>
```

The parameter attribute specifies the Struts module name and bundle key (bundle name) that the message resources factory creates messages for.

So, you could create your own message resources factory that reads the resources from a database. Thankfully, the grunt work of creating such an extension has been done! James Mitchell, a long-time Struts committer, created the OJBMessageResources implementation. This set of classes leverages the object-relational mapping framework OJB to provide an easy-to-use database-driven `MessageResources` implementation.

If you are unfamiliar with OJB, don't let that dissuade you from this Solution. You don't need to know anything about OJB to use the OJBMessageResources. OJB is simply used under the covers to map the relational data to the object data. If you use the table schema specified in the Solution, no additional changes are needed to map the data. However, if you want to use a different schema, you can change the mappings in the OJB XML-based configuration files to suit your needs. You will not need to make any changes to the actual Java code that implements the `MessageResourcesFactory`. OJBMessageResources is well documented and comes with a step-by-step installation and configuration *README* file. The Solution above is derived from those instructions.

To use OJBMessageResources most effectively, it helps to understand how the database schema maps to the object data. First, the schema only requires creation of a single table to hold the message resources (step 6 in the Solution). Using a single table simplifies the data mapping. Table 2-2 describes the columns that make up this table and how they are used in Struts.

Table 2-2. OJBMessageResources schema

Column name	Corresponding Struts concept	Notes and examples
subApp	Module prefix	Not null. Use an empty String("") to represent the default module.

Table 2-2. OJBMessageResources schema (continued)

Column name	Corresponding Struts concept	Notes and examples
bundleKey	Key to locate a set of message resources when using multiple sets. This value must match the value of the key attribute of the message-resources element in the Struts configuration file. This value corresponds to the value for the bundle attribute in the Struts tags (e.g., bean:message bundle="labels"	Not null. Use an empty String to represent the default key. Otherwise, the name is a logical value such as "labels," "headers," and "errors."
Locale	The locale code representing the locale of the message. This value is a combination of the two-letter language code and two-letter country code.	Not null. Use an empty String to represent the default (server's) locale. Examples of values are "en_US" for English/United States and "fr" for French.
msgKey	The message name used to look up the message. This value will be the same for all locales. This value is the same as the left-hand side of a property in a *.properties* file. The value of this column corresponds to the value for the key attribute in the Struts tags that retrieve values from MessageResources.	Not null, and should never be empty. A key value might look something like "title. hello.world".
val	Value corresponding to the msgKey. This is the localized text and corresponds to the right-hand side of a property. This is the value that will be retrieved and displayed by a Struts tag.	Can be null. This is the text that will be displayed on the page. For example, "Hello, World!"

Keep in mind that while OJBMessageResources uses a single database table to hold all message resources, each resource set must still be configured in the *struts-config.xml* with a message-resources element. In other words, you will need to have a message-resource element for each resource set distinguished by a bundleKey and subApp. See Recipe 2.6 for more details.

See Also

Recipe 2.6 describes how to configure Struts to use multiple message resource bundles. Chapter 14 has additional recipes related to internationalizing Struts applications.

OJB is a project under the Apache umbrella. Complete information on OJB can be found online at *http://db.apache.org/ojb*.

An effort is underway to factor out the Struts message resources into a reusable set of common classes. The Commons Resources project, *http://jakarta.apache.org/commons/ sandbox/resources/*, will provide an implementation of message resources backed by properties files as well as other persistence mechanisms including OBJ, Hibernate, Torque, and straight JDBC. It's anticipated that a future version of Struts will deprecate the internal message resources implementation and in favor of Commons Resources.

2.8   Selectively Disabling Actions

Problem

You want to disable an action using a custom property that can be set on the action element in your *struts-config.xml* file; forwarding any requests to the disabled action to an "under construction" page.

Solution

Create a custom `ActionMapping` extension (as shown in Example 2-16) that provides a boolean property indicating if the action is disabled or not.

Example 2-16. Custom ActionMapping

```
import org.apache.struts.action.ActionMapping;

public class DisablingActionMapping extends ActionMapping {

    private String disabled;
    private boolean actionDisabled = false;

    public String getDisabled( ) {
        return disabled;
    }

    public void setDisabled(String disabled) {
        this.disabled = disabled;
        actionDisabled = new Boolean(disabled).booleanValue( );
    }

    public boolean isActionDisabled( ) {
        return actionDisabled;
    }
}
```

This action mapping class can now be specified in the *struts-config.xml* file. You set the disabled property to true if an action is to be disabled:

```
<action-mappings type="com.oreilly.strutsckbk.DisablingActionMapping">

    <!-- Edit mail subscription -->
    <action     path="/editSubscription"
                type="org.apache.struts.webapp.example.EditSubscriptionAction"
            attribute="subscriptionForm"
                scope="request"
             validate="false">
        <set-property property="disabled" value="true"/>
        <forward name="failure"              path="/mainMenu.jsp"/>
        <forward name="success"              path="/subscription.jsp"/>
    </action>
```

Then create a custom `RequestProcessor`, such as the one shown in Example 2-17, that handles the `DisablingActionMapping`.

Example 2-17. Processing requests for disabled actions

```java
import java.io.IOException;

import javax.servlet.ServletException;
import javax.servlet.http.HttpServletRequest;
import javax.servlet.http.HttpServletResponse;

import org.apache.struts.action.Action;
import org.apache.struts.action.ActionForm;
import org.apache.struts.action.ActionForward;
import org.apache.struts.action.ActionMapping;
import org.apache.struts.action.RequestProcessor;

public class CustomRequestProcessor extends RequestProcessor {

    protected ActionForward processActionPerform(HttpServletRequest request,
            HttpServletResponse response, Action action,ActionForm form,
             ActionMapping mapping) throws IOException, ServletException {
        ActionForward forward = null;
        if (!(mapping instanceof DisablingActionMapping)) {
            forward = super.processActionPerform( request, response,
                                                  action, form, mapping);
        }
        else {
            DisablingActionMapping customMapping =
                    (DisablingActionMapping) mapping;
            if (customMapping.isActionDisabled()) {
                forward = customMapping.findForward("underConstruction");
            }
            else {
                forward = super.processActionPerform( request, response,
                                                      action, form, mapping);
            }
        }
        return forward;
    }
}
```

Discussion

Struts supports the capability of providing custom properties to an `Action` through two primary mechanisms. First, every Struts action can be passed through a general purpose parameter value:

```xml
<action    path="/editRegistration"
             type="org.apache.struts.webapp.example.EditRegistrationAction"
         attribute="registrationForm"
             scope="request"
          validate="false"
```

```
            parameter="disabled">
    <forward name="success" path="/registration.jsp"/>
  </action>
```

Second, in the Action implementation, the value of the parameter can be accessed with this code:

```
String parameterValue = mapping.getParameter();
```

However, some of the Struts-provided Action subclasses, such as the DispatchAction, are predicated on the use of the parameter attribute. Since you can specify only one parameter attribute, you will not be able to use the parameter for a custom value if you are using one of these pre-built Action subclasses.

For complete extensibility, you can extend the ActionMapping class, optionally providing accessor and mutator methods for custom properties of your own choosing:

```
package com.oreilly.strutsckbk;

import org.apache.struts.ActionMapping

public class MyCustomActionMapping extends ActionMapping {
    private String customValue;
    public String getCustomValue() { return customValue; }
    public String setCustomValue(String s) { customValue = s; }
}
```

You can reference this custom extension in the *struts-config.xml* file. If the custom action mapping should be used globally for all actions, set the type attribute of the action-mappings element to the fully qualified class name of the custom extension:

```
<action-mappings type="com.oreilly.strutsckbk.MyCustomActionMapping">
```

Otherwise, set the className attribute of the action element for which the custom action mapping is needed. In either case, the set-property element can be used to set values for JavaBean properties in the custom extension for a specific action element:

```
<action    path="/someAction"
           type="com.oreilly.strutsckbk.SomeAction"
      className="com.oreilly.strutsckbk.MyCustomActionMapping">
  <set-property property="customValue" value="some value"/>
</action>
```

 To make your custom mapping as robust as possible, accept only a String value in the *setter* method for a set-property. You can perform any necessary data conversion in the class itself, setting the value to acceptable default if an unexpected value is passed.

The Solution uses a custom RequestProcessor for handling the disabled property of the custom ActionMapping. If you were using a custom ActionMapping for only specific actions, you could access the custom ActionMapping property directly in the Action.execute( ) method:

```
boolean disabled = ((DisablingActionMapping) mapping).isActionDisabled( );
if (disabled) return mapping.findForward("underConstruction");
```

See Also

You could use an authorization servlet filter to solve this problem. Recipe 11.8 shows an approach that could be applied to this problem.

CHAPTER 3

User Interface

3.0   Introduction

Face it: you can create the most architecturally pure, elegant, and robust web application, but if the users don't like the looks of the interface, you are doomed to failure. Some Java developers consider themselves above the use of such mundane technologies as HTML and JavaScript. Whether you like it or not, however, knowledge of these technologies—particularly HTML—can make all the difference when it comes to presentation and usability. If you don't know how to use them to your advantage, you will find it challenging for your application to be endorsed by the user community.

This chapter will introduce some recipes to help you get the most out of your application's presentation. The recipes here don't eliminate the need for a good graphics/user interface designer. However, they do go a long way in helping you leverage HTML via the dynamic capability of Struts. In addition, this chapter will provide alternative solutions based on complementary technologies, such as JSTL.

Some scenarios when working with HTML forms are always challenging. Checkboxes, for example, cause no end of headaches because of the way that unchecked controls are handled. This chapter includes a recipe that specifically tackles this problem. Another common issue in form processing is how to handle date fields. There are many ways to do them and they all have their pros and cons. A recipe that highlights these different approaches is included in this chapter as well.

You'll find various other recipes that address issues such as setting form tab order, generating URLs for use in JavaScript, and working with frames. All in all, if you've got a user interface problem, there is a good chance that you'll find some help in these pages.

3.1   Using JSTL

Problem

You want to use the JSP Standard Tag Library (JSTL) tags in your Struts application.

Solution

Download the Jakarta Taglibs JSTL reference implementation from *http://jakarta.apache.org/taglibs*. Copy the *jstl.jar* and *standard.jar* files from the *lib* folder into your applications *WEB-INF/lib* folder. Then copy the *c.tld*, *fmt.tld*, *sql.tld*, and *x.tld* files from the *tlds* folder into your applications *WEB-INF/lib* folder.

Use the appropriate `taglib` directives on JSP pages where you want to use JSTL:

```
<%@ taglib uri="http://java.sun.com/jstl/core" prefix="c" %>
```

Table 3-1 lists the JSTL tag libraries and the corresponding URIs.

Table 3-1. JSTL tag library URIs

Tag library	JSTL 1.0 Taglib URI	JSTL 1.1 Taglib URI
Core	*http://java.sun.com/jstl/core*	*http://java.sun.com/jsp/jstl/core*
Formatting	*http://java.sun.com/jstl/fmt*	*http://java.sun.com/jsp/jstl/fmt*
SQL	*http://java.sun.com/jstl/sql*	*http://java.sun.com/jsp/jstl/sql*
XML	*http://java.sun.com/jstl/xml*	*http://java.sun.com/jsp/jstl/xml*
Functions	N/A	*http://java.sun.com/jsp/jstl/functions*

Discussion

JSTL is a powerful set of tag libraries that should be a part of any Struts developer's toolkit. JSTL contains tags for outputting JavaBean properties, looping, conditional logic, and URL formatting. There are tags for formatting and parsing dates and numbers. The XML tag library can be used to parse and process XML on a JSP page. The tags of the SQL tag library interact with a relational database. The Functions tag library provides useful functions that can be used in expressions, primarily for string manipulation.

By far the most important of these to have in your bag of developer tricks is the Core tag library. This library contains tags that can be used instead of many of the Struts bean logic tags. Why would you want to use these tags instead of the Struts tags? The answer is a practical one: These tags are more powerful and easier to use than the Struts tags. Make no mistake, however; the folks on the Struts project are not offended by this. Quite the contrary. JSTL has allowed Struts to focus on what it does best: providing the controller glue for robust JSP-based web applications.

Take a look at how you would implement a loop and display output using JSTL tags compared to the Struts tags. First, here's the Struts version:

```
<ul>
    <logic:iterate id="cust" name="branch" property="customers">
        <li>
            <bean:write name="cust" property="lastName"/>,
            <bean:write name="cust" property="firstName"/>
        </li>
    </logic:iterate>
</ul>
```

In JSTL, this becomes a lot simpler:

```
<ul>
    <c:forEach var="cust" items="${branch.customers}">
        <li>
            <c:out value="${cust.lastName}, ${cust.firstName}"/>
        </li>
    </c:forEach>
</ul>
```

The cool part is that you don't have to choose one over the other. JSTL tags can be introduced into an application as you learn it. The JSP Expression Language (EL) enables easy access to data in ActionForms and objects available in the various JSP scopes (page, request, session, and application). The hardest decision you will have to make is not whether to use JSTL, but which version of JSTL to use. If you are using a JSP 2.0/Servlet 2.4 container such as Tomcat 5, you should use JSTL 1.1. Otherwise, you'll need to use JSTL 1.0.

Throughout this book, where appropriate, JSTL examples will be provided along with the pure Struts-based examples. In many cases, examples are provided that use the capabilities of both Struts and JSTL.

See Also

Recipe 3.2 shows how you can use EL expressions with the Struts tags. *JavaServer Pages* by Hans Bergsten (O'Reilly) covers JSTL in great detail and is an invaluable source. Sun provides an excellent tutorial on JSTL that can be found at *http://java.sun.com/tutorials/jstl*.

I've created a handy quick reference guide for JSTL. This guide can be found in PDF format at *http://www.jadecove.com/jstl-quick-reference.pdf*.

3.2   Using the Struts-EL Tags

Problem

You want to be able to use JSTL expressions for attribute values on Struts tags.

Solution

Use the tag libraries supplied with the Struts distribution in the *contrib/struts-el/lib* directory. You will need to copy all the JAR and TLD files from this directory to your application's *WEB-INF/lib* directory. Use the appropriate `taglib` directives on JSP pages where you want to use expressions:

```
<%@ taglib uri="http://jakarta.apache.org/struts/tags-html-el"
        prefix="html-el" %>
```

Table 3-2 lists the Struts-EL tag libraries and the corresponding `taglib` URIs.

Table 3-2. Struts-EL Taglib URIs

Tag library	Struts-EL Taglib URI (1.1)	Struts-EL Taglib URI (1.2)
html-el	*http://jakarta.apache.org/struts/tags-html-el*	*http://struts.apache.org/tags-html-el*
bean-el	*http://jakarta.apache.org/struts/tags-bean-el*	*http://struts.apache.org/tags-bean-el*
logic-el	*http://jakarta.apache.org/struts/tags-logic-el*	*http://struts.apache.org/tags-logic-el*

Discussion

JSTL-style expressions, such as `${foo.bar[4].baz}`, are not supported by the base Struts tags. For example, it would be nice if you could format a tag using an expression like the following:

```
<html:text value="${sessionScope.foo.bar[3]}"/>
```

Instead, these tags require runtime expressions, which is just Java code:

```
<html:text
    value="<%=session.((Foo)getAttribute("foo")).getBar(3)%>"/>
```

Getting the Java code out of your JSP pages makes your pages less brittle and more maintainable. This lack of EL support was identified and the Struts-EL tag libraries were created. These libraries extend the `html`, `bean`, and `logic` Struts tag libraries to add support for EL expressions. If an attribute of a Struts tag supports a runtime expression, the corresponding Struts-EL tag will allow a JSTL expression. It is possible to use the regular Struts tags and the Struts-EL tags in the same application and even on the same JSP page. Just be sure to define unique prefixes in the `taglib` directive for each library.

The Struts-EL tags are not a replacement, however, for JSTL. The Struts-EL tags only provide unique tags for Struts. If a Struts tag can be replaced by a JSTL tag, that tag is not implemented in the Struts-EL tag libraries.

See Also

Recipe 3.1 details how to configure your application to use JSTL.

3.3   Displaying Indexed Properties

Problem

On a JSP page, you need to access data from an indexed property of an object.

Solution

Use bean.property[*index*] to access the indexed value, as shown in Example 3-1.

Example 3-1. Accessing indexed properties

```
<@taglib uri=http://jakarta.apache.org/struts/tags-bean" prefix="bean"%>

<ul>
  <li><bean:write name="foo" property="bar.baz[0]"/></li>
  <li><bean:write name="foo" property="bar.baz[1]"/></li>
  <li><bean:write name="foo" property="bar.baz[2]"/></li>
</ul>
```

JSTL supports access to indexed properties, as shown in Example 3-2.

Example 3-2. Accessing indexed properties (JSTL)

```
<@taglib uri="http://java.sun.com/jstl/core" prefix="c"%>

<ul>
  <li><c:out value="${foo.bar.baz[0]}"/></li>
  <li><c:out value="${foo.bar.baz[1]}"/></li>
  <li><c:out value="${foo.bar.baz[1]}"/></li>
</ul>
```

Discussion

Indexed properties are one of the most misunderstood aspects of the Struts tags. An indexed property is a JavaBean property that represents a set of values, not a single scalar value. Indexed properties are accessed using a getter method of the following form:

```
public Foo getSomeProperty (int index) { ... }
```

Likewise, indexed properties are set using a setter method of this form:

```
public void setFoo(int index, Foo someProperty) { ... }
```

Consider a JavaBean representing a calendar. The CalendarHolder class shown in Example 3-3 has a nested property representing the months in a calendar named monthSet.

Example 3-3. Calendar JavaBean

```
package com.oreilly.strutsckbk;

public class CalendarHolder {

    private MonthSet monthSet;

    public CalendarHolder( ) {
        monthSet = new MonthSet( );
    }

    public MonthSet getMonthSet( ) {
        return monthSet;
    }
}
```

The MonthSet class, shown in Example 3-4, is a class that has an indexed property, month representing the month names ("January," "February," and so forth).

Example 3-4. Class with indexed property

```
package com.oreilly.strutsckbk;

public class MonthSet {
```

Example 3-4. Class with indexed property (continued)

```
    static String[] months = new String[] {
            "January", "February", "March", "April",
            "May", "June", "July", "August",
            "September", "October", "November", "December"
    };

    public String[] getMonths() {
        return months;
    }

    public String getMonth(int index) {
        return months[index];
    }

    public void setMonth(int index, String value) {
        months[index] = value;
    }
}
```

The goal is to access the indexed property month of the monthSet property of the CalendarHolder instance in a JSP page as shown in the following snippet from a JSP:

```
<jsp:useBean id="calendar" class="com.oreilly.strutsckbk.CalendarHolder"/>

<ul>
    <li><bean:write name="calendar" property="monthSet.month[0]"/></li>
    <li><bean:write name="calendar" property="monthSet.month[1]"/></li>
    <li><bean:write name="calendar" property="monthSet.month[2]"/></li>
</ul>
```

If the specific indexed property to display was determined dynamically—that is, the index to use was set using a JSP scripting variable—you would need to use scriptlet to generate the property value as follows:

```
You have selected month number <bean:write name="monthIndex"/>:
<bean:write name="calendar"
        property='<%= "monthSet.month[" + monthIndex + "]" %>'
```

Using the scriptlet approach makes for an extremely hard to read and even harder to maintain JSP page. If you were using JSTL, however, this becomes much cleaner:

```
You have selected month number <c:out value="${monthIndex}"/>:
<c:out value="${calendar.monthSet.month[monthIndex]}"/>
```

More commonly, indexed properties are accessed dynamically in a loop. Say you want to display the list of months using the Struts logic:iterate tag. This tag iterates over Collections and arrays. Here's how you would display all the months in an ordered list:

```
<ol>
<logic:iterate id="monthName" name="calendar" property="monthSet.months">
    <li><bean:write name="monthName"/></li>
</logic:iterate>
</ol>
```

Again, JSTL can be used as an alternative. The JSTL `c:forEach` tag is a bit easier to use than the Struts `logic:iterate` tag. Here's how you would generate the same ordered list using JSTL:

```
<ol>
<c:forEach var="monthName" items="${calendar.monthSet.months}">
    <li><c:out name="${monthName}"/></li>
</c:forEach>
</ol>
```

See Also

Problems come in when you need to create form fields that correspond to indexed properties using the Struts `html` tags. Recipe 3.4 addresses these particular issues. Recipe 3.5 provides more details on using indexed properties in JSTL looping constructs.

3.4   Using Indexed Properties on Forms

Problem

You want to create a set of input fields on a form that corresponds to the indexed properties of a bean.

Solution

Use the `indexed` attribute on tags in the Struts `html` tag library to generate the property value:

```
<html:form action="TestOneAction"><p>
  <logic:iterate name="MyForm" property="stringArray"
                 id="stringValue" indexId="ctr">
    <br/>
    <html:text property="stringArray" indexed="true"/>
</logic:iterate>
</html:form>
```

Discussion

As shown in Recipe 3.3, accessing indexed properties for display purposes is easy. However, using indexed properties in a form can be tricky. If the name of the generated input field is not formatted correctly, Struts can't populate the `ActionForm` when the HTML form is submitted. Struts populates the `ActionForm` with values from the HTTP request using the Jakarta Commons BeanUtils package. Specifically, the `BeanUtils.populate()` method loads the `ActionForm` from the HTTP request data sent when the form is submitted.

For indexed properties, `BeanUtils.populate()` uses the name of the request parameter to determine the proper setter method to call on the `ActionForm`. Table 3-3 illustrates how different form input field names are processed. The table shows the HTML tag, the corresponding HTTP request name/value pair, and the method that is called on the ActionForm when the request is processed.

Table 3-3. ActionForm population samples

HTML form input tag	Generated request pair	Resulting method call
`<input type="text" name="bar">`	bar=someValue	Form.setBar("someValue")
`<input type="text" name="sna.fug">`	sna.fug=blah	Form.getSna( ).setFug("blah");
`<input type="text" name="baz[0]">`	baz[0]=someValue	Form.setBaz(0,"firstVal");
`<input type="text" name="glub[1].waf">`	glub[1].waf=halb	Form.getGlub(1).setWaf("halb");
`<input type="text" name="dog.leg[2]">`	dog.leg[2]=lame	Form.getDog( ).setLeg(2, "lame");

Consider a form that allows a user to enter a list of favorite things such as colors and web sites. The ActionForm to hold this data contains a String property for the user's name, a String array representing the user's favorite colors, and a List of WebLink objects representing the user's favorite web sites. The WebLink class, shown in Example 3-5, defines a simple JavaBean with properties for the site name and URL.

Example 3-5. WebLink JavaBean

```
package com.oreilly.strutsckbk;

public class WebLink {
    public String getName( ) {
        return name;
    }
    public void setName(String name) {
        this.name = name;
    }
    public String getUrl( ) {
        return url;
    }
    public void setUrl(String url) {
        this.url = url;
    }
    private String url;
    private String name;
}
```

The form bean, FavoritesForm, containing properties for the user's name, favorite colors, and favorite links is shown in Example 3-6.

Example 3-6. FavoritesForm form bean

```java
package com.oreilly.strutsckbk;

import java.util.ArrayList;
import java.util.List;

import org.apache.struts.action.ActionForm;

public final class FavoritesForm extends ActionForm  {
    public FavoritesForm( ) {
        webLinks = new ArrayList( );
        for (int i=0; i<5; i++) webLinks.add(new WebLink( ));
        colors = new String[3];
    }
    public String getName( ) {
        return name;
    }
    public void setName(String name) {
        this.name = name;
    }
    public String getColor(int index) {
        return colors[index];
    }
    public void setColor(int index, String color) {
        colors[index] = color;
    }
    public String[] getColor( ) {
        return colors;
    }
    public List getWebLinks( ) {
        return webLinks;
    }
    public WebLink getWebLink(int index) {
        return (WebLink)webLinks.get(index);
    }
    public void setWebLink(int index, WebLink webLink) {
        webLinks.set(index, webLink);
    }

    public void reset( ) {
        webLinks.clear( );
        colors = new String[3];
    }

    private List webLinks;
    private String name;
    private String[] colors;
}
```

Now you can create a JSP page (*favorites.jsp*) that allows a user to input corresponding data on a form, as shown in Example 3-7.

Example 3-7. FavoritesForm JSP

```
<%@ page contentType="text/html;charset=UTF-8" language="java" %>
<%@ taglib uri="/WEB-INF/struts-bean.tld" prefix="bean" %>
<%@ taglib uri="/WEB-INF/struts-html.tld" prefix="html" %>
<%@ taglib uri="/WEB-INF/struts-logic.tld" prefix="logic" %>
<%@ taglib uri="http://java.sun.com/jstl/core" prefix="c" %>

<html:html locale="true">
<head>
<title><bean:message key="index.title"/></title>
<html:base/>
</head>
<body bgcolor="white">
<h2>Favorites Poll</h2>
<html:form action="/admin/ViewFavorites">
    <p>
        What is your name:
        <br/><html:text property="name"/>
    </p>
    <p>
        What are your three favorite colors:
        <br/><html:text property="color[0]"/>
        <br/><html:text property="color[1]"/>
        <br/><html:text property="color[2]"/>
    </p>
    <p>
      What are your favorite links?
      <table>
        <tr>
           <th>Name</th>
           <th>URL</th>
        </tr>
        <tr>
           <td><html:text property="webLink[0].name"/></td>
           <td><html:text property="webLink[0].url"/></td>
        </tr>
      </table>
    </p>
    <html:submit/>
    <html:reset/>
</html:form>
</body>
</html:html>
```

Since the index values in Example 3-7 are hardcoded and not dynamic, the html:text tag property values are easily constructed, so the generated HTML tags have the appropriate name attribute values. However, suppose you wanted to use the logic: iterate tag to generate the repeated input fields. To do this for the color property, you might be tempted to try some JSP code like this:

```
What are your three favorite colors:
  <logic:iterate name="FavoritesForm" id="theColor">
    <br/><html:text property="color" indexed="true"/>
  </logic:iterate>
```

This will *not* generate the needed HTML markup. The indexed attribute applies an index (i.e., [n]) to the value specified for the name attribute of the particular Struts html tag (in this case, html:text). If you were to deploy a JSP using the snippet above, the generated HTML would look something like the following:

```
What are your three favorite colors:
<br/><input type="text" name="org.apache.struts.taglib.html.BEAN[0].color"
value="[Ljava.lang.String;@5f1ba8">
<br/><input type="text" name="org.apache.struts.taglib.html.BEAN[1].color"
value="[Ljava.lang.String;@5f1ba8">
<br/><input type="text" name="org.apache.struts.taglib.html.BEAN[2].color"
value="[Ljava.lang.String;@5f1ba8">
```

The index is not applied to the value for the property. Instead, the value is applied to the internal Struts name for the form bean. Additionally, the value attribute contains the results of calling toString( ) on the array, and not a specific element in the array.

What this means in the long run is that the indexed attribute is useful when you need to set a nested simple property of an indexed property that is a complex object—e.g., a JavaBean. You can generate the input fields for a non-nested property in a logic: iterate tag, but you must resort to scriptlet to generate the array index:

```
What are your three favorite colors:
    <logic:iterate name="FavoritesForm" id="theColor" indexId="ctr">
      <br/><html:text property='<%="color["+ctr+"]"%>'/>
    </logic:iterate>
```

Suppose you wanted to use the logic:iterate tag to generate input fields for the favorite links (the WebLink objects). In this case, the indexed attribute will do exactly what you want:

```
What are your favorite links?
<table>
  <tr>
     <th>Name</th>
     <th>URL</th>
  </tr>
  <logic:iterate id="webLink" name="FavoritesForm" property="webLinks">
    <tr>
       <td><html:text name="webLink" property="name" indexed="true"/></td>
       <td><html:text name="webLink" property="url" indexed="true"/></td>
    </tr>
  </logic:iterate>
<table>
```

Using the indexed attribute with the html tag library can be confusing. This confusion generally stems from the name attribute's new importance. In most cases, when using the html tags, the name attribute can be left off as the value will be based on the form-bean that is declared for the action mapping. However, when using the indexed attribute, the name attribute refers to the nested indexed property of the corresponding ActionForm.

Going back to the problem with the `color` property, you have alternatives other than using scriptlet. You can use the Struts `html-el` tags or JSTL. Both of these alternatives essentially do the same thing as the scriptlet, but they do so using EL (expression language). The cleanest approach utilizes the `html-el` tags:

```
What are your three favorite colors:
  <logic:iterate name="FavoritesForm" id="theColor" indexId="ctr">
    <br/><html-el:text property='color[${ctr}]'/>
  </logic:iterate>
```

If you prefer JSTL, you can generate the required input tag directly instead of using the Struts `html` tags:

```
What are your three favorite colors:
  <logic:iterate id="color" name="FavoritesForm" property="color" indexId="ctr">
    <br/><input type="text" name="color[<c:out value='${ctr}'/>]"
             value="<c:out value='${FavoritesForm.color[ctr]}'/>"/>
  </logic:iterate>
```

This JSTL version is about as ugly as the original version using scriptlet. In addition, since neither the Struts `html:text` nor `html-el:text` tag is used, the HTML `input` tag's value attribute must be explicitly coded. If you were to use the Struts `html:text` tag, the value would be set automatically.

 The Struts-EL tags extend the Struts base tags but are not part of the Struts core. Bug fixes and new features for the base Struts tag take time to find their way to the Struts-EL tags.

See Also

Recipe 3.3 discusses techniques to use when displaying values from indexed properties outside of a form. Recipe 3.5 discusses how to use indexed properties in a JSTL `c:forEach` loop.

The `BeanUtils` package of the Jakarta Commons project defines how the indexed properties are resolved. The package description provides additional details and can be found at *http://jakarta.apache.org/commons/beanutils/api/org/apache/commons/beanutils/package-summary.html#package_description*.

3.5   Using Indexed Properties in a JSTL Loop

Problem

You want to use indexed bean properties with the Struts `html` tags in a JSTL `c:forEach` loop instead of Struts `logic:iterate` loop.

Solution

To create fields for a simple indexed property, use the bean:define tag to expose the loop counter as a scripting variable that can be used in a runtime expression:

```
<c:forEach var="theItem" items="${MyForm.myItems}" varStatus="loopStatus">
  <bean:define id="itemIndex">
    <c:out value="${loopStatus.index}"/>
  </bean:define>
  <br/><html:text property='<%="myItem["+itemIndex+"]"%>'/>
</c:forEach>
```

If the indexed property is a nested bean and you are using the indexed="true" property, then replace the Struts logic:iterate tag with the JSTL c:forEach:

```
<c:forEach var="theNestedItem" items="${MyForm.myNestedItems}">
  <br/><html:text name="theNestedItem"
              property="nestedProperty"
              indexed="true"/>
</c:forEach>
```

Discussion

The c:forEach tag provided by JSTL provides additional functionality and can be easier to use than the logic:iterate tag. The items to loop through can be specified using EL. The JSTL tag permits greater control for looping over a subset of the collection, and details on the loop status are easily obtained. However, as is common to all JSTL tags, no scripting variables are created. As was shown in other recipes in this chapter, runtime expressions may have to be used when dealing with indexed properties. This is particularly true if you are not using the *struts-el* tag libraries.

The bean:define tag can create a scripting variable from a JSTL-created scoped variables. This bean:define tag creates a new scoped variable and a corresponding scripting variable based on the value taken from the value attribute or the body of the tag. This latter facility provides a useful bridge between JSTL and the Struts tags. In the Solution, the bean:define tag is used to create a variable containing the index to use for accessing the indexed property. You can apply this technique to the form for selecting the favorite colors from Recipe 3.4:

```
What are your three favorite colors:
<c:forEach var="theColor" items="${FavoritesForm.color}"
    varStatus="loopStatus">
    <bean:define id="ctr">
        <c:out value="${loopStatus.index}"/>
    </bean:define>
    <br/><html:text property='<%="color["+ctr+"]"%>'/>
</c:forEach>
```

As shown in the Recipe 3.4, you can use the *Struts-El* tags to eliminate the scriptlet altogether:

```
What are your three favorite colors:
<c:forEach var="theColor" items="${FavoritesForm.color}" varStatus="loopStatus">
```

```
        <br/><html-el:text property='color[${ctr}]'/>
    </c:forEach>
```

If you need to create an HTML input field for the nested property of an object, which
is an indexed property, then specify the `indexed="true"` attribute on the Struts `html`
tags. The usage of the `indexed` attribute is identical when used in a JSTL `c:forEach`
loop as when using the `logic:iterate` tag. Here is an example of how this would be
done for the Favorite Links portion of the form from Recipe 3.4:

```
What are your favorite links?
<table>
    <tr>
        <th>Name</th>
        <th>URL</th>
    </tr>
    <c:forEach var="webLink" items="${FavoritesForm.webLinks}">
        <tr>
            <td>
                <html:text name="webLink"
                        property="name" indexed="true"/>
            </td>
            <td>
                <html:text name="webLink"
                        property="url" indexed="true"/>
            </td>
        </tr>
    </c:forEach>
</table>
```

The rendered index values are generated correctly even when using the begin, end,
and step attributes to control the loop. The following use of the `c:forEach` tag demonstrates how to generate input fields for the first and third elements of a collection:

```
<c:forEach var="webLink" items="${FavoritesForm.webLinks}"
        begin="1" end="3" step="2">
    <tr>
        <td>
            <html:text name="webLink" property="name" indexed="true"/>
        </td>
        <td>
            <html:text name="webLink" property="url" indexed="true"/>
        </td>
    </tr>
</c:forEach>
```

This results in the following generated HTML:

```
<tr>
    <td><input type="text" name="webLink[1].name" value=""></td>
    <td><input type="text" name="webLink[1].url" value=""></td>
</tr>

<tr>
    <td><input type="text" name="webLink[3].name" value=""></td>
```

```
        <td><input type="text" name="webLink[3].url" value=""></td>
    </tr>
```

For rendering dynamic data in a loop for display, JSTL works well and should be easier to use than the corresponding Struts tags. As you have seen, JSTL has better support for accessing indexed properties than the Struts tags. For example, the following shows how the favorite colors could be displayed:

```
<c:forEach var="color" items="${favs.color}">
    <li><c:out value="${color}"/></li>
</c:forEach>
```

See Also

Recipe 3.4 demonstrates similar usages of indexed properties. You should consult the JSTL documentation if needed. The specification provides additional details on the tags mentioned here. The specification can be found at *http://java.sun.com/jsp/jstl*.

3.6   Submitting a Form from an Image

Problem

You want the user to be able to submit a form by clicking an image that isn't contained within the HTML form tags.

Solution

Use a link with a JavaScript URL to submit the form:

```
<html:link href="javascript:document.MyForm.submit( )">
    <html:img page="/submit-form.gif"
              alt="Submit" border="0"/>
</html:link>
```

Discussion

Web sites frequently use clickable images instead of HTML submit buttons to trigger form submission. The Struts html:image tag can be used to generate an HTML input type="image" tag that creates such an image. However, with complex HTML layouts, it is not always possible to nest the image within the <form>...</form> tags. In some cases, an HTML page may have multiple forms in one section of a page, with the images for submitting the forms in a separate region of the page.

The Solution above can be used to submit a form from an image located outside of the form tags. The image to display is nested in an html:link tag. The link submits the form by executing a line of JavaScript. In the Solution, the JavaScript will submit the form named MyForm. The form name must match the name attribute from the corresponding action element in the *struts-config.xml*. Here is the HTML that gets generated using the Solution:

```
<a href="javascript:document.MyForm.submit( )">
    <img src="/myApp/struts-power.gif"
        border="0" alt="Submit">
</a>
```

Though you could directly use the above HTML markup instead of the Struts `html` tags, you would lose the features provided by those tags. By using the Struts tags, you don't have to specify the context name, and you have the ability for the image name and alternate text to be retrieved from a resource bundle (if needed).

Another alternative is to use the `onclick` attribute of the `html:img` tag:

```
<html:img page="/submit-form.gif"
        onclick="document.MyForm.submit( );"
            alt="Submit" border="0"/>
```

The disadvantage of this approach is that most browsers won't provide a visual clue that the image is clickable. Since the image is nested in a link, most browsers change the mouse pointer to indicate that the image can be clicked as shown in the Solution.

 If you want to ensure that your web application will function for clients that have disabled JavaScript, a conventional submit button should be provided somewhere on the form.

See Also

Recipe 3.9 describes how to submit a form to an alternate URL from the one specified in the form's `action` attribute.

3.7   Generating JavaScript on the Fly

Problem

You want to generate JavaScript dynamically using data retrieved from your application's Model.

Solution

Use the Struts tags to render data within the JavaScript code just as you would within HTML:

```
<script language="JavaScript">
    function showMessage( ) {
        alert( "Hello, <bean:write name='myForm' property='name'/>!" );
    }
</script>
```

Discussion

The Solution above generates a JavaScript function that pops up a message box with the text "Hello, name!" The value for *name* is generated using the bean:write tag. The Solution shows how the Struts tags can be used to create JavaScript just as easily as they create HTML.

 JSTL can be used in the same manner.

While this solution seems obvious, it is surprising how many times this question comes up. Often the question is posed as, "How do I call a JavaScript function in HTML from Struts?" Technically, you can't *call* a JavaScript function on an HTML page from Struts. Struts—and the underlying JSP technology—runs on the server-side. JavaScript, in contrast, is processed by the browser on the client-side. However, with the dynamic generation capabilities of Struts as shown in the Solution, you can approximate this behavior.

Another important concept that this recipe hinges on is the JSP translation process. A JSP page is composed of JSP declarations, standard JSP tags (such as jsp:useBean), custom JSP tags (such as the Struts and JSTP tags), runtime expressions, and scriptlets. Everything else in the page is *template text*. The template text is anything that isn't processed as part of the JSP translation. People commonly think of template text as the HTML markup, but it is JavaScript or any other non-JSP processed text. The JSP translator does not care what form the template text takes. Therefore, you can as easily generate text into a JavaScript function as you can into an HTML element.

 If you are using JSP *documents* to generate well-formed XHTML, then dynamic JavaScript template text must be specified using a combination of jsp:text elements and CDATA sections. See Hans Bergsten's ONJava article at *http://www.onjava.com/pub/a/onjava/2004/04/21/JSP2part3.html* for more details.

The Solution presents a simple scenario. If the model data being accessed require the use of complex JavaScript data structures, such as Arrays, you could use iteration tags such as logic:iterate and c:forEach to populate those structures.

See Also

Recipe 3.8 uses iteration tags to generate client-side JavaScript arrays.

3.8   Dynamically Changing Select Options Using JavaScript

Problem

You want to use JavaScript to dynamically change the items displayed in an HTML select element based on data retrieved from your application's model.

Solution

Use the Struts logic:iterate tag to create JavaScript arrays for the different option sets. Then use a JavaScript onchange event handler to change the options set at runtime. Example 3-8 shows a complete JSP page where the JavaScript arrays are dynamically created using Struts tags. The changeOptions event handler function resets the options for the select control using the JavaScript arrays.

Example 3-8. Generating DHTML using Struts

```
<%@ page contentType="text/html;charset=UTF-8" language="java" %>
<%@ taglib uri="/WEB-INF/struts-bean.tld" prefix="bean" %>
<%@ taglib uri="/WEB-INF/struts-html.tld" prefix="html" %>
<%@ taglib uri="/WEB-INF/struts-logic.tld" prefix="logic" %>

<html>
<head>
    <title>Struts - JavaScript Example</title>
    <script language="JavaScript">
        // Create the array for the first set of options
        fooArray = new Array();
        <logic:iterate id="fooValue" indexId="ctr"
                    name="MyForm"  property="fooList">
            fooArray[<bean:write name="ctr"/>] =
                new Option("<bean:write name='fooValue'/>",
                            "<bean:write name='fooValue'/>",
                            false, false);
        </logic:iterate>

        // Create the array for the second set of options
        barArray = new Array();
        <logic:iterate id="barValue" indexId="ctr"
                    name="MyForm"  property="barList">
            fooArray[<bean:write name="ctr"/>] =
                new Option("<bean:write name='barValue'/>",
                            "<bean:write name='barValue'/>",
                            false, false);
        </logic:iterate>

        function changeOptions(var control) {
            // control is the triggering control
            // baz is the select control
```

Example 3-8. Generating DHTML using Struts (continued)

```
            baz = document.MyForm.baz;
            baz.options.length=0;

            if (control.value == 'Foo')
                bazArray = fooArray;
            else
                bazArray = barArray;

            for (i=0; i < bazArray.length; i++)
                baz.options[i] = bazArray[i];
        }
    </script>
</head>
<body>
    <html:form name="MyForm" action="processMyForm">
        <html:radio property="fooBar" value="Foo"
                    onclick="changeOptions(this);"/> Foo<br/>
        <html:radio property="fooBar" value="Bar"
                    onclick="changeOptions(this);"/> Bar<br/>
        Baz: <html:select property="baz">
            </html:select>
    </html:form>
</body>
</html>
```

Discussion

You can use Struts to generate JavaScript as you can use it to generate HTML. Some developers consider JavaScript "evil"; in reality, it's only "slightly wicked." Take a pragmatic approach: If JavaScript makes your application better and your users happier, then use it. But, use it in such a way that your business logic stays in the business layer, and not slapped on the web page. Struts helps you do just this.

A concrete example can illustrate this approach. Suppose you want to ask a user to select his favorite programming language and, subsequently, favorite Integrated Development Environment (IDE) for the selected language. The language will be chosen using radio buttons, and the IDE will be selected from a drop-down menu. If the language is Java, then the IDE drop-down will display options such as Eclipse, Net Beans, IDEA, etc. If the language is C#, then the drop-down will display Visual Studio and SharpDevelop.

Example 3-9 shows the action form that holds this data.

Example 3-9. ActionForm for favorite language/IDE

```
package com.oreilly.strutsckbk;

import org.apache.struts.action.ActionForm;

public final class MyForm extends ActionForm {
```

Example 3-9. ActionForm for favorite language/IDE (continued)

```java
    private static String[] javaIdes =
        new String[] {"Eclipse", "IDEA", "JBuilder",
                      "JDeveloper", "NetBeans"};
    private static String[] csharpIdes =
        new String[] {"SharpDevelop", "Visual Studio"};

    public String[] getJavaIdes() {return javaIdes;}
    public String[] getCsharpIdes() {return csharpIdes;}

    public String getLanguage() {
        return language;
    }

    public void setLanguage(String language) {
        this.language = language;
    }

    public String getIde() {
        return ide;
    }
    public void setIde(String ide) {
        this.ide = ide;
    }
    private String language;
    private String ide;
}
```

Example 3-10 shows the JSP (*favorite_language.jsp*) that renders the input page. This example is similar to the Solution.

Example 3-10. JSP Page using Struts-rendered DTHML

```jsp
<%@ page contentType="text/html;charset=UTF-8" language="java" %>
<%@ taglib uri="/WEB-INF/struts-bean.tld" prefix="bean" %>
<%@ taglib uri="/WEB-INF/struts-html.tld" prefix="html" %>
<%@ taglib uri="/WEB-INF/struts-logic.tld" prefix="logic" %>
<html>
<head>
  <title>Struts - JavaScript Example</title>
  <script language="JavaScript">
    // Create the array for the first set of options
    javaIdesArray = new Array();
    <logic:iterate id="ide" indexId="ctr"
                name="MyForm"  property="javaIdes">
        javaIdesArray[<bean:write name="ctr"/>] =
          new Option("<bean:write name='ide'/>",
                     "<bean:write name='ide'/>",
                     false, false);
    </logic:iterate>

    // Create the array for the second set of options
    csharpIdesArray = new Array();
```

Example 3-10. JSP Page using Struts-rendered DTHML (continued)

```
    <logic:iterate id="ide" indexId="ctr"
                name="MyForm"  property="csharpIdes">
        csharpIdesArray[<bean:write name="ctr"/>] =
            new Option("<bean:write name='ide'/>",
                        "<bean:write name='ide'/>",
                        false, false);
    </logic:iterate>

    function changeOptions(control) {
        ideControl = document.MyForm.ide;
        ideControl.options.length=0;

        if (control.value == 'Java')
            ideArray = javaIdesArray;
        else
            ideArray = csharpIdesArray;

        for (i=0; i < ideArray.length; i++)
            ideControl.options[i] = ideArray[i];
    }
  </script>
</head>
<body>
  <html:form action="/admin/ViewFavoriteLanguage">
      What's your favorite programming language?<br/>
      <html:radio property="language" value="Java"
                  onclick="changeOptions(this);"/> Java<br/>
      <html:radio property="language" value="C-Sharp"
                  onclick="changeOptions(this);"/> C-Sharp<br/>
      <p>What's your favorite development tool?<br/>
      IDE: <html:select property="ide"/>
      </p>
      <html:submit/>
  </html:form>
</body>
</html>
```

The `script` block nested in the head element contains the JavaScript. The `logic:iterate` tags loop over JavaBean properties to create two JavaScript arrays: one for the Java IDEs and one for the C# IDEs. Each array contains a set of `Option` JavaScript objects. The `Option` object represents an option of an HTML select control. This object takes four parameters in the constructor: the text value to display, the value to pass when the form is submitted, a Boolean indicating if the value is the default selected value, and another Boolean indicating if the value is currently selected.

The JavaScript function for changing the options comes after the `logic:iterate` loop. This function is pure static JavaScript. The radio button that triggers the change is passed as the parameter to the function. If the current value of the radio button control is Java, then the select control is populated with the `Option` objects representing the Java IDEs. Otherwise, the control is populated with the Option objects representing the C# IDEs.

The HTML body contains the form, rendered using the Struts html tags. The Struts tags support the JavaScript change listeners via the *onfunction* attributes. For radio buttons, the onclick listener works well. The single parameter passed to the function, this, is a reference to the HTML radio button. When the page is initially rendered, the display should look something like Figure 3-1.

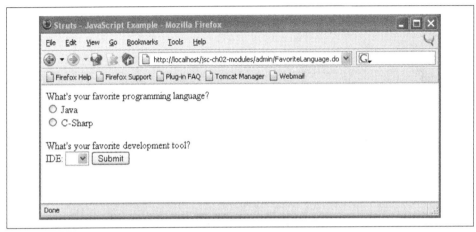

Figure 3-1. Form using DHTML and Struts

Once you click one of the radio buttons, the options in the drop-down list for the IDE field are populated with the data originally from the form bean. Figure 3-2 shows the display when you click the Java radio button.

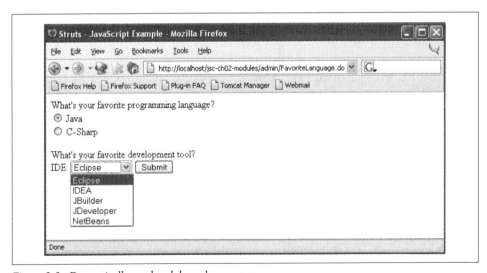

Figure 3-2. Dynamically rendered drop-down menu

Similarly, if you click the C-Sharp radio button, the values in the drop-down list change to reflect the values from the corresponding JavaScript array.

JSTL can be used instead of the Struts bean and logic tags. In this case, you use the JSTL c:forEach and c:out tags instead of logic:iterate and bean:write. These tags generate the JavaScript array in the same manner as the Struts tags:

```
javaIdesArray = new Array();
<c:forEach var="ide" varStatus="status"
        items="${MyForm.javaIdes}">
  javaIdesArray[<c:out value="${status.index}"/>] =
  new Option("<c:out value='${ide}'/>",
             "<c:out value='${ide}'/>",
             false, false);
</c:forEach>
```

JavaScript programming can be frustrating, particularly for the Java developer used to strong typing and compile-time checks. However, providing this type of dynamic client-side interaction can lead to a much richer end-user experience.

See Also

JavaScript: The Definitive Guide by David Flanagan (O'Reilly) is invaluable when it comes to JavaScript programming. If business logic is required to determine the dynamic data, then Recipe 3.9 provides a better approach.

3.9   Generating Dynamic Select List Options

Problem

You want to dynamically change the options displayed in a select element based on a change in another field in the same form, without having to render the set of options in client-side JavaScript.

 This problem isn't about avoiding JavaScript altogether; instead, it shows how to call a Struts action from a client-side JavaScript event listener.

Solution

Use an onchange or onclick JavaScript listener to call a JavaScript function that submits the form to a Struts Action. In the Action, perform the necessary business logic to construct a new collection for the select options, and forward control back to the original JSP page. Example 3-11 shows a JSP page that submits the form to an Action when the user clicks a radio button. The value of the radio button is passed to the Action as a request parameter.

Example 3-11. Submitting a form using JavaScript

```
<%@ page contentType="text/html;charset=UTF-8" language="java" %>
<%@ taglib uri="/WEB-INF/struts-bean.tld" prefix="bean" %>
<%@ taglib uri="/WEB-INF/struts-html.tld" prefix="html" %>
<html>
<head>
  <title>Struts - JavaScript Example</title>
  <script language="JavaScript">
     function getOptions(control) {
         form = control.form;
         form.action = "SetOptions.do?someProp=";
         form.action += control.value;
         form.submit( );
     }
  </script>
</head>
<body>
  <html:form action="ProcessMyForm">
     <html:radio property="someProp1" value="val1"
                 onclick="getOptions(this);"/> Value 1<br/>
     <html:radio property="language" value="val2"
                 onclick="getOptions(this);"/> Value 2<br/>
     SomeProp2:
     <html:select property="someProp2">
         <html:optionsCollection property="prop2Values"/>
     </html:select>
     </p>
     <html:submit/>
  </html:form>
</body>
</html>
```

Discussion

When the requirements for the dynamic interaction of a web page are driven by business logic, then it's best to use an Action, not JavaScript, to perform this function. Encoding business rules into JavaScript functions leads to hard-to-maintain, nonreusable code. A better approach is to execute the behavior on the server-side.

This recipe addresses the same problem as described in Recipe 3.8. However, the Solution here doesn't rely on the incorporation of the data in a JavaScript function. Instead, the function called by the onclick event handler submits the form to a different URL and Action than specified by the form's action attribute. This alternative URL directs control to an Action whose sole purpose is to determine the new set of options to display in the select control. This Action forwards control back to the original JSP page at which point the drop-down menu is populated based on the new values.

Creating a separate Action for changing the values in an HTML control may seem like overkill. However, the technique demonstrated here provides a flexible solution that puts the full power of the server behind the dynamic HTML. Consider the case where you are computing financial data for one field based on the values from another input field on the same form. The service for performing the calculation should be called by an Action. The Solution shown here works well for this scenario.

For a concrete example, the approach used in Recipe 3.8 will be replaced with the approach detailed in this recipe. This example provides an input form where a user can input information about his favorite programming language and IDE. The options for the IDE are contingent upon the selected programming language. Example 3-12 shows the JSP page (*favorite_language2.jsp*) that displays the form.

Example 3-12. Submitting a form to an alternate URL

```
<%@ page contentType="text/html;charset=UTF-8" language="java" %>
<%@ taglib uri="/WEB-INF/struts-html.tld" prefix="html" %>
<html>
<head>
  <title>Struts - JavaScript Example</title>
  <script language="JavaScript">
    function getOptions(control) {
        form = control.form;
        form.action = "GetIdeOptions.do?language=";
        form.action += control.value;
        form.submit( );
    }
  </script>
</head>
<body>
   <html:form action="ViewFavoriteLanguage">
      What's your favorite programming language?<br/>
      <html:radio property="language" value="Java"
                  onclick="getOptions(this);"/> Java<br/>
      <html:radio property="language" value="C-Sharp"
                  onclick="getOptions(this);"/> C-Sharp<br/>
      <p>What's your favorite development tool?<br/>
      IDE:
      <html:select property="ide">
         <html:optionsCollection property="ides"/>
      </html:select>
      </p>
      <html:submit/>
   </html:form>
</body>
</html>
```

The action elements in the *struts-config.xml* file specifies the URL paths used by the form. The first mapping, /FavoriteLanguage2, specifies the action that forwards to the JSP in Example 3-12. The second mapping, /GetIdeOptions, specifies the action that's called when the user clicks the radio button. The last mapping, /ViewFavoriteLanguage, specifies the action that processes the form when Submit is pressed:

```
<action    path="/FavoriteLanguage2"
           name="MyForm"
          scope="session"
           type="org.apache.struts.actions.ForwardAction"
      parameter="/favorite_language2.jsp"/>

<action    path="/GetIdeOptions"
           name="MyForm"
          scope="session"
           type="com.oreilly.strutsckbk.GetIdeOptionsAction">
    <forward name="success" path="/FavoriteLanguage2.do"/>
</action>

<action    path="/ViewFavoriteLanguage"
           name="MyForm"
          scope="session"
           type="org.apache.struts.actions.ForwardAction"
      parameter="/view_favorite_language.jsp"/>
```

The last piece of the puzzle is the GetIdeOptionsAction itself, shown in Example 3-13.

Example 3-13. Action for alternate URL

```
package com.oreilly.strutsckbk;

import java.util.ArrayList;

import javax.servlet.http.HttpServletRequest;
import javax.servlet.http.HttpServletResponse;

import org.apache.struts.action.Action;
import org.apache.struts.action.ActionForm;
import org.apache.struts.action.ActionForward;
import org.apache.struts.action.ActionMapping;
import org.apache.struts.util.LabelValueBean;

public final class GetIdeOptionsAction extends Action {

    public ActionForward execute(ActionMapping mapping,
                ActionForm form,
                HttpServletRequest request,
                HttpServletResponse response)
    throws Exception {
        MyForm myForm = (MyForm) form;
        String language = myForm.getLanguage( );
        ArrayList ides = new ArrayList( );
```

Example 3-13. Action for alternate URL (continued)

```
        if (language.equals("Java")) {
            ides.add(new LabelValueBean("Net Beans","Net Beans"));
            ides.add(new LabelValueBean("Eclipse", "Eclipse"));
            ides.add(new LabelValueBean("jEdit", "jEdit"));
        }
        else if (language.equals("C-Sharp")) {
            ides.add(new LabelValueBean("Sharp Develop", "Sharp Develop"));
            ides.add(new LabelValueBean("Visual Studio", "Visual Studio"));
        }
    myForm.setIdes( ides );

        // Forward control to the specified success URI
        return (mapping.findForward("success"));
    }
}
```

This class is responsible for retrieving the selected language from `MyForm`. The `Action` then sets the collection containing the corresponding IDE names into the form. For simplicity, this `Action` creates the collections directly. In a real-world application, these values would probably come from the business layer, perhaps from a database. Finally, the `Action` returns the *success* forward, looping back to the initial `Action`.

 A consequence of using this approach is that you may need to define the `ActionForm` to be in session scope. This will allow the main JSP page to reflect the changed data when the form is resubmitted back to the original page from the alternate `Action`.

For this example, the built-in `ForwardAction` processes the form, forwarding the request directly to the JSP page. If instead you were using a custom `Action`, consider extending the `DispatchAction` and implementing the ancillary action as a method of the `DispatchAction`. This approach allows you to keep related code together, making the application easier to maintain.

See Also

Recipe 3.8 provides an alternative solution to this problem that utilizes dynamically generated JavaScript arrays. The `DispatchAction` is covered in Recipe 6.8.

3.10   Filtering Text Input

Problem

You want to render data containing HTML tags, and you want that data to be interpreted and processed by the browser as HTML markup.

Solution

This is about as simple as it gets:

```
<bean:write name="myForm" property="freeText" filtered="false"/>
```

You can allow unfiltered values when using JSTL:

```
<c:out value="${myForm.freeText}" escapeXml="false"/>
```

Discussion

When you use the Struts bean:write tag to generate text, by default any special characters sensitive to HTML processing are replaced with their entity equivalents. For example, the greater than character (>) is replaced with the > character entity. This feature is known as response filtering and is enabled by default. In most cases, the filtering is desired, as an unfiltered response can be misinterpreted by the browser. Table 3-4 shows the characters and the corresponding replacement entities that are filtered by the bean:write tag.

Table 3-4. Filtered characters

Character name	Character value	Replacement entity
Less than	<	&lt;
Less than	>	&gt;
Ampersand	&	&amp;
Double quote	"	&quot;
Backslash	\	&#39;

Sometimes, however, you want rendered text to include HTML tags. Suppose you had an online journaling application that allows a user to enter text that will be displayed on a page. Allowing HTML permits the user to use tags that make text appear in bold or italics. The text could contain hyperlinks, different font sizes, and images. In other situations, your application may be retrieving HTML template text from some other source such as another URL, an XML file, a web service, or a database.

By setting the filtered attribute of the bean:write tag to false, you instruct the Struts tag not to replace the special characters with the corresponding entities. First, take a look at how the filtering works. Say a user enters the following text into a form:

```
Struts <b>rocks</b>!
```

Now this text is rendered using the bean:write tag. The text with the character entities replacing the special characters—when the filtered attribute is set to true (the default value)—looks like this:

```
Struts &lt;b&gt;rocks&lt;/b&gt;!
```

This is most likely not what the user wanted. He wanted it to look something like "Struts rocks!". However, since the intent was to allow the user to enter embellishing HTML tags, then setting the `filtered` attribute to false yields the correct rendering:

```
Struts <b>rocks</b>!
```

The browser will recognize the tags and apply the HTML markup as desired.

This is a useful mechanism when rendering a web page. However, care must be taken when using this approach. If the data are not filtered, then the layout of the rendered HTML can be compromised, and the entire page could appear mangled. For example, suppose the following text was entered:

```
Struts <b>rocks<b>!
```

At first glance, this looks fine. However, notice that the forward slash is missing on what should be the closing b (bold) element. This mistake is easily overlooked, and it could make all the text on the rest of the page appear bolded!

Unfortunately, avoiding this error is difficult. The best you can do is to try to ensure that the entered data is valid HTML. One option is to process the data through an XML parser. This will detect problems such as unbalanced tags. Another alternative is to process the data through a parser that will attempt to fix any errors, such as JTidy. Finally, if the data are coming from an uncontrolled source such as a user, you may want to disallow HTML altogether. If you still want the user to be able to enter text enhancements such as bold and italic, and hyperlinks, then you may want to consider using an alternative form of markup such as WikiText or UBB Code.

See Also

JTidy provides a command-line interface and Java API for parsing and tidying up HTML. Details on JTidy can be found at *http://jtidy.sourceforge.net*. UBBCode is a markup form natively supported by PHP. It is possible to process UBBCode using Java. A PHP function for parsing UBBCode that could be rewritten in Java can be found at *http://www.firegemsoftware.com/other/tutorials/ubb.php*.

3.11 Generating a Set of Related Radio Buttons

Problem

You want to generate a set of related radio buttons whose values are dynamically based on values retrieved from a Collection.

Solution

Expose the set of values for the radio buttons as a Collection that can be iterated over using the `logic:iterate` tag. The `idName` attribute of the `html:radio` tag should be the same as the value of the id attribute of the iterate tag. Use the value attribute of the html:radio tag to specify a property of the idName object. The value of this property will be the value for the generated input type="radio" HTML control:

```
<logic:iterate id="loopVar" name="MyForm" property="values">
  <html:radio property="beanValue" idName="loopVar" value="value"/>
   
  <bean:write name="loopVar" property="name"/>
  <br />
</logic:iterate>
```

Discussion

Radio buttons are HTML controls in which one button can be selected at a time. Radio buttons are grouped together based on the name attribute of the HTML input tag. Like other HTML form input elements, the label for the control isn't part of the control itself. Developers label the control however they want using regular text. Typically, radio buttons are labeled with the text to the right of the input tag:

```
<input type="radio" name="skill" value="1"/> Beginner <br />
<input type="radio" name="skill" value="2"/> Intermediate <br />
<input type="radio" name="skill" value="3"/> Advanced <br />
```

In some cases, the set of radio buttons in a group is dynamic. In other words, the radio buttons to render varies. Say you are taking a poll on programming languages and developer tools using a wizard-style interface. On the first page, you display a set of radio buttons where the poll takers pick their favorite language. On the second page, you present a set of related radio buttons where the poll takers pick their favorite IDE. The set of radio buttons for the IDE choices is dynamic, based on the language chosen on the first page.

First, you need to define the form that will be used to hold the selected language and IDE. Since these are simple String properties, you can use a DynaActionForm:

```
<form-bean name="DevPollForm"
           type="org.apache.struts.action.DynaActionForm">
  <form-property name="language" type="java.lang.String" />
  <form-property name="ide" type="java.lang.String" />
</form-bean>
```

Next, create the Java class that holds the set of programming languages and corresponding IDEs, as shown in Example 3-14. The values are hardcoded here for demonstration purposes. The Struts LabelValueBean is used to hold the name/value pairs for the data.

Example 3-14. Language choices JavaBean

```
package com.oreilly.strutsckbk;

import java.util.*;
import org.apache.struts.util.LabelValueBean;
```

Example 3-14. Language choices JavaBean (continued)

```java
public class LanguageChoices {
    public LanguageChoices() {
        // create the set of languages
        languages = new ArrayList();
        languages.add(createBean("Java"));
        languages.add(createBean("C#"));

        languageIdeMap = new HashMap();

        // create the set of Java IDEs
        LabelValueBean[] javaIdes =  new LabelValueBean[] {
                createBean("Eclipse"),
                createBean("NetBeans"),
                createBean("JDeveloper"),
                createBean("IDEA") };

        // create the set of C# IDEs
        LabelValueBean[] csharpIdes =  new LabelValueBean[] {
                createBean("SharpDevelop"),
                createBean("Visual Studio") };

        // relate the language and IDEs
        languageIdeMap.put("Java", javaIdes);
        languageIdeMap.put("C#", csharpIdes);
    }

    private LabelValueBean createBean(String name) {
        return new LabelValueBean(name, name);
    }

    public Map getLanguageIdeMap() {
        return languageIdeMap;
    }

    public List getLanguages() {
        return languages;
    }

    private List languages;
    private Map languageIdeMap;
}
```

The first JSP page (*lang_poll_1.jsp*), shown in Example 3-15, renders the form containing the radio buttons for the language choice.

Example 3-15. Generating related radio buttons via Struts tags

```
<%@ page contentType="text/html;charset=UTF-8" language="java" %>
<%@ taglib uri="/WEB-INF/struts-bean.tld" prefix="bean" %>
<%@ taglib uri="/WEB-INF/struts-html.tld" prefix="html" %>
<%@ taglib uri="/WEB-INF/struts-logic.tld" prefix="logic" %>
<html>
```

Example 3-15. Generating related radio buttons via Struts tags (continued)

```
<head>
  <title>Struts Cookbook - Developer Poll</title>
</head>
<body>
  <jsp:useBean id="languageChoices"
            class="com.oreilly.strutsckbk.LanguageChoices"
            scope="application"/>
  <html:form action="ProcessLanguageChoice">
    What's your favorite programming language?
    <p>
    <logic:iterate id="lang" name="languageChoices" property="languages">
      <html:radio property="language" idName="lang" value="value"/>
       <bean:write name="lang" property="label"/><br />
    </logic:iterate>
    </p>
    <html:submit value="Next >>"/>
  </html:form>
</body>
</html>
```

The LanguageChoices object is placed in application scope using the jsp:useBean standard JSP tag. Alternatively, this object could have been placed in scope using an Action or with a Struts plug-in.

After the bean is instantiated, the form is created. The logic:iterate tag loops over the Language property of the LanguageChoices bean. This property is a java.util.List of org.apache.struts.util.LabelValueBeans. The LabelValueBean class mates a String label and a String value. The label is accessed by the label property and the value by the value property. In this example, the label and value are the same. In a real-world application, the value would probably be some sort of identity value, usually different from the displayed text.

The logic:iterate tag exposes each LabelValueBean in the list as a scoped variable specified by the id attribute: "lang". The html:radio tag creates the actual input type="radio" HTML element. The property attribute identifies the name of the property of the ActionForm that will receive the value of the radio button. The idName attribute identifies the bean that contains the radio button value; in other words, the value exposed by the logic:iterate tag: "lang".

 The idName attribute was added with the release of Struts 1.1. With Struts 1.0, the value for the radio button had to be rendered using a runtime expression:

```
<html:radio property="language" value="<%= lang.getValue( ) %>
"/>
```

After creating the radio button, the label for the button is generated using the bean: write tag. This tag is used to render the label property from the LabelValueBean (lang).

Example 3-16 shows the source that is generated from the JSP page in Example 3-15.

Example 3-16. Generated source for lang_poll_1.jsp

```html
<html>
<head>
  <title>Struts Cookbook - Developer Poll</title>
</head>
<body>
    <form name="DevPollForm" method="post"
        action="/jsc-ch03/ProcessLanguageChoice.do">
        What's your favorite programming language?
        <p>
            <input type="radio" name="language" value="Java">
             Java<br />
            <input type="radio" name="language" value="C#">
             C#<br />
        </p>
        <input type="submit" value="Next >>">
    </form>
</body>
</html>
```

The second page of the poll asks the poll taker to choose a favorite IDE. The choices are based on the programming language selected on the first page. Like the first page, the choices are rendered as a set of radio buttons. Though the second page, shown in Example 3-17, is similar to the first page, this page uses a JSTL c:forEach loop.

Example 3-17. Generating related radio buttons via JSTL

```jsp
<%@ page contentType="text/html;charset=UTF-8" language="java" %>
<%@ taglib uri="/WEB-INF/struts-html.tld" prefix="html" %>
<%@ taglib uri="http://java.sun.com/jstl/core" prefix="c" %>
    <html>
<head>
  <title>Struts Cookbook - Developer Poll</title>
</head>
<body>
    Favorite Language: <b><c:out value="${DevPollForm.language}"/></b>
    <html:form action="ProcessIdeChoice">
        What's your favorite IDE?
        <p>
        <c:forEach var="langIde"
          items="${languageChoices.languageIdeMap[DevPollForm.map.language]}">
            <html:radio property="ide" idName="langIde" value="value"/>
             <c:out value="${langIde.label}"/><br />
        </c:forEach>
        </p>
        <html:submit value="Next >>"/>
    </html:form>
</body>
</html>
```

Accessing Complex Properties with JSTL

More interesting in Example 3-17 is how the JSTL expression language (EL) is used to retrieve the collection of IDEs for the chosen language:

```
${languageChoices.languageIdeMap[DevPollForm.map.language]}
```

The power of EL allows you to access normal JavaBean properties as well as mapped properties in almost any combination. To understand how the expression is evaluated, let's examine how it would be done in Java:

```
// get the language-ide map
Map ideMap = languageChoices.getLanguageIdeMap();

// get the selected language from the form bean
DynaActionFrom form =
  (DynaActionForm) session.getAttribute("DevPollForm");
String language = form.getMap().get("language");

// get the list of IDEs from the language-ide map
List ides = (List) map.get(language);
```

DynaActionForms expose their internal table of name/value pairs via the map property. This allows you to retrieve the chosen language from the DevPollForm dynamic form bean.

The html:radio tag is used just as it was on the first page shown in Example 3-15. Though c:forEach is used instead of logic:iterate, you can use the idName attribute of the radio tag. When using JSTL in this way, the idName should be the same as the value for the var attribute of the JSTL c:forEach tag.

See Also

Ted Husted has some great Struts tips at *http://www.husted.com/struts/tips*. Specifically, a discussion on the intricacies of the using radio buttons can be found at *http://www.husted.com/struts/tips/016.html*.

3.12   Handling Unchecked Checkboxes

Problem

You need to ensure that a Boolean ActionForm property, corresponding to an HTML checkbox, is set to false when the checkbox is unchecked.

Solution

Create a checkbox input field that uses JavaScript to set the value of a hidden Boolean field. Use the logic:equal tag to set the checked property of the checkbox if the value for the hidden field is *true*. The JSP page (*checkbox_test.jsp*) in Example 3-18 uses this approach to guarantee a true or false value is always submitted.

Example 3-18. Guaranteeing checkbox settings

```
<%@ page contentType="text/html;charset=UTF-8" language="java" %>
<%@ taglib uri="http://jakarta.apache.org/struts/tags-html" prefix="html" %>
<%@ taglib uri="http://jakarta.apache.org/struts/tags-logic" prefix="logic" %>
<html>
<head>
  <title>Struts Cookbook - Chapter 4 : Checkbox Test</title>
</head>
<body>
  <html:form method="get" action="/ProcessCheckbox">
    <input type="checkbox" name="foo_"
      onclick="javascript:elements['foo'].value=this.checked;"
      <logic:equal name="CheckboxForm" property="foo" value="true">
        checked
      </logic:equal>
    >
    <html:hidden property="foo"/>
    <html:submit/>
  </html:form>
</body>
</html>
```

Discussion

For such a common little field, the HTML checkbox can cause trouble. If a checkbox is unchecked and the form is submitted, no value for that field will be sent in the request. Suppose you have a form with one checkbox on it:

```
<html:form method="get" action="ProcessFoo">
  <html:checkbox property="foo"/>
  <html:submit/>
</html:form>
```

If the checkbox is checked, then the resultant request URL looks something like this:

```
http://localhost/jsc-ch04/ProcessFoo?foo=on
```

When processed by Struts, your `ActionForm` is populated by `BeanUtils.populate()` method. If `foo` is a `boolean` property, its value is set to true.

The problem occurs when you uncheck the checkbox with the intention of setting the property value to false. If the checkbox is unchecked, the resultant URL looks something like this:

```
http://localhost/jsc-ch04/ProcessFoo?
```

Where did the property value go? One would expect the request query string to contain "foo=off" or "foo=". Unfortunately, no request parameter is generated for an unchecked checkbox. When `BeanUtils.populate()` is called, it doesn't know to set the property value.

This problem can usually be handled by implementing the reset( ) method in your ActionForm. The Struts request processor calls this method before the ActionForm is populated. The method gives you a chance to set the form properties to desired default values. If the HTTP request doesn't contain a name/value pair for a property, then the property retains the value set in the reset( ) method. For checkboxes, set the value to false, as shown here:

```
public void reset( ActionMapping mapping,
                   HttpServletRequest request )
{
    foo = false;
}
```

However, the reset( ) method can't always solve the problem. If you're using a form in session scope in a wizard-style interface, then implementing reset( ) will clear the form when you don't want it to. You need an alternative that guarantees that a value will be sent when the form is submitted. The Solution does that by implementing two fields on the form. The actual form field corresponding to the Boolean ActionForm property isn't the checkbox, but is a hidden field generated using the html:hidden tag. The checkbox is then created using normal HTML (input type="checkbox"). A JavaScript onclick event handler is defined for this control:

```
javascript:elements['foo'].value=this.checked;
```

When a user clicks the checkbox, the value of the hidden field is set. If the checkbox is checked, the value is set to true; otherwise, it is set to false. To ensure that the checkbox renders correctly when the form is initially displayed, the logic:equal tag is used to render the checked attribute for the field.

See Also

This topic comes up fairly frequently on the *struts-user* mailing list. A good thread that discusses this topic is archived at *http://www.mail-archive.com/struts-user@jakarta. apache.org/msg93525.html*.

If you are using the Struts html:multibox control to render a set of checkboxes, a similar problem can occur when the user clears all the values. An archived discussion on this topic can be found at *http://www.mail-archive.com/struts-user@jakarta.apache.org/ msg96487.html*.

3.13   Handling Date Input Fields

Problem

You want to allow a user to input a value for a calendar date.

Solution

First, only use `String` form fields to hold the input date values. If the user can manually type in the date, it helps if you provide graphical Calendar control, either client- or server-based, that can populate the date input fields automatically. When the date value is submitted, validate the input using the Struts Validator.

Here's a `DynaActionForm`, JSP page, and `Action` that demonstrate this approach. The `DynaActionForm` is declared with the following `form-bean` element:

```
<form-bean name="DateForm"
        type="org.apache.struts.validator.DynaValidatorForm">
    <!-- Date 1 -->
    <form-property name="month" type="java.lang.String"/>
    <form-property name="day" type="java.lang.String"/>
    <form-property name="year" type="java.lang.String"/>
    <!-- Birth Date-->
    <form-property name="birthDateString" type="java.lang.String"/>
    <!-- Date 3 -->
    <form-property name="monthOpt" type="java.lang.String"/>
    <form-property name="dayOpt" type="java.lang.String"/>
    <form-property name="yearOpt" type="java.lang.String"/>
</form-bean>
```

The JSP page shown in Example 3-19 (*date_test.jsp*) renders fields for inputting data for these three variations of date formats. The first variation uses three numeric fields to accept the month, day, and year. The second variation accepts the date as a single value in *mm/dd/yyyy* format. This variation utilizes a JavaScript calendar that can be used to pick the value. The third variation uses drop-down menus for selecting the month, day, and year.

Example 3-19. Date input methods and formatting

```
<%@ page contentType="text/html;charset=UTF-8" language="java" %>
<%@ taglib uri="http://jakarta.apache.org/struts/tags-html" prefix="html" %>
<%@ taglib uri="http://java.sun.com/jstl/core" prefix="c" %>
<%@ taglib uri="http://java.sun.com/jstl/fmt" prefix="fmt" %>
  <html>
<head>
  <title>Struts Cookbook - Chapter 4 : Date Test</title>
  <script language="JavaScript" src="scripts/CalendarPopup.js"></script>
  <!-- This prints out the default stylehseets used by the DIV style calendar.
     Only needed if you are using the DIV style popup -->
  <script language="JavaScript">document.write(getCalendarStyles());</script>
</head>
<body>
  <html:errors/>
  <html:form action="/ProcessDate">
    Date 1 (mm|dd|yyyy):
    <html:text size="2" property="month"></html:text>
    <html:text size="2" property="day"></html:text>
    <html:text size="4" property="year"></html:text>
```

Example 3-19. Date input methods and formatting (continued)

```
   <br />
 <c:if test="${not empty date1}">
   Date 1: <b><fmt:formatDate dateStyle="full" value="${date1}"/></b>.
 </c:if>
 <p></p>
   <script language="JavaScript" type="text/javascript" id="jscal1x">
     var cal1x = new CalendarPopup("testdiv1");
     cal1x.showNavigationDropdowns();
     cal1x.setYearSelectStartOffset(60);
   </script>
   Birth Date (mm/dd/yyyy):
   <html:text size="8" property="birthDateString"/>
   <a href="" onClick="cal1x.select(document.forms[0].birthDateString,'anchor1x','MM/dd/
yyyy'); return false;" TITLE="cal1x.select(document.forms[0].
birthDateString,'anchor1x','MM/dd/yyyy'); return false;" NAME="anchor1x" ID="anchor1x">
select</A>
   <br />
 <c:if test="${not empty birthDate}">
   Birth Date: <b><fmt:formatDate dateStyle="full" value="${birthDate}"/></b>.
 </c:if>
 <p></p>
   Date 3 (month day, year):
   <html:select property="monthOpt">
     <option value="1">January</option>
     <option value="2">February</option>
     <option value="3">March</option>
     <option value="4">April</option>
     <option value="5">May</option>
     <option value="6">June</option>
     <option value="7">July</option>
     <option value="8">August</option>
     <option value="9">September</option>
     <option value="10">October</option>
     <option value="11">November</option>
     <option value="12">December</option>
   </html:select>
   <html:select property="dayOpt">
     <option>1</option>
     <option>2</option>
     <option>3</option>
     <option>4</option>
     <option>5</option>
     <option>6</option>
     <option>7</option>
     <option>8</option>
     <option>9</option>
     <option>10</option>
     <option>11</option>
     <option>12</option>
     <option>13</option>
     <option>14</option>
     <option>15</option>
```

Example 3-19. Date input methods and formatting (continued)

```
            <option>16</option>
            <option>17</option>
            <option>18</option>
            <option>19</option>
            <option>20</option>
            <option>21</option>
            <option>22</option>
            <option>23</option>
            <option>24</option>
            <option>25</option>
            <option>26</option>
            <option>27</option>
            <option>28</option>
            <option>29</option>
            <option>30</option>
            <option>31</option>
      </html:select>,  
      <html:select property="yearOpt">
            <option>2001</option>
            <option>2002</option>
            <option>2003</option>
            <option>2004</option>
            <option>2005</option>
      </html:select>
   <c:if test="${not empty date3}">
      Date 3: <b><fmt:formatDate dateStyle="full" value="${date3}"/></b>.
   </c:if>
   <p></p>
      <html:submit/>
   </html:form>
   <DIV ID="testdiv1" STYLE="position:absolute;visibility:hidden;background-color:
white;layer-background-color:white;"></DIV>
</body>
</html>
```

The generated page should look something like Figure 3-3.

The "select" link beside the Birth Date field displays a JavaScript calendar pop up. The birth date input field is populated with a correctly formatted value when the user selects a date from the pop up. Figure 3-4 shows the pop up.

Discussion

There are four primary rules of thumb that apply to handling dates. The first two are considered Struts best practices that apply to all form fields:

- ActionForms should only contain String properties.
- Validate all input fields, always on the server side and optionally on the client side.

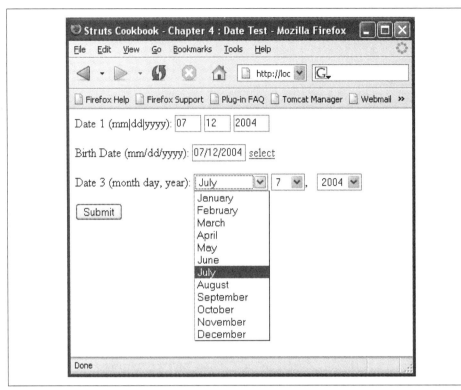

Figure 3-3. Sample date fields

- Make the date format apparent to the user by showing an accepted format pattern or example beside the field.

- For Date fields, use a Calendar control for better usability and to minimize typographical errors.

Working with dates can be aggravating; if you're not careful, it's easy for the user to input bad data. As a developer, using separate fields for the month, day, and year components of the date would seem to be a good approach. But users don't like having to move from field to field to enter a date; they would prefer entering the date in a single field. This mismatch of requirements can be frustrating for developers and users alike.

A compromise can be made by using a client-side calendar. (The calendar in the Solution was written by Matt Kruse.) This excellent calendar tool can be used to populate a single field with specific formatting as with the Birth Date field, or multiple fields as in the first and third date inputs shown in the Solution. If users have JavaScript turned off, then they can still manually key in the date.

Regardless of what approach you take, you should always validate the data. Recipe 8.6 provides all the details on date validation using the Struts Validator.

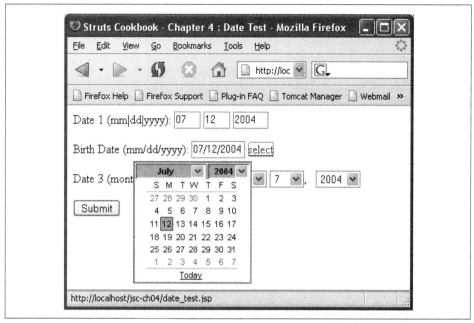

Figure 3-4. JavaScript calendar

See Also

Recipe 8.6 shows the different ways you can validate date fields using the Validator's built-in rules, regular expressions, or your own custom rules.

Matt Kruse's awesome calendar pop up can be found at *http://www.mattkruse.com/javascript/calendarpopup/*. While some web purists may frown on the use of JavaScript, the pragmatic developer can see how helpful a tool like this can be.

3.14   Setting Tab Order

Problem

You want to control the tab order of the elements on a page.

Solution

Use the `tabindex` attribute of the Struts `html` tags to sequence the fields:

```
<html:form action="/SomeAction">
  <table>
    <tr>
      <td><html:text property="field1" tabindex="1"/></td>
      <td><html:text property="field4" tabindex="4"/></td>
    </tr>
```

```
      <tr>
        <td><html:text property="field2" tabindex="2"/></td>
        <td><html:text property="field5" tabindex="5"/></td>
      </tr>
      <tr>
        <td><html:text property="field3" tabindex="3"/></td>
        <td><html:text property="field6" tabindex="6"/></td>
      </tr>
    </table>
  </html:form>
```

Discussion

On most most browsers, users can use the Tab and Backtab keys to set the form input fields, buttons, and hyperlinks that have the current focus. By default, the browser changes focus from field to field in the order that the elements appear in the source HTML document. This generally equates to a top-to-bottom, left-to-right sequencing. While this default ordering works fine in most cases, sometimes you need to control the tab ordering manually. Struts provides the `tabindex` attribute on most tags in the Struts `html` tag library for manually controlling the ordering. This attribute takes a positive integer value that indicates the sequence of the element.

In the Solution, an HTML table lays out the text fields of the form in a two-column fashion. You want the user to be able to tab down the fields in the first column and then down the fields in the second column. This newspaper-style column interface is more common than you might think. A web page that allows a user to enter a billing address on the left and the shipping address on the right could use such a layout.

The default tab sequencing won't provide the desired navigation. To override the browsers default ordering, the `tabindex` attribute is used. This attribute is a pass-through attribute to the actual HTML element rendered. In other words, the value of the attribute passes through unaltered to the value of the corresponding attribute of the rendered HTML element. The value for the `tabindex` should be a non-negative integer. Its value represents the relative tab ordering sequence of the element. The first element in a form might have a `tabindex` equal to "1," the second field "2," and so forth.

The browser determines the tab sequence of the fields using the `tabindex`. If an element does not have a `tabindex` attribute, then its position in the sequence is based on its order in the source document. If the `tabindex` is 0, the element will be skipped when tabbing. The browser starts navigation with the element that has the lowest nonzero `tabindex` value. As you press Tab, the browser changes focus to the element with the next highest value.

 The tab indices don't have to be sequential; you can skip values.

On a JSP page, the value for the tabindex can be dynamically generated using a scriptlet, or if you are using the Struts-EL libraries, a JSP 2.0 expression. This capability could be used, for example, if you were generating a dynamic set of fields in an iteration loop. A beneficial technique when using tab indices is to use non-sequential values. Instead of using 1, 2, 3, etc., use 5, 10, 15, and so on. With this approach, if you need to add a new field to the page, you won't have to re-sequence the tabindex values for all the elements. Add the field and set the sequence to an unused value so the fields are ordered as desired.

See Also

HTML: The Definitive Guide by David Flanagan (O'Reilly) is the quintessential reference for HTML.

3.15 Generating URLs

Problem

You want to generate a hyperlink URL for use in a JavaScript function, using the same mechanisms available to the Struts html:link tag.

Solution

Use the Struts html:rewrite tag to generate the URL in the function as needed:

```
<script language="JavaScript">
  function popupHelp( ) {
    window.open('<html:rewrite forward="showHelp"/>');
  }
</script>
```

Discussion

The Struts html:link tag can be used to generate hyperlinks that are based on a Struts action (Struts 1.2), a global forward, the name of a JSP page, or any other URL. Sometimes, however, you need to generate a URL for uses other than as the value of the href attribute of an HTML anchor (a) element. The Struts html:rewrite tag addresses this issue.

A common example of this usage occurs when a URL is needed within JavaScript. In the Solution, the html:rewrite tag generates the URL for the JavaScript window.open( ) function. This function opens a new browser window using the URL—the first argument of the function—as the browser location. Without the html:rewrite tag, you would have to hardcode the real path for the URL. Furthermore, if you needed to use URL rewriting to maintain the session ID, you would have to hardcode this as well. The html:rewrite tag properly handles URL rewriting just like the html:link tag. Like the Struts html:link tag, the html:rewrite tag can refer to a global forward, an action, a context-relative page, or an absolute URL. Exactly one of the following attributes must be specified:

forward
> The value of this attribute is the name of a global `ActionForward` specified as a forward element in the Struts configuration file.

action
> The value of this attribute is the name of an `action` element in the Struts configuration file. This attribute is only available in Struts 1.2.

page
> The value of this attribute, taken as a module-relative path, is used to generate a server-relative URI, including the context path and module prefix.

href
> The value of this attribute is passed through unchanged.

Request parameters can be added to the query string of the URL using the `paramId`, `paramName`, and `paramProperty` elements as with the `html:link` tag. If you need to add more than one parameter, use the technique shown in Recipe 3.16.

See Also

The Struts documentation for the rewrite tag can be found at *http://jakarta.apache. org/struts/userGuide/struts-html.html#rewrite*. Recipe 3.7 shows some other techniques for generating dynamic JavaScript using the Struts tags.

3.16   Adding Request Parameters to a Link

Problem

You want to add an arbitrary set of request parameters to a hyperlink or URL created using the Struts `html:link` or `html:rewrite` tags.

Solution

Create a `java.util.HashMap` as a page-context bean using the `jsp:useBean` tag. Populate the map using the JSTL `c:set` tag. Then reference the created map using the `name` attribute of the `html:link` and `html:rewrite` tags:

```
<%@ taglib prefix="c"    uri="http://java.sun.com/jstl/core" %>
<%@ taglib prefix="html" uri="http://jakarta.apache.org/struts/tags-html" %>

<!-- header stuff here -->

<jsp:useBean id="params" class="java.util.HashMap"/>

<c:set target="${params}" property="user" value="${user.username}"/>
<c:set target="${params}" property="product" value="${product.productId}"/>
```

```
<html:link action="/BuyProduct" name="params">Buy Product Link</html:link>
<a href="javascript:window.open(
        <html:rewrite action='/BuyProduct' name='params'/>)">
    Buy Product Popup
</a>
```

Discussion

The Struts `html:link` and `html:rewrite` tags allow you to add name/value parameters to the generated URL by referring to a `Map` property of a JavaBean. The map key is the parameter name and the map value is the parameter value.

While this approach is functional, it smells like a hack. You are forced to create Java code to represent something used only used to create an HTML link. Granted, the data comes from your business objects—which is the Model—but the parameter names are purely part of the View. A more practical problem with this approach is that the values for the parameters may come from different objects. Forcing developers to cobble together a class on the serverside to render a link reeks of a bad technique.

The Solution avoids this problem by utilizing the JSP, Struts, and JSTL tag libraries in concert. The `jsp:useBean` tag creates a `java.util.HashMap` as a page-scoped variable, and the JSTL `c:set` tag populates the map with name/value pairs. The `property` attribute is the map key and the value is the map value. The JSTL `c:set` tag provides an added benefit so you have the full power of the JSTL expression language to retrieve the value.

You can avoid the Struts tags altogether and use the JSTL `c:url` tag to create the URL:

```
<c:url="/BuyProduct.do" var="buyLink">
  <c:param name="user" value="${user.username}"/>
  <c:param name="product" value="${product.productId}"/>
</c:url>
<a href='<c:out value="${buyLink}"/>'>
Buy Product Link
</a>
<a href="javascript:window.open('<c:out value="${buyLink}"/>')">
    Buy Product Popup
</a>
```

Nesting the `c:param` tags within the `c:url` feels more natural than the `HashMap` approach supported by Struts. This approach, however, has a major disadvantage compared with the Struts tags: You cannot refer to your Struts actions or global forwards defined in your *struts-config.xml*. The Struts tags allow you to render the links with a transaction token. You surrender these features when you don't use the Struts `html:link` and `html:rewrite` tags.

See Also

If you are unfamiliar with JSTL, refer to Recipe 3.1. It has all the details you need to get started using these powerful tags. Another important source is the Struts documentation for the html tag library, which can be found at *http://struts.apache.org/userGuide/dev_html.html*. The Struts transaction token handling facility is discussed in Recipe 7.9.

3.17   Using Frames

Problem

You need to reference an Action or JSP page from within one frame to another.

Solution

Use the Struts html:frame tag to create frame elements with the proper URLs for your Struts application, as in Example 3-20 (*frame_test.jsp*).

Example 3-20. Generating a frame set with Struts

```
<%@ page contentType="text/html;charset=UTF-8" language="java" %>
<%@ taglib uri="http://jakarta.apache.org/struts/tags-html" prefix="html" %>
<frameset cols="50%,*">
  <html:frame frameName="_frame1"
                  page="/frame1.jsp"
          marginwidth="10"
          marginheight="10"
            scrolling="auto"
          frameborder="1"/>
  <html:frame frameName="_frame2"
                  page="/frame2.jsp"
          marginwidth="10"
          marginheight="10"
            scrolling="auto"
          frameborder="1"/>
</frameset>
```

Within the individual frame's source JSP, use the target attribute on the html:link and html:form tags to refer to the other frame. The JSP in Example 3-21 (*frame1.jsp*) demonstrates this approach.

Example 3-21. Frame with link to other frame

```
<%@ page contentType="text/html;charset=UTF-8" language="java" %>
<%@ taglib uri="http://jakarta.apache.org/struts/tags-html" prefix="html" %>
<%@ taglib uri="http://java.sun.com/jstl/core" prefix="c" %>

<html>
<head>
```

Example 3-21. Frame with link to other frame (continued)

```
  <title>Struts Cookbook - Chapter 04: Frame Test</title>
</head>
<body bgcolor="white">
<h2>Frame 1</h2>
  <html:link href="frame2.jsp?calledBy=FRAME_1" target="_frame2">
    Call Frame2
  </html:link>
  <p>
  Message received: 
  <c:out value="${FrameForm.map.message}"/>
</body>
</html>
```

Likewise, *frame2.jsp* shown in Example 3-22 defines a form that submits to an Action and directs the result to *_frame1* using the target attribute.

Example 3-22. Frame that submits to other frame

```
<%@ page contentType="text/html;charset=UTF-8" language="java" %>
<%@ taglib uri="http://jakarta.apache.org/struts/tags-html" prefix="html" %>
<%@ taglib uri="http://java.sun.com/jstl/core" prefix="c" %>

<html>
<head>
  <title>Struts Cookbook - Chapter 04: Frame Test</title>
<body bgcolor="white">
<h2>Frame 2</h2>
  Send a message to frame 1!
  <html:form action="CallFrame1" target="_frame1">
    <html:text property="message"/>
    <html:submit/>
  </html:form>
  <c:forEach var="paramValue" items="${paramValues}">
    <br />
    Parameter: <c:out value="${paramValue.key}"/><br />
    Values:
    <c:forEach var="theValue" items="${paramValue.value}">
      <c:out value="${theValue}"/><br />
    </c:forEach>
  </c:forEach>
</body>
</html>
```

Discussion

There are two key concerns when using HTML frames within a Struts application. First, the URLs of the frame elements within the frameset tag should be generated using the same rules used by the Struts html:link and html:rewrite tags—i.e., enter the html:frame tag. It supports the same action, page, and href attributes as the html:link and html:rewrite tags. The html:frame tag supports additional attributes specific to the

HTML frame element. Most of these attributes are pass-throughs, and the attribute value is passed through without modification to the generated frame element.

Second, with frame-to-frame interaction, you will probably need a user request, made on one frame, to affect the display of another frame displayed on the same page. The key to making this communication work is the use of the target attribute on the html:form and html:link tags.

The target attribute specifies the window or frame that receives the results of a request. The request can come from a form submission or link. In the Solution, a frameset is created that contains two frames—_frame1_ and _frame2_—positioned on the left and right, respectively. Frame 1, as shown in Example 3-21, defines a link with the page attribute set to _frame2.jsp_ and the target set to _frame2_. Parameters are passed on the query string that will be displayed by _frame2.jsp_:

```
<html:link href="frame2.jsp?calledBy=FRAME_1" target="_frame2">
    Call Frame2
</html:link>
```

Similarly, _frame2.jsp_, shown in Example 3-22, defines a form where the target is specified as _frame1_:

```
<html:form action="CallFrame1" target="_frame1">
```

The form-bean and action for this example are defined in the _struts-config.xml_ file:

```
<form-bean name="FrameForm" type="org.apache.struts.action.DynaActionForm">
  <form-property name="message" type="java.lang.String"/>
</form-bean>
...
<action    path="/CallFrame1"
          name="FrameForm"
         scope="request"
          type="org.apache.struts.actions.ForwardAction"
       parameter="/frame1.jsp"/>
```

When you first access _frame_test.jsp_ and click the link on the lefthand frame, you'll see the data displayed in Frame 2. Likewise, when you submit the form on the righthand frame, you will see the results displayed in Frame 1. Figure 3-5 shows the frames after this series of interaction.

If the target attribute was omitted, the output would be displayed in the same frame from where the request was made. Think of a frame as a browser within a browser. The Solution works the way it does because _frame1_ and _frame2_ are both part of the same frameset.

Other specially named targets are relevant to frames that are handled in specific ways by the browser. These special targets in described in Table 3-5.

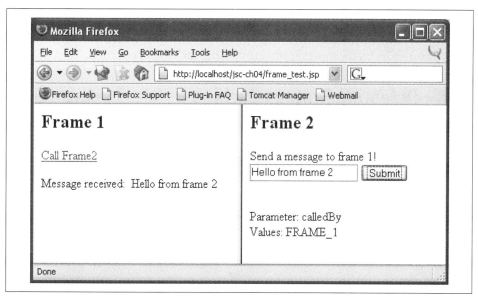

Figure 3-5. frame_test.jsp

Table 3-5. Special frame target values

Frame	Description
_blank	The browser loads the received request into a new browser window. This target is useful for creating pop ups.
_self	The browser loads the received request into the current window or frame. This is the default setting when the target is not specified.
_parent	The browser loads the received request into the parent window or frameset directly containing this frame. If the current reference is a top-level frame or window, this is equivalent to _self.
_top	The browser loads the received request into the window at the top of the hierarchy. This results in the request being displayed in the entire browser window.

Frames can get complicated, particularly if you use frames within frames as well as hidden frames. Many people prefer to steer clear of frames because of this complexity. Carefully consider your requirements when using frames. You may find that you can get similar behavior without the complexity of inter-frame communication using JSP includes or Tiles.

See Also

The Struts documentation for the html tag library provides complete details on the html:frame tag as well as the use of the target attribute. You can find this at *http://struts.apache.org/userGuide/struts-html.html*.

A great reference for details on frames can be found in *HTML and XHTML: The Definitive Guide* by Chuck Musciano and Bill Kennedy (O'Reilly).

Recipe 14.1 provides the basics of setting up Tiles for your application.

3.18   Defeating Browser Caching

Problem

You want to force the browser to display an up-to-date JSP page instead of showing the page from the browser's cache.

Solution

Set the nocache attribute to true for the `controller` element in your *struts-config.xml* file.

```
<controller nocache="true"/>
```

Discussion

To speed processing, browsers frequently keep a copy of a visited page on the client's local system. If an identical URL for the original page is requested and that page hasn't expired, the browser may display the page from the local cache instead of issuing a new request. This caching reduces network traffic and improves the user experience significantly. However, this can cause problems for dynamically generated pages. Consider a JSP page that renders data retrieved from the HTTP session. If data stored in the session changes, the browser won't be aware of the change. When the browser receives a new request for the page, it serves up the old page instead.

The easiest means of solving this problem for a Struts application is to configure the Struts `RequestProcessor` to generate a nocache header entry for every generated HTTP response. Set the nocache attribute to true on the `controller` element, as shown in the Solution. If the nocache attribute is not specified, the default value is false.

While this solves the problem, a consequence of its use is that every page accessed through a Struts `Action` results in a new request being sent to the server, even if the data haven't changed. One alternative solution is to generate a dummy request parameter with some unique value, such as the current time in milliseconds. This guarantees that the browser issues a new request. This technique works when the request uses the HTTP GET method; however, it may fail if the URL is accessed via an HTTP POST, or the URL is the result of a servlet forward to the URL.

Given these conditions, it would be nice if there were a way to indicate selectively which actions should be cached or not. You can delve into this by taking a look at how the Struts `RequestProcessor` handles the nocache attribute. The code below

shows the actual implementation of the processNocache( ) method from the org.
apache.struts.action.RequestProcessor class:

```
/**
 * Set the no-cache headers for all responses, if requested.
 * <strong>NOTE</strong> - This header will be overridden
 * automatically if a <code>RequestDispatcher.forward( )</code> call is
 * ultimately invoked.
 *
 * @param request The servlet request we are processing
 * @param response The servlet response we are creating
 */
protected void processNoCache(HttpServletRequest request,
                             HttpServletResponse response) {

    if (moduleConfig.getControllerConfig().getNocache( )) {
        response.setHeader("Pragma", "No-cache");
        response.setHeader("Cache-Control", "no-cache");
        response.setDateHeader("Expires", 1);
    }
}
```

You can provide a similar response handling on a per-Action basis by utilizing a custom action mapping. The custom action mapping, shown in Example 3-23, allows
specification of the nocache attribute on a per-action basis.

Example 3-23. A custom action mapping for avoiding browser caching

```
package com.oreilly.strutsckbk;

import org.apache.struts.action.ActionMapping;

public class NocacheActionMapping extends ActionMapping {

    private String nocache;
    private boolean nocacheEnabled = false;

    public String getNocache( ) {
        return nocache;
    }

    public void setNocache(String nocache) {
        this.nocache = nocache;
        nocacheEnabled = new Boolean(nocache).booleanValue( );
    }

    public boolean isNocacheEnabled( ) {
        return nocacheEnabled;
    }
}
```

A custom RequestProcessor evaluates the nocache setting for each request. Example 3-24 shows the custom RequestProcessor that checks the caching property of the custom ActionMapping, setting the HTTP response headers as appropriate.

Example 3-24. Nocache request processor

```
package com.oreilly.strutsckbk;

import java.io.IOException;

import javax.servlet.ServletException;
import javax.servlet.http.HttpServletRequest;
import javax.servlet.http.HttpServletResponse;

import org.apache.struts.action.Action;
import org.apache.struts.action.ActionForm;
import org.apache.struts.action.ActionForward;
import org.apache.struts.action.ActionMapping;
import org.apache.struts.action.RequestProcessor;

public class NocacheRequestProcessor extends RequestProcessor {

    protected ActionForward processActionPerform(HttpServletRequest request,
            HttpServletResponse response, Action action,ActionForm form,
            ActionMapping mapping) throws IOException, ServletException {
      ActionForward forward = null;
      if (mapping instanceof NocacheActionMapping) {
        NocacheActionMapping customMapping =
                (NocacheActionMapping) mapping;
        if (customMapping.isNocacheEnabled( )) {
          response.setHeader("Pragma", "No-cache");
          response.setHeader("Cache-Control", "no-cache");
          response.setDateHeader("Expires", 1);
        }
      }
      forward = super.processActionPerform( request, response,
                                            action, form, mapping);
      return forward;
    }
}
```

To complete the solution, you need to define the custom action mapping and request processor in your *struts-config.xml* file (see Example 3-25).

Example 3-25. Struts Config for action-based response caching

```
<?xml version="1.0" encoding="ISO-8859-1" ?>

<!DOCTYPE struts-config PUBLIC
        "-//Apache Software Foundation//DTD Struts Configuration 1.1//EN"
        "http://jakarta.apache.org/struts/dtds/struts-config_1_1.dtd">
<struts-config>
  <action-mappings type="com.oreilly.strutsckbk.NocacheActionMapping">
```

Example 3-25. Struts Config for action-based response caching (continued)

```
    <action    path="/main"
               type="org.apache.struts.actions.ForwardAction"
        parameter="/index.jsp">
      <set-property property="nocache" value="true"/>
    </action>
  </action-mappings>
  <controller
    processorClass="com.oreilly.strutsckbk.NocacheRequestProcessor"/>
</struts-config>
```

See Also

The Struts documentation for the controller element can be found at *http://jakarta. apache.org/struts/userGuide/configuration.html#controller_config*. Recipe 2.8 demonstrates another way that you can use custom action mappings.

CHAPTER 4

Tables, Sorting, and Grouping

4.0   Introduction

Chapter 3 covered many techniques for solving user interface problems. This chapter focuses specifically on ways to use HTML tables to solve a number of presentation-related problems.

The chapter starts by showing you some clever ways of using tables for simple histogram-style bar charts. The techniques in these recipes can liven data reporting web pages without relying on complex graphics generation.

A number of recipes discuss problems and solutions applicable to displaying tabular data in a grid. The recipes will show you how to alternate row colors in tables for improved readability, sort the displayed by clicking on a table header, and separate rows of data onto separate pages. You will find a recipe that combines all of these features using an easy-to-use open source tag library.

4.1   Creating a Horizontal Bar Chart

Problem

You want to create a simple data-driven horizontal bar chart on a web page without using an applet or graphics library.

Solution

Use nested HTML tables with the width percentages calculated dynamically:

```
<table border="0">
  <logic:iterate id="row" name="foo" property="bar">
    <tr>
      <td align="right" width="20%">
        <bean:write name"row" property="label"/>
      </td>
      <td align="left" width="80%">
```

```
        <table width='<bean:write name="row"
                              property="percentage"/>%'
             bgcolor="blue">
          <tr>
            <td align="right">
              <font color="white">
                <bean:write name="row"
                      property="percentage"/>%
              </font>
            </td>
          </tr>
        </table>
      </td>
    </tr>
  </logic:iterate>
</table>
```

Discussion

Displaying tables of raw numeric data may satisfy the functional requirements of your application, but outputting this information in a graph can make a tremendous difference to your end users. However, as soon as you start talking about graphics, the groans begin. Should you buy a reporting engine? What about a graphics-rendering framework? Do you need both? In many situations, if your application requirements can be met fairly by bar graphs, a combination of some clever HTML and Struts can do the work for you.

Consider a web application that displays weather forecast information. The application needs to display a bar chart that shows the chance of precipitation for the upcoming week. You'll create the WeeklyWeather class that holds the weather forecast as shown Example 4-1.

Example 4-1. JavaBean containing weather-related data

```
package com.oreilly.strutsckbk.ch04;

import java.util.ArrayList;
import java.util.List;

public class WeeklyWeather {

    public WeeklyWeather( ) {
        weekForecast = new ArrayList( );
        weekForecast.add(new DailyForecast("Sunday", 70));
        weekForecast.add(new DailyForecast("Monday", 40));
        weekForecast.add(new DailyForecast("Tuesday", 20));
        weekForecast.add(new DailyForecast("Wednesday", 5));
        weekForecast.add(new DailyForecast("Thursday", 50));
        weekForecast.add(new DailyForecast("Friday", 40));
        weekForecast.add(new DailyForecast("Saturday", 90));
    }
```

Example 4-1. JavaBean containing weather-related data (continued)

```
    public List getWeekForecast( ) {
        return weekForecast;
    }

    private List weekForecast;
}
```

The WeeklyWeather class uses the DailyForecast class, shown in Example 4-2, to encapsulate the pairing of the day and the chance of precipitation,

Example 4-2. Value object for daily forecast data

```
package com.oreilly.strutsckbk.ch04;

public class DailyForecast {

    public DailyForecast(String day, int chanceOfPrecip) {
        this.day = day;
        this.chancePrecip = chanceOfPrecip;
    }

    public int getChancePrecip( ) {
        return chancePrecip;
    }

    public void setChancePrecip(int chancePrecip) {
        this.chancePrecip = chancePrecip;
    }
    public String getDay( ) {
        return day;
    }
    public void setDay(String day) {
        this.day = day;
    }

    private String day;
    private int chancePrecip;

}
```

Now that the Model has been created for the application, the JSP (*horizontal_chart. jsp*) to render the chart can be written as shown in Example 4-3.

Example 4-3. Precipitation graph JSP

```
<%@ page contentType="text/html;charset=UTF-8" language="java" %>
<%@ taglib uri="http://jakarta.apache.org/struts/tags-bean" prefix="bean" %>
<%@ taglib uri="http://jakarta.apache.org/struts/tags-logic" prefix="logic" %>
<%@ taglib uri="http://java.sun.com/jstl/core" prefix="c" %>

<html>
<head>
```

Example 4-3. Precipitation graph JSP (continued)

```
  <title>Struts Cookbook - Chapter 04</title>
</head>
<body bgcolor="white">
<h2>Struts Cookbook Chapter 4 Examples</h2>
<div align="center">
  <hr />
  <h3>Color Bar Chart (horizontal)</h3>
  <jsp:useBean id="weeklyWeather"
            class="com.oreilly.strutsckbk.ch04.WeeklyWeather"/>
  <table border="0" width="60%">
  <logic:iterate id="dayEntry" name="weeklyWeather" property="weekForecast">
    <tr>
      <td align="right" width="20%">
        <bean:write name="dayEntry" property="day"/></td>
      <td align="left" width="80%">
        <table width='<bean:write name="dayEntry"
                            property="chancePrecip"/>%'
             bgcolor="#003366">
          <tr>
            <td align="right">
              <font color="white">
                <bean:write name="dayEntry"
                        property="chancePrecip"/>%
              </font>
            </td>
          </tr>
        </table>
      </td>
    </tr>
  </logic:iterate>
  </table>
</div>
</body>
</html>
```

Figure 4-1 shows the resultant web page.

The horizontal chart is generated by iterating over the weekForecast property of the
WeeklyWeather bean. A row of the table is generated for each element of the
weekForecast property, with each row consisting of two columns. The first (left-
most) column holds the name of the day of the week, and the second column displays the bars of the graph. The JSP page enables the graphing magic by specifying a
nested HTML table within the cell. The nested table uses the chancePrecip property
of the DailyForecast to set the width of the table as a percentage:

```
<table width='<bean:write name="dayEntry"
                      property="chancePrecip"/>%'
     bgcolor="#003366">
```

This percentage indicates the fractional amount of space that the table will occupy
within the containing table cell. This nested table is then filled to this percentage

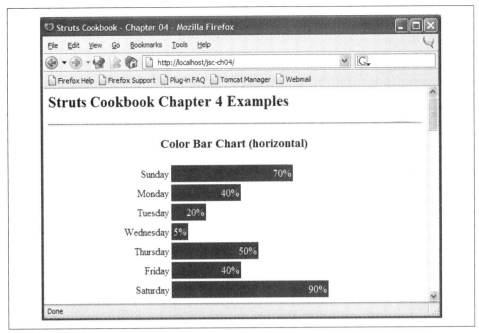

Figure 4-1. Simple HTML horizontal bar graph

with the background color specified by the bgcolor attribute. The actual content of this inner table is the percentage value text. By displaying the numeric percentage along with the graphic, you can pack a lot of information in a small space. If you didn't want to display the raw percentage data here, you could have set the cell contents to a nonblank space:

```
<td> </td>
```

In the Solution and in the Weekly Forecast example, the data to be graphed were in the form of a percentage value. The value was used without modification as the width percentage for the table. In many cases, the data is not a percentage but a raw scalar value. The main purpose for the chart may be to show a relative comparison of the data. You can compute the percentage value for the table width using simple arithmetic.

Continuing with the weather theme, suppose that you wanted to display the expected number of inches of rainfall per day for next week (starting with Sunday). Here is the raw forecast data from the weather service:

Day of week	Rainfall (inches)
Sunday	1.5
Monday	2.0
Tuesday	1.0

Day of week	Rainfall (inches)
Wednesday	0.2
Thursday	0.8
Friday	1.0
Saturday	3.0

To turn these values into percentages for comparison purposes, you would use the following formula:

```
Percentage = (rainfall / max(rainfall)) * 100
```

With this formula, the day with the *maximum* rainfall amount will yield a percentage of 100 percent. Since the percentage calculation is used for presentation purposes, performing the calculation on the JSP page is acceptable. The JSP expression language (EL) available with JSTL supports arithmetic. EL does not, however, provide an easy way to calculate the maximum value. You will code this calculation to the WeeklyForecast Java class. You'll want to add the rainfallAmount float property to the DailyForecast object. Then, you'll want to add a method to the WeeklyForecast that calculates and returns the maximum rainfall.

Now you can use this data to create the bar graph. Example 4-4 shows the JSP page (*horizontal_chart_jstl.jsp*) to create the graph. In addition to its calculation abilities, the JSTL fmt:formatNumber tag formats the text representing the numeric value. This page shows how to use an image instead of background color to fill the graph.

Example 4-4. Expected rainfall JSP

```
<%@ page contentType="text/html;charset=UTF-8" language="java" %>
<%@ taglib uri="http://jakarta.apache.org/struts/tags-bean" prefix="bean" %>
<%@ taglib uri="http://jakarta.apache.org/struts/tags-logic" prefix="logic" %>
<%@ taglib uri="http://java.sun.com/jstl/core" prefix="c" %>
<%@ taglib uri="http://java.sun.com/jstl/fmt" prefix="fmt" %>

<html>
<head>
  <title>Struts Cookbook - Chapter 04</title>
</head>
<body bgcolor="white">
<h2>Struts Cookbook Chapter 4 Examples</h2>
<div align="center">
  <h3>Expected Rainfall</h3>
  <table border="0" width="60%">
  <c:forEach var="dayEntry" items="${weeklyWeather.weekForecast}">
    <tr>
      <td align="right" width="20%">
        <bean:write name="dayEntry" property="day"/>
      </td>
      <td align="left" width="80%">
        <table background="images/raincloud.gif"
```

Example 4-4. Expected rainfall JSP (continued)

```
        width="<c:out value='${(dayEntry.rainfall div weeklyWeather.maxRainfall) *
100}'/>%">
        <tr>
          <td align="right">
            <span style="{color:black;background-color:white}">
              <fmt:formatNumber value="${dayEntry.rainfall}" pattern="##.0"/>"
            </span>
          </td>
        </tr>
      </table>
    </td>
  </tr>
  </c:forEach>
  </table>
</div>
</body>
</html>
```

The key to making the chart work is the calculation of the width percentage using JSTL:

```
        width="<c:out value='${(dayEntry.rainfall div weeklyWeather.maxRainfall) * 100}'/>%
```

The rendered bar chart is shown in Figure 4-2; it's obviously going to be a wet week.

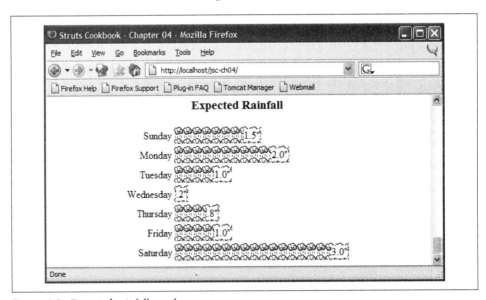

Figure 4-2. Expected rainfall graph

See Also

The graphics shown in this recipe are created through a clever use of HTML. More complex graphics can be created by dynamically generating actual graphic images using graphic support provided by Java. Jason Hunter shows some of these techniques in *Java Servlet Programming* (O'Reilly).

If you are unfamiliar with JSTL you'll want to check out Recipe 3.1. Recipe 4.2 demonstrates how to render a more traditional vertical bar chart.

4.2 Creating a Vertical Bar Chart

Problem

You want to create a data-driven vertical bar chart on a web page without having to use an applet or a graphics library.

Solution

Use nested HTML tables with the `height` percentages calculated dynamically:

```
<table height="500" width="60%">
  <tr>
    <logic:iterate id="row"
                name="foo"
             property="bar">
      <td valign="bottom">
        <table height='<bean:write name="row"
                                  property="percentage"/>%'
               width="100%" bgcolor="#003366">
          <tr>
            <td align="center" valign="top">
              <font color="white">
                <bean:write name="row"
                        property="percentage"/>%
              </font>
            </td>
          </tr>
        </table>
      </td>
    </logic:iterate>
  </tr>
  <tr align="center" height="10%">
    <logic:iterate id="row"
                name="foo"
             property="bar">
      <td align="center" width="50">
        <bean:write name="row" property="label"/>
      </td>
    </logic:iterate>
  </tr>
</table>
```

Discussion

In Recipe 4.1, the chart is generated using a `logic:iterate` loop. On each pass through the loop, a table row is generated. The first column of the each row holds the label, and the second column contains the bar graph. The graph is generated using a numeric value to specify the width percentage for a nested table that has a different background color.

A vertical bar chart can be thought of as a horizontal bar chart flipped on its side. The table for a horizontal chart has n rows by two columns, in which n is the size of the Collection being iterated over, and the two columns are for the label and the bar. The vertical bar chart, on the other hand, uses n columns by two rows. Instead of each pass through the loop generating a row, each pass generates a column. So, to generate a vertical bar chart, you use two iteration loops. The first loop generates the top row containing the bars. The second loop generates the bottom row containing the labels.

The mechanism for creating the bar is similar to that used for the horizontal bar chart: a table is nested within a table cell. For the vertical chart, the height percentages are set instead of the width.

```
<table height='<bean:write name="dayEntry"
                property="chancePrecip"/>%'
       width="100%" bgcolor="#003366">
```

You should locate the text containing the numeric value for each bar at the top end of the graphic. You set the value of the `valign` attribute for the `td` cell to top to get this alignment.

A concrete example helps pull this all together. You can use the same `WeeklyForecast` JavaBean and related classes that are used in Recipe 4.1 (shown in Examples 4-1 and 4-2). Example 4-5 shows the JSP page (*vertical_chart.jsp*) that generates the vertical bar chart.

Example 4-5. Vertical bar chart JSP

```
<%@ page contentType="text/html;charset=UTF-8" language="java" %>
<%@ taglib uri="http://jakarta.apache.org/struts/tags-bean" prefix="bean" %>
<%@ taglib uri="http://jakarta.apache.org/struts/tags-logic" prefix="logic" %>
<%@ taglib uri="http://java.sun.com/jstl/core" prefix="c" %>

<html>
<head>
  <title>Struts Cookbook - Chapter 04</title>
</head>
<body bgcolor="white">
<h2>Struts Cookbook Chapter 4 Examples</h2>
<div align="center">
  <hr />
  <h3>Color Bar Chart (vertical)</h3>
  <table height="500" width="60%">
```

Example 4-5. Vertical bar chart JSP (continued)

```
    <tr>
      <logic:iterate id="dayEntry"
                     name="weeklyWeather"
               property="weekForecast">
        <td valign="bottom">
          <table height='<bean:write name="dayEntry"
                                     property="chancePrecip"/>%'
                 width="100%" bgcolor="#003366">
            <tr>
              <td align="center" valign="top">
                <font color="white">
                  <bean:write name="dayEntry"
                              property="chancePrecip"/>%
                </font>
              </td>
            </tr>
          </table>
        </td>
      </logic:iterate>
    </tr>
    <tr align="center" height="10%">
      <logic:iterate id="dayEntry"
                     name="weeklyWeather"
               property="weekForecast">
        <td align="center" width="50">
          <bean:write name="dayEntry" property="day"/>
        </td>
      </logic:iterate>
    </tr>
  </table>
</div>
</body>
</html>
```

The rendered chart is shown in Figure 4-3.

If you look closely, you'll notice that the width of the bars is inconsistent. That's because the width of the label (day of week) displayed on the bottom row determines the width for the each column. You can normalize the column widths by specifying a size large enough to hold the widest label. Alternatively, you can calculate—using Struts and JSTL—a uniform percentage for the width—which you can apply to each column.

You use the Struts bean:size tag to create a scoped variable whose value is the number of columns. Then use a JSTL expression to turn that value into a percentage:

```
<bean:size id="cols" name="weeklyWeather" property="weekForecast"/>
<tr align="center" height="10%">
  <logic:iterate id="dayEntry" name="weeklyWeather" property="weekForecast">
    <td align="center" width="<c:out value='${100 div cols}'/>%">
      <bean:write name="dayEntry" property="day"/>
```

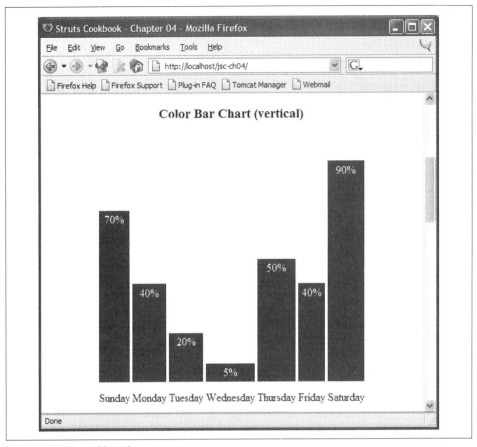

Figure 4-3. Vertical bar chart

```
        </td>
    </logic:iterate>
</tr>
```

See Also

Recipe 4.1 shows how to create similar charts as in this example but with a horizontal bar graph. Recipe 3.1 shows how to use JSTL in your Struts application.

4.3   Alternating Table Row Colors

Problem

You need to build an HTML table where the rows alternate in color or style.

Solution

Example 4-6 shows a JSP page (*struts_table.jsp*) that uses Struts tags to display tabular data where the background colors alternate between orange and yellow.

Example 4-6. Alternating table row colors using Struts

```
<%@ page contentType="text/html;charset=UTF-8" language="java" %>
<%@ taglib uri="http://jakarta.apache.org/struts/tags-bean" prefix="bean" %>
<%@ taglib uri="http://jakarta.apache.org/struts/tags-logic" prefix="logic" %>
  <html>
<head>
  <title>Struts Cookbook - Chapter 4 : Tables</title>
  <style>
  /* Even row */
  .row1 {background-color:orange;}

  /* Odd row */
  .row0 {background-color:yellow;}
  </style>
</head>
<body>
  <jsp:useBean id="weeklyWeather"
           class="com.oreilly.strutsckbk.ch04.WeeklyWeather"/>
  <table>
    <tr>
      <th>Day of Week</th>
      <th>Chance of Precipitation</th>
      <th>Expected Precipitation (inches)</th>
    </tr>
    <logic:iterate id="forecast" indexId="count"
               name="weeklyWeather" property="weekForecast">
      <tr>
        <td class='row<%= count.intValue( ) % 2 %>'>
          <bean:write name="forecast" property="day"/>
        </td>
        <td class='row<%= count.intValue( ) % 2 %>'>
          <bean:write name="forecast" property="chancePrecip"/>
        </td>
        <td class='row<%= count.intValue( ) % 2 %>'>
          <bean:write name="forecast" property="rainfall"/>
        </td>
      </tr>
    </logic:iterate>
  </table>
</body>
</html>
```

Example 4-7 (*jstl_table.jsp*) shows a cleaner solution that uses JSTL EL instead of relying on JSP scriptlet.

Example 4-7. Alternating table row colors using JSTL

```
<%@ page contentType="text/html;charset=UTF-8" language="java" %>
<%@ taglib uri="http://java.sun.com/jstl/core" prefix="c" %>
<html>
<head>
  <title>Struts Cookbook - Chapter 4 : Tables</title>
  <style>
  /* Even row */
  .evenRow {background-color:orange;}

  /* Odd row */
  .oddRow {background-color:yellow;}
  </style>
</head>
<body>
  <jsp:useBean id="weeklyWeather"
          class="com.oreilly.strutsckbk.ch04.WeeklyWeather"/>
  <table>
    <tr>
      <th>Day of Week</th>
      <th>Chance of Precipitation</th>
      <th>Expected Precipitation (inches)</th>
    </tr>
    <c:forEach var="forecast"
            items="${weeklyWeather.weekForecast}"
          varStatus="loop">
      <c:set var="tdclass" value="oddRow"/>
      <c:if test="${loop.count % 2 == 0}">
        <c:set var="tdclass" value="evenRow"/>
      </c:if>
      <tr>
        <td class='<c:out value="${tdclass}"/>'>
          <c:out value="${forecast.day}"/>
        </td>
        <td class='<c:out value="${tdclass}"/>'>
          <c:out value="${forecast.chancePrecip}"/>
        </td>
        <td class='<c:out value="${tdclass}"/>'>
          <c:out value="${forecast.rainfall}"/>
        </td>
      </tr>
    </c:forEach>
  </table>
</body>
</html>
```

Discussion

It doesn't take a usability expert to show you that alternating the color or style of tabular data rows makes the table more readable. Both approaches shown in the Solution—the first using Struts tags and the second using JSTL—render a table with alternating row colors. In each approach, the style element in the head defines two styles for alternation. In the first approach, the styles are identified as *row1* and *row0*. The logic:iterate loop iterates over the data Collection. The indexId attribute creates a scripting variable that holds the current value of the loop index. This value starts at 0 and increments by one on each iteration of the loop. The modulus (remainder) operation is used to calculate a 0 or 1. The style to use is specified by concatenating row to the calculated modulus:

```
class='row<%= count.intValue() % 2 %>
```

Since count is a java.lang.Integer object, you must use the intValue() method when performing the calculation. The calculation returns the remainder from dividing count by 2. Therefore, if the loop index is an even number—2, 4, etc.—then the style ID for the class attribute will be *row0*. If the loop index is an odd number, *row1* will be used. The result is that the rows alternate in color. Figure 4-4 shows the rendered page generated by the first approach.

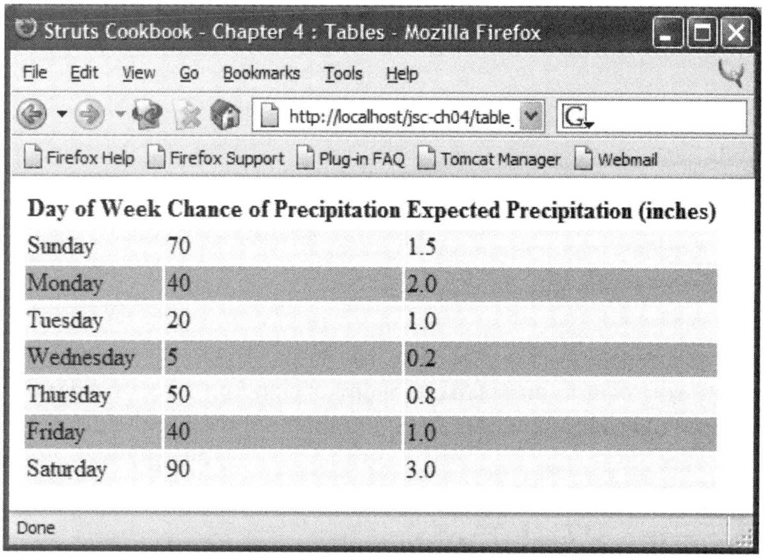

Figure 4-4. HTML table with alternating colors

The use of Cascading Style Sheet (CSS) styles makes this solution flexible. The style allows for a myriad of presentation effects to be applied in addition to the basic background color. However, this solution does force you to name each style in a contrived fashion—the name must end in a 0 or 1.

The second approach uses JSTL only, and no Struts tags are used. The generated HTML is identical to the first, but three significant differences occur between the JSTL approach and the Struts-based one. First, the remainder calculation to determine if a row is odd or even is handled using EL instead of scriptlet. Second, the c:if tag directly determines the style to apply; you aren't forced to name the styles *row0* and *row1*.

The third difference is subtle, yet important. When the `varStatus` attribute is used, the `c:forEach` loop exposes an object that indicates the status of the loop. This object has properties that represent the `index` of the underlying collection and the `count` of the number of loops that have occurred. This property is useful if the `c:forEach` iterates over a portion of a collection by specifying the `begin`, `end`, or `step` attributes. For example, consider the following `c:forEach` loop:

```
<c:forEach var="bar" items="fooList" begin="3" step="2" varStatus="loopStat">
    Index: <c:out value="${loopStat.index}"/><br />
    Count: <c:out value="${loopStat.count}"/> <br />
</c:forEach>
```

This loop starts with the fourth element (begin="3") and displays every other element (step="2"). The output from this loop would look something like:

```
Index: 3
Count: 1
Index: 5
Count: 2
Index: 7
Count: 3
...
```

If the index, instead of the count, were used to calculate the modulus, the colors would never alternate.

See Also

Recipe 3.1 provides the basics needed to use JSTL in your application. Recipe 4.4 shows how to sort data in an HTML table by clicking on a row header. Recipe 4.6 shows you how to create the effects shown in this recipe using the display tags open source tag library.

4.4   Sorting HTML Tables

Problem

You need to sort the results of a displayed table by clicking on a column header.

Solution

Create an `Action`, as shown in Example 4-8, that uses the `BeanComparator` class of the Jakarta Commons BeanUtils library to sort the underlying Collection.

Example 4-8. Sorting tabular data with an Action

```java
package com.oreilly.strutsckbk.ch04;

import java.util.ArrayList;
import java.util.Collections;
import java.util.Comparator;
import java.util.List;

import javax.servlet.http.HttpServletRequest;
import javax.servlet.http.HttpServletResponse;

import org.apache.commons.beanutils.BeanComparator;
import org.apache.commons.collections.comparators.ReverseComparator;
import org.apache.struts.action.Action;
import org.apache.struts.action.ActionForm;
import org.apache.struts.action.ActionForward;
import org.apache.struts.action.ActionMapping;

public class ViewForecastAction extends Action {

  public ActionForward execute(ActionMapping mapping,
      ActionForm form,
      HttpServletRequest request,
      HttpServletResponse response) throws Exception {
    // create the weather bean
    WeeklyWeather weather = new WeeklyWeather();

    // create a list to hold the forecast
    List list = new ArrayList();
    list.addAll( weather.getWeekForecast() );

    // get the sort by request param
    String sortBy = request.getParameter("sortBy");

    // get the reverse request param
    boolean reverse = false;
    String reverseParam = request.getParameter("reverse");
    if (reverseParam != null)
        reverse = Boolean.valueOf(reverseParam).booleanValue();

    // sort the list
    if (sortBy != null) {
      Comparator comparator = new BeanComparator(sortBy);
      if(reverse) comparator = new ReverseComparator(comparator);
      Collections.sort( list, comparator );
    }

    // add the list as a request attribute and forward to the JSP
    request.setAttribute( "weekForecast", list );
    return mapping.findForward("success");
  }
}
```

Then create an action element in the *struts-config.xml* that uses ViewForecastAction and forwards to the JSP page that displays the table:

```
<action path="/ViewForecast"
        type="com.oreilly.strutsckbk.ch04.ViewForecastAction">
    <forward name="success" path="/sorted_struts_table.jsp"/>
</action>
```

On the JSP page (*sorted_struts_table.jsp*), shown in Example 4-9, the table header cells contain links to the ViewForecast action. Each link sets request parameters that indicate the property name to sort by and if the sort order is reversed (i.e., descending).

Example 4-9. Using table column headers for sorting

```
<%@ page contentType="text/html;charset=UTF-8" language="java" %>
<%@ taglib uri="http://jakarta.apache.org/struts/tags-bean" prefix="bean" %>
<%@ taglib uri="http://jakarta.apache.org/struts/tags-logic" prefix="logic" %>
  <html>
<head>
  <title>Struts Cookbook - Chapter 4 : Sorted Struts Table</title>
</head>
<body>
  <table width="60%" border="2">
    <tr>
      <th>Day of Week<br />
        <a href="ViewForecast.do">unsort</a>
      </th>
      <th>Chance of Precipitation<br />
        <a href="ViewForecast.do?sortBy=chancePrecip">asc</a>
        <a href="ViewForecast.do?sortBy=chancePrecip&reverse=true">desc</a>
      </th>
      <th>Expected Precipitation (inches)<br />
        <a href="ViewForecast.do?sortBy=rainfall">asc</a>
        <a href="ViewForecast.do?sortBy=rainfall&reverse=true">desc</a>
      </th>
    </tr>
    <logic:iterate id="forecast" name="weekForecast">
      <tr>
        <td>
          <bean:write name="forecast" property="day"/>
        </td>
        <td>
          <bean:write name="forecast" property="chancePrecip"/>
        </td>
        <td>
          <bean:write name="forecast" property="rainfall"/>
        </td>
      </tr>
    </logic:iterate>
  </table>
</body>
</html>
```

Discussion

The approach shown in the solution performs an in-memory sort of the data displayed in an HTML table.

 If the tabular data were stored in a database, you would need to store the data collection in the session or refetch the data from the database between requests.

The table is sorted by creating a `java.util.Comparator` based on the name of the property to sort by. The `BeanComparator` class provides the intelligence to create the comparator using JavaBean introspection. The created `Comparator` sorts the data based on the natural ordering of the property. If a reverse or descending order sort is desired, a `ReverseComparator` is created from the `BeanComparator`.

Comparing Java Objects

The value passed to the `BeanComparator` must implement the `java.lang.Comparable` interface. How that object implements `Comparable` determines that object's natural ordering. For `Strings`, the ordering is lexicographic, in other words, dictionary ordering. For numbers, the ordering is numeric.

What's sweet about the `BeanComparator` is that it does all the sorting for you, yet allows you to control the order. Return an object from the property getter that implements the `Comparable` interface. In the `compareTo(Object obj)` method, you can enforce whatever ordering you want. For more information on comparing Java objects, check out Budi Kurniawan's *ONJava* article at *http://www.onjava.com/pub/a/onjava/2003/03/12/java_comp.html*.

The Solution for this problem is easy. The grunt work of creating the `Comparators` is handled by the `BeanComparator`. If you add a new property to the object in the collection, it can be sorted by passing in a request parameter with the name of that property. If you want to return the collection to its natural, unsorted state, don't pass in the sortBy parameter.

Sorting in ascending or descending order is handled via the reverse request parameter. This parameter is mapped to a Boolean variable. If reverse is true, a `ReverseComparator` is used.

The JSP page adds sorting capability by providing links that forward to the `ViewForecast` action. Each link specifies a sortBy parameter corresponding to the column to be sorted. The link for sorting in descending order adds the reverse parameter. Figure 4-5 shows the resultant web page for the Solution. Here the "desc" link in the third column was clicked to order the data by greatest expected rainfall. You can see the generated URL for the "desc" link in the browser's status bar.

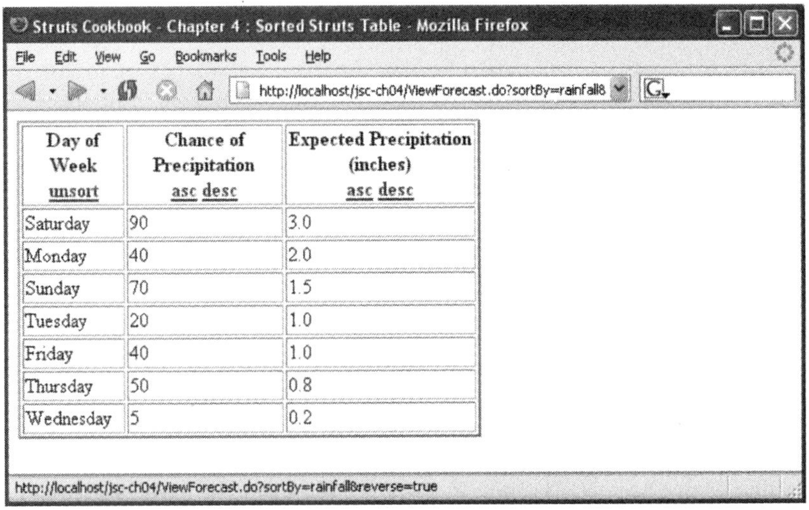

Figure 4-5. Sorted table

See Also

This Solution was based in-part on suggestions made in the *struts-user* mailing list. One useful thread posting by Henri Yandell is archived at *http://www.mail-archive.com/ struts-user%40jakarta.apache.org/msg95356.html*.

JSTL tags can be used to create the table instead of the Struts logic:iterate and bean:write tags. Recipe 4.3 shows examples of JSTL to create tables. Recipe 4.6 shows you how to provide table sorting using the *display tags* open source tag library. You do not need to code any special Java sorting actions if you use this popular tag library.

For further information on the BeanUtils sorting capabilities, check out the Java-Docs at *http://jakarta.apache.org/commons/beanutils/api/org/apache/commons/ beanutils/BeanComparator.html*.

4.5   Paging Tables

Problem

Instead of creating a long page to display a large number of tabular items, you want to display a limited fraction of the data on a page, allowing the user to navigate between the pages.

Solution

The simplest way to perform paging without resorting to a third-party tag library is to leverage the arithmetic capabilities of JSTL EL and the features of JSTL's `c:forEach` tag. The JSP page (*paged_data.jsp*) of Example 4-10 presents a complete page that supports paging through a Collection.

Example 4-10. Using JSTL for data paging

```
<%@ page contentType="text/html;charset=UTF-8" language="java" %>
<%@ taglib uri="http://jakarta.apache.org/struts/tags-bean" prefix="bean" %>
<%@ taglib uri="http://java.sun.com/jstl/core" prefix="c" %>
<html>
<head>
  <title>Struts Cookbook - Chapter 4 : Paging</title>
</head>
<body>
  <jsp:useBean id="pagedData" class="com.oreilly.strutsckbk.ch04.PagedData"/>
  <bean:size id="listSize" name="pagedData" property="data"/>
  <c:set var="pageSize" value="10"/>
  <c:set var="pageBegin" value="${param.pageBegin}"/>
  <c:set var="pageEnd" value="${pageBegin + pageSize - 1}"/>
  <c:if test="${(pageBegin - pageSize) ge 0}">
    <a href='<c:url value="paged_data.jsp">
              <c:param name="pageBegin" value="${pageBegin - pageSize}"/>
             </c:url>'>
      Prev
    </a>
  </c:if>
   
  <c:if test="${(listSize gt pageSize) and (pageEnd lt listSize)}">
    <a href='<c:url value="paged_data.jsp">
              <c:param name="pageBegin" value="${pageBegin + pageSize}"/>
             </c:url>'>
      Next
    </a>
  </c:if>
  <table border="2">
    <tr>
      <th>First Name</th>
      <th>Last Name</th>
      <th>Term of Office</th>
    </tr>
    <c:forEach var="pres" items="${pagedData.data}"
            begin="${pageBegin}" end="${pageEnd}">
      <tr>
        <td>
          <c:out value="${pres.firstName}"/>
        </td>
        <td>
          <c:out value="${pres.lastName}"/>
        </td>
        <td>
```

Example 4-10. Using JSTL for data paging (continued)

```
            <c:out value="${pres.term}"/>
          </td>
        </tr>
      </c:forEach>
    </table>
  </body>
</html>
```

Discussion

An application's usability improves when the user doesn't have to scroll around, vertically or horizontally, to see all the data on a web page. For a business application, this usability, or lack thereof, can make a measurable difference in productivity. This recipe addresses the problem of displaying a collection of data of indeterminate length. This frequently occurs in database-driven applications where the data is rendered in tabular fashion.

The Solution provided can be completely implemented at the presentation level. No requirements are made on the model of the data or on any controller Actions that process the data.

This solution provides presentation-level paging. It doesn't restrict the data amount initially received from the underlying persistent store.

In the Solution, the data being paged through is hardcoded into the JavaBeans shown in Example 4-11. In a real application, these data would more likely come from a persistence store such as a database or filesystem.

Example 4-11. JavaBean that holds data collection

```
package com.oreilly.strutsckbk.ch04;

import java.util.ArrayList;
import java.util.List;

public class PagedData {

    private List list;

    public PagedData( ) {
        list = new ArrayList( );
        list.add( new President( "Washington", "George", "1789-97") );
        list.add( new President( "Adams", "John", "1797-1801") );
        list.add( new President( "Jefferson", "Thomas", "1801-09") );
        list.add( new President( "Madison", "James", "1809-17") );
        list.add( new President( "Monroe", "James", "1817-25") );
        list.add( new President( "Jackson", "Andrew", "1829-37") );
        list.add( new President( "Van Buren", "Martin", "1837-41") );
        list.add( new President( "Harrison", "William Henry", "1841") );
```

Example 4-11. JavaBean that holds data collection (continued)

```
        list.add( new President( "Tyler", "John", "1841-45") );
        list.add( new President( "Polk", "James", "1845-49") );
        list.add( new President( "Taylor", "Zachary", "1849-50") );
        list.add( new President( "Fillmore", "Millard", "1850-53") );
        list.add( new President( "Pierce", "Franklin", "1853-57") );
        list.add( new President( "Buchanan", "James", "1857") );
        list.add( new President( "Lincoln", "Abraham", "1861-65") );
        list.add( new President( "Johnson", "Andrew", "1865-69") );
        list.add( new President( "Grant", "Ulysses S.", "1869-77") );
        list.add( new President( "Hayes", "Rutherford B.", "1877-81") );
        list.add( new President( "Garfield", "James", "1881") );
        list.add( new President( "Arthur", "Chester", "1881-85") );
        list.add( new President( "Cleveland", "Grover", "1885-89") );
        list.add( new President( "Harrison", "Benjamin", "1889-93") );
        list.add( new President( "Cleveland", "Grover", "1893-97") );
        list.add( new President( "McKinley", "William", "1897-1901") );
        list.add( new President( "Roosevelt", "Theodore", "1901-09") );
        list.add( new President( "Taft", "William H.", "1909-13") );
        list.add( new President( "Wilson", "Woodrow", "1913-21") );
        list.add( new President( "Jackson", "Andrew", "1829-37") );
        list.add( new President( "Harding", "Warren", "1921-23") );
        list.add( new President( "Coolidge", "Calvin", "1923-29") );
        list.add( new President( "Hoover", "Herbert", "1929-33") );
        list.add( new President( "Roosevelt", "Franklin D.", "1933-45") );
        list.add( new President( "Truman", "Harry", "1945-53") );
        list.add( new President( "Eisenhower", "Dwight", "1953-61") );
        list.add( new President( "Kennedy", "John F.", "1961-63") );
        list.add( new President( "Johnson", "Lyndon", "1963-69") );
        list.add( new President( "Nixon", "Richard", "1969-74") );
        list.add( new President( "Ford", "Gerald", "1974-77") );
        list.add( new President( "Carter", "Jimmy", "1977-81") );
        list.add( new President( "Reagan", "Ronald", "1981-89") );
        list.add( new President( "Bush", "George H.W.", "1989-93") );
        list.add( new President( "Clinton", "William J.", "1993-2001") );
        list.add( new President( "Bush", "George W.", "2001-present") );
    }

    public List getData( ) {
        return list;
    }
}
}
```

The President class encapsulates information about a president, as shown in Example 4-12.

Example 4-12. Value object representing a President

```
package com.oreilly.strutsckbk.ch04;

public class President {
    public President(String lname, String fname, String term) {
        lastName = lname;
```

Example 4-12. Value object representing a President (continued)

```
        firstName = fname;
        this.term = term;
    }

    public String getFirstName( ) {
        return firstName;
    }
    public void setFirstName(String firstName) {
        this.firstName = firstName;
    }
    public String getLastName( ) {
        return lastName;
    }
    public void setLastName(String lastName) {
        this.lastName = lastName;
    }
    public String getTerm( ) {
        return term;
    }
    public void setTerm(String term) {
        this.term = term;
    }

    private String lastName;
    private String firstName;
    private String term;
}
```

The JSP page (Example 4-10) contains all the logic that handles paging. Though this JSP could have been implemented using only Struts tags, it would have required a substantial amount of scripting to perform the necessary arithmetic. A better approach is to use JSTL. JSTL easily supports arithmetic calculations in expressions; in addition, the JSTL c:forEach tag is designed to allow for specification of beginning and ending indices for the collection being iterated. This ability is a natural fit for the requirements of paging.

Paging requires you to track the current page that the user is on. When the page is initially displayed, you want to display the first *n* rows, where *n* is the desired page size. In the Solution, this value—pageSize—is set to 10:

```
    <c:set var="pageSize" value="10"/>
```

The JSP page is designed to accept a request parameter that identifies the beginning index for the current page: pageBegin. The ending index, pageEnd, is calculated by adding the page size to the value of the beginning index. The calculation subtracts 1 from this result because the indices in a c:forEach loop are zero-based.

```
    <c:set var="pageEnd" value="${pageBegin + pageSize - 1}"/>
```

The JSP page is designed to generate links for the previous and next pages. The link loops back to the current page with the URL query string containing the calculated beginning index. The beginning index for the link to the previous page is calculated as follows:

```
pageBegin - pageSize
```

The beginning index for the link to the next page is likewise calculated:

```
pageBegin + pageSize
```

Additionally, you don't want the links to display if they aren't valid. In other words, you don't want a link to the previous page when you are displaying the first page. Similarly, there shouldn't be a link to the next page when the last page is displayed. For this requirement, the JSP page needs to know the total size—essentially the number of rows—in the list. This value is determined using the Struts bean:size tag:

```
<bean:size id="listSize" name="pagedData" property="data"/>
```

The JSTL Length Function

JSTL 1.0 doesn't provide a mechanism for determining the size of a Collection; instead, you can use the Struts bean:size tag. However, the function tag library available with JSTL 1.1 will provide this capability. The bean:size tag could be replaced by including the JSTL function tag library and using the fn:length function:

```
<%@ taglib uri="http://java.sun.com/jsp/jstl/core"
    prefix="c" %>
<%@ taglib uri="http://java.sun.com/jsp/jstl/functions"
    prefix="fn" %>
<c:set var="listSize"
    value="${fn:length(pagedData.data)}"/>
```

Most of the other JSTL functions perform common String manipulations. Check out Hans Bergsten's *ONJava* article at *http://www.onjava.com/pub/a/onjava/2003/11/05/jsp.html?page=1* for more details.

The JSTL c:url tag is used to generate the href attribute for the HTML links:

```
<a href='<c:url value="paged_data.jsp">
        <c:param name="pageBegin" value="${pageBegin - pageSize}"/>
      </c:url>'>
    Prev
</a>
```

This results in a link rendered something like the following:

```
<a href='paged_data.jsp?pageBegin=20'>
  Prev
</a>
```

Though the Struts html:link tag could have been used, it doesn't add any significant advantage over using the JSTL c:url tag.

A good practice to use when building JSP pages is to minimize mixing tag libraries when it doesn't add to the overall functionality of the page.

If you examine the Solution, you may notice what appears to be a defect: the ending index is calculated by adding the beginning index to the page size. With the examples, the list being iterated has over 42 elements—e.g., the number of U.S. presidents to date. The first page displays elements 0–9, the second displays 10–19, etc. For the last page, begin will be set to 40 and end will be set to 49. Yet only 42 elements are in the list: end should be set to 41. Fear not, for JSTL is smart enough not to overrun the list. When the c:forEach loop reaches the end of the list, it gracefully discontinues iteration regardless of the value of the end attribute.

Now take a look at the resulting web pages. First, Figure 4-6 shows the rendered web page when the JSP page is initially accessed.

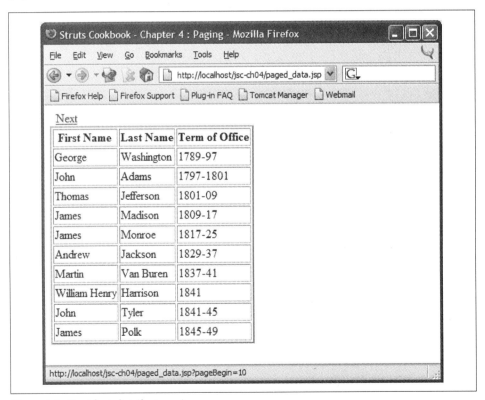

Figure 4-6. *Presidents list (first page)*

Figure 4-7 shows the web page after paging forward two pages to display the third page (the 31st through 40th presidents).

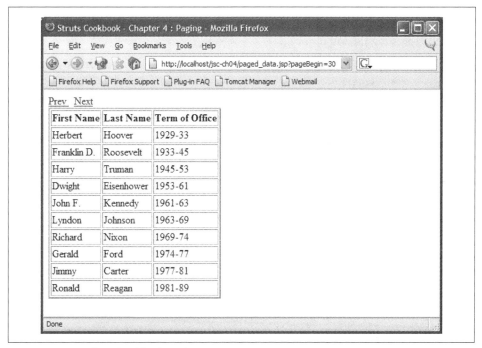

Figure 4-7. Presidents list (third page)

Though the Solution presented satisfies many application requirements, if the size of the data to be displayed is a large result set from a database and the number of rows could be significantly higher—say in the thousands—then you'll need to consider additional alternatives. Look to your underlying persistence mechanism for solutions that manage large data sets at the persistence level.

See Also

The Pager Tag Library is a popular JSP tag library that supports paging. It provides a presentation that can emulate the paging style of search engines such as Google and Alta Vista. Information on this library can be found at *http://jsptags.com/tags/ navigation/pager/index.jsp*.

The *display tag* library is an open source JSP tag library that is well suited for the display of tabular data. It supports paging in various manners and is discussed in Recipe 4.6.

4.6   Using the Display Tag Library

Problem

You want an easier way of displaying tabular data that supports paging and sorting.

Solution

Use the *Display tag* JSP tag library.

Example 4-13 shows a JSP page that displays the list of U.S. presidents using the model data from Recipe 4.5. This JSP page displays a table rendered using the display tag library. The displayed page has alternating table row colors, allows for paging, and offers column sorting, all without requiring any custom Java coding.

Example 4-13. Display tag example

```
<%@ page contentType="text/html;charset=UTF-8" language="java" %>
<%@ taglib uri="http://displaytag.sf.net/el" prefix="display" %>
<html>
<head>
  <title>Struts Cookbook - Chapter 4 : Display Tag Example</title>
  <style>
  .even {background-color:orange;}
  .odd {background-color:yellow;}
  </style>
</head>
<body>
  <h2>Display Tag Examples</h2>
  <jsp:useBean id="pagedData" class="com.oreilly.strutsckbk.ch04.PagedData"/>
  <display:table id="pres" name="${pagedData.data}"
                 sort="list" pagesize="10" defaultsort="3">
    <display:caption>United States Presidents</display:caption>
    <display:setProperty name="basic.show.header" value="true"/>
    <display:column property="firstName" title="First Name"
                    sortable="true"/>
    <display:column property="lastName" title="Last Name"
                    sortable="true"/>
    <display:column property="term" title="Term of Office"
                    sortable="true"/>
  </display:table>
</body>
</html>
```

Discussion

The *display* tag library is an open source tag library that can be used to render highly functional displays of tabular data. The Solution shown above creates the page shown in Figure 4-8.

The web page shown in Figure 4-8 packs a lot of functionality for a table created using a handful of custom tags. If you compare this Solution to the previous recipes that were used to provide alternate row colors, paging, and sorting, you can see why this tag library has become quite popular.

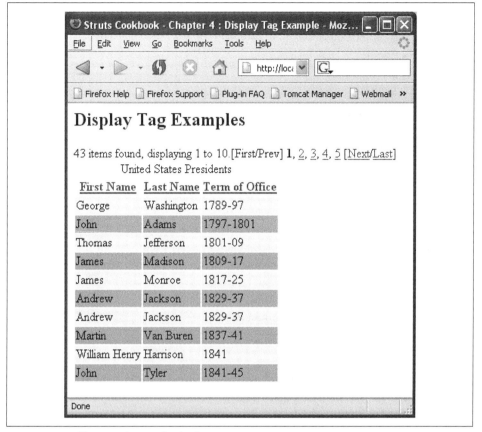

Figure 4-8. Table created using the display tags

This solution provides presentation-level paging. It doesn't restrict the amount of data initially received from the underlying persistent store.

To use the *display* tag library, you will need to download it from *http://displaytag.sourceforge.net*. Once downloaded, copy the *displaytag.jar* file into your web application's *WEB-INF/lib* folder. You will need to copy a tag library descriptor (*.tld*) file into this folder as well. The *display* tags provide a couple of choices here. The Solution uses the *displaytags-el.tld* file. These tags support JSTL expressions for attribute values.

The EL-version of the display tags requires that the *jstl.jar* and *standard.jar* JAR files be present in the *WEB-INF/lib* folder.

The *display* tag library depends on Version 2.0 or later of the Jakarta Commons Lang library, *commons-lang-2.0.jar*.

At the time of this writing, the Struts 1.1 distribution shipped with an earlier version of Commons Lang, and Struts 1.2 didn't include any version of Commons Lang. You can download the *commons-lang-2.0.jar* from *http://jakarta.apache.org/commons*. Replace *commons-lang.jar* with *commons-lang-2.0.jar* in your web application's *WEB-INF/lib* folder. From here on, you should not have any other incompatibility or dependency problems.

The display tags provide a lot of functionality and are easy to use. First, the `display:table` tag specifies information about the entire table:

```
<display:table id="pres" name="${pagedData.data}"
         sort="list" pagesize="10" defaultsort="3">
```

The `id` attribute creates a scoped variable that can be used to refer to the current row. The `name` attribute identifies the collection to be rendered. The `sort` attribute indicates how the data should be sorted: "list" indicates that the entire list is sorted, and "page" indicates that only the visible data on the current page is to be sorted. The value of the `pagesize` attribute is the number of rows to display per page.

Setting the `pagesize` attribute automatically enables paging.

The `defaultsort` attribute specifies the column (starting with 1) on which the data is initially sorted. In the Solution, this value is set to 3, which sorts the data by the "Term of Office" column.

The `display:caption` tag renders the table caption displayed above the column headers:

```
<display:caption>United States Presidents</display:caption>
```

The `display:column` tag specifies information about each column to be displayed:

```
<display:column property="firstName" title="First Name"
           sortable="true"/>
```

The `property` attribute specifies the JavaBean property that holds the data for the column. The `title` attribute specifies the text to display in the column header. The `sortable` attribute specifies if the data can be sorted by this column. If this value is set to true, then clicking the column header will sort the data by that column.

The *display* tag library provides functionality for exporting displayed tabular data to XML, Excel spreadsheets, and comma-separated value (*.csv*) files. This functionality can be enabled by registering some servlet filters provided with the library. Then you set the `export` attribute of the `display:table` tag to true. The documentation provided with display tags has all the details on setting up the export capability.

See Also

Complete details on the *display* tag library can be found at its web site: *http://displaytag.sourceforge.net*. Recipes 4.3, 4.4, and 4.5 show how to provide similar functionality. While these "roll your own" recipes may not be necessary if you're using the *display* tags, they will help you understand how the functionality is implemented.

## CHAPTER 5

Processing Forms

5.0   Introduction

ActionForms are key components of any Struts application. They transport data between the Controller—that is, your Actions—and the View—your JSP pages. They protect your business layer components by acting as a firewall; they only let in expected data received from the HTTP request.

An ActionForm is a JavaBean that extends the org.apache.struts.ActionForm class. ActionForms declare properties that correlate to form fields and data displayed on a presentation page using getter (getXXX( )) and setter (setXXX( )) methods. An ActionForm can override two additional methods that the Struts framework calls when processing a servlet request:

reset( )
> Prepares an ActionForm to receive data from an HTTP request. This method primarily serves as a place for you to reset checkbox properties.

validate( )
> Performs data validation on ActionForm properties before the data is sent to your Action.

In addition to providing JavaBean-style properties that accept HTTP request data, the ActionForm can contain additional data that don't directly correspond to an HTML input field. This data could be used directly on the HTML form, such as the options displayed in an HTML select (drop-down) control. Typically, these "extra" ActionForm data provide contextual information for the form being displayed. Many developers prefer to use the ActionForm as the JavaBean that provides *all* data for a page: the properties on the form and properties for ancillary data. Others prefer to keep the ActionForm focused on providing only the properties needed to support the form. In this latter approach, the JSP page accesses the ancillary data through other scoped variables external to the ActionForm.

Both of these approaches are valid and acceptable. Either way, understanding the different types of `ActionForms`, how they work, and how to use them will make your Struts development go a lot smoother.

5.1   Creating Dynamic Action Forms

Problem

You want to create `ActionForms` for use on your pages without having to handcode a unique Java class for each form.

Solution

Create a `form-bean` in the *struts-config.xml* file using the built-in `DynaActionForm` type or any of its subclasses. Then define the properties of the form using nested `form-property` elements:

```
<form-beans>
  <form-bean name="MyForm" type="org.apache.struts.action.DynaActionForm">
    <form-property name="foo" type="java.lang.String"/>
    <form-property name="bar" type="java.lang.String"/>
    <form-property name="baz" type="java.lang.Boolean"/>
    <form-property name="blindMice" type="java.lang.String[]"
                   size="3"/>
  </form-bean>
<form-beans>
```

You can retrieve the data from the form using methods of the `DynaActionForm` or generically using the Jakarta Commons `PropertyUtils` class. The `Action` shown in Example 5-1 uses this technique to get the form property values by name.

Example 5-1. Using PropertyUtils with ActionForms

```
package com.oreilly.strutsckbk.ch05;

import javax.servlet.http.HttpServletRequest;
import javax.servlet.http.HttpServletResponse;

import org.apache.commons.beanutils.PropertyUtils;
import org.apache.struts.action.Action;
import org.apache.struts.action.ActionForm;
import org.apache.struts.action.ActionForward;
import org.apache.struts.action.ActionMapping;

public class ProcessAction extends Action {

  public ActionForward execute(ActionMapping mapping,
      ActionForm form,
      HttpServletRequest request,
      HttpServletResponse response) throws Exception {
```

Example 5-1. Using PropertyUtils with ActionForms (continued)

```
      String foo =
          (String) PropertyUtils.getSimpleProperty(form, "foo");
      String bar =
          (String) PropertyUtils.getSimpleProperty(form, "bar");
      Boolean baz =
          (Boolean) PropertyUtils.getSimpleProperty(form, "baz");
      String[] mice =
          (String[]) PropertyUtils.getProperty(form, "blindMice");
      return mapping.findForward("success");
  }
}
```

Discussion

Struts 1.1 introduced the ability to create ActionForms without writing any Java code; you create the ActionForm declaratively in your *struts-config.xml* file. This feature simplifies the application and reduces the amount of Java source code that you have to write and maintain. Prior to Struts 1.1, you could only create a custom ActionForm by extending the Struts base class, org.apache.struts.action.ActionForm. Your custom class consisted of getter and setter methods for the form properties and validation for the property values. Then along came the Struts Validator. Developers no longer needed to code the validate( ) method; they could provide form validation using an XML-based configuration file. Once the validation was removed from the custom ActionForm, the class became a group of trivial getter and setter methods.

Struts 1.1 relieves the burden of writing these trivial classes through the use of dynamic action forms. The dynamic action form is implemented by the org.apache.struts.action.DynaActionForm class. This class implements the DynaBean interface provided by the Jakarta Commons BeanUtils package. The interface provides methods that allow a class to contain a dynamic set of properties, much like a java.util.Map. The main benefit of a DynaBean over a simple map is that its values can be accessed just like standard JavaBean properties using the BeanUtils introspection utilities.

 If you aren't using the Validator or you have to code a custom validate( ) method, you lose the benefit of the DynaActionForm and you might as well code a conventional ActionForm subclass.

You create a dynamic action form in the *struts-config.xml* file by specifying the value for the type attribute of the form-bean element as the fully qualified class name of the DynaActionForm—org.apache.struts.action.DynaActionForm—or one of its subclasses. The form-property elements specify the name and type of the properties that make up the form. While DynaActionForms officially support a number of different types, you should stick with Strings and Booleans.

Booleans—that is, true/false values—are commonly used for check-boxes.

DynaActionForms do support other types, such as java.lang.Long and java.sql.Date. However, these types can cause problems with form validation and should be avoided in all action forms.

Use Strings for Form Properties

Form property types that aren't Strings or Booleans are problematic because the ActionForm is populated prior to being validated.

If a user enters alphabetic characters into a field corresponding to a property of a numeric type—e.g., java.lang.Integer—then the form can't be populated and a runtime exception will be thrown by the BeanUtils.populate( ) method.

But if you use String properties, then the form can be populated successfully regardless of the input. Once populated, form validation, implemented in the validate( ) method, can check the data for correctness.

If the data pass validation, then the values can be converted as needed and passed on to other business objects. If not, control returns to the input page where the values can be redisplayed and the user can correct them.

The DynaActionForm allows a property to be defined as a *scalar*, or single value, or as an array of values by using the [ ] notation following the type value. In the Solution, the form property blindMice is defined as an array of Strings with an array size of three elements:

```
<form-property name="blindMice"
               type="java.lang.String[]"
               size="3"/>
```

 The size attribute applies only to array properties.

When it comes to retrieving the values from the DynaActionForm, you can use the API of the DynaActionForm class or use the property accessor utility classes provided by the Jakarta Commons BeanUtils package.

See Also

Recipe 5.2 describes how to set initial values for form properties. Recipe 5.6 goes into greater detail about accessing the values from action forms.

Complete details on how the Jakarta Commons BeanUtils utility classes work can be found in the JavaDoc package description at *http://jakarta.apache.org/commons/beanutils/api/index.html*.

5.2   Setting DynaActionForm Initial Values

Problem

You need to initialize the properties in a dynamic action form declared in the *struts-config.xml* file.

Solution

Specify an initial value for a property of a DynaActionForm using the initial attribute of the form-property element.

```
<form-bean name="MyForm" type="org.apache.struts.action.DynaActionForm">
  <form-property name="firstName" type="java.lang.String"
            initial="George"/>
  <form-property name="lastName" type="java.lang.String"
            initial="Burdell"/>
  <form-property name="javaCoder" type="java.lang.Boolean"
            initial="true"/>
  <form-property name="friend" type="java.lang.String[]"
              size="3"
            initial="Larry,Moe,Curly"/>
</form-bean>
```

Discussion

DynaActionForms simplify your life as a Struts developer. There is no Java code to write, and when requirements change and you must add fields to a form, you need only change some XML and the Actions that use the form. When working with these forms, a common question that comes up is how to populate the form with initial values. The Solution shows how this can be done using the initial attribute of the form-property element. This attribute specifies a default value for a property. The property is set to this value when the form is created or when the initialize( ) method is called on the form. The time of creation depends on the scope of the form. If the scope is "request," a new form is created for each new request that uses the form. For session scope, the form is created when it can't be found in the current HTTP session.

The initial value, like any other XML attribute value, is specified as a double-quoted text string. Since most form properties should be Strings, specifying an initial value is straightforward. Care must be taken if the initial value contains embedded quotes or other special characters, though. These characters should be escaped by preceding the character with a leading backslash:

```
<form-property name="quotation"
               initial="John Dunne wrote \"No man is an island\""/>
```

If the property type is java.lang.Boolean, then the initial value should be set to true or false, ignoring case. Boolean properties are false by default.

If the property is an array type, the value for the initial attribute can represent multiple values. String values are listed as comma or space-separated values. If the Strings contain spaces, then wrap the value in single quotes. If the value contains an embedded single or double quotation mark or other character that may cause parsing problems, then escape the character by preceding it with a backslash. If an array value should be blank, you use the empty String (""). Here are some examples of acceptable syntax for the initial value of a String array property, and the equivalent String array literal:

```
initial="Larry,Moe,Curly" → {"Larry","Moe","Curly"}
initial="Fine,Horward" → {"Fine","Howard"}
initial="Larry Moe Curly" → {"Larry","Moe","Curly"}
initial="'Larry','','Curly'" → {"Larry","","Curly"}
initial="'O\'Reilly','Struts','Cook Book'" → {"O'Reilly","Struts","Cook book"}
```

The size attribute of the form-property element applies to array-based properties. This attribute sets the number of elements in the array. If the initial value specifies more elements than the size attribute, the size of the array is set to the larger value—i.e., the number of initial values.

In a beta version of Struts 1.1, calling reset( ) on a DynaActionForm set the property values to the initial values. With Struts 1.1 final, this behavior was aligned with that of conventional action forms—i.e., the form's initial values are only set when the form is created. The initialize( ) method, however, will reset the property values to their initial values. If you need the reset( ) method to work like Struts 1.1 beta, you can create a subclass of DynaActionForm that overrides the reset( ) method. Example 5-2 shows a DynaActionForm subclass that reinitializes the values on form reset.

Example 5-2. DynaActionForm extension for resetting properties

```
package com.oreilly.strutsckbk.ch05;

import javax.servlet.http.HttpServletRequest;

import org.apache.struts.action.ActionMapping;
import org.apache.struts.action.DynaActionForm;

public class ResettingDynaActionForm extends DynaActionForm {

    public void reset(ActionMapping mapping, HttpServletRequest request) {
        initialize(mapping);
    }
}
```

You can specify this class as the value of the type attribute of the form-bean element.

```
<form-bean name="MyFooForm"
           type="com.oreilly.strutsckbk.ch05.ResettingDynaActionForm">
  <form-property name="foo" type="java.lang.String"
           initial="bar"/>
</form-bean>
```

The primary disadvantage of the initial attribute is that it forces you to hardcode the values. In many cases, this meets requirements; at other times, you want the values to be determined dynamically at runtime. In this situation, the DynaActionForm can be populated from Java code, typically in the Action preceding a forward to the JSP page that displays the form. The DynaActionForm values can be set using the DynaActionForm.set( ) methods or the introspection utilities provided by the PropertyUtils class in Jakarta Commons BeanUtils package. Example 5-3 shows both of these techniques.

Example 5-3. Populating a DynaActionForm

```
package com.oreilly.strutsckbk.ch05;

import javax.servlet.http.HttpServletRequest;
import javax.servlet.http.HttpServletResponse;

import org.apache.commons.beanutils.PropertyUtils;
import org.apache.struts.action.Action;
import org.apache.struts.action.ActionForm;
```

Example 5-3. Populating a DynaActionForm (continued)

```java
import org.apache.struts.action.ActionForward;
import org.apache.struts.action.ActionMapping;
import org.apache.struts.action.DynaActionForm;

public class ViewFormAction extends Action {

    public ActionForward execute(ActionMapping mapping,
      ActionForm form,
      HttpServletRequest request,
      HttpServletResponse response) throws Exception {

        DynaActionForm myForm = (DynaActionForm) form;

        PropertyUtils.setSimpleProperty(myForm, "firstName", "Bill");

        myForm.set("lastName", "Siggelkow");

    return mapping.findForward("success");
    }
}
```

See Also

Recipe 5.5 shows how to create and use a dynamic form that allows for the properties to be determined completely at runtime. Recipe 5.6 shows additional solutions for populating forms in an Action.

The Struts User's Guide discusses dynamic action forms in the section *http://struts.apache.org/userGuide/building_controller.html#dyna_action_form_classes*.

5.3   Using a List-Backed Form Property

Problem

You want to create and use a form property backed by a java.util.List. You want to be able to access the entire list of data through one method as well as specific values in the list using indexed properties.

Solution

Create the form property as an indexed property, backed by a java.util.List, as shown in Example 5-4.

Example 5-4. List-backed form property

```java
package com.oreilly.strutsckbk.ch05;

import java.util.ArrayList;
import java.util.List;
```

Example 5-4. List-backed form property (continued)

```java
import javax.servlet.http.HttpServletRequest;

import org.apache.struts.action.ActionForm;
import org.apache.struts.action.ActionMapping;

public class ListForm extends ActionForm {

    private int size = 3;
    private List friends = new ArrayList(size);

    public List getFriends() {
        return friends;
    }

    public String getFriend(int index) {
        return (String) friends.get(index);
    }

    public void setFriend(int index, String name) {
        friends.set(index, name);
    }

    public void reset(ActionMapping mapping, HttpServletRequest request) {
        // prepopulate the list with empty strings
        friends = new ArrayList();
        for (int i=0; i<size;i++) friends.add("");
    }
}
```

Example 5-5 (*list_form_test.jsp*) shows how the property values can be accessed on a JSP page. The form is created by accessing individual elements as indexed properties. The results are output by iterating over the list.

Example 5-5. Accessing list-backed form properties

```jsp
<%@ page contentType="text/html;charset=UTF-8" language="java" %>
<%@ taglib uri="http://jakarta.apache.org/struts/tags-html" prefix="html" %>
<%@ taglib uri="http://java.sun.com/jstl/core" prefix="c" %>
<html>
<head>
    <title>Struts Cookbook - Chapter 5 : List-backed Form Property</title>
</head>
<body>
    <h2>List Form Test</h2>
    <html:form action="/ProcessListForm">
        Who are your 3 friends:<br />
        Friend 1: <html:text property="friend[0]"/><br />
        Friend 2: <html:text property="friend[1]"/><br />
        Friend 3: <html:text property="friend[2]"/><br />
        <html:submit/>
    </html:form>
    <hr />
```

Example 5-5. Accessing list-backed form properties (continued)

```
    <c:forEach var="item" items="${ListForm.friends}">
        <c:out value="${item}"/><br />
    </c:forEach>
</body>
</html>
```

Discussion

Sometimes you need a form property to represent a list of values instead of a single value. The value type may be simple like a String or number, or it may be a complex type composed of other types. An ActionForm can have a property of a simple or complex type that is backed by an implementation of a java.util.List.

So, how do you make a list-backed property accessible from an HTML form? First, you provide getter and setter methods that follow the JavaBean convention for indexed properties:

```
    public Foo getFoo(int index);
    public void setFoo(int index, Foo foo);
```

As long as the property follows this convention, it can be accessed regardless of the underlying implementation. If the property values are stored in an implementation of java.util.List, such as a java.util.ArrayList, then the getter method will call list.get(*index*) and the setter method will call list.set(*index, obj*).

Though a List, unlike an array, is resizable, you must ensure the getter and setter methods don't attempt to access a value at an index greater than the List size. Doing so will result in an IndexOutOfBoundsException. You can preload the List in the ActionForm's reset( ) method, or you can dynamically resize the list as needed in the getter and setter methods:

```
    public Foo getFoo(int index) {
        if (index >= list.size( )) {
            list.add(index, new Foo( ));
        }
        return (Foo) list.get(index)
    }

    public void setFoo(int index, Foo foo) {
        if (index < list.size( )) {
            list.set(index, foo);
        }
        else {
            list.add(index, foo);
        }
    }
```

See Also

Recipe 5.4 discusses how to use Maps for properties in a similar fashion. Recipe 5.5 discusses forms that are even more dynamic; the properties themselves are not determined until runtime.

Check out Recipe 3.4 for details on using multivalue properties on a form.

5.4 Using a Map-Backed Form Property

Problem

You have a form with a property defined as a Map, and you want to access a value in that Map using a key.

Solution

Define getter and setter methods that use the following pattern:

```
public Object getFoo(String key) {...}
public void setFoo(String key, Object value) {...}
```

In Example 5-6, the skill property is a Map-backed property.

Example 5-6. Map-backed form

```
package com.oreilly.strutsckbk.ch05;

import java.util.HashMap;
import java.util.Map;

import org.apache.struts.action.ActionForm;

public class MapForm extends ActionForm {

    private static String[] skillLevels =
        new String[] {"Beginner","Intermediate","Advanced"};
    private Map skills = new HashMap( );

    public Object getSkill(String key) {
        return skills.get(key);
    }

    public void setSkill(String key, Object value) {
        skills.put(key, value);
    }

    public Map getSkills( ) {
        return skills;
    }
}
```

Example 5-6. Map-backed form (continued)

```
    public String[] getSkillLevels() {
        return skillLevels;
    }
}
```

The Map-backed property value is accessed from the Struts tags on a JSP page (*map_form_test.jsp*) using the property="value(key)" syntax as shown Example 5-7.

Example 5-7. Accessing Map-backed form properties

```
<%@ page contentType="text/html;charset=UTF-8" language="java" %>
<%@ taglib uri="http://jakarta.apache.org/struts/tags-html" prefix="html" %>
<%@ taglib uri="http://java.sun.com/jstl/core" prefix="c" %>
<html>
<head>
  <title>Struts Cookbook - Chapter 5 : Map-backed Form</title>
</head>
<body>
    <h2>Map Form Test</h2>
    <html:form action="/ProcessMapForm">
        Java Skill:
        <html:select property="skill(java)">
            <html:options property="skillLevels"/>
        </html:select><br />
        JSP Skill:
        <html:select property="skill(jsp)">
            <html:options property="skillLevels"/>
        </html:select><br />
        Struts Skill:
        <html:select property="skill(struts)">
            <html:options property="skillLevels"/>
        </html:select><br />
        <html:submit/>
    </html:form>
    <hr />
    <c:if test="${not empty MapForm.skills}">
        Java Skill: <c:out value="${MapForm.skills.java}"/><br />
        JSP Skill: <c:out value="${MapForm.skills.jsp}"/><br />
        Struts Skill: <c:out value="${MapForm.skills.struts}"/><br />
    </c:if>
</body>
</html>
```

Discussion

The value of a Map-backed form property is accessed using its key. The key and value are used to add or replace a value in the map. Map-backed form properties provide a good way of creating a property that can hold an indeterminate set of values.

In the Solution above, the MapForm action form defines the property skill. The getters and setters use the following pattern:

```
public Value getValue(String key);
public void setValue(String key, Object value);
```

Using this pattern allows the value to be accessed on a JSP page from most Struts tags using the property attribute syntax of value(key). value corresponds to the property name, and key corresponds to the actual key into the map. For Map-backed properties, the keys should always be Strings. A Map-backed property can be accessed in this way by any Struts tag where the property attribute is used to access JavaBean properties:

```
<html:text property="skill(java)"/>
<bean:write name="MapForm" property="skill(java)"/>
```

JSTL doesn't support accessing properties that use the getValue(String key) pattern. Map-backed properties can, however, be accessed using a JSTL expression provided the actual Map is exposed via a public getter method. The Solution shows how the JSTL c:out tag is used to render the data from the map:

```
<c:out value="${MapForm.skills.java}"/>
```

JSTL accesses the Map directly and extracts values by the specified key. If you don't need to use JSTL to access Map-backed properties, then exposing the Map in a public method is not required.

See Also

Recipe 5.3 shows how to use lists to back a form property.

5.5   Lazy Dynamic Action Forms

Problem

You want to create a form where the properties are variable and completely determined at runtime.

Solution

Use Niall Pemberton's Lazy DynaBean forms available for download from *http://www.niallp.pwp.blueyonder.co.uk/*.

Declare the form-bean to use in the *struts-config.xml*:

```
<form-bean name="LazyForm" type="lib.framework.struts.LazyValidatorForm"/>
```

Then, use the form on a JSP page as you would a normal ActionForm. Example 5-8 shows a JSP page (*lazy_form_test.jsp*) that will utilize the LazyForm declared previously.

Example 5-8. Using the LazyValidatorForm on an HTML form

```
<%@ page contentType="text/html;charset=UTF-8" language="java" %>
<%@ taglib uri="http://jakarta.apache.org/struts/tags-html" prefix="html" %>
<%@ taglib uri="http://jakarta.apache.org/struts/tags-bean" prefix="bean" %>
<html>
<head>
  <title>Struts Cookbook - Chapter 5 : Lazy Form</title>
</head>
<body>
  <h2>Lazy Form Test</h2>
  <html:form action="/ProcessLazyForm">
    What is your name:<br />
      First Name: <html:text property="firstName"/><br />
      Last Name: <html:text property="lastName"/><br />
    Do you want to subscribe to our newsletter?<br />
      <html:checkbox property="subscribe"/><br />
    Who are your 3 friends:<br />
      Friend 1: <html:text property="friend[0].name"/><br />
      Friend 2: <html:text property="friend[1].name"/><br />
      Friend 3: <html:text property="friend[2].name"/><br />   
    <html:submit/>
  </html:form>
  <hr />
  Your name is: <bean:write name="LazyForm" property="firstName"/> 
              <bean:write name="LazyForm" property="lastName"/><br />
  Your friends are:<br />
  <bean:write name="LazyForm" property="friend[0].name"/><br />
  <bean:write name="LazyForm" property="friend[1].name"/><br />
  <bean:write name="LazyForm" property="friend[2].name"/><br />
</body>
</html>
```

In the Action that receives the form, cast the form into a DynaBean (org.apache.
commons.beanutils.DynaBean). You then access the properties using the get("*name*")
method. Since the LazyValidatorForm extends ValidatorForm, you can define standard Struts Validator validation rules in your *validation.xml* file.

Discussion

Occasionally, you may need to display a group of data input fields that are not
known until runtime. Consider an application that allows a potential buyer to configure a product for purchase—e.g., the online purchase of a computer. The available configuration options vary based on the product and current promotions; the
configuration data actually comes from a database, so the page needs to be built on
the fly.

The LazyValidatorForm and the LazyValidatorActionForm allow form properties to be
created automatically as they are needed. In particular, indexed properties in these
classes are backed by a LazyList. The list will resize as necessary instead of throwing
an IndexOutOfBoundsException if you attempt to access an index beyond the current

size. Like the DynaActionForm, these forms implement the DynaBean interface and store their properties in a Map. Unlike the DynaActionForm, however, new properties can be added to them at any time. In the Solution, you declare the form in your *struts-config.xml* file as you would define a custom ActionForm; no form-property elements are specified.

On the JSP page that uses the form, the Struts tags are used as if you were working with a normal ActionForm. In the Solution, two text fields (firstName and lastName), a Boolean field (subscribe), and three values of an indexed property (friend[i].name) are created.

You may not find common uses for these classes; however, they can be helpful in certain scenarios. One such idea is to use these classes when you are prototyping a new application or new feature. Once you nail down the requirements, you can replace the lazy action from with a normal ActionForm or DynaActionForm.

A word of warning: Using the lazy action forms removes the firewall that ActionForms usually provide. In other words, the lazy ActionForm instance will get populated with all the request parameters, whether or not you were expecting them. Make sure that you don't blindly accept the values and pass them onto your business model. Instead, only pull out the specific values that you are expecting.

See Also

Niall Pemberton's web site, *http://www.niallp.pwp.blueyonder.co.uk/*, has the latest information about these forms as well as some other useful Struts utilities.

Similar capabilities can be achieved using Map-backed form properties. Recipe 5.4 provides more details on this approach.

5.6   Populating Value Objects from ActionForms

Problem

You don't want to have to write numerous getters and setters to pass data from your action forms to your business objects.

Solution

Use the introspection utilities provided by the Jakarta Commons BeanUtils package in your Action.execute( ) method:

```
import org.apache.commons.beanutils.*;

// other imports omitted

  public ActionForward execute(ActionMapping mapping,
      ActionForm form,
```

```
        HttpServletRequest request,
        HttpServletResponse response) throws Exception {

    BusinessBean businessBean = new BusinessBean();
    BeanUtils.copyProperties(businessBean, form);

    // ... rest of the Action
```

Discussion

A significant portion of the development effort for a web application is spent moving data to and from the different system tiers. Along the way, the data may be transformed in one way or another, yet many of these transformations are required because the tier to which the data is moving requires the information to be represented in a different way.

Data sent in the HTTP request is represented as simple text. For some data types, the value can be represented as a String object throughout the application. However, many data types should be represented in a different format in the business layer than on the view. Date fields provide the classic example. A date field is retrieved from a form's input field as a String. Then it must be converted to a java.util.Date in the model. Furthermore, when the value is persisted, it's usually transformed again, this time to a java.sql.Timestamp. Numeric fields require similar transformations.

The Jakarta Commons BeanUtils package supplied with the Struts distribution provides some great utilities automating the movement and conversion of data between objects. These utilities use JavaBean property names to match the source property to the destination property for data transfer. To leverage these utilities, ensure you give your properties consistent, meaningful names. For example, to represent an employee ID number, you may decide to use the property name employeeId. In all classes that contain an employee ID, you should use that name. Using empId in one class and employeeIdentifier in another will only lead to confusion among your developers and will render the BeanUtils facilities useless.

The entire conversion and copying of properties from ActionForm to business object can be performed with one static method call:

```
    BeanUtils.copyProperties(businessBean, form);
```

This copyProperties() method attempts to copy each JavaBean property in *form* to the property with the same name in *businessBean*. If a property in *form* doesn't have a matching property in *businessBean*, that property is silently ignored. If the data types of the matched properties are different, BeanUtils will attempt to convert the value to the type expected. BeanUtils provides converters from Strings to the following types:

- java.lang.BigDecimal
- java.lang.BigInteger

- boolean and java.lang.Boolean
- byte and java.lang.Byte
- char and java.lang.Character
- java.lang.Class
- double and java.lang.Double
- float and java.lang.Float
- int and java.lang.Integer
- long and java.lang.Long
- short and java.lang.Short
- java.lang.String
- java.sql.Date
- java.sql.Time
- java.sql.Timestamp

While the conversions to character-based and numeric types should cover most of your needs, date type fields (as shown in Recipe 3.13) can be problematic. A good solution suggested by Ted Husted is to implement transformation getter and setter methods in the business object that convert from the native type (e.g. java.util.Date) to a String and back again.

 Because BeanUtils knows how to handle DynaBeans and the DynaActionForm implements DynaBean, the Solution will work unchanged for DynaActionForms and normal ActionForms.

As an example, suppose you want to collect information about an employee for a human resources application. Data to be gathered includes the employee ID, name, salary, marital status, and hire date. Example 5-9 shows the Employee business object. Most of the methods of this class are getters and setters; for the hireDate property, however, helper methods are provided that get and set the value from a String.

Example 5-9. Employee business object

```
package com.oreilly.strutsckbk.ch05;

import java.math.BigDecimal;
import java.text.DateFormat;
import java.text.ParseException;
import java.text.SimpleDateFormat;
import java.util.Date;

public class Employee {

    private String employeeId;
    private String firstName;
```

Example 5-9. Employee business object (continued)

```
    private String lastName;
    private Date hireDate;
    private boolean married;
    private BigDecimal salary;

    public BigDecimal getSalary( ) {
        return salary;
    }
    public void setSalary(BigDecimal salary) {
        this.salary = salary;
    }
    public String getEmployeeId( ) {
        return employeeId;
    }
    public void setEmployeeId(String employeeId) {
        this.employeeId = employeeId;
    }
    public String getFirstName( ) {
        return firstName;
    }
    public void setFirstName(String firstName) {
        this.firstName = firstName;
    }
    public String getLastName( ) {
        return lastName;
    }
    public void setLastName(String lastName) {
        this.lastName = lastName;
    }
    public boolean isMarried( ) {
        return married;
    }
    public void setMarried(boolean married) {
        this.married = married;
    }
    public Date getHireDate( ) {
        return hireDate;
    }
    public void setHireDate(Date HireDate) {
        this.hireDate = HireDate;
    }
    public String getHireDateDisplay( ) {
        if (hireDate == null)
            return "";
        else
            return dateFormatter.format(hireDate);
    }
    public void setHireDateDisplay(String hireDateDisplay) {
        if (hireDateDisplay == null)
            hireDate = null;
        else {
            try {
```

Example 5-9. Employee business object (continued)

```
            hireDate = dateFormatter.parse(hireDateDisplay);
        } catch (ParseException e) {
            e.printStackTrace( );
        }
    }
}

    private DateFormat dateFormatter = new SimpleDateFormat("mm/DD/yy");
}
```

Example 5-10 shows the corresponding ActionForm that will retrieve the data from the HTML form. The hire date is represented in the ActionForm as a String property, hireDateDisplay. The salary property is a java.lang.String, not a java.math. BigDecimal, as in the Employee object of Example 5-9.

Example 5-10. Employee ActionForm

```
package com.oreilly.strutsckbk.ch05;

import java.math.BigDecimal;

import org.apache.struts.action.ActionForm;

public class EmployeeForm extends ActionForm {

    private String firstName;
    private String lastName;
    private String hireDateDisplay;
    private String salary;
    private boolean married;

    public String getEmployeeId( ) {
        return employeeId;
    }
    public void setEmployeeId(String employeeId) {
        this.employeeId = employeeId;
    }
    public String getFirstName( ) {
        return firstName;
    }
    public void setFirstName(String firstName) {
        this.firstName = firstName;
    }
    public String getLastName( ) {
        return lastName;
    }
    public void setLastName(String lastName) {
        this.lastName = lastName;
    }
    public boolean isMarried( ) {
        return married;
    }
```

Example 5-10. Employee ActionForm (continued)

```
    public void setMarried(boolean married) {
        this.married = married;
    }
    public String getHireDateDisplay( ) {
        return hireDateDisplay;
    }
    public void setHireDateDisplay(String hireDate) {
        this.hireDateDisplay = hireDate;
    }
    public String getSalary( ) {
        return salary;
    }
    public void setSalary(String salary) {
        this.salary = salary;
    }
}
```

If you wanted to use a DynaActionForm, you would configure it identically as the
EmployeeForm class. The form-bean declarations from the *struts-config.xml* file show
the declarations for the EmployeeForm and a functionally identical DynaActionForm:

```
    <form-bean name="EmployeeForm"
               type="com.oreilly.strutsckbk.ch05.EmployeeForm"/>
    <form-bean name="EmployeeDynaForm"
               type="org.apache.struts.action.DynaActionForm">
        <form-property name="employeeId" type="java.lang.String"/>
        <form-property name="firstName" type="java.lang.String"/>
        <form-property name="lastName" type="java.lang.String"/>
        <form-property name="salary" type="java.lang.String"/>
        <form-property name="married" type="java.lang.Boolean"/>
        <form-property name="hireDateDisplay" type="java.lang.String"/>
    </form-bean>
```

The following is the action mapping that processes the form. In this case, the name
attribute refers to the handcoded EmployeeForm. You could, however, change this to use
the EmployeeDynaForm without requiring any modifications to the SaveEmployeeAction or
the *view_emp.jsp* JSP page:

```
    <action    path="/SaveEmployee"
               name="EmployeeForm"
               scope="request"
               type="com.oreilly.strutsckbk.ch05.SaveEmployeeAction">
        <forward name="success" path="/view_emp.jsp"/>
    </action>
```

The data is converted and copied from the form to the business object in the
SaveEmployeeAction shown in Example 5-11.

Example 5-11. Action to save employee data

```
package com.oreilly.strutsckbk.ch05;

import javax.servlet.http.HttpServletRequest;
import javax.servlet.http.HttpServletResponse;

import org.apache.commons.beanutils.BeanUtils;
import org.apache.struts.action.Action;
import org.apache.struts.action.ActionForm;
import org.apache.struts.action.ActionForward;
import org.apache.struts.action.ActionMapping;

public class SaveEmployeeAction extends Action {

    public ActionForward execute(ActionMapping mapping,
                                 ActionForm form,
                                 HttpServletRequest request,
                                 HttpServletResponse response)
                      throws Exception {

        Employee emp = new Employee( );

        // Copy to business object from ActionForm
        BeanUtils.copyProperties( emp, form );

        request.setAttribute("employee", emp);
        return mapping.findForward("success");

    }
}
```

Finally, two JSP pages complete the example. The JSP of Example 5-12 (*edit_emp.jsp*) renders the HTML form to retrieve the data.

Example 5-12. Form for editing employee data

```
<%@ page contentType="text/html;charset=UTF-8" language="java" %>
<%@ taglib uri="http://jakarta.apache.org/struts/tags-bean" prefix="bean" %>
<%@ taglib uri="http://jakarta.apache.org/struts/tags-html" prefix="html" %>
<%@ taglib uri="http://java.sun.com/jstl/core" prefix="c" %>
<html>
<head>
  <title>Struts Cookbook - Chapter 5 : Add Employee</title>
</head>
<body>
  <h2>Edit Employee</h2>
  <html:form action="/SaveEmployee">
    Employee ID: <html:text property="employeeId"/><br />
    First Name: <html:text property="firstName"/><br />
    Last Name: <html:text property="lastName"/><br />
    Married? <html:checkbox property="married"/><br />
    Hired on Date: <html:text property="hireDateDisplay"/><br />
    Salary: <html:text property="salary"/><br />
```

Example 5-12. Form for editing employee data (continued)

```
    <html:submit/>
  </html:form>
</body>
</html>
```

The JSP in Example 5-13 (*view_emp.jsp*) displays the results. This page is rendering data from the business object, and not an ActionForm. This is acceptable since the data on this page is for display purposes only. This approach allows for the formatting of data, (salary and hireDate) to be different than the format in which the values were entered.

Example 5-13. View of submitted employee data

```
<%@ page contentType="text/html;charset=UTF-8" language="java" %>
<%@ taglib uri="http://jakarta.apache.org/struts/tags-bean" prefix="bean" %>
<%@ taglib uri="http://java.sun.com/jstl/core" prefix="c" %>
<html>
<head>
  <title>Struts Cookbook - Chapter 5 : View Employee</title>
</head>
<body>
  <h2>View Employee</h2>
    Employee ID: <bean:write name="employee" property="employeeId"/><br />
    First Name: <bean:write name="employee" property="firstName"/><br />
    Last Name: <bean:write name="employee" property="lastName"/><br />
    Married? <bean:write name="employee" property="married"/><br />
    Hired on Date: <bean:write name="employee" property="hireDate"
                      format="MMMMM dd, yyyy"/><br />
    Salary: <bean:write name="employee" property="salary" format="$##0.00"/><br />
</body>
</html>
```

When you work with this example, swap out the handcoded form for the DyanActionForm to see how cleanly BeanUtils works. When you consider how many files need to be changed for one additional form input, the use of BeanUtils in conjunction with DynaActionForms becomes obvious.

See Also

Recipe 3.13 discusses additional considerations when working with Date fields specifically. Complete documentation on the BeanUtils package can be found at *http://jakarta.apache.org/commons/beanutils/api/org/apache/commons/beanutils/BeanUtils.html*.

DynaActionForms are discussed in Recipe 5.1.

5.7   Automatically Creating ActionForms

Problem

You want to create a `DynaActionForm` (or subclass) automatically from your business objects without having to configure the `form-bean` and `form-property` elements ahead of time.

Solution

Use Hubert Rabago's *Formdef* plug-in. You can download *formdef.jar* from *https://formdef.dev.java.net/* and copy it to your application's *WEB-INF/lib* directory. *Formdef* allows you to define form definitions in an XML file, as shown in Example 5-14. This file should be placed in the *WEB-INF* folder of your web application and given a meaningful name such as *form-defs.xml*.

Example 5-14. Formdef form definitions

```
<?xml version="1.0" encoding="ISO-8859-1"?>
<!DOCTYPE form-definition PUBLIC "-//FormDef//FormDef Form Definition//EN"
                          "form-defs_0_5.dtd">
<form-definition>
    <formset>
        <form name="EmployeeForm"
           beanType="com.oreilly.strutsckbk.ch05.EmployeeFd"/>
    </formset>
</form-definition>
```

The `form` element maps a form named with the `name` element to a business object whose class is specified by the `beanType` attribute.

Next, add a `plug-in` element for *Formdef* to your *struts-config.xml* file:

```
<plug-in className="formdef.plugin.FormDefPlugIn">
    <set-property property="defnames"
                  value="/WEB-INF/form-defs.xml"/>
</plug-in>
```

The form named in the `form` element can be used in your application as if you had explicitly declared the form using a `form-bean` element in the *struts-config.xml* file. Here's an action that uses the `EmployeeFdForm`:

```
<action    path="/SaveEmployeeFd"
           name="EmployeeFdForm"
          scope="request"
           type="com.oreilly.strutsckbk.ch05.SaveEmployeeFdAction">
    <forward name="success" path="/view_emp_fd.jsp"/>
</action>
```

Discussion

Formdef was created by Hubert Rabago, who remains the project lead. *Formdef* is an open-source project licensed under the Apache Software License. At the time of this writing, the latest available version was 0.5.

Formdef maps the business objects of your application's domain model map to your `ActionForm`s. With Struts 1.1, dynamic action forms (see Recipe 5.1) made life easier by allowing you to create an `ActionForm` declaratively. The *Formdef* Struts extension takes this notion further by allowing you to create a `DynaActionForm` behind the scenes that maps to the properties of a business object. An XML file holds the relationship between the form name and the business object.

Foremost, *Formdef* provides a runtime-created `DynaActionForm` for a specified business object. Using *Formdef*, you save yourself the hassle of specifying `form-bean` and `form-property` elements in the *struts-config.xml* file. More importantly, when a new property is added to the business object, you don't have to add a corresponding `form-property` in the *struts-config.xml*. The new property will get picked up at runtime and will be available to your form. In this respect, *Formdef* is similar to capabilities discussed in Recipe 5.5.

Formdef allows you to group together, in the *formdefs.xml* file, a form definition and its corresponding Struts Validator rules. This feature can make a project more manageable since related data is kept together.

Mapping business objects to web forms is a big affair. Business objects tend to represent data in native formats; forms represent data as strings. A date is represented by the `java.util.Date`, and numbers are represented by primitives or classes such as `java.math.BigDecimal`. Business objects can be composed of other business objects. A `Person` object contains an `Address` object, and that object, in turn, contains separate properties for the street, city, state, and postal code.

Formdef addresses these issues by allowing you to define how data is converted from a business object to an `ActionForm` and back again. A *Formdef* form definition can define and include *converters*, specialized classes that convert data from one type or format to another.

Formdef includes some utility methods that will transfer data from an `ActionForm` to your business object applying the specified conversions where needed. These utilities replace the use of the `BeanUtils.copyProperties()` method. If your business object contains complex types, properties with types other than primitives and Strings. If you want to perform intelligent data transfer between the `ActionForm` and the business object, you will need to use a converter. Here's one way you could define a converter for a field of type `java.util.Date`:

```
<form    name="EmployeeFdForm"
    beanType="com.oreilly.strutsckbk.ch05.Employee"/>
    <field property="hireDate">
```

```
        <converter param="mm/DD/yy"/>
    </field>
</form>
```

You can localize property conversion by using the key attribute of the converter element. At runtime, the key attribute is used to retrieve the format string from your Struts MessageResources properties file.

```
<form      name="EmployeeFdForm"
        beanType="com.oreilly.strutsckbk.ch05.Employee"/>
    <field property="hireDate">
        <converter key="format.date.us"/>
    </field>
</form>
```

In the MessageResources properties file, you would have an entry like:

```
format.date.us=mm/DD/yyyy
```

In this case, the converter uses the default date converter provided with *Formdef*. The converter element is used to specify the expected format of the date field. You can register your own converter. A converter can be defined as global; it will apply to any property that has the type or name that the converter is defined for. Say you wanted to be able to convert a form input into a phone number object, where the phone number object maintained separate properties for area code, seven-digit number, and extension.

```
<global-converter for="property-type"
        target="com.foo.PhoneNumber"
        type="com.foo.util.PhoneNumber "/>
```

The for="property-type" indicates that the converter is to be applied to all properties of the type specified by the target attribute. Converters can be defined for a target property name.

```
<global-converter for="converter-name"
        target="salary"
        param="###,###,##0.00"/>
```

This converter will be applied to any property named salary, regardless of the property's type.

Keep your eye one the *Formdef* project. If your application frequently maps business objects to forms on a one-to-one basis, then *Formdef* may provide a good solution. It allows rapid development by automatically creating ActionForms that remain in synch with your business objects. *Formdef* is in the early development, so here's your opportunity to contribute!

See Also

At the time of this writing, the *Formdef* project was being migrated from Hubert Rabago's site (*http://www.rabago.net/struts/formdef/*) to Java.net (*https://formdef.dev. java.net/*).

Like Recipe 5.5, this recipe shows ways to reduce the manual effort needed to create `ActionForms`.

CHAPTER 6

Leveraging Actions

6.0   Introduction

Actions control the flow of data and navigation in a Struts application. Each Action acts like a decision point in a flow chart. It's the place where you can decide what data to create, what data to save, and where to send users based on their input. A Struts application doesn't require that every request be routed through an Action, but doing so gives you a level of control that will allow your application to adapt as requirements and new features are changed and added.

Do you feel like your application is exploding with hundreds of custom Actions? If it is, you aren't alone. This condition can be acceptable, but you may not be leveraging Struts Actions to their full extent. Using the recipes in this chapter will enable you to get more reuse from your Actions and reduce the number of custom classes that you have to maintain.

A number of the recipes in this chapter utilize Action subclasses included with Struts. These pre-built actions are found in the org.apache.struts.actions package. Some of these actions are designed to be extended, and others are used as is. The DispatchAction and its provided subclasses, LookupDispatchAction and MappingDispatchAction, fall into this first category. These actions reduce the amount of code you have to write by replacing multiple related Actions with a single Action that supports multiple operations.

You use two other pre-built actions, ForwardAction and IncludeAction, directly—no subclassing required. These actions perform the same functions as the javax. servlet.RequestDispatcher provided by the Java Servlet API. The ForwardAction forwards an HTTP request to another resource such as a servlet, JSP, or static HTML page. The IncludeAction includes content from another resource, such as a servlet or JSP, which generates a partial HTTP response.

Struts provides a SwitchAction used to change the current Struts module and a LocaleAction used to change the current locale. This chapter covers the SwitchAction (however, the LocaleAction is discussed in Recipe 12.4) and some programming techniques and guidelines specifically related to working with Actions.

6.1   Creating a Base Action

Problem

You want to implement and enforce a common feature or behavior across all of your Actions.

Solution

Implement an abstract base class that incorporates the behavior in its execute( ) method. As shown by the class in Example 6-1, the execute( ) method calls abstract methods that are implemented by subclasses.

Example 6-1. Abstract base action

```
package com.oreilly.strutsckbk.ch06;

import javax.servlet.http.HttpServletRequest;
import javax.servlet.http.HttpServletResponse;

import org.apache.struts.action.Action;
import org.apache.struts.action.ActionForm;
import org.apache.struts.action.ActionForward;
import org.apache.struts.action.ActionMapping;

public abstract class BaseAction extends Action {

    public ActionForward execute( ActionMapping mapping,
                                  ActionForm form,
                                  HttpServletRequest request,
                                  HttpServletResponse response) throws Exception {
        executeBefore( );

        // call the abstract method
        ActionForward forward = executeAction( mapping, form, request, response );

        executeAfter( );

        return forward;
    }

    protected abstract ActionForward executeAction( ActionMapping mapping,
                                                    ActionForm form,
                                                    HttpServletRequest request,
                                                    HttpServletResponse response)
                                      throws Exception;
    private void executeBefore( ) {
        //Real stuff goes here
    }
```

Example 6-1. Abstract base action (continued)

```
    private void executeAfter( ) {
        //Real stuff goes here
    }
    protected CommonServices getCommonServices( ) {...}
}
```

Discussion

For some applications, you may want to apply global business rules any time a user accesses the application, submits a form, or clicks on a link. Here are some common examples of these rules:

- Users must be logged in.
- Users can only access the page if they have been granted permission.
- You want to track every time users hit a page.
- The user's first name and last name should be displayed at the top of every page.

You can enforce these across-the-board features using an abstract base Action class that your custom Actions extend. The Solution above shows such a base Action. BaseAction extends org.apache.struts.action.Action and implements the standard execute( ) method. The execute( ) method calls the private method executeBefore( ) and then the abstract method executeAction( ). executeAction( ) returns an ActionForward, which is stored in a local variable. Next, the private method executeAfter( ) is called. The execute( ) method ends by returning the ActionForward referenced by the local variable.

Your concrete actions extend this BaseAction. Each concrete action implements the executeAction( ) method as if it were the execute( ) method inherited from org.apache.struts.action.Action.

If you are familiar with design patterns, you will probably recognize the Solution as the Template Method from *Design Patterns of Object-Oriented Software* by Erich Gamma, et al. (Addison-Wesley). The Template Method pattern is characterized by a base abstract class that defines the steps of an algorithm. In the Solution, the steps are comprised of a pre-execution step, the execution step, and a post-execution step.

If you want subclasses to be able to override the common behavior in the pre- and post-execution steps, make the methods protected; otherwise, they should be private. The signature of the executeAction( ) method is identical to the execute( ) method; however, this is not required. In general, you'll want to pass through at least the set of parameters available to the execute( ) method. In addition, you may want to pass additional references to objects that are created in the base class, such as a user object representing the current user.

Base actions can provide access to global objects and services that concrete actions will need. For example, you might want to provide a getUser( ) method that returns a user object for the current session. Chapter 11 provides more detail on this specific case.

See Also

Chuck Cavaness discusses the use of a base `Action` class in *Programming Jakarta Struts* (O'Reilly). The timeless book *Design Patterns of Object-Oriented Software* by Erich Gamma, et al. (Addison-Wesley) is the bible of design patterns. In its pages is an assortment of low-level design approaches applicable to any object-oriented application.

6.2   Relaying Actions

Problem

You want to link one action directly to another.

Solution

Use a local or global forward that specifies its destination URL as another action:

```
<action    path="/FirstAction"
           type="com.foo.FirstAction">
    <forward name="success" path="/SecondAction.do"/>
</action>
<action    path="/SecondAction"
           type="com.foo.SecondAction">
    <forward name="success" path="/second_page.jsp"/>
</action>
```

Discussion

The actions configured in your *struts-config.xml* are commonly used as the target action of forms on a JSP page. These actions subsequently forward requests to JSP pages for rendering of the view. However, nothing prohibits an action from forwarding the request to another action. This technique is referred to as *action relaying*.

As you can see from the Solution, setting up a relay from one action to another is easy. The motivation for doing so, however, isn't as apparent, particularly if you have just started developing your Struts application. By relaying actions, you can hook together application features that you had not originally intended.

Consider a point-of-sale web application for a retail business. Salespersons use the application to make sales and to track and maintain data about customers and their purchases. The application supports two main workflows: one for making purchases and one for updating customer data. The developer on this project has created an action with the path `/UpdateCustomer.do` that allows retrieval and editing of customer information. After an initial release of the application, the developer is given a new requirement: Every time a customer makes a purchase, the salesperson should make updates to the customer data. Though the developer hadn't planned for this workflow, the steps in the flow can be easily linked using the technique shown in the Solution. The action that completes the purchase has the path /SavePurchase.do. The desired workflow can be set up as follows:

```
<action    path="/SavePurchase"
           type="com.foo.SavePurchaseAction">
     <forward name="success" path="/UpdateCustomer.do"/>
</action>
```

Avoid Chaining Actions

While relaying can be a convenient mechanism, a pitfall is related to this technique. Once you have developed a number of actions, you may find that you can reuse application functionality by relaying many of these actions together. This practice of setting up relays to relays is known as *action chaining*. This approach can be attractive if you have coded your business logic into your Action classes instead of delegating logic to a service layer. Essentially, you have created your business API with Struts actions instead of with Java classes and methods. Chaining the actions together in a sequence, as you would call methods of an API, may appear to be a valid approach.

Beware this temptation! If you follow this path, you've essentially substituted Java method calls with HTTP requests. It doesn't take a rocket scientist to know that an HTTP request is much slower than a Java method call. If this chaining—that is, relay to relay to relay—seems useful to you, consider refactoring logic in your Action classes into a service layer interface. This gives you the reuse without sacrificing performance or maintainability.

See Also

The Struts User's mailing list has some good discussions on the implications of hooking actions together. Ted Husted discusses this in more detail in a thread archived at *http://www.mail-archive.com/struts-user@jakarta.apache.org/msg96565.html*.

6.3   Returning the HTTP Response

Problem

You want to create a response in the Action and send that response to the client instead of forwarding to another action or JSP page.

Solution

Use the standard methods provided by the HttpServletResponse object to write the response. Then return null instead of an ActionForward from the execute( ) method

---

of the Action. Example 6-2 shows an `Action` that creates and returns a simple response.

Example 6-2. Writing the HTTP response in an action

```
package com.oreilly.strutsckbk.ch06;

import java.io.PrintWriter;

import javax.servlet.http.HttpServletRequest;
import javax.servlet.http.HttpServletResponse;

import org.apache.struts.action.Action;
import org.apache.struts.action.ActionForm;
import org.apache.struts.action.ActionForward;
import org.apache.struts.action.ActionMapping;

public class ResponseWriterAction extends Action {

    public ActionForward execute( ActionMapping mapping,
                                  ActionForm form,
                                  HttpServletRequest request,
                                  HttpServletResponse response)
            throws Exception {
        response.setContentType("text/html");
        PrintWriter out = response.getWriter( );
        out.write("<html><head></head><body>Hello World!</body></html>");
        return null;
    }

}
```

Discussion

The typical `Action` returns an `ActionForward` from its execute( ) method. The returned `ActionForward` is evaluated and processed by the Struts request processor. The returned forward specifies the path to a resource, like a JSP page, that generates the actual HTTP response. However, you can generate the response in the `Action`. If you do so, you must return `null` from the `Action`'s execute( ) method. This tells the Struts request processor no `ActionForward` will follow; therefore, the response should be returned to the client.

Many scenarios exist in which you may want to write the response. Applications that dynamically generate non-HTML content from binary data can use this approach. These applications can write binary content, such as images and PDF documents, directly to the response and can set the content type in the HTTP header to the appropriate MIME type for handling by the browser.

Though the `Action` may return the response, the `Action` should delegate the writing of the response to a custom class not tied to the Struts API.

See Also

The traditional Java mechanism for creating an HTTP response is the servlet. If you are writing the response in your Action, you may want to consider using a servlet to do this instead. Your Action would forward the request to that servlet using an ActionForward. The ForwardAction described in Recipe 6.5 shows a technique for wrapping access to servlets with Struts actions.

6.4   Writing Thread-Safe Actions

Problem

Your Action classes must operate correctly in a multi-threaded environment.

Solution

In your custom Action, never use instance variables to carry per-request state; only use local variables. If you want to have local methods called from the execute( ) method, pass values to these methods as arguments instead of using instance variables. The Action class in Example 6-3 demonstrates this approach.

Example 6-3. Thread-safe action

```
package com.oreilly.strutsckbk.ch06;

import javax.servlet.http.HttpServletRequest;
import javax.servlet.http.HttpServletResponse;

import org.apache.struts.action.Action;
import org.apache.struts.action.ActionForm;
import org.apache.struts.action.ActionForward;
import org.apache.struts.action.ActionMapping;

public class ThreadSafeAction extends Action {

    // This variable is not thread-safe
    private SecurityUtil securityUtil = new SecurityUtil.instance( );

    public ActionForward execute( ActionMapping mapping,
                                  ActionForm form,
                                  HttpServletRequest request,
                                  HttpServletResponse response) throws Exception {

        // the 'user' variable is thread-safe
        User user = (User) request.getSession( ).getAttribute("user");

        // pass the user to the private method
        doSomething(user);

        // ...
```

Example 6-3. Thread-safe action (continued)

```
        return mapping.findForward("success");
    }

    private void doSomething(User user) throws Exception {
        // authenticate the user
        securityUtil.authenticate(user);
    }
}
```

Discussion

A Struts Action is subject to the same threading issues as a servlet. Internally, Struts maintains and reuses each Action instance to service requests. Your Action's execute( ) method will probably be called by multiple concurrent threads. You might be tempted to synchronize the execute( ) method, but avoid this temptation! Synchronizing the execute( ) method will degrade performance and you should avoid it. If you need to synchronize behavior in your application, perform the synchronization in the service layer of your application.

If you use a base Action, as described in Recipe 6.1, you need to follow these guidelines. A base Action should refrain from using client-state instance variables like any other well-behaved Action class.

See Also

The Struts User's guide addresses this specific issue, and other Action class design guidelines, in the section at *http://struts.apache.org/userGuide/building_controller.html#action_design_guide*. A recent *JavaWorld* article, "Writing thread-safe Servlets" by Phillip Bridgham, discusses this issue with respect to servlets and can be found at *http://www.javaworld.com/javaworld/jw-07-2004/jw-0712-threadsafe.html*. You can find discussions in the archives of the Struts user and developer mailing lists.

6.5   Forwarding Requests

Problem

You want to provide an action that forwards a request to any action, JSP page, servlet, or other resource of your web application.

Solution

Use a forwarding action. Specifying the module-relative path to the resource as the value of the forward attribute is the most convenient way:

```
<action  path="/ForwardTest"
    forward="/forward_test.jsp"/>
```

Alternatively, if you use a custom `RequestProcessor`, which overrides the `processForwardConfig()` method, you must use the Struts built-in `ForwardAction`, specifying the context-relative path for the value of the parameter attribute.

```
<action  path="/ForwardActionTest"
         type="org.apache.struts.actions.ForwardAction"
      parameter="/forward_test.jsp"/>
```

Discussion

Struts provides two mechanisms for creating an action that forwards directly to a specified resource. You can use the `forward` attribute or the `ForwardAction`. In most situations, the `forward` attribute will work just fine. The value of the attribute is treated as a module-relative path. At request time, the `RequestProcessor` checks the action mapping specifies a forward attribute. If so, it converts the `forward` attribute value to a context-relative path by adding the module prefix to the front of the path. The request processor then hands the request and response to the `RequestDispatcher.forward()` method and immediately returns.

The `ForwardAction` is a Struts prebuilt action class included with the Struts distribution. This `Action` forwards the request to the path specified as the value of the `parameter` attribute in an `action` mapping. The `parameter` attribute may contain an HTTP query string for passing request parameters.

```
<action  path="/SendToLegacyServlet"
         type="org.apache.struts.actions.ForwardAction"
      parameter="/LegacyServlet?foo=bar"/>
```

Unlike handling the `forward` attribute, when you use the `ForwardAction`, the `RequestProcessor` routes the request through all steps of the process. This difference is relevant if you are using a custom `RequestProcessor`, which overrides the `processForwardConfig()` method, for custom processing of action forwards. If so, you should use the `ForwardAction` to preserve your custom processing.

Whether using the `forward` attribute or `ForwardAction`, your action acts as a bridge between requests. Since the action performs a forward and not a redirect, request data is maintained.

If you are prototyping a Struts application, a forwarding action can save you significant time and effort as your application develops. A forwarding action allows you to define your action paths—the URIs that link the application together—prior to coding the actual custom `Action` classes. Suppose your web designers have created a prototype comprised of static HTML pages and simple JSP pages. Instead of linking directly from page to page, create a forwarding action in your *struts-config.xml* that routes the request to the path of the prototype page.

You can use the action URI for hyperlinks and HTML form actions instead of the prototype JSP page name. As you create the real functionality of the application, reconfigure the action element to use your own custom `Action` class. You'll need to make changes to the JSPs, but you will already have established the workflow. This is a great development approach, particularly if you want to have a working prototype available.

This practice allows your application to take advantage of application-wide services provided by Struts. These services may be Struts-provided, like a role-based access, or they may be custom behaviors that you implement by extending the Struts RequestProcessor. Forwarding actions are useful for creating proxies to resources, such as traditional servlets. If you are adding Struts to an existing servlet-based application, you can use a forwarding action to route requests to the servlet. Once you have the proxy in place, you can replace the servlet with a JSP without breaking the application.

See Also

If you need to link to a servlet that is used to include a portion of the HTTP response, Recipe 6.6 provides a similar proxy ability as a forwarding action.

The Struts documentation on the ForwardAction can be found at *http://jakarta. apache.org/struts/api/org/apache/struts/actions/ForwardAction.html*.

The difference between the forward attribute and the ForwardAction has been discussed on the Struts-users mailing list. Searching the archives for "Forward attribute vs. Forward Action" will return several threads of interest.

6.6   Including the Response from a Servlet or JSP

Problem

You want to retrieve and include a partial HTTP response from a servlet or JSP, but you want control to go through Struts.

Solution

Employ an including action. Specifying the module-relative path to the resource as the value of the include attribute is the most convenient way:

```
<action  path="/IncludeContent"
       include="/LegacyIncludeServlet"/>
```

Alternatively, if you use a custom RequestProcessor, which overrides the processForwardConfig( ) method, you must use the Struts built-in IncludeAction, specifying the context-relative path for the value of the parameter attribute:

```
<action path="/IncludeContent"
        type="org.apache.struts.actions.IncludeAction"
     parameter="/LegacyIncludeServlet"/>
```

Discussion

This recipe addresses a problem similar to that in Recipe 6.6. The solution is similar as well; you can use the `include` attribute of the action element, or you can use the Struts-provided `IncludeAction`. The `IncludeAction` uses the value specified for the `parameter` attribute to indicate the resource whose response is to be included.

You may have legacy code that includes content, using `RequestDispatcher.include()` or `jsp:include`, from another servlet or JSP. You can replace direct references to the included resources with an including action defined in your *struts-config.xml* file.

Like the `ForwardAction`, you only need to use the `IncludeAction` if you are using a custom `RequestProcessor`, which overrides the `processForwardConfig()` method, to handle requests. Using an including action ensures that the request is routed through your application's control layer provided by Struts's `ActionServlet` and `RequestProcessor`. An including action essentially decorates the legacy resource with Struts functionality. You use this action as you would the original resource. In other words, you would change JSP tags that look like this:

```
<jsp:include page="/LegacyIncludeServlet"/>
```

to this:

```
<jsp:include page="/IncludeContent.do"/>
```

See Also

Recipe 6.5 shows how to use a similar approach that provides the equivalent replacement for calls to the `RequestDispatcher.forward()`.

6.7   Changing the Current Module

Problem

You want to allow the user to switch to a different module at runtime.

Solution

In the *struts-config.xml* file of the module that you will be switching (referred to as the "source" module), create an `action` that uses a type of `org.apache.struts.actions.SwitchAction`:

```
<action path="/ChangeModuleTest"
        type="org.apache.struts.actions.SwitchAction"/>
```

To use the action, pass request parameters that indicate the module and page within the module to switch to. The module is specified as the value of the `prefix` request parameter. The page is specified as the value for the `page` request parameter and defines the module-relative location of the resource to access.

```
<html:link page="/ChangeModuleTest.do?prefix=moduleName&page=/SomeAction.do">
    Change Module
</html:link>
```

Since the page value is a location, if you are linking to an action, you must include the action extension (e.g., .do) as part of the parameter value.

Discussion

SwitchAction changes the application's current module to another module and forwards control to a specified module-relative URL. Like ForwardAction and IncludeAction, the SwitchAction doesn't require subclassing.

A *module* is an in-memory, application-relative context maintained by Struts. Modules partition a web application context into *subcontexts*. A module is defined by creating a separate Struts configuration XML file for the module. This file is referenced using an initialization parameter for the Struts ActionServlet in the web application's *web.xml* file. The name of the initialization parameter specifies the module's prefix. The following servlet definition creates three modules: the default module, /mod1, and /mod2:

```
<servlet>
    <servlet-name>action</servlet-name>
    <servlet-class>org.apache.struts.action.ActionServlet</servlet-class>
    <init-param>
        <param-name>config</param-name>
        <param-value>/WEB-INF/struts-config.xml</param-value>
    </init-param>
    <init-param>
        <param-name>config/mod1</param-name>
        <param-value>/WEB-INF/struts-config-mod1.xml</param-value>
    </init-param>
    <init-param>
        <param-name>config/mod2</param-name>
        <param-value>/WEB-INF/struts-config-mod2.xml</param-value>
    </init-param>
    <load-on-startup>1</load-on-startup>
</servlet>
```

You might assume that you can switch from one module to another by using the module prefix on a URL of a link or action. For example, say that you have created a module for administration features called *admin*. You want to create a link from your application's main page, in the default module, to the main page of the admin module. You might be inclined to create the link using something like this:

```
<html:link action="/admin/Main.do">Admin Module</html:link>
```

If you were to code this, you would find that the link would not work!

To switch to an action in another module, the request must go through the Struts controller layer. If you issue a request directly to a JSP page in another module, it won't have access to module-specific Struts objects, such as message resources, plug-ins, and global forwards. The `SwitchAction` ensures that the request goes through the controller.

Since you can't link directly to JSP in another module, create an `action` in the Struts configuration file for the module you are linking from that uses the `SwitchAction` type. Then reference the path of that action in the link, passing the module prefix and page as request parameters:

```
<html:link page="/SwitchModule.do?prefix=admin&page=/Main.do">
    Admin Module
</html:link>
```

The `SwitchAction` determines the module and the URL of the page or action to forward to based on the `prefix` and `page` request parameters. Table 6-1 describes these parameters and provides some examples.

Table 6-1. Switch action parameters

Parameter	Description	Examples
prefix	The name of the module to switch to. This value should start with a leading /.. Use an empty string to denote the default module.	prefix="" prefix="/admin"
page	The module-relative URL of the JSP or Action to execute.	page="/main.jsp" page="/AddEmployee.do?id=5"

Use global forwards to predefine module links in the Struts configuration file. If the module prefix or page to execute should change, you only need to change the global forward:

```
<global-forwards>
    <forward name="goToDefaultModule"  contextRelative="true"
            path="/default_module.jsp"/>
    <forward name="goToDefaultModuleViaAction"
            path="/SwitchModule.do?prefix=&amp;page=/default_module.jsp"/>
    <forward name="goToModule2"
            path="/SwitchModule.do?prefix=/mod2&amp;page=/module2.jsp"/>
</global-forwards>
```

Setting `contextRelative="true"` indicates that you will be switching to the default module. If you are switching to a module other than the default module, the action referenced by the `path` must be a `SwitchAction`. To create a link that switches to the module, specify the value of the `html:link` tag's `forward` attribute as the name of the global forward:

```
<html:link forward="goToModule2">
    Module2
</html:link>
```

When specifying request parameters on a path attribute in a Struts configuration XML file, the ampersand character (&) can't be used literally. Instead, use the & character entity. The resulting attribute value will be parsed correctly when it's processed and read by Struts.

Struts 1.2 has added additional support for modules that makes it easier to create links between modules. You can use the html:link tag to create a link to an action in a different module without having to use the SwitchAction or a global forward. When used with the action attribute of the html:link tag, the module attribute specifies the prefix name of the module containing the action mapping specified by the action attribute. Use the empty string ("") to denote the default module. The module attribute is only valid when used with the action attribute:

```
<html:link module="/mod2" action="module2Action.do">
    Module2
</html:link>
```

If you need to link to a JSP page in another module, you must pass the request through the controller using the SwitchAction.

See Also

If you are unfamiliar with Struts modules, Recipe 2.5 provides complete information. The Struts User Guide has describes the module switching. The specific section can be found at *http://struts.apache.org/userGuide/configuration.html#module_config-switching*.

6.8   Managing Related Operations from a Central Action

Problem

You want to use a single Action class to handle related operations instead of having to write separate Action classes for each operation.

Solution

Extend the DispatchAction with your own class. Provide methods for each operation that you wish to be accessible as an Action. Each method should have the same signature as the execute( ) method except for the method name. The Action class shown in Example 6-4 provides three related operations in one class: create( ), update( ), and delete( ).

Example 6-4. Dispatch action for related operations

```
package com.oreilly.strutsckbk.ch06;

import javax.servlet.http.HttpServletRequest;
import javax.servlet.http.HttpServletResponse;

import org.apache.struts.action.ActionForm;
import org.apache.struts.action.ActionForward;
import org.apache.struts.action.ActionMapping;
import org.apache.struts.actions.DispatchAction;

public class MyDispatchAction extends DispatchAction {
    public ActionForward create( ActionMapping mapping,
                                 ActionForm form,
                                 HttpServletRequest request,
                                 HttpServletResponse response) throws Exception {
        // create data
        request.setAttribute("dispatchedTo","create");
        return mapping.findForward("success");
    }
    public ActionForward update( ActionMapping mapping,
                                 ActionForm form,
                                 HttpServletRequest request,
                                 HttpServletResponse response) throws Exception {
        // update data
        request.setAttribute("dispatchedTo","update");
        return mapping.findForward("success");
    }
    public ActionForward delete( ActionMapping mapping,
                                 ActionForm form,
                                 HttpServletRequest request,
                                 HttpServletResponse response) throws Exception {
        // delete data
        request.setAttribute("dispatchedTo","delete");
        return mapping.findForward("success");
    }
}
```

In the actions that use your DispatchAction, specify the request parameter whose value will be the method to call:

```
<action   path="/DispatchActionTest"
          name="TestForm"
          scope="request"
          type="com.oreilly.strutsckbk.ch06.MyDispatchAction"
      parameter="methodToCall">
  <forward name="success" path="/dispatch_test.jsp"/>
</action>
```

On a form that submits to this action, use JavaScript to set the parameter for the method to call. The name of the request parameter must match the value of the parameter attribute from the action mapping. The value of the request parameter is the name of the method. To dispatch to a method from a hyperlink, set the method parameter on the URL. Example 6-5 (*dispatch_test.jsp*) shows the different ways that you can specify the method parameter for a DispatchAction.

Example 6-5. JSP for submitting to a DispatchAction

```
<%@ page contentType="text/html;charset=UTF-8" language="java" %>
<%@ taglib uri="http://struts.apache.org/tags-html" prefix="html" %>
<%@ taglib uri="http://java.sun.com/jstl/core" prefix="c" %>

<html>
<head>
  <title>Struts Cookbook - Chapter 6 : Dispatch Action Test</title>
</head>
<body bgcolor="white">
  <h2>Dispatch Action Test</h2>
  <html:form method="get" action="/DispatchActionTest">
    Name: <html:text property="name"/>
    <input type="hidden" name="methodToCall">
    <script>
      function set(target) {
        document.forms[0].methodToCall.value=target;
      }
    </script>
    <p>
    <html:submit onclick="set('create');">New</html:submit>
    <html:submit onclick="set('update');">Edit</html:submit>
    <html:link href="javascript:set('touch');document.forms[0].submit();">
        <html:img border="0" srcKey="image.touch"/>
    </html:link>
    </p>
  </html:form>
  <html:link page="/DispatchActionTest.do?methodToCall=delete">Remove</html:link>
</body>
</html>
```

Discussion

The DispatchAction enables a single custom class to process multiple requests for similar operations. Performing create/read/update/delete(CRUD) operations for the same business object exemplifies the classic use case for the DispatchAction. Traditionally, four custom Action classes would be written, one for each operation. Since the operations are for the same business object, a significant amount of code would be duplicated.

The DispatchAction allows you to use a more natural programming approach. Instead of creating separate classes, you create one class with methods corresponding to the desired operations. A DispatchAction is created by subclassing org.apache.struts.actions.DispatchAction. You don't override the execute( ) method as you would for a normal custom Action. Instead, you implement methods corresponding to the operations you wish to support. Common behavior can be implemented by private methods that you call from the main dispatch operations. The method signature of each operation must be the same as the signature as the execute method:

```
public ActionForward someOperation(
        ActionMapping mapping,
        ActionForm form,
        HttpServletRequest request,
        HttpServletResponse response) throws Exception {
    // custom code
    return mapping.findForward("success");
}
```

The execute( ) method of the base DispatchAction calls a given method of your subclass using the value of a specific HTTP request parameter.

Is the DispatchAction Safe?

A common misconception is that the DispatchAction allows *any* method of your subclass to be called. In fact, the only methods that can be called are those that accept the same arguments as those passed to the execute( ) method.

However, the DispatchAction initially shipped with Struts 1.1 had a serious flaw because it didn't test if the "method to call" was the execute( ) or perform( ) method. This oversight opened the door for an accidental or malicious recursive call. This bug was identified and has been eliminated in Struts 1.2. If you are using Struts 1.1, you can eliminate this issue in your own DispatchAction subclass by overriding the dispatchMethod( ) method as follows:

```
protected ActionForward dispatchMethod(
        ActionMapping mapping,
        ActionForm form,
        HttpServletRequest request,
        HttpServletResponse response,
        String name) throws Exception {
    if ("execute".equals(name) || "perform".equals(name)) {
        throw new ServletException(
            "Accidental recursive call in DispatchAction"
        );
    }
    return super.dispatchMethod(mapping,
                                form,
                                request,
                                response,
                                name);

}
```

The parameter attribute of the action element in the *struts-config.xml* file dictates the name of that request parameter:

```
<action    path="/DispatchActionTest"
           type="com.foo.MyDispatchAction"
       parameter="methodToCall">
   <forward name="success" path="/some_page.jsp"/>
</action>
```

If the action is called on form submission, use a hidden field with the value set using JavaScript. You'll want to use the HTML `<input type="hidden" name="`*methodToCall*`">` tag instead of the Struts `<html:hidden property="`*methodToCall*`"/>`. Using the Struts tag forces you to create an artificial property in your `ActionForm` to hold the *methodToCall* parameter.

If you want to use an image to perform the submission instead of a button, wrap the image in a link. Set the `href` attribute of the link so it sets the *methodToCall* property appropriately and submits the form:

```
<script>
    function set(target) {
        document.forms[0].methodToCall.value=target;
    }
</script>
<html:link href="javascript:set('create');document.forms[0].submit();">
    <html:img border="0" srcKey="image.create"/>
</html:link>
```

Finally, all `DispatchActions` support the ability to define default behavior if the name of the method to call can't be resolved; that is, no matching method is defined in the `DispatchAction` subclass. The default behavior is implemented by overriding the protected method named unspecified( ). This method, like other custom operational methods of `DispatchActions`, takes the same arguments as the execute( ) method. Use the unspecified( ) method if the `DispatchAction` has a primary default operation; then you won't have to use an additional request parameter to access this primary flow. If you don't provide an implementation of unspecified( ), then a `ServletException` will be thrown if an unknown method is specified.

See Also

Recipe 6.9 provides similar functionality as the `DispatchAction` without requiring the use of JavaScript on the JSP page.

6.9   Submitting a Form from Localized Form Controls

Problem

You want to use a single `Action` class to process related operations where each button, which has a localized value, on a form corresponds to a specific method in the `Action` class.

Solution

Extend the Struts pre-built `LookupDispatchAction` with your own class. Provide methods for each operation you wish to be called. Each method should have the same signature as the `execute( )` method. Implement the `getKeyMethodMap( )` method, mapping the button label resource bundle key to the corresponding method name to call. The `Action` class shown in Example 6-6 provides three related operations in one class: `create( )`, `update( )`, and `delete( )`. The `getKeyMethodMap( )` method returns a map where the map key is a `MessageResources` key for the button label, and the map value is the corresponding method name.

Example 6-6. LookupDispatchAction for related operations

```java
package com.oreilly.strutsckbk.ch06;

import java.util.HashMap;
import java.util.Map;

import javax.servlet.http.HttpServletRequest;
import javax.servlet.http.HttpServletResponse;

import org.apache.struts.action.ActionForm;
import org.apache.struts.action.ActionForward;
import org.apache.struts.action.ActionMapping;
import org.apache.struts.actions.LookupDispatchAction;

public class MyLookupDispatchAction extends LookupDispatchAction {

    public MyLookupDispatchAction() {
        keyMethodMap = new HashMap();
        keyMethodMap.put("button.add", "create");
        keyMethodMap.put("button.edit", "update");
        keyMethodMap.put("button.remove", "delete");
    }

    protected Map getKeyMethodMap() {
        return keyMethodMap;
    }

    public ActionForward create( ActionMapping mapping,
                                 ActionForm form,
```

Example 6-6. LookupDispatchAction for related operations (continued)

```
                                HttpServletRequest request,
                                HttpServletResponse response) throws Exception {
        // create data
        request.setAttribute("dispatchedTo","create");
        return mapping.findForward("success");
    }
    public ActionForward update( ActionMapping mapping,
                                 ActionForm form,
                                 HttpServletRequest request,
                                 HttpServletResponse response) throws Exception {
        // update data
        request.setAttribute("dispatchedTo","update");
        return mapping.findForward("success");
    }
    public ActionForward delete( ActionMapping mapping,
                                 ActionForm form,
                                 HttpServletRequest request,
                                 HttpServletResponse response) throws Exception {
        // delete data
        request.setAttribute("dispatchedTo","delete");
        return mapping.findForward("success");
    }
}
```

In the actions that use your LookupDispatchAction, specify the request parameter whose value will be the button's value. When your custom Action receives the request, the base LookupDispatchAction performs a reverse lookup on the MessageResources, retrieving the matching key for the value from the bundle:

```
<action    path="/LookupDispatchActionTest"
           name="TestForm"
           type="com.oreilly.strutsckbk.ch06.MyLookupDispatchAction"
        parameter="methodToCall">
    <forward name="success" path="/lookup_dispatch_test.jsp"/>
</action>
```

On a form that submits to this action, use the bean:message tag as the body for each submit button rendered using html:submit. The property attribute value on the html:submit tag must match the parameter attribute value for the corresponding action in the *struts-config.xml* file. Struts will look up the method to call from your LookupDispatchAction implementation, using the map returned in the getKeyMethodMap( ) method. The JSP page in Example 6-7 (*lookup_dispatch_test.jsp*) specifies three submit buttons corresponding to the three operations provided by the class in Example 6-6.

Example 6-7. JSP that submits to a LookupDispatchAction

```
<%@ page contentType="text/html;charset=UTF-8" language="java" %>
<%@ taglib uri="http://struts.apache.org/tags-bean" prefix="bean" %>
<%@ taglib uri="http://struts.apache.org/tags-html" prefix="html" %>
<%@ taglib uri="http://java.sun.com/jstl/core" prefix="c" %>
```

Example 6-7. JSP that submits to a LookupDispatchAction (continued)

```
<html>
<head>
  <title>Struts Cookbook - Chapter 6 : Lookup Dispatch Action Test</title>
</head>
<body bgcolor="white">
<h2>Lookup Dispatch Action Test</h2>
  <html:form method="get" action="/LookupDispatchActionTest">
    Name: <html:text property="name"/>
    <p>
    <html:submit property="methodToCall">
        <bean:message key="button.add"/>
    </html:submit>
    <html:submit property="methodToCall">
        <bean:message key="button.edit"/>
    </html:submit>
    <html:submit property="methodToCall">
        <bean:message key="button.remove"/>
    </html:submit>
    </p>
  </html:form>
  <hr />
  <c:if test="${not empty TestForm.map.name}">
    Name: <c:out value="${TestForm.map.name}"/><br />
    Dispatch Method: <b><c:out value="${dispatchedTo}"/></b>
  </c:if>
</body>
</html>
```

Discussion

The LookupDispatchAction, included with Struts, performs the same function as the DispatchAction that it extends. It is designed to allow for a single Action class to service related operations triggered by clicking submit buttons on a form. Unlike the DispatchAction, the LookupDispatchAction doesn't require the use of JavaScript to set a request parameter. Instead, you add a method to your subclass of LookupDispatchAction that returns a map of key/value pairs. The *key* matches the MessageResources key for the corresponding button label, and the *value* represents the name of the corresponding method to call.

In the Solution, the relevant key/value pairs values defined in the MessageResources properties file are shown here:

```
button.add = Add Me
button.edit = Change Me
button.remove = Remove Me
```

Each property value—that is, the right-side of the pair—is retrieved using the bean: message tag:

```
<html:submit property="methodToCall">
    <bean:message key="button.add"/>
</html:submit>
```

When you click this button, the URL will look something like:

```
http://localhost/jsc-ch06/LookupDispatchActionTest.do?name=Bill&methodToCall=Add+Me
```

Struts will use the value of the *methodToCall* request parameter to look up the key for the value from the MessageResources. For this example, it will retrieve the key "button.add". Struts then uses the Map returned in your class's getKeyMethodMap( ) method to determine the method to call. For the example, this will be the create( ) method. The method is discovered and invoked using Java reflection.

 The performance of reflection operations has improved in JDK 1.4. In particular, reflective method invocation, used by the DispatchAction (and subclasses), and object instantiation have been rewritten. These operations perform several times faster than in previous releases of the JDK. For Struts applications the overhead of using reflection is minimal.

Using the LookupDispatchAction can seem a little tricky at first. Once you understand how it works, it can reduce substantially the number of classes you have to maintain. It ties nicely into Struts support for internationalization. If you are localizing button labels using Struts bean:message tags, you have the necessary presentation hooks in place to leverage the LookupDispatchAction.

See Also

If you are using images as submit buttons instead of text-based buttons, use the DispatchAction shown in Recipe 6.8 and set the *methodToCall* request parameter using JavaScript. For an alternative approach when using image buttons, check out Michael McGrady's page on the Struts Wiki at *http://wiki.apache.org/struts/StrutsCatalogMultipleImageButtonsWithNoJavaScript*.

6.10 Dispatching to Related Operations with Action Mappings

Problem

You want to use a single Action class to process related operations yet allow the form type, validation rules, and other action attributes to vary for each operation.

Solution

Extend the Struts pre-built MappingDispatchAction (only available in Struts 1.2 or later) with your own subclass. Provide methods for each operation you wish to be callable. Each method should have the same signature as the execute( ) method. The class shown in Example 6-8 provides three related operations: create( ), update( ), and delete( ).

Example 6-8. MappingDispatchAction for related operations

```java
package com.oreilly.strutsckbk.ch06;

import java.util.HashMap;
import java.util.Map;

import javax.servlet.http.HttpServletRequest;
import javax.servlet.http.HttpServletResponse;

import org.apache.commons.beanutils.PropertyUtils;
import org.apache.struts.action.ActionForm;
import org.apache.struts.action.ActionForward;
import org.apache.struts.action.ActionMapping;
import org.apache.struts.actions.MappingDispatchAction;

public class MyMappingDispatchAction extends MappingDispatchAction {

    public ActionForward create( ActionMapping mapping,
                ActionForm form,
                HttpServletRequest request,
                HttpServletResponse response) throws Exception {
        PropertyUtils.setSimpleProperty(form, "dispatchedTo", "create");
        return mapping.findForward("success");
    }
    public ActionForward update( ActionMapping mapping,
                ActionForm form,
                HttpServletRequest request,
                HttpServletResponse response) throws Exception {
        PropertyUtils.setSimpleProperty(form, "dispatchedTo", "update");
        return mapping.findForward("success");
    }
    public ActionForward delete( ActionMapping mapping,
                ActionForm form,
                HttpServletRequest request,
                HttpServletResponse response) throws Exception {
        PropertyUtils.setSimpleProperty(form, "dispatchedTo", "delete");
        return mapping.findForward("success");
    }
}
```

In the actions that use your MappingDispatchAction, specify the value of the method to call as the value of the parameter attribute. Unlike the DispatchAction and LookupDispatchAction, a different action form, identified by the name attribute, can be specified for each action mapping:

```xml
<action    path="/AddAction"
            name="AddForm"
            type="com.oreilly.strutsckbk.ch06.MyMappingDispatchAction"
        parameter="create">
    <forward name="success" path="/mapping_dispatch_test.jsp"/>
</action>
<action    path="/ChangeAction"
            name="ChangeForm"
```

```
            type="com.oreilly.strutsckbk.ch06.MyMappingDispatchAction"
        parameter="update">
      <forward name="success" path="/mapping_dispatch_test.jsp"/>
    </action>
    <action    path="/RemoveAction"
            name="RemoveForm"
            type="com.oreilly.strutsckbk.ch06.MyMappingDispatchAction"
        parameter="delete">
      <forward name="success" path="/mapping_dispatch_test.jsp"/>
    </action>
```

Reference the path of the action to use as the value for the action attribute on the
html:form tag. The JSP in Example 6-9 (*mapping_dispatch_test.jsp*) contains three separate forms, each corresponding to the three actions defined in the *struts-config.xml*
file.

Example 6-9. JSP that submits to a mapping dispatch action

```
<%@ page contentType="text/html;charset=UTF-8" language="java" %>
<%@ taglib uri="http://struts.apache.org/tags-bean" prefix="bean" %>
<%@ taglib uri="http://struts.apache.org/tags-html" prefix="html" %>
<%@ taglib uri="http://java.sun.com/jstl/core" prefix="c" %>

<html>
<head>
  <title>Struts Cookbook - Chapter 6 : Mapping Dispatch Action Test</title>
</head>
<body bgcolor="white">
<h2>Mapping Dispatch Action Test</h2>
  <hr />
  <h3>Add Action</h3>
  <html:form method="get" action="/AddAction">
    Name: <html:text property="name"/>
    <p><html:submit/></p>
  </html:form>
  <p>
  Name: <c:out value="${AddForm.map.name}"/><br />
  Dispatch Method: <b><c:out value="${AddForm.map.dispatchedTo}"/></b>
  <hr />
  <h3>Change Action</h3>
  <html:form method="get" action="/ChangeAction">
    Name: <html:text property="name"/>
    <p><html:submit/></p>
  </html:form>
  <p>
  Name: <c:out value="${ChangeForm.map.name}"/><br />
  Dispatch Method: <b><c:out value="${ChangeForm.map.dispatchedTo}"/></b>
  <hr />
  <h3>Remove Action</h3>
  <html:link page="/RemoveAction.do?name=Test">Remove Me</html:link>
```

Example 6-9. JSP that submits to a mapping dispatch action (continued)

```
<p>
Name: <c:out value="${RemoveForm.map.name}"/><br />
Dispatch Method: <b><c:out value="${RemoveForm.map.dispatchedTo}"/></b>
</body>
</html>
```

Discussion

The `MappingDispatchAction`, included with Struts 1.2, extends the `DispatchAction`. Whereas the operational methods implemented in a `DispatchAction` or `LookupDispatchAction` are tied to a request parameter, the method to call in a `MappingDispatchAction` is tied to an action definition in the *struts-config.xml* file. The parameter attribute of the action element identifies the method to call.

The `MappingDispatchAction` allows you to group together related methods. However, the `ActionForm` can vary per method. This allows for greater flexibility when dispatching related operations. You get the benefits of grouping the related operations, yet you aren't required to use a common form if it doesn't make sense. Consider a concrete `Action` for performing the traditional CRUD functionality. Though the `create( )` and `update( )` operations most likely use the same `ActionForm`, the `read( )` and `delete( )` operations only require a single form property representing the object's primary identifier or key.

Because the form can vary per method, the validation rules can vary since these rules are related to the form type. The `MappingDispatchAction` provides a more elegant solution than the other `DispatchAction` types because it doesn't rely on JavaScript or the use of reverse `MessageResource` lookups. However, this action is new to Struts and is available with Struts Version 1.2 or later.

See Also

If you are using Struts 1.1 and want to use a `DispatchAction` for related operations, Recipes 6.8 and 6.9 show how this can be accomplished. A short tutorial on using the `MappingDispatchAction` can be found in the weblog entry at *http://frustratedprogrammer. blogspot.com/2004/07/struts-121-mappingdispatchaction.html*. You should also read over the JavaDocs for the `MappingDispatchAction`. These can be found at *http://struts.apache. org/api/org/apache/struts/actions/MappingDispatchAction.html*.

## CHAPTER 7

Execution Control

7.0 Introduction

This chapter presents problems related to controlling execution of your web application. Some of the solutions use *listener* features provided by the Servlet container. These classes and interfaces allow your application to receive notification of servlet container events. Servlet listeners can be used on any Java web application and container that supports the Servlet 2.3 API.

Managing workflow in a web application can be a challenge due to the stateless nature of HTTP. This chapter covers some approaches for handling navigation within a Struts application. Finally, this chapter will look at some specific problems and solutions you'll encounter when working with files. You'll find solutions for enabling and processing file uploads as well as displaying content—in varying formats—from files on the server.

7.1 Performing Tasks at Application Startup

Problem

You want to be notified when your web application is initialized so you can preload application-scope data or execute other startup functions.

Solution

Create a class that implements the ServletContextListener interface. The class shown in Example 7-1 stores the current date and time in the servlet context when the application is started.

Example 7-1. Servlet context data loader

```
package com.oreilly.strutsckbk.ch07;

import java.util.Date;

import javax.servlet.ServletContextEvent;
import javax.servlet.ServletContextListener;

public class ContextLoader implements ServletContextListener {
    public void contextInitialized(ServletContextEvent event) {
        ServletContext ctx = event.getServletContext();
        ctx.setAttribute("dateStarted", new Date());
    }
    public void contextDestroyed(ServletContextEvent event) {
        // clean up here
    }
}
```

Declare the class with a listener element in your web application's *web.xml* file. The listener element is supported by Version 2.3 or 2.4 of the Servlet specification; the DTD must specify Version 2.3 or 2.4:

```
<?xml version="1.0" encoding="ISO-8859-1" ?>
<!DOCTYPE web-app PUBLIC
    "-//Sun Microsystems, Inc.//DTD Web Application 2.3//EN"
    "http://java.sun.com/dtd/web-app_2_3.dtd">

<web-app>
  <display-name>Struts Cookbook - Chapter 7 Examples</display-name>

  <listener>
     <listener-class>com.oreilly.strutsckbk.ch07.ContextLoader</listener-class>
  </listener>
  ... rest of web.xml
```

Discussion

Every Java web application has one single servlet context. This context is the place where application-scoped attributes are stored. The servlet container creates the servlet context for a web application when the application is started. You can create a class that gets notified when this context is created (or destroyed) by implementing the ServletContextListener interface. Your listener class receives notifications immediately after the servlet context is created and immediately before the context is destroyed. These events coincide with the startup and shutdown of the web application.

The ServletContextListener interface defines two methods: contextInitialized() and contextDestroyed(). The container passes a ServletContextEvent to these methods. This class provides access to the ServletContext itself. With the servlet context, you can add, remove, and replace application-scope objects as servlet context attributes. The class in Example 7-1 uses the ServletContext.setAttribute(*name,value*) method to store the current a Date object in the servlet context. You could access this data from a JSP page as an application-scoped object:

```
Running since: <bean:write name="dateStarted"
                            scope="application"
                            format="MM/dd/yy"/>
```

Servlet context listeners make an excellent choice for this kind of data loading, but for a Struts application you may prefer to use a Struts plug-in. A plug-in can do anything a context listener can do, and a plug-in gives you access to your entire application's Struts configuration through the `ActionServlet`. You can pass parameters to a plug-in using the `set-property` element, making plug-ins more flexible and reusable than listeners. Because you declare plug-ins in the *struts-config.xml* file, you get a side benefit as your application's configuration will be centralized in one place.

See Also

Recipe 2.1 gives complete details on writing and configuring Struts plug-ins. Recipe 7.2 describes how to create classes that monitor HTTP sessions.

If you are unfamiliar with servlet programming, then you should check out *Java Servlet Programming* by Jason Hunter (O'Reilly). This classic work will give you all the information you need to create highly functional servlets and servlet-related classes.

7.2   Tracking Client Sessions

Problem

You need to keep track of the number of clients currently using your application.

Solution

Create a class that implements the `HttpSessionListener` interface, like the one shown in Example 7-2, that keeps count of the total number of active sessions.

Example 7-2. Session-counting listener

```
package com.oreilly.strutsckbk.ch07;

import javax.servlet.ServletContext;
import javax.servlet.http.HttpSessionEvent;
import javax.servlet.http.HttpSessionListener;

public class SessionCounter implements HttpSessionListener {
    public void sessionCreated(HttpSessionEvent event) {
        ServletContext ctx = event.getSession().getServletContext();
        Integer numSessions = (Integer) ctx.getAttribute("numSessions");
        if (numSessions == null) {
            numSessions = new Integer(1);
        }
```

Example 7-2. Session-counting listener (continued)

```
        else {
            int count = numSessions.intValue( );
            numSessions = new Integer(count + 1);
        }
        ctx.setAttribute("numSessions", numSessions);
    }
    public void sessionDestroyed(HttpSessionEvent event) {
        ServletContext ctx = event.getSession().getServletContext( );
        Integer numSessions = (Integer) ctx.getAttribute("numSessions");
        if (numSessions == null) {
            numSessions = new Integer(0);
        }
        else {
            int count = numSessions.intValue( );
            numSessions = new Integer(count - 1);
        }
        ctx.setAttribute("numSessions", numSessions);
    }
}
```

Declare your class in a listener element of your application's *web.xml* file. The listener element is supported by Version 2.3 or 2.4 of the Servlet specification—the DTD must specify Version 2.3 or 2.4:

```
<?xml version="1.0" encoding="ISO-8859-1" ?>
<!DOCTYPE web-app PUBLIC
    "-//Sun Microsystems, Inc.//DTD Web Application 2.3//EN"
    "http://java.sun.com/dtd/web-app_2_3.dtd">

<web-app>
  <display-name>Struts Cookbook - Chapter 7 Examples</display-name>

  <listener>
      <listener-class>com.oreilly.strutsckbk.ch07.SessionCounter</listener-class>
  </listener>
  ... rest of web.xml
```

Discussion

In the Solution, any time a session is created, a counter—stored in the servlet context—is incremented. Every time a session is destroyed, that counter is decremented. In practical terms, this custom class tracks the number of users currently using your application.

Web applications use HTTP sessions to maintain state between requests. The Servlet 2.3 specification added support for session listeners that receive notifications when any session is created or destroyed. You can write a class that receives these events by implementing the HttpSessionListener interface.

This interface defines two methods: sessionCreated( ) and sessionDestroyed( ). The container calls sessionCreated( ) after a session is created and sessionDestroyed( )

before the session is destroyed or invalidated. The container passes an HttpSessionEvent to each of these methods. This event object has a getSession( ) method that gives you a handle to the particular session.

Once you've got the HttpSession, you can do anything you want to with it. If the session was just created, you can add objects as session-scoped attributes. If destroyed, then you have the opportunity to dispose of session objects that require special handling. The HttpSession provides the getAttribute( ), setAttribute( ), and removeAttribute( ) methods for manipulating session attributes. You can get a reference to your application's servlet context via the getServletContext( ) method.

See Also

While session listeners receive notification of session lifecycle events, servlet context listeners receive notification of application life-cycle events. These listeners are discussed in Recipe 7.1. If you want notifications specifically when objects are added to or removed from the session, use a session attribute listener discussed in Recipe 7.3.

If you are unfamiliar with servlet programming, you should check out *Java Servlet Programming* by Jason Hunter (O'Reilly). This classic work will give you all the information you need to create highly functional servlets and servlet-related classes.

7.3   Monitoring User Logins

Problem

You want to know when a user has logged into your application.

Solution

Create a class that implements the HttpSessionAttributeListener for session-scoped objects. The class shown in Example 7-3 tracks the number of logged-in users of an application by listening for the addition and removal of a User object to or from the session.

Example 7-3. Session attribute listener

```
package com.oreilly.strutsckbk.ch07;

import javax.servlet.ServletContext;
import javax.servlet.http.HttpSessionAttributeListener;
import javax.servlet.http.HttpSessionBindingEvent;

public class UserCounter implements HttpSessionAttributeListener {

    public void attributeAdded(HttpSessionBindingEvent event) {
        if (attributeIsUser(event))
            adjustUserCounter(event.getSession().getServletContext(), true);
    }
```

Example 7-3. Session attribute listener (continued)

```
    public void attributeRemoved(HttpSessionBindingEvent event) {
        if (attributeIsUser(event))
            adjustUserCounter(event.getSession().getServletContext( ), false);
    }

    public void attributeReplaced(HttpSessionBindingEvent event) {
    }

    private boolean attributeIsUser(HttpSessionBindingEvent event) {
        String name = event.getName( );
        Object value = event.getValue( );
        return "user".equals(name) &&
                value instanceof com.oreilly.strutsckbk.ch07.User;
    }

    private void adjustUserCounter(ServletContext ctx, boolean userAdded) {
        Integer counterObj = (Integer) ctx.getAttribute("numUsers");
        int counter = (counterObj == null ? 0 : counterObj.intValue( ));
        if (userAdded) {
          counter++;
        }
        else {
            if (counter > 0) counter--;
        }
        ctx.setAttribute("numUsers", new Integer(counter));
    }
}
```

Like the other servlet listeners, you declare the class as a `listener` element in your web application's *web.xml* file. The `listener` element is supported by Version 2.3 or 2.4 of the Servlet specification; the DTD must specify Version 2.3 or 2.4:

```
    <?xml version="1.0" encoding="ISO-8859-1" ?>
    <!DOCTYPE web-app PUBLIC
        "-//Sun Microsystems, Inc.//DTD Web Application 2.3//EN"
        "http://java.sun.com/dtd/web-app_2_3.dtd">

    <web-app>
      <display-name>Struts Cookbook - Chapter 7 Examples</display-name>

      <listener>
          <listener-class>com.oreilly.strutsckbk.ch07.UserCounter</listener-class>
      </listener>
      ... rest of web.xml
```

Discussion

The Servlet 2.3 specification added support for various listener types. Attribute listeners allow you to receive event notifications when an object is added, removed, or replaced in the session and application scopes. A class that implements the `HttpSessionAttributeListener` interface monitors session-scope objects.

The Solution shown in Example 7-3 shows how an attribute listener can track the number of users logged into your application. When an attribute is added to the session under the name "user," a counter object—maintained in the servlet context—is incremented. Likewise, when the user object is removed from the session, the counter is decremented. The session listener of Recipe 7.2 provided a similar function. However, using an attribute listener gives you finer-grained monitoring.

The `HttpSessionAttributeListener` specifies three methods: `attributeAdded()`, `attributeReplaced()`, and `attributeRemoved()`. The servlet container calls `attributeAdded()` when an object is added to the session or servlet context under a new name. If an attribute is added using the name of an existing attribute, the `attributeReplaced()` method is called. When an object is removed from the session or servlet context, the container calls `attributeRemoved()`. When an `HttpSession` is invalidated, the servlet container will call the `removeAttribute()` method of any `HttpSessionAttributeListeners` for each object in the session. This allows you to perform any necessary cleanup on those objects before the session is destroyed.

 Objects can be added, replaced, or removed from the `HttpSession` and `ServletContext` using the `setAttribute()` and `removeAttribute()` methods. You can manipulate these objects from a JSP page using custom tags like the standard `jsp:useBean`, Struts' `bean:define`, and JSTL's `c:set`.

The session attribute that caused the event is accessible via the `HttpSessionBindingEvent` object passed to each notification method. The `getValue()` method retrieves the object and the `getName()` retrieves the attribute's name.

See Also

You can monitor attributes added to the ServletContext using a `ServletContextAttributeListener`. Furthermore, the Servlet 2.4 specification adds a `ServletRequestAttributeListener` and lets you monitor objects added to any servlet request.

The `HttpSessionBindingListener` interface allows objects being managed as session attributes to be notified when they're bound or unbound from the session. The methods of this interface are triggered by the same events as the `HttpSessionAttributeListener`. The JavaDocs for the session binding listener can be found at *http://java.sun.com/products/servlet/2.3/javadoc/javax/servlet/http/ HttpSessionBindingListener.html*.

If you are unfamiliar with servlet programming, you should check out *Java Servlet Programming* by Jason Hunter (O'Reilly). This classic work will give you all the information you need to create highly functional servlets and servlet-related classes.

7.4 Forwarding Users to Alternate Destinations

Problem

You want to define locations, such as other servlets, JSPs, or Struts components that you can forward users to from your application code.

Solution

Define the global forwards in the *struts-config.xml* file. If the forward is for a specific module, define it in that module's *struts-config.xml* file:

```
<form-beans>
  <!-- snipped ... -->
</form-beans>
<global-forwards>
    <forward name="main" path="/index.jsp"
        redirect="true"/>
    <forward name="logon" path="/Logon.do"
        contextRelative="true" redirect="true"/>
    <forward name="logoff" path="/Logoff.do"
        contextRelative="true" redirect="true"/>
</global-forwards>
<global-exceptions>
  <!-- snipped ... -->
</global-exceptions>
```

Discussion

The URL paths you use in your application commonly evolve and change as your application develops. You can create logical references to application paths using a Struts *forward*. Global forwards—defined using forward elements nested in the global-forwards element—create logical destinations that can be accessed from anywhere in your application. The Struts html:link, html:rewrite, and html:frame tags all support the forward attribute that accepts the name of a global forward. The tag uses the logical path for that forward to generate the actual URL.

Local forwards are specific to a given action. Local forwards are specified as nested elements of an action element:

```
<action   path="/LoadData"
          type="com.oreilly.strutsckbk.ch07.LoadDataAction"
        scope="request"
         name="TestForm">
    <forward name="success" path="/show_data_form.jsp"/>
</action>
```

Local forwards are used by action classes to specify a logical destination. The ActionMapping.findForward( ) method retrieves a forward by name. This method finds a matching local forward for the given name. If none can be found, it searches the global forwards. Here's how a typical custom Action uses the findForward( ) method to retrieve and return an ActionForward:

```
public ActionForward execute(ActionMapping mapping, ActionForm form,
        HttpServletRequest request, HttpServletResponse response)
    throws Exception {
// perform action here

    // forward to the logical "success" location
    return mapping.findForward("success");
}
```

The forward element, whether global or local, accepts the attributes shown in Table 7-1.

Table 7-1. Forward attributes

Attribute	Description
className	Fully qualified Java class name of the ActionForward subclass to use for this object. If unspecified, the class org.apache.struts.action.ActionForward is used. You only need to use this if you extend the Struts ActionForward to provide unique behavior.
contextRelative	Set this to true if the path is relative to the entire application and not this module. This attribute, added in Struts 1.1, is deprecated in Struts 1.2. The default value is false; that is, the path is considered module-relative.
module	The module prefix to use with this path. This value begins with a slash (for example, /adminModule). If unspecified, the module prefix defaults for the current module will be used. A single slash (/) indicates the root module.
name	A module-unique logical identifier for this forward. This value is used to retrieve the forward using the ActionMapping.findForward(String name) method.
path	The module-relative or context-relative URI path to the resource for this ActionForward. This value begins with a slash (for example, /somePage.jsp).
redirect	Set this to true if a redirect instruction should be issued to the browser so a new request is issued to the resource for this forward. The default value is false.

The URI generated for the forward is determined by the contextRelative, module, and path attributes. For Struts 1.1 applications, the contextRelative attribute lets you create forwards between modules. For Struts 1.2, use the module attribute instead of contextRelative. Specifying a module value of / is the same as setting contextRelative to true.

The path attribute contains the location to the desired resource. You can include request parameters by appending a query string. Just be sure to use the ampersand character entity (&amp) to separate name-value pairs. Table 7-2 contains some example global forwards and the resulting URIs.

Table 7-2. Sample forwards

Forward definition	Resultant URL

`<forward name="home"`
`    path="/index.jsp"`
`    redirect="true"`
`/>`
	http://localhost/jsc-ch07/index.jsp

`<forward name="goToModule1"`
`    module="/mod1"`
`    path="/module1.jsp"`
`/>`
	http://localhost/jsc-ch07/mod1/module1.jsp

`<forward name="goToDefaultModule"`
`    contextRelative="true"`
`    path="/default_module.jsp"`
`/>`
	http://localhost/jsc-ch07/default_module.jsp

`<forward name="goToDefaultModule2"`
`    module="/"`
`    path="/default_module.jsp"`
`/>`
	http://localhost/jsc-ch07//default_module.jsp

See Also

Using a global forward specifically to switch to a page in a different module is covered in Recipe 7.5. More information on switching between modules can be found in Recipe 6.7. Global forwards can be used like bridges between workflows as described in Recipe 6.5.

The Struts User Guide provides additional information on configuring and using global and local forwards. The relevant section can be found at *http://struts.apache.org/ userGuide/building_controller.html#config*.

7.5   Forwarding Users to a Module

Problem

You want to forward control from one module to a page in another module.

Solution

If the link is for a JSP page and not an action, create an action of type `ForwardAction` for that page in the target module's *struts-config.xml* file. Specify the path to the JSP page as the value of the parameter attribute:

```
<action   path="/module1Menu"
          type="org.apache.struts.actions.ForwardAction"
       parameter="/mod1/module1Menu.jsp"/>
```

Then define a global forward, in the *struts-config.xml* file of the source module, with the `module` attribute set to the target module prefix and the `path` attribute set to the name of the action you just created:

```
<forward name="goToModule1" module="/mod1" path="/module1.do"/>
```

If the link is for an action in the other module, then specify the path to the action, making sure to include the Struts `ActionServlet` prefix or suffix (for example, `.do`):

```
<html:link forward="goToModule1">Go To Module 1</html:link>
```

Discussion

You would think that you could create a link to a page in another module by specifying the `module` attribute on the global forward:

```
<forward name="goToModule1" module="/mod1" path="/module1.jsp"/>
```

Unfortunately, this will not work. The URL to the page is correctly generated as *http://localhost/jsc-ch07/mod1/module1.jsp*; however, internally Struts still thinks that you are in the source module. Module-specific Struts entities such as global forwards and message resources will not be available on the target page because Struts has not switched the module context. In short, you can't link between pages in a module but only between actions.

To force Struts to switch the module context, the URL must go through the Struts controller, which is the `ActionServlet`. To achieve this, create an `action` in the Struts configuration XML file of the target module that uses the `ForwardAction`. Specify the name of the JSP page as the value for the parameter attribute. Then define a global forward, setting the module attribute to the target module and the path attribute to the path to the forwarding action. Make sure to include the extension (for example, */module1.do*).

See Also

Module support has been enhanced in Struts 1.2. Check the online user's guide for the latest updates. The Struts User Guide can be found at *http://struts.apache.org/userGuide/index.html*. Some other recipes that relate are Recipes 6.7 and 7.4.

7.6   Creating a Wizard-Style Page Flow

Problem

You want users to have a wizard-style page flow experience.

Solution

Implement a subclass of `LookupDispatchAction` that supports operations for the navigational functions—previous, next, and finish—and template methods for the business logic. For each discrete step of the workflow, extend this subclass, placing the business logic for each step in the provided template methods. (See Example 7-4.)

Example 7-4. LookupDispatchAction for wizards

```
package com.oreilly.strutsckbk.ch07;

import java.util.HashMap;
import java.util.Map;

import javax.servlet.http.HttpServletRequest;
import javax.servlet.http.HttpServletResponse;

import org.apache.struts.action.ActionForm;
import org.apache.struts.action.ActionForward;
import org.apache.struts.action.ActionMapping;
import org.apache.struts.actions.LookupDispatchAction;

public class WizardLookupDispatchAction extends LookupDispatchAction {

    public WizardLookupDispatchAction( ) {
        keyMethodMap = new HashMap( );
        keyMethodMap.put("button.previous", "doPrevious");
        keyMethodMap.put("button.next", "doNext");
        keyMethodMap.put("button.finish", "doFinish");
    }

    public ActionForward doPrevious( ActionMapping mapping,
            ActionForm form,
            HttpServletRequest request,
            HttpServletResponse response) throws Exception {
        processPrevious(mapping, form, request, response);
        return mapping.findForward("previous");
    }

    protected void processPrevious( ActionMapping mapping,
            ActionForm form,
            HttpServletRequest request,
            HttpServletResponse response) throws Exception {
    }

    public ActionForward doNext( ActionMapping mapping,
            ActionForm form,
            HttpServletRequest request,
            HttpServletResponse response) throws Exception {
        processNext(mapping, form, request, response);
        return mapping.findForward("next");
    }

    protected void processNext( ActionMapping mapping,
            ActionForm form,
            HttpServletRequest request,
            HttpServletResponse response) throws Exception {
    }
```

Example 7-4. LookupDispatchAction for wizards (continued)

```
    public ActionForward doFinish( ActionMapping mapping,
          ActionForm form,
          HttpServletRequest request,
          HttpServletResponse response) throws Exception {
      processFinish(mapping, form, request, response);
      return mapping.findForward("finish");
    }

    protected void processFinish( ActionMapping mapping,
          ActionForm form,
          HttpServletRequest request,
          HttpServletResponse response) throws Exception {
    }

    protected Map getKeyMethodMap( ) {
        return keyMethodMap;
    }
}
```

Specify the workflow for the wizard in the *struts-config.xml* file:

```
    <!-- Wizard mappings -->
    <!-- Step 1 -->
    <action    path="/ViewStep1"
             name="WizardForm"
             scope="session"
             type="org.apache.struts.actions.ForwardAction"
        parameter="/step1.jsp"/>
    <action    path="/ProcessStep1"
             name="WizardForm"
             scope="session"
             type="com.oreilly.strutsckbk.ch07.WizardLookupDispatchAction"
        parameter="methodToCall">
      <forward name="next" path="/ViewStep2.do"/>
    </action>

    <!-- Step 2 -->
    <action    path="/ViewStep2"
             name="WizardForm"
             scope="session"
             type="org.apache.struts.actions.ForwardAction"
        parameter="/step2.jsp"/>
    <action    path="/ProcessStep2"
             name="WizardForm"
             scope="session"
             type="com.oreilly.strutsckbk.ch07.WizardLookupDispatchAction"
        parameter="methodToCall">
      <forward name="previous" path="/ViewStep1.do"/>
      <forward name="next" path="/ViewStep3.do"/>
    </action>

    <!-- Step 3 -->
    <action    path="/ViewStep3"
```

```
              name="WizardForm"
          scope="session"
          type="org.apache.struts.actions.ForwardAction"
       parameter="/step3.jsp"/>
    <action    path="/ProcessStep3"
              name="WizardForm"
          scope="session"
          type="com.oreilly.strutsckbk.ch07.WizardLookupDispatchAction"
       parameter="methodToCall">
    <forward name="previous" path="/ViewStep2.do"/>
    <forward name="finish" path="/wizard_done.jsp"/>
</action>
```

Discussion

The topic of wizard-style applications comes up frequently on the Struts mailing lists. Struts doesn't have a silver bullet solution for this problem. Wizard interfaces can be built many ways; there is no "right way" to do it. The Solution leverages the ability of the LookupDispatchAction and the use of a session-scoped form to pass data from page to page. If it doesn't meet your needs, it will at least provide the basis of a custom solution.

The WizardLookupDispatchAction subclasses LookupDispatchAction, implementing the getKeyMethodMap( ) method to map a button label key to the corresponding method. Methods are provided for handling *previous*, *next*, and *finish* buttons. Each of these methods delegates processing to a no-op protected method. The business logic for processing the form from each JSP would be added to the processNext( ) method. Business logic required when clicking previous would be implemented in the processPrevious( ) and logic to be handled when clicking finish is implemented in the processFinish( ) method.

A benefit of this Solution is you can see the flow from page to page in the *struts-config.xml*. You can look at the mappings and follow the steps in the flow:

```
<forward name="previous" path="/ViewStep1.do"/>
<forward name="next" path="/ViewStep3.do"/>
```

The solution works even if the user clicks the browser's back or forward buttons instead of using the navigation buttons.

One common gripe about the LookupDispatchAction is it doesn't work well if you are using images for buttons. In this case, you may want to extend DispatchAction and set the dispatch action using JavaScript.

See Also

Use of the LookupDispatchAction is presented in Recipe 6.9. The DispatchAction is shown in Recipe 6.8. The basic approach shown here is similar to that presented in the Struts Newbie FAQ at *http://struts.apache.org/faqs/newbie.html#wizard*.

An extension to Struts for complex workflows has been developed by Matthias Bauer and can be found at *http://www.livinglogic.de/Struts/index.html*. This extension utilizes a custom `ActionMapping` and `RequestProcessor`. In addition to the basic workflow steps discussed in this recipe, it supports workflow branching and custom authentication.

7.7 Determining the Action Based on User Input

Problem

You want to change the target action for a form based on user input.

Solution

Call a JavaScript function, like the one shown in Example 7-5, from an event handler on the HTML control that determines the action.

Example 7-5. JavaScript function to change a form's action

```
<script>
    function swapAction(control) {
      formAction = document.getElementById("empForm").action;
      if (control.checked)
        newAction = '<html:rewrite page="/CreateEmployee.do"/>';
      else
        newAction = '<html:rewrite page="/UpdateEmployee.do"/>';
      document.getElementById("empForm").action = newAction;
    }
</script>
<html:form styleId="empForm" action="/UpdateEmployee">
    New Employee: <html:checkbox property="create"
      onclick='swapAction(this)"'/><br />
    ... rest of the page
```

Discussion

JavaScript makes this problem easy to solve. You might be tempted to hardcode the new value for the action in the function. However, the function will be a lot more robust if you use the `html:rewrite` tag. Using this tag ensures the action URI includes the appropriate application context prefix. It generates the session token if cookies are disabled. You can verify this works by disabling cookies on your browser. If you clicked the "New Employee" checkbox and submit the form you'd see a URL like the following:

```
http://localhost/jsc-ch05/CreateEmployee.
do;jsessionid=C0691FF1D538431815A448C4278BA999
```

If you had hardcoded the action, you'd lose the session. The drawback to this solution is you must specify the Struts `ActionServlet` mapping prefix or extension (for example, */action* or *.do*). Unlike the `html:link` tag, the Struts 1.1 `html:rewrite` tag doesn't support the action attribute, which would eliminate this problem. Struts 1.2 corrects this annoyance; the `html:rewrite` tag supports the action attribute like the `html:link` tag.

See Also

An interesting thread on this discussion from the struts-user mailing list can be found at *http://marc.theaimsgroup.com/?l=struts-user&m=107885895821471&w=2.*

7.8   Using Wildcards in Action Paths

Problem

You want to reduce the number of action mappings by combining similar action mappings into a single generic mapping.

Solution

```
<action
        path="/Edit*"
        type="com.oreilly.strutsckbk.ch07.Edit{1}Action"
        name="{1}Form"
        scope="request"
        validate="false">
    <forward
        name="success"
        path="/edit_{1}.jsp"/>
</action>

<action
        path="/Save*"
        type="com.oreilly.strutsckbk.ch07.Save{1}Action"
        name="{1}Form"
        scope="request"
        validate="true"
        input="edit_{1}.jsp">
    <forward
        name="success"
        path="/saved_{1}.jsp"/>
</action>
```

Discussion

Many developers find that their action mappings start to follow similar patterns. In fact, many applications use standard conventions for naming action paths, `Action` classes, and `ActionForms`, making their application easier to organize and maintain.

Struts 1.2 allows you to leverage these conventions in your *struts-config.xml* file. Create your action elements using an asterisk (*) as a wildcard in the path attribute. When Struts finds the action mapping for a given request path, it attempts to find an exact match. If an exact match is not found, it attempts a match using the wildcards.

In the Solution, for example, when a request comes in for */EditEmployee.do*, the action mapping with the path of /Edit* will match. The {1} notation represents the part of the request URL value that matches the wildcard, minus any extension. In this case, {1} has the value of Employee.

Wildcard mappings reduce the number of action elements you have to write and can enforce a workflow of your own design. Figure 7-1 illustrates the workflow for the Solution when applied to editing employee data.

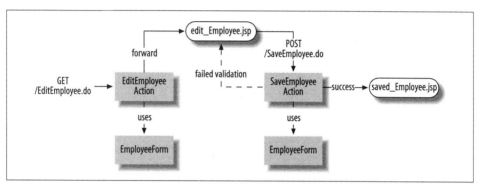

Figure 7-1. Common workflow applied to editing employee data

Suppose you need to edit and save different information, such as vendor data. Without wildcard mappings, you would create action mappings such as the following:

```
<action
       path="/EditVendor"
       type="com.oreilly.strutsckbk.ch07.EditVendorAction"
       name="VendorForm"
       scope="request"
       validate="false">
    <forward
        name="success"
        path="/edit_Vendor.jsp"/>
</action>

<action
       path="/SaveVendor"
       type="com.oreilly.strutsckbk.ch07.SaveVendorAction"
       name="VendorForm"
       scope="request"
       validate="true"
       input="edit_Vendor.jsp">
    <forward
        name="success"
```

```
            path="/saved_Vendor.jsp"/>
    </action>
```

But with the wildcard mappings shown in the Solution, you can use one common set of action elements for employee and vendor data. Of course, you need to create the JSPs, Actions, and ActionForms specific to vendor data.

The action element attributes that can use wildcard-matched strings via the {*n*} notation are the following:

- type
- name
- roles
- parameter
- attribute
- forward
- include
- input

You can use the placeholders in the path attribute of nested local forward elements.

If the mappings for a particular application feature no longer fit the pattern, create standard action mappings without wildcards that exactly match the request path. An exact-match mapping takes precedence over a wildcard mapping.

 The algorithm and code used for wildcard matching was derived from similar features in the Apache Cocoon project.

You can use other wildcard characters in addition to the "*" in your path attribute. Table 7-3 shows the complete set of supported characters.

Table 7-3. Supported wildcard characters

*	Matches zero or more characters, excluding the slash (/) character.
**	Matches zero or more characters, including the slash (/) character.
\character	The backslash character is used as an escape sequence. Thus, * matches the character asterisk (*), and \\ matches the character backslash (\).

As was shown in the Solution, the wildcard-matched values can be accessed with the {*n*} notation. *n* is a number from 1 to 9 that indicates the position of the wildcard-matched value to substitute. The entire request URI can be accessed with the {0} token.

See Also

The Struts User's guide discusses wildcard mapping. The specific section can be found at *http://struts.apache.org/userGuide/building_controller.html#action_mapping_wildcards*. If you're using Struts 1.1 and want to use wildcard mapping, earlier versions are available. Consult *http://www.twdata.org/struts-wildcard/* for details, documentation, and downloads.

As mentioned, the DispatchAction can be used to provide a single action that serves multiple purposes. The DispatchAction and its related subclasses are discussed in Chapter 6.

7.9   Preventing Double Form Submissions

Problem

You need to stop users from inadvertently submitting a form twice.

Solution

Use the Struts token facility to reject a duplicate request. First, as shown in Example 7-6, save a token in the HTTP request in the Action which precedes the JSP containing the form.

Example 7-6. Action that saves token

```
package com.oreilly.strutsckbk.ch06;

import javax.servlet.http.HttpServletRequest;
import javax.servlet.http.HttpServletResponse;

import org.apache.struts.action.Action;
import org.apache.struts.action.ActionForm;
import org.apache.struts.action.ActionForward;
import org.apache.struts.action.ActionMapping;

public class SaveTokenAction extends Action {
    public ActionForward execute(ActionMapping mapping, ActionForm form,
            HttpServletRequest request, HttpServletResponse response)
            throws Exception {
        // save a token
        saveToken(request);

        // load the data to view
        BusinessService.loadData( );

        return mapping.findForward("success");
    }
}
```

You don't have to make any changes to the JSP that displays the form as long as you create the form using the html:form tag (as shown in Example 7-7).

Example 7-7. JSP page for token handling

```
<%@ page contentType="text/html;charset=UTF-8" language="java" %>
<%@ taglib uri="http://struts.apache.org/tags-html" prefix="html" %>

<html>
<head>
  <title>Struts Cookbook - Chapter 7 : Token Test</title>
</head>
<body bgcolor="white">
<h2>Token Test</h2>
  <html:errors/>
  <html:form action="/SaveData">
      <html:text property="name"/>
      <html:submit/>
  </html:form>
  <html:link action="/SaveData" transaction="true">Save</html:link>
</body>
</html>
```

In the Action that processes the form, shown in Example 7-8, check the token. If the token is invalid, reject the request by throwing an exception or returning errors; otherwise, continue normal processing.

Example 7-8. Action that checks token validity

```
package com.oreilly.strutsckbk.ch06;

import javax.servlet.http.HttpServletRequest;
import javax.servlet.http.HttpServletResponse;

import org.apache.struts.Globals;
import org.apache.struts.action.Action;
import org.apache.struts.action.ActionError;
import org.apache.struts.action.ActionErrors;
import org.apache.struts.action.ActionForm;
import org.apache.struts.action.ActionForward;
import org.apache.struts.action.ActionMapping;

public class CheckTokenAction extends Action {
    public ActionForward execute(ActionMapping mapping, ActionForm form,
            HttpServletRequest request, HttpServletResponse response)
            throws Exception {
        if (isTokenValid(request)) {
            // reset the token
            resetToken(request);

            // save data
            BusinessService.saveData();
        }
```

Example 7-8. Action that checks token validity (continued)

```
            else {
                ActionErrors errors = new ActionErrors( );
                errors.add(ActionErrors.GLOBAL_ERROR,
                        new ActionError("Invalid token"));
                saveErrors(request, errors);
                return new ActionForward(mapping.getInput( ));
            }
            return mapping.findForward("success");
    }
}
```

Discussion

Inadvertent or duplicate form submissions cause real problems with many web applications. When the form being submitted results in financial transactions, real dollars can be erroneously lost or gained. A couple of common scenarios result in double form submission. If the server's form processing takes several seconds, the user may be tempted to resubmit the form, thinking the first submit wasn't received. Users get in the habit of refreshing a page when the browser isn't responding. The typical user may not realize that pressing Refresh resubmits the form.

Another common problem is double-clicks. Users are conditioned by the operating system to use double-click to open applications. Users unaccustomed to web browsing commonly use double-click when they need to single-click. The double-click problem happens because users have a "loose trigger finger."

Struts provides a mechanism for managing these problems. This mechanism can't prevent a user from submitting a form twice (see the sidebar "Preventing Double-Clicks Using JavaScript"), but it does allow for an Action to check if the request was received as expected. If the request wasn't expected, the action can reject the request and generate an appropriate error or exception.

The Solution shows the basic pattern for utilizing tokens. You need an Action that forwards to the JSP page containing the form. Usually this pre-form Action is responsible for loading the data to be displayed. In this Action, call the saveToken(HttpServletRequest request) method provided by the base Struts Action class (org.apache.struts.action.Action). This method generates a unique String value, as a token for the current transaction and saves that value under a known attribute name in the HTTP request.

When the form is rendered on the JSP page, Struts generates an HTML hidden field containing the token value. You can generate the token value as request parameter on a hyperlink by setting transaction=true on the html:link tag. The token value, whether rendered as a hidden field or a request parameter, is only generated if a token is found in the current request for the JSP. The generated page source from the JSP is shown in Example 7-9.

Example 7-9. Generated form with Struts token

```
<html>
<head>
  <title>Struts Cookbook - Chapter 7 : Token Test</title>
</head>
<body bgcolor="white">
<h2>Token Test</h2>

<form name="TestForm" method="post" action="/jsc-ch07/SaveData.do">
  <input type="hidden" name="org.apache.struts.taglib.html.TOKEN"
         value="8f72ef608fb385fd757513ff5fc1b091">
  <input type="text" name="name" value="">
  <input type="submit" value="Submit">
</form>
<a href="/jsc-ch07/SaveData.do?org.apache.struts.taglib.html.
TOKEN=8f72ef608fb385fd757513ff5fc1b091">
  Save Data
</a>
  <hr />
  <a href="/jsc-ch07/index.jsp">Home</a>
</body>
</html>
```

You check the token value in the `Action` that is the target of the form or link using the `isTokenValid( )` method of the base Struts `Action`. If the token is invalid, you can generate an appropriate error or throw an exception. If it is, then you should clear the token using the `resetToken( )` method.

Preventing Double-Clicks Using JavaScript

JavaScript can be used to prevent a user from submitting a form twice. A JavaScript function is called as an `onclick` event handler. The function checks the value of a global variable indicating if the form has been submitted. If the value isn't set, the indicator is set to true and the form is submitted. If the value has been set, then the request is ignored. This solution doesn't prevent the user from refreshing the page, so you will want to use the Struts token facility on the server-side.

See Also

The methods for generating, saving, checking, and resetting tokens are all defined in the Struts Action class. JavaDocs for this class can be found at *http://struts.apache. org/api/org/apache/struts/action/Action.html*.

The *JavaWorld* online magazine has a good article on the Struts token handling and can be found at *http://www.javaworld.com/javatips/jw-javatip136_p.html*. The topic

---

comes up frequently on the struts-user mailing list; search for "token" and you'll find a number of discussions.

The "Introduce Synchronizer Token" refactoring presented in the book *Core J2EE Patterns* by Deepak Alur, John Crupi, and Dan Malks (Sun Microsystems Press) was based, in part, on the Struts token facility.

7.10   Allowing Users to Upload Files

Problem

You need to allow users to upload file content to a web application.

Solution

Create an `ActionForm` that uses the Struts `FormFile` object as a property as shown in Example 7-10.

Example 7-10. ActionForm with FormFile property

```
package com.oreilly.strutsckbk.ch04;

import org.apache.struts.action.ActionForm;
import org.apache.struts.upload.FormFile;

public class UploadForm extends ActionForm {
    private FormFile content;

    public FormFile getContent() {
        return content;
    }
    public void setContent(FormFile content) {
        this.content = content;
    }
}
```

Then use the `html:file` tag on the JSP page (*upload_test.jsp*) that contains the form as shown in Example 7-11. For file uploads, the enctype attribute of the `html:form` tag must be set to *multipart/form-data* and the method attribute set to POST.

Example 7-11. JSP for file upload

```
<%@ page contentType="text/html;charset=UTF-8" language="java" %>
<%@ taglib uri="http://jakarta.apache.org/struts/tags-html" prefix="html" %>
  <html>
<head>
  <title>Struts Cookbook - Chapter 4 : Upload Test</title>
</head>
<body>
  <html:form action="/ProcessUpload"
            method="POST"
```

Example 7-11. JSP for file upload (continued)

```
          enctype="multipart/form-data">
    <html:file property="content"/>
    <html:submit/>
  </html:form>
</body>
</html>
```

 The default value for the method attribute of the html:form tag is POST, so the attribute isn't required here. In this case, however, explicitly setting the value reduces the risk of the method type being changed by another developer.

When the form is processed, use the FormFile object to retrieve the uploaded file content. The ProcessUploadAction shown in Example 7-12 retrieves the file contents in an InputStream and writes this data to a file.

Example 7-12. Action that processes uploaded file

```
package com.oreilly.strutsckbk.ch04;

import java.io.BufferedOutputStream;
import java.io.FileOutputStream;
import java.io.InputStream;
import java.io.OutputStream;

import javax.servlet.http.HttpServletRequest;
import javax.servlet.http.HttpServletResponse;

import org.apache.struts.action.Action;
import org.apache.struts.action.ActionForm;
import org.apache.struts.action.ActionForward;
import org.apache.struts.action.ActionMapping;
import org.apache.struts.upload.FormFile;

public class ProcessUploadAction extends Action {

  public ActionForward execute(ActionMapping mapping,
      ActionForm form,
      HttpServletRequest request,
      HttpServletResponse response) throws Exception {

    // Get the form file property from the form
    UploadForm uploadForm = (UploadForm) form;
    FormFile content = uploadForm.getContent( );

    InputStream in = null;
    OutputStream out = null;

    try {
      // Get an input stream on the form file
      in = content.getInputStream( );
```

Example 7-12. Action that processes uploaded file (continued)

```
    // Create an output stream to a file
    out = new BufferedOutputStream (new FileOutputStream("temp.txt"));

    byte[] buffer = new byte[512];
    while (in.read(buffer) != -1) {
      out.write(buffer);
    }
  }
  finally {
    if (out != null) out.close();
    if (in != null) in.close();
  }

  return mapping.findForward("success");
  }
}
```

Discussion

Handling a file upload for a Java-based web application can be critical and down-right intimidating for many developers. Thankfully, Struts provides an API for file uploads that simplifies this task. The API is accessed primarily through a single class (FormFile) you can use as a property on your ActionForm.

You can handle file uploads by using the FormFile class as the type for a property of an ActionForm. On the JSP page that displays the form, use the html:file tag to refer to the FormFile property. The html:file tag generates the HTML that lets a user upload a file:

```
<input type="file">.
```

The FormFile object encapsulates the uploaded file. It contains information about the name and type of the uploaded file as well as the actual file contents. The getFileName( ) method returns the actual filename from the client's machine. This filename may have been keyed in by the user directly, or, more commonly, the filename was set when the user chose the file using the "Browse..." button. Figure 7-2 shows the displayed JSP page after the user picked a file from his local system.

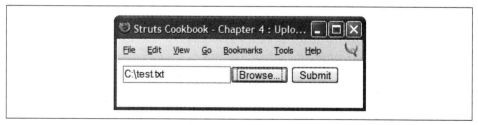

Figure 7-2. File upload page

If you're going to save the uploaded file to the server's filesystem, don't make the mistake of using this filename. The filename and path won't be correct for the server and will probably not be valid for the server's operating system. However, you may want to preserve the filename and other information about the file as metadata. You could include the name of the user that uploaded the file as well as the date and time it was uploaded.

The `ProcessUploadAction`, shown in Example 7-12, handles the `FormFile` property. The `uploadForm.getContent()` method returns the `FormFile` property. The `getInputStream()` method of `FormFile` returns an input stream for reading the file contents. Data is read from the stream in 512-KB chunks and written using an output stream to the *temp.txt* file.

So where does this file get saved to when it is written? The answer varies by application server. On Tomcat, the filename is relative to the directory from which Tomcat was started, usually *<CATALINA_HOME>/bin*. Check your application server's documentation for more information.

See Also

The underlying implementation of the Struts file upload capability is provided by the Jakarta Commons FileUpload project. Details can be found at *http://jakarta.apache.org/commons/fileupload/*. The API documenaton for the Struts `html:file` tag can be found online at *http://struts.apache.org/userGuide/struts-html.html#file*.

The Struts source distribution includes a file upload example, similar to this recipe, contained within the *struts-examples* sample web application.

7.11   Displaying a File from the Server

Problem

You need to display the contents of a file on your server's filesystem that isn't part of your web application.

Solution

Use a servlet, similar to the one shown in Example 7-13, to read the file from the filesystem and write the file contents to the HTTP response.

Example 7-13. File viewer servlet

```
package com.oreilly.strutsckbk.ch07;

import java.io.File;
import java.io.FileReader;
import java.io.IOException;
import java.io.PrintWriter;
```

Example 7-13. File viewer servlet (continued)

```java
import javax.servlet.ServletException;
import javax.servlet.http.HttpServlet;
import javax.servlet.http.HttpServletRequest;
import javax.servlet.http.HttpServletResponse;

public class FileViewerServlet extends HttpServlet {

    protected void doGet(HttpServletRequest request, HttpServletResponse response)
            throws ServletException, IOException {
        doPost(request, response);
    }
    protected void doPost(HttpServletRequest request, HttpServletResponse response)
            throws ServletException, IOException {
        String fileName = (String) request.getAttribute("fileName");
        fileName = "temp.txt";
        FileReader in = null;
        PrintWriter out = null;
        response.setContentType("text/plain");
        File dir = (File) getServletContext().getAttribute("javax.servlet.context.
tempdir");
        File f = new File(dir, "test.tmp");
        try {
            // Get an input stream on the form file
            in = new FileReader(f);

            // Get an output stream for the response
            out = response.getWriter();

            // Write from the input stream to the output stream
            char[] buffer = new char[512];
            int chars = 0;
            while ((chars = in.read(buffer)) != -1) {
                out.write(buffer, 0, chars);
            }
        }
        finally {
            if (out != null) out.close();
            if (in != null) in.close();
        }
    }
}
```

Discussion

This servlet reads a file from the filesystem and writes it out to the response; it's written to handle a file uploaded using the Solution from Recipe 7.10. The file is read from the servlet's *temp* directory; however, the location of the file could be any place accessible to the server, even a database.

The servlet shown in Example 7-13 can be used for any Java web application and not just a Struts application.

Here are the primary steps to render content from a servlet, regardless of where the file is located:

1. Determine the file to retrieve.
2. Set the HTTP response content type to the correct MIME type for the file.
3. Acquire a `java.io.Reader` on the file.
4. Acquire a `java.io.Writer` on the response.
5. In a buffered fashion, read the data from the `Reader` and write to the `Writer`.
6. Ensure the `Reader` and `Writer` are always closed on completion.

See Also

Jason Hunter's classic text, *Java Servlet Programming* (O'Reilly), is the bible of servlet programming. This text has loads more information on the details and nuances of rendering content in this fashion.

Recipe 6.5 shows a good technique for integrating a servlet like this into a Struts application.

## CHAPTER 8

Input Validation

8.0 Introduction

Ensuring that users enter data correctly can make the difference between a production-ready application and one relegated to remain in the Quality Assurance department. Web applications need to verify the data entered is valid. Data validation takes two forms: syntactic and semantic. *Syntactic validity* indicates the data is in the correct format; for example, making sure that a numeric field contains only numeric digits. *Semantic validity* indicates the data means what it should in the functional context of the application. For example, if a user enters his or her birthdate, that date can't be in the future.

The recipes in this chapter cover some advanced uses of the Struts Validator. Some of the recipes use new features of the Validator such as the validwhen *validator*. A validator is a reusable type of validation. Several recipes show you how easy it is to create your own validators. Providing locale-specific validators to support internationalization is covered. If you're familiar with the Validator, skip ahead to the particular recipes that interest you.

Struts was designed from the beginning to support validation. Every Struts ActionForm has a validate( ) method.

If a validation check requires access to a back-end business service, like an EJB or the database, place the call to the business service in the Action that processes the form and not the ActionForm itself.

You can add your own data validation checks for form data in this method. The method returns an ActionErrors object, a collection of ActionError objects.

In Struts 1.2, the ActionError class has been deprecated and replaced by the ActionMessage class. The ActionErrors class, however, isn't deprecated. In Struts 1.2, ActionErrors contain a collection of ActionMessage objects. See Recipe 9.5 for more details.

If your validate( ) method returns an ActionErrors object with one or more errors, then the validation check fails. Struts routes control back to the page set as the value for the input attribute of the action element in the *struts-config.xml*. Example 8-1 shows a simple ActionForm that validates that the username and password fields each have a non-blank value; in other words, they are required.

Example 8-1. Custom action form with validation

```
package com.oreilly.strutsckbk.ch08;

import javax.servlet.http.HttpServletRequest;

import org.apache.struts.action.ActionError;
import org.apache.struts.action.ActionErrors;
import org.apache.struts.action.ActionForm;
import org.apache.struts.action.ActionMapping;

public class MyLoginForm extends ActionForm {

    public String getPassword( ) {
        return password;
    }
    public void setPassword(String password) {
        this.password = password;
    }
    public String getUsername( ) {
        return username;
    }
    public void setUsername(String username) {
        this.username = username;
    }

    public ActionErrors validate(ActionMapping mapping, HttpServletRequest request) {
        ActionErrors errors = new ActionErrors( );
        if (username == null || "".equals(username)) {
            errors.add("username",
                new ActionError("errors.required","The username"));
        }
        if (password == null || "".equals(password)) {
            errors.add("password",
                new ActionError("errors.required","The password"));
        }
        return errors;
    }
```

Example 8-1. Custom action form with validation (continued)

```
    private String username;
    private String password;
}
```

Basic syntax checks, such as those shown in Example 8-1, comprise the vast majority of validation needs. Coding each one of these checks in Java can be tedious and repetitive. Thankfully, the Struts Validator, available to Struts applications since Struts 0.5, has been developed under the Jakarta Commons project.

Struts provides an integration layer with the Validator, which allows you to define validations for form fields in an XML file. You use the Validator for JavaScript-based client-side checks as well as server-side ones. You can write your own validators (see Recipe 8.7); however, the Validator bundles a full-featured set of validators, as shown in Table 8-1.

Table 8-1. Bundled pluggable validators

required	Checks that a field value is non-null and not an empty string.
requiredif	Only available for Struts 1.1. This validator allows one field to be specified as required if another field is null, not null, or equal to a specified value. This validator is deprecated, in favor of validwhen, in releases after Struts 1.1.
validwhen	Designed to replace requiredif, this validator is available in releases after Struts 1.1. This validator relies on a user-specified test expression that can include references to other fields, field values, and logical relationships.
minlength	Checks that the number of characters in the field value is greater than or equal to a specified minimum.
maxlength	Checks that the number of characters in the field value is less than or equal to a specified maximum.
mask	Validates the field value using a regular expression to determine a match. If the value matches the regular expression, the field is valid.
byte	Checks that the field value is a valid byte value.
short	Checks that the field value is a valid short integer value.
integer	Checks that the field value is a valid integer value.
long	Checks that the field value is a valid long value.
float	Checks that the field value is a valid floating-point value.
double	Checks that the field value is a valid double value.
date	Checks that the field value matches a specified date format pattern (e.g., MM/dd/yyyy). The match can be strict or lenient; "strict" would require May 10, 1963 to be formatted (using the MM/dd/yyyy pattern) as 05/10/1963; "lenient" would allow 5/10/1963.
range	Checks that the field value is within a specified numeric range. This valdiator has been deprecated in favor of the type-specific range checks (intRange, floatRange, etc.).
intRange	Checks that the field value is within a range bounded by two int values.
floatRange	Checks that the field value is within a range bounded by two float values.
doubleRange	Checks that the field value is within a range bounded by two double values.
creditCard	Verifies that the format of the field value is valid for a credit card number. This validator is convenient to use instead of using mask.

Table 8-1. Bundled pluggable validators (continued)

`email`	Verifies that the format of the field value is valid for an electronic mail address (e.g., foo@bar.com). This validator is convenient to use instead of working with `mask`.
`url`	Verifies that the value entered is a valid uniform resource locator. Use this validator when you want to validate an input web location or hyperlink value.

The most up-to-date listing of the bundled validators can be found at *http://struts. apache.org/userGuide/dev_validator.html#builtin*.

Configuring the Validator

To use the Validator, first specify a `plug-in` element in your *struts-config.xml* file:

```
<plug-in className="org.apache.struts.validator.ValidatorPlugIn">
    <set-property property="pathnames"
                  value="/WEB-INF/validator-rules.xml,
                         /WEB-INF/validation.xml"/>
</plug-in>
```

The pathnames property value specifies the Validator configuration files you're using. Typically, you specify one or more files here. The first file, *validator-rules.xml*, defines and declares the pluggable validators, listed in Table 8-1, which are bundled with the Struts distribution. The second file, *validation.xml*, declares how the validators are applied to your application.

 You can specify more than these two files if needed.

A good approach is to have separate validation XML files for each major functional area of your application. For a large application, you might have a dozen of these files. The Validator supports multiple *validation* documents in the same manner that Struts supports *struts-config* documents (see Recipe 2.4).

To use the Validator with a hand-coded `ActionForm`, the `ActionForm` must extend `org.apache.struts.action.ValidatorForm` (or one of its subclasses). For a dynamic action form, the type must be `org.apache.struts.action.DynaValidatorForm` (or one of its subclasses). You specify how the validators apply to the form in the *validation.xml* file. Example 8-2 shows a portion of a *validation.xml* file that validates that the username and password are required on the form named MyLoginForm. This Validator form establishes minimum and maximum lengths for the password field.

Example 8-2. Validation for a login form

```
<?xml version="1.0" encoding="ISO-8859-1" ?>
<!DOCTYPE form-validation PUBLIC
 "-//Apache Software Foundation//DTD Commons Validator Rules Configuration 1.1//EN"
 "http://jakarta.apache.org/commons/dtds/validator_1_1_3.dtd">
```

Example 8-2. Validation for a login form (continued)

```
<form-validation>
    <formset>
        <form name="MyLoginForm">
            <field property="username"
                    depends="required">
                <arg key="prompt.username"/>
            </field>
            <field property="password"
                    depends="required, minlength,maxlength">
                <arg key="prompt.password"/>
                <arg key="${var:minlength}" name="minlength"
                    resource="false"/>
                <arg key="${var:maxlength}" name="maxlength"
                    resource="false"/>
                <var>
                    <var-name>maxlength</var-name>
                    <var-value>16</var-value>
                </var>
                <var>
                    <var-name>minlength</var-name>
                    <var-value>3</var-value>
                </var>
            </field>
        </form>
    <formset>
<form-validation>
```

 The value of the name attribute specified in the form element is the name of the form from the form-bean element in the *struts-config.xml* file and not the type (class name) of the form.

You might think of a validation set as applying to all the fields of an ActionForm, and you can tie the validation set to an *action path* instead of the form name. This feature is referred to as *action-based* or *path-based* validation. The Validator applies this feature if the form subclasses ValidatorActionForm or DynaValidatorActionForm. When such a form is submitted to an Action, only the Validator form element, in which the name matches the *path*, applies, and only those fields specified in that validation set are checked. In this snippet from a *validation.xml* file, the username will be validated when the form is submitted to the action path */ProcessStep1*:

```
<form name="/ProcessStep1">
    <field property="username"
            depends="required">
        <arg key="prompt.username"/>
    </field>
</form>
<form name="/ProcessStep2">
    <field property="password"
            depends="required">
```

```
            <arg key="prompt.password"/>
        </field>
    </form>
```

Validation is enabled for an action mapping by setting the `action` element's `validate` attribute to true. If validation fails, Struts forwards to the resource identified by the `input` attribute. The value of the `input` attribute represents the path to the resource, typically a JSP page, to forward control so the user can reinput data.

```
<action     path="/Login"
            type="com.oreilly.strutsckbk.ch08.LoginAction"
            scope="request"
            name="MyLoginForm"
        validate="true"
           input="/login.jsp">
    <forward name="success" path="/login_success.jsp"/>
</action>
```

 You can set the `inputForward` attribute to true on the controller element in a Struts configuration file so Struts will treat the value of the `input` attribute as the name of a local or global forward (see Recipe 7.4).

You're ready to apply validation across your application! Once you get in the groove of configuring validations and verifying that it all works as desired, you will be well on your way to creating a web application that will be robust enough to support the demands of those pesky creatures known as users.

 Like most application features driven by XML configuration files, typographical mistakes may cause silent failures in your application that can be hard to diagnose and debug. If you find your application misbehaving after setting up the validations, you can turn off the validation by setting `validate="false"` in the action mapping. If everything works correctly down this "happy path," then you know that something is amiss with your validation setup.

See Also

For more of the basics on using the Validator, check out *Programming Jakarta Struts* by Chuck Cavaness (O'Reilly).

8.1   Reusing Validator Attribute Values

Problem

You want to define, in one place, a common value you can reference wherever needed in a Validator form.

Solution

Define the value as a global or form-set constant in one of your *validation* documents, as shown in Example 8-3.

Example 8-3. Defining global and form-set validator constants

```
<?xml version="1.0" encoding="ISO-8859-1" ?>
<!DOCTYPE form-validation PUBLIC
 "-//Apache Software Foundation//DTD Commons Validator Rules Configuration 1.1//EN"
 "http://jakarta.apache.org/commons/dtds/validator_1_1_3.dtd">
<form-validation>
    <global>
        <constant>
            <constant-name>globalVarName</constant-name>
            <constant-value>globalVarValue</constant-value>
        </constant>
    </global>
    <formset>
        <constant>
            <constant-name>formsetVarName</constant-name>
            <constant-value>formsetVarValue</constant-value>
        </constant>
        <form name="MyForm">
            <field property="myfield"
                   depends="someRule,anotherRule">
                <var>
                    <var-name>someRule</var-name>
                    <var-value>${globalVarName}</var-value>
                </var>
                <var>
                    <var-name>anotherRule</var-name>
                    <var-value>${formsetVarName}</var-value>
                </var>
            </field>
        </form>
    <formset>
<form-validation>
```

Discussion

Good developers understand the Don't Repeat Yourself (DRY) principle of software engineering. But if they fail to follow this principle, they could end up all wet. The Validator embraces this guideline, making it an excellent choice for input validation. If you have an attribute value shared by multiple field elements, you can define the value as a named constant. You can reference the constant value by name wherever an attribute value can be used.

If the value applies across the entire application, define it as a *global* constant. If the value only applies to a specific form and it's used multiple times on that form, define it as a *formset* constant. In Example 8-4, the minimum length for the username is

defined as a global constant. For the `RegistrationForm`, the maximum length for the
first and last name is defined as a formset constant.

Example 8-4. Using global and formset constants

```xml
<?xml version="1.0" encoding="ISO-8859-1" ?>
<!DOCTYPE form-validation PUBLIC
 "-//Apache Software Foundation//DTD Commons Validator Rules Configuration 1.1//EN"
 "http://jakarta.apache.org/commons/dtds/validator_1_1_3.dtd">
<form-validation>
    <global>
        <constant>
            <constant-name>usernameMinLength</constant-name>
            <constant-value>7</constant-value>
        </constant>
    </global>
    <formset>
        <constant>
            <constant-name>nameMaxLength</constant-name>
            <constant-value>40</constant-value>
        </constant>
        <form name="RegistrationForm">
            <field property="username"
                    depends="required,minlength">
                <arg key="prompt.username"/>
                <arg key="${var:minlength}" name="minlength"
                   resource="false"/>
                <var>
                    <var-name>minlength</var-name>
                    <var-value>${usernameMinLength}</var-value>
                </var>
            </field>
            <field property="firstName"
                    depends="required,maxlength">
                <arg key="prompt.firstName"/>
                <arg key="${var:maxlength}" name="maxlength"
                   resource="false"/>
                <var>
                    <var-name>maxlength</var-name>
                    <var-value>${nameMaxLength}</var-value>
                </var>
            </field>
            <field property="lastName"
                    depends="required,minlength,maxlength">
                <arg key="prompt.lastName"/>
                <arg key="${var:minlength}" name="minlength"
                   resource="false"/>
                <arg key="${var:maxlength}" name="maxlength"
                   resource="false"/>
                <var>
                    <var-name>minlength</var-name>
                    <var-value>2</var-value>
                </var>
```

Example 8-4. Using global and formset constants (continued)

```
                <var>
                    <var-name>maxlength</var-name>
                    <var-value>${nameMaxLength}</var-value>
                </var>
            </field>
        </form>
    <formset>
<formset-validation>
```

Validator constants are handy for those fields you use throughout your application. If you use the mask validator to check fields such as Social Security Numbers (SSNs) and phone numbers, using a Validator constant means you only have to maintain the regular expression in one place.

See Also

The mask validator is discussed in Recipe 8.2.

8.2   Validating Using Regular Expressions

Problem

You want to validate data using a regular expression.

Solution

Use the mask validation type provided by the Validator:

```
<form name="ValidationTestForm">
    <!-- Validate Social Security Number -->
    <field property="ssn"
            depends="required,mask">
        <arg key="prompt.ssn"/>
        <var>
            <var-name>mask</var-name>
            <var-value>^[0-9]{3}-[0-9]{2}-[0-9]{4}$</var-value>
        </var>
    </field>
</form>
```

Discussion

A regular expression uses a general pattern notation that can be used to describe and parse text. Regular expressions have been around in one form or another since the 1960s. Using regular expressions, you can validate that a user's input matches a specific pattern. The pattern, simple or complex, is specified as a mask value that uses the regular expression pattern language. Without regular expressions, you would have to write a significant amount of custom code. Despite the power of regular expressions, many developers aren't comfortable using them. If you don't know regular expressions, learn them now because it could change your life. A good place to start is *Mastering Regular Expressions* by Jeffrey E. F. Friedl (O'Reilly).

The Validator supports the use of regular expressions through the mask bundled validator. A validation passes if the field value matches a given regular expression. You specify the regular expression through a Validator variable, defined in a var element. The name of the variable must be mask, and the value is the regular expression to use. If the field value matches the pattern, the validation passes; otherwise, the validation fails.

```
<var>
    <var-name>mask</var-name>
    <var-value>^[0-9]{3}-[0-9]{2}-[0-9]{4}$</var-value>
</var>
```

 If you are using Struts 1.1 or later, the regular expression must start with a caret (^) and end with the dollar sign ($). This restriction wasn't in place prior to Struts 1.1. Its inclusion, however, makes complete sense in the context of regular expressions. The caret notates the start of the string, and the dollar sign the end of the string. Supplying these values indicates you are validating the entire input string.

Regular expressions can look downright cryptic, but they are not that hard to understand once you get the basic notation. The expression shown in the Solution describes a pattern for validating an SSN. An SSN contains three digits, a hyphen, two digits, another hyphen, and four more digits. Valid values would be *123-45-6789*, *000-00-0000*, but not *123-84-Ab45* or *12-12-1234*.

The best way to understand a regular expression is to put it into words. Here's how this would be done for the SSN expression. First, here's the expression:

^[0-9]{3}-[0-9]{2}-[0-9]{4}$

This expression would be interpreted as the following:

The beginning of the text (^), followed by three characters ({3}) each between 0 and 9 ([0-9]), followed by a hyphen (-), followed by two characters ({2}) each between 0 and 9 ([0-9]), followed by a hyphen (-), followed by four characters ({4}) each between 0 and 9 ([0-9]), followed by the end of the text ($).

The [0-9] is known as a *character class*. There are character classes for lowercase and uppercase alphabetic characters, numbers, and other character types. The {3} syntax is known as a *quantifier*. It specifies the quantity of the preceding character (or parenthesized character group). Additional quantifiers include * (0 or more), + (1 or more), and ? (0 or 1, i.e. optional).

Several shorthand notations exist for certain predefined character classes. For example, \d represents a digit and equates to using [0-9]. Knowing this, the SSN expression can be rewritten as:

```
^\d{3}-\d{2}-\d{4}$
```

When used by the Validator, a regular expression specified by the mask validator does replace the basic required validator. If you were to remove required from the Solution and no data was input, the form would pass validation though the mask validator was in place. At first glance this seems wrong; however, it works well in practice. If a field needs to be required, use required. Then, if the data needs to follow a certain text pattern, you can apply a regular expression validation using mask. This allows you to use mask on optional fields, and the mask only gets applied when the field has a non-empty value.

See Also

Regular expressions are powerful but important; it would be a disservice to cover the syntax and nuances of these expressions here. A better option is to consult a print or online reference.

Mastering Regular Expressions remains an essential tutorial and reference for regular expressions. This book has been recently updated to include, among other things, information relating to Java-based use of regular expressions. If you are new to regular expressions, this book provides a great start.

If you are familiar with regular expressions, *Regular Expression Pocket Reference* by Tony Stubblebine (O'Reilly) is a handy reference for the advanced programmer.

Steve Ramsay has put together a concise explanation of regular expressions at *http://etext.lib.virginia.edu/helpsheets/regex.html*.

The Validator uses the regular expression engine of the Jakarta ORO project (*http://jakarta.apache.org/commons/oro*). The Jakarta ORO JavaDocs provide an overview of the supported Perl 5-compliant regular expression syntax and can be found at *http://jakarta.apache.org/oro/api/org/apache/oro/text/regex/package-summary.html*.

8.3 Validating Dependent Fields in Struts 1.1

Problem

You are using Struts 1.1 and you want to validate a field based on the value of another related field.

Solution

Use the requiredif validator. The field element, in this snippet from a *validation. xml* file, indicates that the zipCode field is required if the city or state field is null:

```
<!-- zipCode is required if city is null or state is null -->
<field property="zipCode" depends="requiredif">
    <arg key="prompt.zipCode"/>
    <var>
        <var-name>field[0]</var-name>
        <var-value>city</var-value>
    </var>
    <var>
        <var-name>fieldTest[0]</var-name>
        <var-value>NULL</var-value>
    </var>
    <var>
        <var-name>field[1]</var-name>
        <var-value>state</var-value>
    </var>
    <var>
        <var-name>fieldTest[1]</var-name>
        <var-value>NULL</var-value>
    </var>
    <var>
        <var-name>fieldJoin</var-name>
        <var-value>OR</var-value>
    </var>
</field>
```

Discussion

The Struts Validator has always worked well for single-field validations. Cross-field validation, that is validating two or more dependent fields, wasn't supported by the Validator until Struts 1.1. The requiredif validation rule was introduced at that time to address the problem. Interestingly enough, the requiredif rule lifespan will be short. It is being deprecated in Struts 1.2 and is being replaced by the validwhen rule, discussed in Recipe 8.4.

The validation shown in the Solution would be used on a form where you were retrieving a user's address. If users specify a zip code, then they can omit the city and state; these values would be looked up based on the zip code. On the other hand, if the city or state is not specified, then the zip code is required.

 The requiredif validator can't be used for client-side validation, only server-side validation.

Before Struts 1.1, cross-field validations like this had to be hand coded in the ActionForm or Action. With Struts 1.1, you can use the requiredif rule to indicate

---

that a field is required if the value of other fields meet certain criteria. The criteria are defined by specifying variable names and values for the rule using the var element.

Each criterion for a dependent field is identified by an index. In the Solution, the indices are used to create two criterion sets for the dependent fields; city and state. The index is used to group together a field name, test type, and value. These values combine to represent an expression. The corresponding var-value for the field[i] variable refers to a form property:

```
<var>
    <var-name>field[0]</var-name>
    <var-value>property name</var-value>
</var>
```

The fieldTest[i] variable defines the type of test:

```
<var>
    <var-name>fieldTest[i]</var-name>
    <var-value>test type</var-value>
</var>
```

The following test types are accepted:

NULL
> The field must be null or an empty string.

NOTNULL
> The field must not be null or an empty string.

EQUAL
> The field value must be equal to a specific value.

If the field test is NULL or NOTNULL, then the criterion for that index is complete. If the field test is EQUAL, the fieldValue[i] variable contains the literal value to compare against:

```
<var>
    <var-name>fieldValue[i]</var-name>
    <var-value>literal value</var-value>
</var>
```

If the property is numeric, the literal value will be converted to a number; otherwise, it is treated as literal text for a String comparison.

If more than one field is specified for a requiredif validation—there is more than one criterion—you can logically connect the criterion using the fieldJoin variable:

```
<var>
    <var-name>fieldJoin</var-name>
    <var-value>logical operator</var-value>
</var>
```

Valid values for the logical operator are AND and OR. Using a logical AND indicates that the validation passes if *all* the requiredif field criteria are true. A value of OR indicates that the validation passes if *any* one of the field criteria is true.

If `fieldJoin` isn't specified, then `AND` will be assumed.

See Also

If you are using Struts 1.2, the `requiredif` validator is deprecated. Instead, use the `validwhen` validator described in Recipe 8.4.

The latest documentation on `requiredif` can be found in the Struts Validator Guide, available online at *http://struts.apache.org/userGuide/dev_validator.html*.

8.4   Validating Dependent Fields in Struts 1.2

Problem

You are using Struts 1.2 and you want to validate a field based on the value of another related field.

Solution

Use the `validwhen` validator. The `field` element in the following snippet from a *validation* document indicates that the `zipCode` is valid when the following occurs:

- The `city` and `state` properties are not `null` (regardless of the `zipCode` value).
- The `zipCode` is not `null`:

```
<form name="AddressForm">
  <field property="zipCode" depends="validwhen">
      <arg key="prompt.zipCode"/>
      <var>
          <var-name>
              test
          </var-name>
          <var-value>
              (((city != null) and (state != null)) or (*this* != null))
          </var-value>
      </var>
  </field>
<form name="AddressForm">
```

Discussion

The `validwhen` validator, available with Struts 1.2, replaces `requiredif` for performing cross-field validations.

The `validwhen` validator, like `requiredif`, can't be used for client-side validation, only server-side validation.

As in Recipe 8.3, the Solution shows how you would set up the validation on a form where you were retrieving a user's address. If users specify a zip code, then they can omit the city and state; otherwise, if the city or state is not specified, the zip code is required.

With `validwhen`, you can code a single expression that takes the place of multiple XML elements needed for `requiredif`. The `validwhen` validator is more powerful than `requiredif`, though it can be trickier to get the logic correct. With `requiredif`, your validation makes the assertion "this field is required if...." The `validwhen` validator is different in that it asserts the statement "this field is valid when..." followed by a boolean expression. The criteria that make up the expression are open-ended.

 When you create the test expression for `validwhen`, ensure that the expression has a way to evaluate to true; otherwise, the page will never pass validation.

In the Solution, the validation ensures that a zip code must have a value if the city or state is `null`. Likewise, if the city and state aren't `null`, then the zip code doesn't have to be specified; it can be `null`. The following expression from the Solution enforces this logic:

```
(((city != null) and (state != null)) or (*this* != null))
```

The `*this*` notation in the expression represents the value of the field being validated, the zip code. If the zip code isn't `null` the expression will be true regardless of the city and state values. If the city or state is `null` and the zip code is `null`, the expression evaluates to false; the zip code isn't valid. Finally, if the city and state have values, the zip code can be any value, including `null`.

The kinds of values allowed in a `validwhen` expression are the following:

- Single- or double-quoted string literals
- Integer literals in decimal, hex, or octal format
- The value null, which will match against `null` *or* an empty string
- Other fields in the form referenced by field name, such as `customerAge`
- Indexed fields in the form referenced by an explicit integer, such as `childLastName[2]`
- Indexed fields in the form referenced by an implicit integer, such as `childLastName[]`, which will use the same index into the array as the index of the field being tested

- Properties of an indexed fields in the form referenced by an explicit or implicit integer, such as child[].lastName, which will use the same index into the array as the index of the field being tested
- The literal *this*, which contains the value of the field currently being tested

The Validator parses the test expression using the ANTLR parser.

 The expression syntax is strict and unforgiving.

The entire expression must be enclosed in parentheses. Each logical statement, such as (foo == bar), contained in the expression must be enclosed in parentheses; using an editor that matches parentheses can help. Here are some practical guidelines for crafting validwhen expressions:

- Think completely through the logic of the test expression. Ensure the expression can evaluate to true under some set of circumstances.
- Be precise with the parentheses and whitespace in the expression.
- In testing, if the validation unexpectedly fails, check the container's log file or console output before you starting questioning your logic. You have made a typo in the *validation.xml* file or the validwhen expression can't be parsed for some reason.

See Also

If you are using Struts 1.1, validwhen is not available. You may be able to use the requiredif rule, discussed in Recipe 8.3.

The latest documentation on the built-in pluggable validators can be found in the Struts Validator Guide available at *http://struts.apache.org/userGuide/dev_validator.html*.

8.5   Validating an Indexed Property

Problem

You want to validate a field that is a nested property of an object in an array or Collection.

Solution

Set the indexedListProperty attribute for the field element to the name of the property that returns the array or Collection. The value of the property attribute will be interpreted as the name of a nested property of an element within the Collection. If you're using Struts 1.2, you can reference the indexed property in a test for a validwhen rule. Example 8-5 shows a complete form element from *validation.xml* for a form containing the array property "orders."

Example 8-5. Validations for an indexed list property (partial)

```
<form name="IndexedListForm">
    <field property="partNumber" indexedListProperty="orders"
            depends="minlength">
        <arg position="0" key="prompt.partNumber"/>
        <arg position="1" key="${var:minlength}" resource="false"/>
        <var>
            <var-name>minlength</var-name>
            <var-value>5</var-value>
        </var>
    </field>
    <field property="quantity" indexedListProperty="orders"
            depends="intRange,validwhen">
        <arg position="0" key="prompt.quantity"/>
        <arg position="1" key="${var:min}" resource="false"/>
        <arg position="2" key="${var:max}" resource="false"/>
        <msg name="validwhen" key="error.quantity.invalid"/>
        <var>
            <var-name>min</var-name>
            <var-value>5</var-value>
        </var>
        <var>
            <var-name>max</var-name>
            <var-value>20</var-value>
        </var>
        <var>
            <var-name>test</var-name>
            <var-value>
                (((orders[].partNumber != null) and (*this* != null)) or
                 ((orders[].partNumber == null) and (*this* == null)))
            </var-value>
        </var>
    </field>
</form>
```

Discussion

The indexedListProperty permits you to define one set of validation rules applied to repeated fields on a form. Say you have a JSP page like the one shown in Example 8-6 (*indexed_list_test2.jsp*) that allows a user to place orders for specific part numbers and quantities.

Example 8-6. JSP for rendering indexed properties

```
<%@ page contentType="text/html;charset=UTF-8" language="java" %>
<%@ taglib uri="http://struts.apache.org/tags-bean" prefix="bean" %>
<%@ taglib uri="http://struts.apache.org/tags-html" prefix="html" %>
<%@ taglib uri="http://struts.apache.org/tags-logic" prefix="logic" %>
```

Example 8-6. JSP for rendering indexed properties (continued)

```
<html>
<head>
  <title>Struts Cookbook Chapter 8 : Indexed List Validation</title>
</head>
<body bgcolor="white">
<h2>Struts Cookbook Chapter 8 :  Indexed List Validation</h2>
  <html:form action="/ProcessIndexedListTest2">
    <table>
        <tr>
            <th><bean:message key="prompt.partNumber"/></th>
            <th><bean:message key="prompt.quantity"/></th>
        </tr>
         <logic:iterate name="IndexedListForm" property="orders"
                        id="orders" indexId="ndx">
            <tr>
                <td>
                    <html:text name="orders" property="partNumber"
                            indexed="true"/><br /> 
                    <html:messages id="error"
                            property='<%="orders["+ndx+"].partNumber"%>'>
                        <font color="red"><bean:write name="error"/></font>
                    </html:messages>
                </td>
                <td>
                    <html:text name="orders" property="quantity"
                            indexed="true"/><br /> 
                    <html:messages id="error"
                            property='<%="orders["+ndx+"].quantity"%>'>
                        <font color="red"><bean:write name="error"/></font>
                    </html:messages>
                </td>
            </tr>
        </logic:iterate>
    </table>
    <html:submit/>
  </html:form>
</body>
</html>
```

The rendered HTML form for the JSP in Example 8-6 is shown in Example 8-7.

Example 8-7. Generated HTML for indexed properties

```
<html>
<head>
  <title>Struts Cookbook Chapter 8 : Indexed List Validation</title>
</head>
<body bgcolor="white">
<h2>Struts Cookbook Chapter 8 :  Indexed List Validation</h2>
  <form name="IndexedListForm" method="post"
      action="/jsc-ch08/ProcessIndexedListTest2.do">
    <table>
```

Example 8-7. Generated HTML for indexed properties (continued)

```
<tr>
    <th>Part number</th>
    <th>Quantity</th>
</tr>
    <tr>
        <td>
            <input type="text" name="orders[0].partNumber" value="">
            <br /> 
        </td>
        <td>
            <input type="text" name="orders[0].quantity" value="">
            <br /> 
        </td>
    </tr>
    <tr>
        <td>
            <input type="text" name="orders[1].partNumber" value="">
            <br /> 
        </td>
        <td>
            <input type="text" name="orders[1].quantity" value="">
            <br /> 
        </td>
    </tr>
    <tr>
        <td>
            <input type="text" name="orders[2].partNumber" value="">
            <br /> 
        </td>
        <td>
            <input type="text" name="orders[2].quantity" value="">
            <br /> 
        </td>
    </tr>
    <tr>
        <td>
            <input type="text" name="orders[3].partNumber" value="">
            <br /> 
        </td>
        <td>
            <input type="text" name="orders[3].quantity" value="">
            <br /> 
        </td>
    </tr>
    <tr>
        <td>
            <input type="text" name="orders[4].partNumber" value="">
            <br /> 
        </td>
        <td>
            <input type="text" name="orders[4].quantity" value="">
            <br /> 
```

Example 8-7. Generated HTML for indexed properties (continued)

```
                </td>
            </tr>
    </table>
    <input type="submit" value="Submit">
  </form>
</body>
</html>
```

By setting property="partNumber" and indexedListProperty="orders", you define a validation rule that will be evaluated for each indexed property submitted. In the Solution, each part number is checked using the minlength rule.

```
<field property="partNumber" indexedListProperty="orders"
       depends="minlength">
    <arg position="0" key="prompt.partNumber"/>
    <arg position="1" key="${var:minlength}" resource="false"/>
    <var>
        <var-name>minlength</var-name>
        <var-value>7</var-value>
    </var>
</field>
```

The rule only applies if the property being validated has a non-blank value. Users don't have to enter five part numbers if they don't want to. If you wanted to force the users to enter a value for every part number field, you would specify the required rule as well.

In the Solution, the quantity is validated. The intRange rule validates that an entered quantity is between 5 and 20. This field uses the validwhen rule with a rather verbose test.

```
<var>
    <var-name>test</var-name>
    <var-value>
        (((orders[].partNumber != null) and (*this* != null)) or
         ((orders[].partNumber == null) and (*this* == null)))
    </var-value>
</var>
```

The test ensures that if a quantity is entered, a part number must also be entered. Likewise, if a part number isn't entered, the quantity should be blank. The operand, orders[].partNumber, allows you to refer to a nested property of an indexed object. The [] notation tells the Validator that the expression applies to each object in the array. You can refer to a specific index in the property attribute value or a validwhen expression. If you wanted to require that a part number and quantity were entered for the first row, use the following:

```
<field property="orders[0].partNumber"
       depends="required">
    <arg position="0" key="prompt.partNumber"/>
</field>
```

A common problem when validating multiple rows is that one error message is generated for each rule type for a field. In the Solution, for example, the quantity range validation is generated for the first failing property. You can see the practical results of this behavior in Figure 8-1. Though both quantity fields are invalid, the error is generated for the first quantity field.

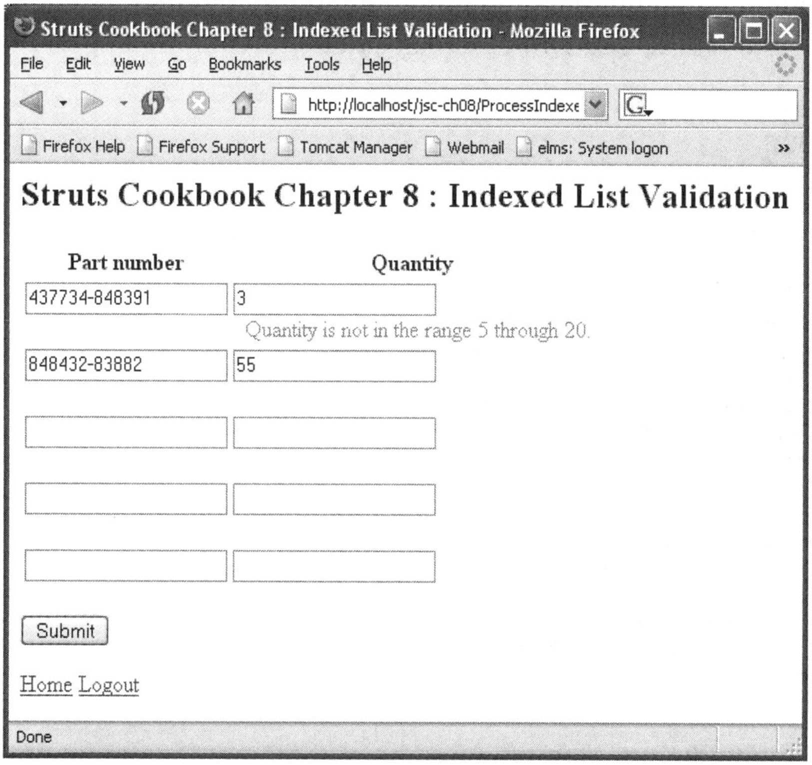

Figure 8-1. Indexed list JSP with errors

Unfortunately, this is a quirk of the Validator when using indexed properties. When the Validator encounters the first error for a particular field, it won't continue to check additional indices of the same field. If this presents a problem, you may want to go back to displaying the errors at the top of the page or take the tried and true method and hand code the validate( ) method to do what you want.

See Also

For additional details on using indexed properties in forms see Recipe 3.4. The validwhen rule is discussed in Recipe 8.4.

For custom rendering of error messages, look at Recipe 9.6.

You'll find a number of interesting discussions on the struts-user mailing list; search on "indexedListProperty" and "array validation."

8.6   Validating Dates

Problem

You want to validate a calendar date and time field by specifying a specific format pattern.

Solution

Use the Validator's date rule to specify the expected pattern that the date must match. Example 8-8 shows some different ways of using this rule.

Example 8-8. Using the Validator's date rule

```
<field property="date1" depends="date">
    <arg key="Date1" resource="false"/>
    <var>
        <var-name>datePattern</var-name>
        <var-value>MM/dd/yyyy</var-value>
    </var>
</field>

<field property="date2" depends="date">
    <arg key="Date2" resource="false"/>
    <var>
        <var-name>datePatternStrict</var-name>
        <var-value>MM/dd/yyyy</var-value>
    </var>
</field>

<field property="dateTime" depends="date">
    <arg key="DateTime" resource="false"/>
    <var>
        <var-name>datePattern</var-name>
        <var-value>MM/dd/yy HH:mm</var-value>
    </var>
</field>
```

Discussion

Calendar dates have got to be one of the hardest field types to work with in a web application. The developer wants to ensure that only valid data gets into the system, but the users want to be able to enter the date in various formats. The Validator helps mitigate these conflicting desires by providing a robust rule for validating dates and times.

The date rule uses a Validator variable (`var`) to specify the pattern that a property value must match. The `datePattern` variable specifies the pattern for formatting the value using the `java.text.SimpleDateFormat` class. If `SimpleDateFormat` can format the value into a date, then the validation passes; otherwise, the validation fails.

If `datePatternStrict` is used instead of `datePattern`, the length of the value must match the length of the pattern. Suppose you are validating against the pattern of MM/dd/yyyy. The user inputs 5/10/1963 to represent May 10, 1963. If `datePattern` is used, the value will pass validation. If `datePatternStrict` is used, however, the validation won't pass because the month portion has one digit, not two, as specified by the pattern.

The date rule allows the `SimpleDateFormat` to interpret the input value leniently. For example, the value of 07/32/2004 passes validation! It's interpreted as August 1, 2004. Though you can't change the date rule to use strict parsing, you can add the mask rule to enforce stricter formats.

See Also

The JavaDocs for the `SimpleDateFormat` class have all the information you need to come up with a suitable formatting patterns. This documentation can be found at *http://java.sun.com/j2se/1.4.2/docs/api/java/text/SimpleDateFormat.html*.

Use of the mask rule is described in Recipe 8.2. Other considerations when working with dates are discussed in Recipe 3.13.

8.7   Validating Field Equality with a Custom Validator

Problem

You want to create a reusable validator in Struts 1.1 that can validate that the value of one field is equal to the value of another.

Solution

Use Matt Raible's *TwoFields* custom validator. Start by creating a class with a static method that implements the rule, as shown in Example 8-9.

Example 8-9. TwoFields validation rule class

```
package com.oreilly.strutsckbk.ch08;

import javax.servlet.http.HttpServletRequest;

import org.apache.commons.validator.Field;
import org.apache.commons.validator.GenericValidator;
```

Example 8-9. TwoFields validation rule class (continued)

```java
import org.apache.commons.validator.ValidatorAction;
import org.apache.commons.validator.util.ValidatorUtils;
import org.apache.struts.action.ActionErrors;
import org.apache.struts.validator.Resources;

public class CustomValidatorRules {

    public static boolean validateTwoFields( Object bean,
                                             ValidatorAction va,
                                             Field field,
                                             ActionErrors errors,
                                             HttpServletRequest request ) {
        String value = ValidatorUtils.getValueAsString(bean, field.getProperty( ));
        String sProperty2 = field.getVarValue("secondProperty");
        String value2 = ValidatorUtils.getValueAsString(bean, sProperty2);

        if (!GenericValidator.isBlankOrNull(value)) {
            try {
                if (!value.equals(value2)) {
                    errors.add(
                            field.getKey( ),
                            Resources.getActionError(request, va, field));
                    return false;
                }
            } catch (Exception e) {
                errors.add(
                        field.getKey( ),
                        Resources.getActionError(request, va, field));
                return false;
            }
        }

        return true;
    }
}
```

Next, add the following validator element, shown in Example 8-10, as a sub-element of the global element in the *validator-rules.xml* file.

Example 8-10. TwoFields validator rule

```xml
<validator name="twofields"
      classname="com.oreilly.strutsckbk.ch08.CustomValidatorRules"
         method="validateTwoFields"
   methodParams="java.lang.Object,
                 org.apache.commons.validator.ValidatorAction,
                 org.apache.commons.validator.Field,
                 org.apache.struts.action.ActionErrors,
                 javax.servlet.http.HttpServletRequest"
      depends="required"
          msg="errors.twofields">
    <javascript><![CDATA[
```

Example 8-10. TwoFields validator rule (continued)

```
    function validateTwoFields(form) {
        var bValid = true;
        var focusField = null;
        var i = 0;
        var fields = new Array();
        oTwoFields = new twofields();
        for (x in oTwoFields) {
            var field = form[oTwoFields[x][0]];
            var secondField = form[oTwoFields[x][2]("secondProperty")];

            if (field.type == 'text' ||
                field.type == 'textarea' ||
                field.type == 'select-one' ||
                field.type == 'radio' ||
                field.type == 'password') {

                var value;
                var secondValue;
                // get field's value
                if (field.type == "select-one") {
                    var si = field.selectedIndex;
                    value = field.options[si].value;
                    secondValue = secondField.options[si].value;
                } else {
                    value = field.value;
                    secondValue = secondField.value;
                }

                if (value != secondValue) {

                    if (i == 0) {
                        focusField = field;
                    }
                    fields[i++] = oTwoFields[x][1];
                    bValid = false;
                }
            }
        }

        if (fields.length > 0) {
            focusField.focus();
            alert(fields.join('\n'));
        }

        return bValid;
    }]]></javascript>
</validator>
```

Next, add an error message with the key of errors.twofields to your applications
MessageResources properties file:

```
    errors.twofields={0} must be equal to {1}.
```

To use the *TwoFields* validator, in your *validation.xml* file change the `field` element for one of the related fields to be dependent on the `twofields` rule. In Example 8-11, the `password2` field must be equal to the `password` field for the validation of `password2` to succeed.

Example 8-11. Applying the TwoFields rule

```
<?xml version="1.0" encoding="ISO-8859-1" ?>
<!DOCTYPE form-validation PUBLIC
        "-//Apache Software Foundation//DTD Commons Validator Rules Configuration
1.1//EN"
        "http://jakarta.apache.org/commons/dtds/validator_1_1_3.dtd">
<form-validation>
    <formset>
        <form name="RegistrationForm">
            <field property="emailAddress"
                    depends="required,email">
                <arg0 key="prompt.emailAddress"/>
            </field>
            <field property="password"
                    depends="required">
                <arg0 key="prompt.password"/>
            </field>
            <field property="password2"
                    depends="required,twofields">
                <arg0 key="prompt.password2"/>
                <arg1 key="prompt.password"/>
                <var>
                    <var-name>secondProperty</var-name>
                    <var-value>password</var-value>
                </var>
            </field>
        </form>
    </formset>
</form-validation>
```

Discussion

This recipe provides a solution for checking field equality and shows you how to create a custom validator. It's easier than you might suppose.

You implement a custom validator as a static method of a class of your choosing. By convention, the method should be named validate*RuleName*. The precise method signature when developing under Struts 1.1 is the following:

```
public static boolean validateRuleName( Object bean,
                                  ValidatorAction va,
                                  Field field,
                                  ActionErrors errors,
                                  HttpServletRequest request)
```

This method returns a `boolean`, which indicates if the validation passes (`true`) or fails (`false`). Table 8-2 describes the method arguments and how they are used.

Table 8-2. Validator rule arguments

Name	Type	Purpose
bean	Object	The ActionForm being validated. You retrieve the input values from this object's properties.
Va	ValidatorAction	Object representation of the pluggable validator element from the *validator-rules.xml* file for the particular rule. Used to generate the error message for the rule.
field	Field	Object representation of the field element from the *validation.xml* file. Provides access to the nested variables (var) and arguments (arg).
errors	ActionErrors	An instance of ActionErrors you populate with ActionError objects. For Struts 1.2, this variable is an ActionMessages instance that you populate it ActionMessage objects.
request	HttpServletRequest	The HTTP servlet request. Used by the Resources utility class to retrieve the MessageResources for creating an ActionError.

The implementation of the *TwoFields* rule does the following:

1. Gets the value for the field from the ActionForm (bean).
2. Gets the value for the field variable named secondProperty that represents a bean property name.
3. Using the bean property name acquired in step 2, retrieves the form value for the property from the ActionForm.
4. Checks if the field value acquired in step 1 is blank or null. If it is either, true is returned; otherwise, processing continues.
5. Tests if the two values are equal using the equals( ) method.
6. If the values are unequal, adds a new ActionError to the errors and returns false.
7. If an Exception is thrown in step 5 or 6, the rule adds a new ActionError to the errors and return false.
8. If no Exception is thrown, the validation passes and returns true.

Once you have the Java coded for the validator, you need to link the implementation to the Validator by creating a validator element in the *validator-rules.xml* file. Here's the validator element used for *TwoFields*:

```
<validator name="twofields"
      classname="com.oreilly.strutsckbk.ch08.CustomValidatorRules"
         method="validateTwoFields"
   methodParams="java.lang.Object,
               org.apache.commons.validator.ValidatorAction,
               org.apache.commons.validator.Field,
               org.apache.struts.action.ActionErrors,
               javax.servlet.http.HttpServletRequest"
         depends="required"
            msg="errors.twofields">
```

The name attribute specifies the name that you'll use to refer to the validator wherever it's applied. The classname, method, and methodParams attributes are used by the Validator to determine the class and method to call. If you are using Struts 1.2, be sure to change ActionErrors to ActionMessages.

The depends attribute specifies other rules triggered before this rule is fired. For the twofields rule, you need to validate the field if there's a value for it. You can enforce this by setting depends to required. The last attribute, msg, identifies the MessageResources key of the default error message used by this rule. This value can be overridden when the rule is applied.

The *TwoFields* rule shown in Example 8-10 includes JavaScript for client-side validation. For a Validator rule, you enclose the JavaScript code in a CDATA section of the javascript element nested in the validator element:

```
<validator name="twofields" ...
  <javascript>
      <![CDATA[
      function validateTwoFields(form) {
          var bValid = true;
          // body of the JavaScript function ...
          return bValid;
      }]]>
  </javascript>
</validator>
```

The JavaScript function, like the Java method name, should be named using the validate*RuleName* convention. The function must return a boolean value that indicates if the validation rule passes (true) or fails (false).

 For custom rules that don't use client-side validation, you can omit the javascript element.

The last piece of the puzzle (whew!) is to apply the rule to a specific form field:

```
<field property="password2"
    depends="twofields">
    <arg0 key="prompt.password2"/>
    <arg1 key="prompt.password"/>
    <var>
        <var-name>secondProperty</var-name>
        <var-value>password</var-value>
    </var>
</field>
```

The arg0 and arg1 values specify the message resource keys for the labels of the two fields. These values are substituted into the error message if the validation fails. The var element specifies the name of the second field. This value doesn't necessarily have to be a field on the form (though in this case it probably would be); it can be any JavaBean property on the `ActionForm`.

See Also

If you are using Struts 1.2, an easier solution is discussed in Recipe 8.8.

The *TwoFields* validator was originally presented on Matt Raible's weblog. It can be found on his site at *http://www.raibledesigns.com/page/rd/20030226*. The Validator User's Guide discusses custom Validators in the section found at *http://struts.apache. org/userGuide/dev_validator.html#plugs*.

The Recipe 8.9 presents a custom Validator for Struts 1.2 that you may want to read up on as well.

8.8   Validating Field Equality in Struts 1.2

Problem

You want to validate that two fields on a form have the same value, taking advantage of the new features provided by the Validator in Struts 1.2.

Solution

Use the `validwhen` rule with a `test` expression that checks if the validated field is equals the other field. In Example 8-12, the test expression specifies the `password2` field (*this*) must equal the `password` field for the validation to pass.

Example 8-12. Validating field equality with validwhen

```
<?xml version="1.0" encoding="ISO-8859-1" ?>
<!DOCTYPE form-validation PUBLIC
        "-//Apache Software Foundation//DTD Commons Validator Rules Configuration
1.1//EN"
        "http://jakarta.apache.org/commons/dtds/validator_1_1_3.dtd">
<form-validation>
    <formset>
        <form name="RegistrationForm">
            <field property="emailAddress"
                    depends="required,email">
                <arg key="prompt.emailAddress"/>
            </field>
            <field property="password"
                    depends="required">
                <arg key="prompt.password"/>
            </field>
            <field property="password2"
                    depends="required,validwhen">
                <arg position="0" key="prompt.password2"/>
                <arg position="1" key="prompt.password"/>
```

Example 8-12. Validating field equality with validwhen (continued)

```
                <msg name="validwhen" key="error.password.match"/>
                <var>
                    <var-name>test</var-name>
                    <var-value>(*this* == password)</var-value>
                </var>
            </field>
        </form>
    </formset>
</form-validation>
```

Discussion

If you compare this Solution with Recipe 8.7, you can see the same business rule is implemented without requiring a custom Validator rule. The validwhen rule used here accepts a test expression, which it evaluates. If the expression returns true, the validation passes; otherwise, the validation fails.

With validwhen, you can create expressions that reference the value of the field being validated and the value of any other property on the ActionForm. With this power in hand, creating an expression to test the equality of two fields is easy:

```
(*this* == password)
```

The left-hand operand, *this*, represents the value of the field under validation. The right-hand operand, password, represents the value of the password property from the RegistrationForm.

See Also

The validwhen rule is discussed in more detail in Recipe 8.4.

If you can't use validwhen because you are using Struts 1.1, Recipe 8.7 provides an alternate solution using a custom rule.

8.9   Validating Two or More Choices

Problem

You need to check that two or more choices have been picked from a set of check-boxes or a list of options.

Solution

Use my minchoices pluggable Validator rule. The rule implementation is shown in Example 8-13.

Example 8-13. Validating minimum choices

```java
package com.oreilly.strutsckbk.ch08;

import java.util.Collection;

import javax.servlet.http.HttpServletRequest;

import org.apache.commons.beanutils.PropertyUtils;
import org.apache.commons.validator.Field;
import org.apache.commons.validator.ValidatorAction;
import org.apache.struts.action.ActionMessages;
import org.apache.struts.validator.Resources;

public class ValidatorRules {

    public static boolean validateMinChoices(Object bean,
                                              ValidatorAction va,
                                              Field field,
                                              ActionMessages errors,
                                              HttpServletRequest request) {
        try {
            Object values = PropertyUtils.getProperty(bean, field.getProperty( ));
            int minChoices = Integer.parseInt(field.getVarValue("minChoices"));
            if (!(values == null)) {
                int numChoices = 0;
                if (values instanceof Object[]) {
                    numChoices = ((Object[])values).length;
                }
                else if (values instanceof Collection) {
                    numChoices = ((Collection) values).size( );
                }
                else {
                    errors.add(field.getKey( ),
                            Resources.getActionMessage(request, va, field));
                    return false;
                }
                if (numChoices < minChoices) {
                    errors.add(field.getKey( ),
                            Resources.getActionMessage(request, va, field));
                    return false;
                }
            }
        }
        catch (Exception e) {
            errors.add(field.getKey( ),
                    Resources.getActionMessage(request, va, field));
            return false;
        }

        return true;
    }
}
```

Then add the corresponding validator element to the *validator-rules.xml* file:

```
<validator name="minchoices"
       classname="com.oreilly.strutsckbk.ch08.ValidatorRules"
          method="validateMinChoices"
    methodParams="java.lang.Object,
                   org.apache.commons.validator.ValidatorAction,
                   org.apache.commons.validator.Field,
                   org.apache.struts.action.ActionMessages,
                   javax.servlet.http.HttpServletRequest"
         depends="required"
             msg="errors.minChoices"/>
```

Finally, you can apply the rule where needed:

```
<field property=""
        depends="minchoices">
    <arg position="0" key="prompt.language"/>
    <arg position="1" key="${var:minChoices}"
         resource="false"/>
    <var>
        <var-name>minChoices</var-name>
        <var-value>3</var-value>
    </var>
</field>
```

Discussion

You often need to verify that users have checked at least one choice from a set of checkboxes or selected one or more options from a select list. Both of these validations can be performed using the Validator's predefined `required` rule. However, validating users who have chosen *more* than one item requires a custom rule like the one shown in the Solution.

You create the `minchoices` rule using the same basic steps outlined in Recipe 8.7. The rule requires that the validated field must be an array or a `Collection`. If it's not, then the validation fails and an error is returned. Otherwise, the value of the `minChoices` variable is retrieved. If the size of the array or Collection is less than `minChoices`, the validation fails; otherwise, the validation passes.

This pluggable validator was developed using the Struts 1.2 API. It uses the `ActionMessages` and `ActionMessage` classes instead of `ActionErrors` and `ActionError`. The signature of the `validateMinChoices()` method and the `methodParams` attribute of the validator element specify `ActionMessages`.

If the `methodParams` specified in the `validator` element doesn't match the method signature of the rule's Java method, the Validator will be unable to find the method to invoke.

See Also

Recipe 8.7 provides an additional example of creating custom pluggable validators.

8.10 Adding a Custom Validation to a Validator Form

Problem

You need to add a custom ad hoc validation check to a Validator `ActionForm`.

Solution

Extend the `ValidatorForm` or `ValidatorActionForm` and override the `validate( )` method, ensuring you call `super.validate( )` to perform the Validator's validation. (See Example 8-14.)

Example 8-14. Extending the ValidatorForm

```
import javax.servlet.http.HttpServletRequest;

import org.apache.struts.action.ActionError;
import org.apache.struts.action.ActionErrors;
import org.apache.struts.action.ActionMapping;
import org.apache.struts.validator.ValidatorForm;

public final class MyForm extends ValidatorForm {
    private String foo;
    private String bar;

    public String getFoo( ) {
        return foo;
    }
    public void setFoo(String s) {
        foo = s;
    }
    public String getBar( ) {
        return bar;
    }
    public void setBar(String s) {
        bar = s;
    }
    public ActionErrors validate(ActionMapping mapping,
                                 HttpServletRequest request) {
        // Perform validator framework validations
        ActionErrors errors = super.validate(mapping, request);

        // Add crossfield and business validations here
        if (!checkFooBarValid(foo, bar)) {
            errors.add("foo", new ActionError("errors.invalidFooBar"));
```

Example 8-14. Extending the ValidatorForm (continued)

```
        }
        // additional validations ...

        return errors;
    }

    private boolean checkFooBarValid(Foo foo, Bar bar) {
        boolean valid = false;
        // perform custom validation
        valid = FooBarUtil.checkFooBar(foo, bar);
        return valid;
    }
}
```

If you're using a dynamic form defined in the *struts-config.xml*, extend the type being used (e.g., DynaValidatorForm), and override the validate( ) method as the class does in Example 8-15.

Example 8-15. Extending the DynaValidatorForm

```
package com.mycompany.myapp;

import javax.servlet.http.HttpServletRequest;

import org.apache.struts.action.ActionError;
import org.apache.struts.action.ActionErrors;
import org.apache.struts.action.ActionMapping;
import org.apache.struts.validator.DynaValidatorForm;

public final class MyDynaForm extends DynaValidatorForm {
    public ActionErrors validate(ActionMapping mapping,
                                 HttpServletRequest request) {
        // Perform validator framework validations
        ActionErrors errors = super.validate(mapping, request);

        // get the needed property values
        String foo = (String) get("foo");
        String bar = (String) get("bar");

        // Add crossfield and business validations here
        if (!checkFooBarValid(foo, bar)) {
          errors.add("foo", new ActionError("errors.invalidFooBar"));
        }
        // additional validations ...

        return errors;
    }

    private boolean checkFooBarValid(Foo foo, Bar bar) {
        boolean valid = false;
        // perform custom validation
```

Example 8-15. Extending the DynaValidatorForm (continued)

```
        valid = FooBarUtil.checkFooBar(foo, bar);
        return valid;
    }
}
```

Then change the `form-bean` element to use this new class:

```
<form-bean name="SomeForm"
          type="com.mycompany.myapp.MyDynaForm">
    <form-property name="foo" type="java.lang.String"/>
    <form-property name="bar" type="java.lang.String"/>
</form-bean>
```

Discussion

Though the Validator offloads much of your hand-written code to a configuration file, more complex validations may be required. Two general types of validation exist: syntactic and semantic. Syntactic validation verifies the syntax of the data, and semantic validation verifies that the data is meaningful from a business sense. The Validator does syntactic checks well but isn't purposed for semantic validation. Usually, this validation needs to be hand-written.

Fortunately, the Validator doesn't prohibit you from providing additional custom validations. For conventional hand-coded `ActionForms` that extend `ValidatorForm` or `ValidatorActionForm`, override the `validate( )` method to add the additional validation checks. In your `validate( )` method, call `super.validate( )` to allow the Validator to perform its verifications. Then perform additional validations in your own method as required. If an error occurs, add it to the `ActionErrors` object returned from `super.validate( )`.

If you are using the Validator with dynamic action forms, then your form bean typically uses a type of `DynaValidatorForm` or `DynaValidatorActionForm`. Apply the same technique for extending these classes as with conventional nondynamic form classes. You extend the form class and override the `validate` method. To access properties of a `DynaValidatorForm`, you'll need to use the get(*property*) methods.

See Also

Recipe 5.1 discusses how to create and use dynamic action forms.

8.11 Validating a Wizard Form

Problem

You need to perform validations on a form shared across pages as part of a wizard-style interface.

Solution

Use the Validator's built-in support for wizards via the page attribute. Example 8-16 configures the Validator use of this attribute. Validations will be performed on fields where the page attribute value is less than or equal to the page property of the ActionForm.

Example 8-16. Use of the Validator page attribute

```
<form name="WizardForm">
    <field property="username" page="1"
            depends="required">
        <arg key="prompt.username"/>
    </field>
    <field property="password" page="2"
            depends="required">
        <arg key="prompt.password"/>
    </field>
    <field property="ssn" page="3"
            depends="required,mask">
        <arg key="prompt.ssn"/>
        <var>
            <var-name>mask</var-name>
            <var-value>^\d{3}-\d{2}-\d{4}$</var-value>
        </var>
    </field>
</form>
```

If the form used for the wizard uses the DynaValidatorForm (or one of its sub-classes), add a form-property with the name of page. The property must be of type java.lang.Integer:

```
<form-bean name="WizardForm"
            type="org.apache.struts.validator.DynaValidatorForm">
    <form-property name="username" type="java.lang.String"/>
    <form-property name="password" type="java.lang.String"/>
    <form-property name="ssn" type="java.lang.String"/>
    <form-property name="page" type="java.lang.Integer"/>
</form-bean>
```

For conventional ActionForms that subclass ValidatorForm (or one of its subclasses), no changes are necessary. The ValidatorForm already provides a page property. Because the page instance variable is protected, it can be accessed by subclasses. (See Example 8-17.)

Example 8-17. Action Form for wizard interface

```
package com.oreilly.strutsckbk.ch08;

import javax.servlet.http.HttpServletRequest;

import org.apache.struts.action.ActionErrors;
import org.apache.struts.action.ActionMapping;
```

Example 8-17. Action Form for wizard interface (continued)

```
import org.apache.struts.action.ActionMessage;
import org.apache.struts.validator.ValidatorForm;

public class WizardForm extends ValidatorForm {

    public String getUsername( ) {
        return username;
    }
    public void setUsername(String username) {
        this.username = username;
    }
    public String getPassword( ) {
        return password;
    }
    public void setPassword(String password) {
        this.password = password;
    }
    public String getSsn( ) {
        return ssn;
    }
    public void setSsn(String ssn) {
        this.ssn = ssn;
    }

    private String username;
    private String password;
    private String ssn;
}
```

Discussion

The Validator supports validation of session-scoped `ActionForms` used in wizard-style interfaces. You can specify a page attribute for each `field` element in your *validation.xml* file. When you submit the form from a step in the wizard, you set the page property to a number representing the current step. This property can be set in the `Action` preceding the page, or it can be hardcoded on the JSP itself; either way, it's usually rendered as a hidden field.

When the Validator validates the form, it checks those fields whose page attribute value is less than or equal to the current page. The Solution, for example, is based on a wizard interface with three pages; the first page handles the username, the second page handles the password, and the last page handles the SSN.

The Validator validates prior pages and the current page primarily for thoroughness. Because of programming errors, a step in the flow could be accidentally skipped. On a more ominous note, a hacker could circumvent the wizard's flow by submitting directly to an out-of-sequence URL. By validating prior pages in addition to the current page, no assumptions are made about how the current page was accessed; all prior fields are validated.

If you override the `ValidatorForm.validate( )` method in your own subclass, you can account for the page property as the Validator does. This code snippet shows how you could override the `validate( )` of the `ActionForm` in Example 8-17:

```
public ActionErrors validate(ActionMapping mapping,
                             HttpServletRequest request) {
    ActionErrors errors = super.validate(mapping, request);
    if (page >= 2) {
        if (username.equals(password)) {
            errors.add( "password",
                new ActionMessage("password",
                    "errors.password.sameAsUsername"));
        }
    }
    return errors;
}
```

This method calls `super.validate( )` to perform the Validator validations. It then performs a business logic validation, verifying that the username and password are different. If the validation fails, an `ActionMessage` (or `ActionError` in Struts 1.1) is added to the set of errors. Just like the Validator, this validation accounts for the current page. In this case, the validation is only performed for page 2 and beyond.

See Also

Recipe 8.10 shows Solutions for adding custom validations by extending Validator forms. Recipe 7.6 considers additional details about setting up a wizard-style interface.

8.12   Localizing Validation Rules

Problem

You need to specify different validation rules for a specific language or country for certain fields on a form.

Solution

First, define the form validation rules for all form fields within the global `formset` element in the *validation.xml* file:

```
<formset>
    <form name="LocalizedForm">
        <field property="employeeId"
                depends="required">
            <arg key="prompt.employeeId"/>
        </field>
        <field property="hourlyRate"
                depends="required,mask">
            <arg key="prompt.hourlyRate"/>
            <var>
```

```
            <var-name>mask</var-name>
            <var-value>^\d+\.\d{2}$</var-value>
          </var>
        </field>
      </form>
    </formset>
```

Then create a new `formset` element using localization attributes—`language`, `country`, and `variant`—for the specific locale. Within this `formset`, you can configure locale-specific validation rules for those fields that require special treatment:

```
<formset language="fr">
    <form name="LocalizedForm">
        <field property="hourlyRate"
                depends="required,mask">
            <arg key="prompt.hourlyRate"/>
            <var>
                <var-name>mask</var-name>
                <var-value>^\d+,\d{2}$</var-value>
            </var>
        </field>
    </form>
</formset>
```

Discussion

You can tell the Validator to use specific field validation rules for a particular locale. The `formset` supports the standard locale properties with these attributes:

- `language`
- `country`
- `variant`

At runtime, the Validator searches the `formsets`, based on locale, for a matching `form` definition. It evaluates the locale using the standard search algorithm used for resource bundles; that is, if it can't find its match for the language and country, then it searches just for the language, etc. Validations specified for a specific language *and* country override the same validation configured for the language.

 Ensure that the `formset` for the default locale contains an element for *every* field you may validate. If the Validator doesn't have a fallback rule for a field, it won't be able to apply the locale-specific rule.

Suppose you have an application that allows the user to enter a currency amount. For English-speaking users, you want to validate that the value contains one or more digits to the left of the decimal, a decimal point, and then two digits to the right of the decimal. You can state using a regular expression:

```
^\d+\.\d{2}$
```

The period, or full-stop, character (.) is a special character in a regular expression that matches any character. To match an actual decimal point, you need to escape the period by preceding it with a back-slash (\.).

French users, however, use a comma (,) as the decimal separator instead of a period (.). Here's the regular expression for this rule:

```
^\d+,\d{2}$
```

In the Solution, the employeeId field is required regardless of locale. For the hourlyRate field, however, you want to allow French-speaking users to enter the value using their natural format for currency.

For each field that you configure in a locale-specific format, you must specify *all* the rules that apply in the depends attribute. At runtime, the Validator merges the fields between formsets, but it doesn't merge individual rules a field depends on. In the Solution, for example, hourlyRate depends on the required and mask rules. Therefore, all of these dependencies are listed within the French formset.

See Also

The Validator User's Guide at *http://struts.apache.org/userGuide/dev_validator.html* has a section on localizing validations.

A good thread from the struts-user mailing list discussed how the Validator and the order that it processes fields and form sets. The thread can be traced from *http://marc.theaimsgroup.com/?l=struts-user&m=104793541428623&w=2*.

## CHAPTER 9

Exception and Error Handling

9.0   Introduction

Any application can shine under normal conditions; how an application responds to unexpected conditions reveals much more about its robustness and production-readiness. As you saw in Chapter 8, the Struts Validator provides a means for handling unexpected user input. However, applications need to handle unexpected system behavior. This behavior typically manifests as exceptions. These exceptions may be business-related, may have meaning to the end user, or they may be system- and coding-related, or may have meaning to system administrators and developers. This chapter will show you some good solutions for handling both of these cases.

9.1   Simplifying Exception Processing in an Action

Problem

You want to reduce the number of try...catch blocks within your Action classes.

Solution

Remove the exception-handling code from your Action, and define global and local exception handlers in your *struts-config.xml* file, as shown in Example 9-1.

Example 9-1. Global and local exception handling (partial)

```
...
<global-exceptions>
    <exception key="error.unknown.user"
            type="com.oreilly.strutsckbk.ch09.UnknownUserException"
            path="/securityError.jsp"/>
</global-exceptions>
...
```

Example 9-1. Global and local exception handling (partial) (continued)

```
<action-mappings>
    <action    path="/Login"
               type="com.oreilly.strutsckbk.ch09.LoginAction"
               scope="request"
               name="LoginForm"
            validate="true"
               input="/login.jsp">
        <exception key="error.password.match"
                   type="com.oreilly.strutsckbk.ch09.PasswordMatchException">
        <forward name="success" path="/login_success.jsp"/>
    </action>
...
```

Discussion

Prior to Struts 1.1, the handling of exceptions was left to the devloper's devices. Exceptions returned from calls to the business layer from an Action had to be handled individually in your code. Because the perform( ) method of Struts 1.0 only allowed you to throw IOException and ServletException, you didn't have much choice in the matter:

```
public ActionForward perform( ActionMapping mapping,
                              ActionForm form,
                              HttpServletRequest request,
                              HttpServletResponse response)
        throws IOException, ServletException { ...
```

Any checked exception thrown within the body of perform( ) had to be caught and handled. In some cases, it was appropriate to catch the exception, generate an ActionError, and forward to the input page, much like a validation failure. But more often, the exception couldn't be handled by the application, so the developer returned a ServletException wrapped around the application exception. With Struts 1.1, the perform( ) method was deprecated and the execute( ) method was introduced. Unlike perform( ), execute( ) can throw any exception, and once an exception is thrown, you can process using exception handlers configured in your *struts-config.xml* file.

If you migrated an Action class from Struts 1.0 to Struts without using declarative exception handling, the class might look something like Example 9-2.

Example 9-2. Action without declarative exception handling

```
package com.oreilly.strutsckbk.ch09;

import java.io.IOException;

import javax.servlet.http.HttpServletRequest;
import javax.servlet.http.HttpServletResponse;

import org.apache.commons.beanutils.PropertyUtils;
import org.apache.struts.action.Action;
```

Example 9-2. Action without declarative exception handling (continued)

```java
import org.apache.struts.action.ActionError;
import org.apache.struts.action.ActionErrors;
import org.apache.struts.action.ActionForm;
import org.apache.struts.action.ActionForward;
import org.apache.struts.action.ActionMapping;

public class LoginAction extends Action {
    public ActionForward execute(ActionMapping mapping,
                                 ActionForm form,
                                 HttpServletRequest request,
                                 HttpServletResponse response)
            throws Exception {

        String username = null;
        String password = null;

        ActionErrors errors = new ActionErrors();

        try {
            username = (String) PropertyUtils.getSimpleProperty(form, "username");
            password = (String) PropertyUtils.getSimpleProperty(form, "password");
        } catch (Exception e) {
            throw new IOException("Unable to retrieve username and password");
        }

        SecurityService service = new SecurityService();
        try {
            service.authenticate( username, password);
        } catch (UnknownUserException e1) {
            errors.add(ActionErrors.GLOBAL_ERROR,
                new ActionError("error.unknown.user"));
            saveErrors(request, errors);
            return mapping.findForward("securityError");
        } catch (PasswordMatchException e) {
            errors.add(ActionErrors.GLOBAL_ERROR,
            new ActionError("error.password.match"));
        }

        // Report any errors we have discovered back to the original form
        if (!errors.isEmpty()) {
            saveErrors(request, errors);
            return (mapping.getInputForward());
        }

        User user = new User();
        user.setUsername(username);
        request.getSession().setAttribute("user", user);

        return mapping.findForward("success");
    }
}
```

There's a lot of code here whose sole purpose is handling exceptions. The first try ...catch block handles *technical* exceptions thrown in getting data from the form. The more interesting application exceptions are thrown by the SecurityService. The UnknownUserException is handled by generating an error, saving the errors in the request, and forwarding to a Struts forward. The PasswordMatchException is handled similarly, except that the page is forwarded to the input path for the action, where the error will probably be reported and the user can try again.

All of this exception-handling code can be eliminated by using declarative exception handling. Example 9-3 shows the LoginAction with the exception handling removed.

Example 9-3. LoginAction without exception handling

```
package com.oreilly.strutsckbk.ch09;

import javax.servlet.http.HttpServletRequest;
import javax.servlet.http.HttpServletResponse;

import org.apache.commons.beanutils.PropertyUtils;
import org.apache.struts.action.Action;
import org.apache.struts.action.ActionForm;
import org.apache.struts.action.ActionForward;
import org.apache.struts.action.ActionMapping;

public class LoginAction extends Action {

    public ActionForward execute(ActionMapping mapping,
                                 ActionForm form,
                                 HttpServletRequest request,
                                 HttpServletResponse response)
            throws Exception {

        String username = (String)
            PropertyUtils.getSimpleProperty(form, "username");
        String password = (String)
            PropertyUtils.getSimpleProperty(form, "password");

        SecurityService service = new SecurityService( );
        service.authenticate( username, password);

        User user = new User( );
        user.setUsername(username);
        request.getSession( ).setAttribute("user", user);

        return mapping.findForward("success");
    }
}
```

The exceptions are now handled declaratively, as shown in the Solution. The UnknownUserException is declared as a global exception:

```
<global-exceptions>
    <exception key="error.unknown.user"
```

```
        type="com.oreilly.strutsckbk.ch09.UnknownUserException"
        path="/securityError.jsp"/>
    ...
</global-exceptions>
```

The key specifies a `MessageResources` message that will be used to generate an `ActionError`. The path specifies the name of the resource to forward to. If path is omitted, the input page for an action will be used. The generated `ActionError` is stored in an `ActionErrors` object and can be displayed on the destination page using the `<html:errors/>` tag.

 Any `ActionErrors` stored in the request by your `Action` will be replaced if your `Action` throws an exception handled declaratively. If you want to preserve existing `ActionErrors`, you'll need to create a custom `ExceptionHandler`.

Because this exception is declared as a `global-exception`, any action that throws an `UnknownUserException` will be handled by this declaration unless overridden by a local exception.

A local exception is defined by nesting the exception element within the `action` element to which it applies. It defines action-specific handling for specified types of exceptions. The `PasswordMatchException` is handled by a local exception:

```
<action path="/Login" ...>
    <exception key="error.password.match"
            type="com.oreilly.strutsckbk.ch09.PasswordMatchException"
            path="/login.jsp"/>
    <forward .../>
</action>
```

So what happens when you throw an exception that doesn't have a declared handler? These exceptions will be wrapped in a `ServletException` and ultimately thrown by the `ActionServlet.service( )` method to be handled by the application server.

See Also

For more information on custom display of error messages, see Recipe 9.6.

You can provide custom exception handling by extending the Struts exception handler. This approach is discussed in Recipe 9.2.

If you want to provide a fallback exception-handling approach instead of relying on the container, take a look at Recipe 9.4.

9.2   Custom Processing for Declared Exceptions

Problem

Your application requires specialized handling for certain types of exceptions.

Solution

Extend the Struts ExceptionHandler with your own class such as the one shown in Example 9-4.

Example 9-4. Extending the Struts exception handler

```
package com.oreilly.strutsckbk.ch09;

import javax.servlet.ServletException;
import javax.servlet.http.HttpServletRequest;
import javax.servlet.http.HttpServletResponse;

import org.apache.struts.action.ActionForm;
import org.apache.struts.action.ActionForward;
import org.apache.struts.action.ActionMapping;
import org.apache.struts.action.ActionMessage;
import org.apache.struts.action.ExceptionHandler;
import org.apache.struts.config.ExceptionConfig;

public class CustomExceptionHandler extends ExceptionHandler {

    public ActionForward execute(Exception ex, ExceptionConfig ae,
            ActionMapping mapping, ActionForm formInstance,
            HttpServletRequest request, HttpServletResponse response)
            throws ServletException {
        // TODO Add custom code here to completely control handling
        return super.execute(ex, ae, mapping, formInstance, request, response);
    }
    protected void logException(Exception e) {
        // TODO Add custom code here for exception logging
        System.out.println("Customized logException for:"+e);
        super.logException(e);
    }
    protected void storeException(HttpServletRequest request, String property,
            ActionMessage error, ActionForward forward, String scope) {
        // TODO Add custom code here for storing errors
        System.out.println("Customized error storing for:"+error);
        super.storeException(request, property, error, forward, scope);
    }
}
```

In your *struts-config.xml* file, specify your ExceptionHandler's class name as the value for the handler attribute on each exception element you want to use the handler:

```
<exception key="error.exception"
        type="com.oreilly.strutsckbk.ch09.CustomException"
```

```
        handler="com.oreilly.strutsckbk.ch09.CustomExceptionHandler"
          path="/some_error_page.jsp"/>
```

Discussion

You might think that if you use declarative exceptions you are "locked in" to the
Struts-way of processing exceptions. In fact, you are not bound to the Struts exception-
handling process for two oft overlooked reasons; Struts was designed for extensibility, and Struts is open source.

When an `Action` throws an `Exception`, the `RequestProcessor` handles it in the
`processException` method:

```
protected ActionForward processException(HttpServletRequest request,
                                         HttpServletResponse response,
                                         Exception exception,
                                         ActionForm form,
                                         ActionMapping mapping)
    throws IOException, ServletException {
    // Is there a defined handler for this exception?
    ExceptionConfig config = mapping.findException(exception.getClass());
    if (config == null) {
        log.warn(getInternal().getMessage("unhandledException",
                                exception.getClass()));
        if (exception instanceof IOException) {
            throw (IOException) exception;
        } else if (exception instanceof ServletException) {
            throw (ServletException) exception;
        } else {
            throw new ServletException(exception);
        }
    }

    // Use the configured exception handling
    try {
        ExceptionHandler handler = (ExceptionHandler)
          RequestUtils.applicationInstance(config.getHandler());
        return (handler.execute(exception, config, mapping, form,
                            request, response));
    } catch (Exception e) {
        throw new ServletException(e);
    }

}
```

First, the method searches for an exception configuration—represented as an
`ExceptionConfig` object—for the exception type. It searches for a local declarative
exception; if none can be found, it looks for a global declarative exception. The
search mechanism takes object inheritance into account—that is, if `FooException`
extends `BarException` and there is an exception element for `BarException`, then
`mapping.findException()` will use that configuration when `FooException` is thrown. If

a declarative exception is found, Struts instantiates the associated `ExceptionHandler` and calls the handler's execute( ) method.

An `ExceptionHandler` mimics an `Action`. Its execute( ) method accepts the same arguments as `Action.execute( )` plus additional arguments for the `Exception` and `ExceptionConfig` objects. You create a custom exception handler by extending the `ExceptionHandler`.

The base `ExceptionHandler` defines two protected methods designed for extension. The first, `logException( )`, is called to log the thrown exception. Here's the source for this method from the `ExceptionHandler` class:

```
protected void logException(Exception e){
    log.debug(messages.getMessage("exception.log"), e);
}
```

If you need to provide custom logging behavior, you can override this method; however, you should investigate the Struts logging mechanism before you start adding a lot of custom code (see Recipe 13.2).

The second protected method, `storeException( )`, is somewhat misnamed because it stores an `ActionMessage` (`ActionError` in Struts 1.1), created for the exception in the `ExceptionHandler.execute( )` method, in the `HttpServletRequest` or `HttpSession`. Here's the source for this method from the `ExceptionHandler` class:

```
protected void storeException(
        HttpServletRequest request,
        String property,
        ActionMessage error,
        ActionForward forward,
        String scope) {

    ActionMessages errors = new ActionMessages( );
    errors.add(property, error);

    if ("request".equals(scope)) {
        request.setAttribute(Globals.ERROR_KEY, errors);
    } else {
        request.getSession( ).setAttribute(Globals.ERROR_KEY, errors);
    }
}
```

The errors are stored in the request or session based on the value of the scope attribute for the declarative exception. You override `storeException( )` if you want to change or augment the base behavior. For example, let's say you wanted to store the error message in a database:

```
protected void storeException(HttpServletRequest request, String property,
        ActionMessage error, ActionForward forward, String scope) {
    MessageResources msgRes =
        MessageResources.getMessageResources("ApplicationResources");
    String msg = msgRes.getMessage(error.getKey( ));
```

```
        saveMessage(msg);
        super.storeException(request, property, error, forward, scope);
    }

    private void saveMessage(String msg) {
        // store error message in database ...
    }
```

If you need to do more than customize the logging or storing of the exception, you will need to override the execute( ) method. Start by cutting and pasting the code from the base ExceptionHandler's execute( ) method, shown in Example 9-5, into your handler's execute( ) method and modify as needed.

Example 9-5. Base ExceptionHandler's execute method

```
public ActionForward execute(
        Exception ex,
        ExceptionConfig ae,
        ActionMapping mapping,
        ActionForm formInstance,
        HttpServletRequest request,
        HttpServletResponse response)
        throws ServletException {

    ActionForward forward = null;
    ActionMessage error = null;
    String property = null;

    // Build the forward from the exception mapping if it exists
    // or from the form input
    if (ae.getPath( ) != null) {
        forward = new ActionForward(ae.getPath( ));
    } else {
        forward = mapping.getInputForward( );
    }

    // Figure out the error
    if (ex instanceof ModuleException) {
        error = ((ModuleException) ex).getActionMessage( );
        property = ((ModuleException) ex).getProperty( );
    } else {
        error = new ActionMessage(ae.getKey(), ex.getMessage( ));
        property = error.getKey( );
    }

    logException(ex);

    // Store the exception
    request.setAttribute(Globals.EXCEPTION_KEY, ex);
    storeException(request, property, error, forward, ae.getScope( ));

    return forward;

}
```

The execute( ) method takes the following steps:

1. The forward path is determined from the ExceptionConfig. If no path is specified, then the action's input path is used (accessed using mapping.getInputForward( )).

2. If the exception is a ModuleException, the contained ActionMessage is retrieved. Otherwise, a new ActionMessage is generated using the key from the ExceptionConfig.

3. The exception is logged using the logException( ) method.

4. The exception is added as an attribute to the HttpServletRequest.

5. The error is stored by calling storeException( ).

6. The forward is returned.

The ActionMessage generation (step 2) is a common function you might want to customize. Recipe 9.3 shows an example of this.

See Also

If you want to change the logging of exceptions, consider using the customization features of Struts' logging mechanism instead of a custom exception handler. Recipe 13.2 has details on this approach. You can find information at *http://struts.apache.org/ userGuide/configuration.html#config_logging*.

The Struts User's Guide discusses custom exception handlers in the section found at *http://struts.apache.org/userGuide/building_controller.html#exception_handler*.

Recipe 9.1 shows you how to configure exception handling in your *struts-config.xml* file. Recipe 9.3 shows a more ambitious use of customized exception handling.

9.3   Using Exception Error Codes

Problem

You want to use an exception class that accepts a logical error code or key and optional arguments that can be used to display a localized error message.

Solution

Use or extend my ErrorCodeException, shown in Example 9-6.

Example 9-6. Exception that accepts a numeric error code

```
package com.oreilly.strutsckbk.ch09;

public class ErrorCodeException extends Exception {

    public ErrorCodeException(int code) {
        this.code = code;
```

Example 9-6. Exception that accepts a numeric error code (continued)

```
    }
    public ErrorCodeException(int code, Object[] args) {
        this.code = code;
        this.args = args;
    }
    public ErrorCodeException(int code, Object[] args, String msg) {
        super(msg);
        this.code = code;
        this.args = args;
    }
    public ErrorCodeException(int code, Object[] args, String msg, Throwable cause) {
        super(msg, cause);
        this.code = code;
        this.args = args;
    }

    public int getCode( ) {
        return code;
    }

    public Object[] getArgs( ) {
        return args;
    }
    private Object[] args;
    private int code;
}
```

Use my `ErrorCodeExceptionHandler`, shown in Example 9-7, to handle these exception types.

Example 9-7. Exception handler for the ErrorCodeException

```
package com.oreilly.strutsckbk.ch09;

import javax.servlet.ServletException;
import javax.servlet.http.HttpServletRequest;
import javax.servlet.http.HttpServletResponse;

import org.apache.struts.Globals;
import org.apache.struts.action.ActionForm;
import org.apache.struts.action.ActionForward;
import org.apache.struts.action.ActionMapping;
import org.apache.struts.action.ActionMessage;
import org.apache.struts.action.ExceptionHandler;
import org.apache.struts.config.ExceptionConfig;

public class ErrorCodeExceptionHandler extends ExceptionHandler {

    public ActionForward execute(
            Exception ex,
            ExceptionConfig ae,
            ActionMapping mapping,
```

Example 9-7. Exception handler for the ErrorCodeException (continued)

```
                ActionForm formInstance,
                HttpServletRequest request,
                HttpServletResponse response)
                throws ServletException {

        if (!(ex instanceof ErrorCodeException)) {
            return super.execute(ex, ae, mapping, formInstance, request, response);
        }

        ErrorCodeException errCodeEx =(ErrorCodeException) ex;
        ActionForward forward = null;
        ActionMessage error = null;
        String property = null;

        // Build the forward from the exception mapping if it exists
        // or from the form input
        if (ae.getPath( ) != null) {
            forward = new ActionForward(ae.getPath( ));
        } else {
            forward = mapping.getInputForward( );
        }

        ErrorCodeException ece =(ErrorCodeException) ex;
        String code = Integer.toString(ece.getCode( ));
        error = new ActionMessage(code, ece.getArgs( ));
        property = error.getKey( );

        logException(ex);

        // Store the exception
        request.setAttribute(Globals.EXCEPTION_KEY, ex);
        storeException(request, property, error, forward, ae.getScope( ));

        return forward;
    }
}
```

Finally, declare a global exception handler in your *struts-config.xml* for this exception:

```
<global-exceptions>
    ...
    <exception key="error.exception"
            type="com.oreilly.strutsckbk.ch09.ErrorCodeException"
         handler="com.oreilly.strutsckbk.ch09.ErrorCodeExceptionHandler"
            path="/error_page.jsp"/>
</global-exceptions>
```

Discussion

A lot of large software applications report problems using error codes as well as text. The Oracle database reports errors using an error code formatted as ORA-*9999*. You can use an Oracle utility program to retrieve the meaning of the error code. This approach allows the application to localize text messages based on the user's language and country. The ErrorCodeException shown in Example 9-6 can be used in a similar manner in your Struts application. You create this exception class using a numeric error code and an optional set of Object arguments. The error code serves as a key for retrieving a localized message from your MessageResources properties file. The arguments are used at runtime as substitution parameters in that message.

When an Action or business service creates an ErrorCodeException, it can populate the exception with an appropriate error code and an array of arguments for message substitution. The ErrorCodeExceptionHandler shown in Example 9-7 is designed to process ErrorCodeExceptions. The code in the execute( ) method was originally copied from the Struts base ExceptionHandler (org.apache.struts.action.ExceptionHandler) and modified as needed. This custom handler first checks if the error is of type ErrorCodeException; if not, it allows the Struts exception handler to process the Exception by calling super.execute( ). Otherwise, the exception is handled as follows:

1. The path to forward to is determined from the ExceptionConfig. If no path is specified, the action's input path is used (accessed using mapping.getInputForward( )).

2. The error code is retrieved from the ErrorCodeException and converted to a String.

3. An ActionMessage is created using the error code String and the Object array from the ErrorCodeException.

4. The exception is logged using the logException( ) method (implemented by the super class).

5. The exception is added as an attribute to the HttpServletRequest.

6. The error is stored by calling storeException( ) (implemented by the super class).

7. The forward is returned.

Only steps 2 and 3 are specific to this handler. The other steps are identical to the handling in the base ExceptionHandler.

Though not required, you can extend the ErrorCodeException class to create exception types for specific functional areas of your application. Using this approach allows you to control exception processing based on type, yet give the benefits provided by using an error code and message arguments.

If you have an existing application that relies heavily on predefined error codes, this Solution can help bridge the gap with exception handling. The error codes and corresponding error messages can be defined in your application's default MessageResources file, or they can be stored in their own properties file. Since you are coding the exception handler, you can do it how you want.

The ErrorCodeException and corresponding handler are useful if you need to localize the generated message in support of internationalization. Since the exception handler

---

Exception Handling 101

Use only the *type* of the exception—not its properties—to drive exception-handling logic in Java code. In other words, you don't want to have try...catch blocks such as the following:

```
try {
    callService();
} catch (ErrorCodeException ece) {
        // bad code!
    switch (ece.getCode()) {
        case -1:
            return
                mapping.findForward("somewhere.jsp");
        case 100:
            // do something
        case 110:
            // do something else
    }
    throw ece;
}
```

Using the properties of an exception to control the flow of your application can cause serious performance problems. When an exception occurs, the Java Virtual Machine must wait on any method called in the try block to complete before control is yielded to the catch block, essentially forcing synchronization of these methods. A better approach is to subclass the ErrorCodeException and use a catch block for each type.

---

uses MessageResources, the message can be localized by creating a properties file for specific locales.

See Also

Best practices for localizing exceptions have been discussed a number of times on the struts-user mailing list. You'll find the thread at *http://marc.theaimsgroup.com/?l=struts-user&m=109474569119868&w=2* to be particularly interesting.

Creating a custom exception handler is easier than you think. See Recipe 9.2 for details.

9.4   Using a Global Error Page

Problem

Your application should display the same error page for any server error or uncaught exception thrown from a Struts Action, a servlet, or a JSP page.

Solution

Declare a global error page, such as the one shown in Example 9-8, to handle all exceptions and errors in your *web.xml* file as well as your *struts-config.xml* file.

Example 9-8. Global JSP error page

```
<!DOCTYPE HTML PUBLIC "-//W3C//DTD HTML 4.01 Transitional//EN">
<%@ page language="java" isErrorPage="true" %>
<%@ taglib uri="http://java.sun.com/jstl/core" prefix="c" %>
<%@ taglib uri="http://java.sun.com/jstl/fmt" prefix="fmt"%>
<%@ taglib uri="http://struts.apache.org/tags-bean" prefix="bean" %>
<%@ taglib uri="http://struts.apache.org/tags-html" prefix="html" %>
<%@ taglib uri="http://struts.apache.org/tags-logic" prefix="logic" %>

<html:html>
<head>
    <title>Struts Cookbook Chapter 9 : Global error page</title>
    <style type="text/css">
        h2{background:darkblue;color:white}
        h3{background:darkblue;color:white}
    </style>
</head>
<body>
<div align="center">
    <c:choose>
        <c:when test="${not empty pageContext.exception}">
            <c:set var="problemType">JSP Exception</c:set>
            <c:set var="appException" value="${pageContext.exception}"/>
            <c:set var="causeException" value="${appException.cause}"/>
        </c:when>
        <c:when test="${not empty requestScope['javax.servlet.error.exception']}">
            <c:set var="problemType">Servlet Exception</c:set>
            <c:set var="appException" value="${requestScope['javax.servlet.error.
exception']}"/>
            <c:set var="causeException" value="${appException.rootCause}"/>
        </c:when>
        <c:when test="${not empty requestScope['org.apache.struts.action.EXCEPTION']}">
            <c:set var="problemType">Struts Exception</c:set>
            <c:set var="appException" value="${requestScope['org.apache.struts.action.
EXCEPTION']}"/>
            <c:set var="causeException" value="${appException.cause}"/>
        </c:when>
        <c:otherwise>
            <c:set var="problemType">Unidentified Server Error</c:set>
        </c:otherwise>
    </c:choose>
        <!-- end determine error -->

<!-- start framework -->
<table cellpadding="0" cellspacing="0" border="0" width="750">
    <tr>
        <td valign="top" colspan="2">
```

Example 9-8. Global JSP error page (continued)

```
<table cellpadding="4" cellspacing="0" border="0" width="100%">
    <tr valign="top">
        <td>
            <!-- start user review -->
            <table cellpadding="4" cellspacing="0" border="0" width="100%">
                <tr>
                    <td>
                        <h2>System problem</h2>
                    </td>
                </tr>
            </table>
            <table cellpadding="2" cellspacing="1" border="0" width="80%">
                <tr>
                    <td colspan="2">
                        A system error has occured. If the
                        problem persists, please contact the User Helpdesk.
                    </td>
                </tr>
                <tr><td colspan="2">
                    <html:errors/>
                </td></tr>
                <tr valign="top">
                    <td>
                        <b>Problem type</b>
                        <br/><c:out value="${problemType}"/>
                    </td>
                    <td>
                        <b>Problem details</b>
                        <c:if test="${not empty
                         requestScope['javax.servlet.error.message']}">
                         <br/>
                        <c:out value=
                          "${requestScope['javax.servlet.error.message']}"
                        />
                        </c:if>
                        <c:if test="${not empty appException}">
                            <br/><c:out value="${appException.message}"/> 
                        </c:if>
                    </td>
                </tr>
                <c:if test="${not empty causeException}">
                <tr>
                    <td>
                        <b>Caused by</b>
                        <br/><c:out value="${causeException}"/>
                    </td>
                    <td>
                        <b>Cause details</b>
                        <br/><c:out value="${causeException.message}"/> 
                    </td>
                </tr>
                </c:if>
```

Example 9-8. Global JSP error page (continued)

```
        </table>
        <table id="showDetailsLinkDiv" style="{display:inline}"
            cellpadding="2" cellspacing="1" border="0" width="80%">
          <tr>
            <td align="left">
              [ <a href="javascript:showDetails()">Show details</a> ]
            </td>
          </tr>
        </table>
        <table id="hideDetailsLinkDiv" style="{display:none}"
            cellpadding="2" cellspacing="1" border="0" width="80%">
          <tr>
            <td align="left">
              [ <a href="javascript:hideDetails()">Hide details</a> ]
            </td>
          </tr>
        </table>
<!-- begin details -->
        <div id="stackTraceDiv" style="{display:none}">
        <c:if test="${not empty appException}">
          <p></p>
          <table cellpadding="4" cellspacing="0"
              border="0" width="100%">
            <tr>
              <td>
                    <h3>Exception stack trace</h3>
              </td>
            </tr>
          </table>
          <b><c:out value="${appException}"/></b>
          <br/>
          <table align="center" cellpadding="0" cellspacing="0"
              border="0" width="90%" class="pod">
            <c:forEach var="stackItem"
                    items="${appException.stackTrace}">
              <tr><td><c:out value="${stackItem}"/></td></tr>
            </c:forEach>
          </table>
        </c:if>
        <c:if test="${not empty causeException}">
          <p></p>
          <table cellpadding="4" cellspacing="0"
              border="0" width="100%">
            <tr>
              <td>
                    <h3>Cause stack trace</h3>
              </td>
            </tr>
          </table>
          <b><c:out value="${causeException}"/></b>
          <br/>
          <table align="center" cellpadding="0" cellspacing="0"
```

Example 9-8. Global JSP error page (continued)

```
                        border="0" width="90%" class="pod">
                    <c:forEach var="stackItem"
                        items="${causeException.stackTrace}">
                        <tr><td><c:out value="${stackItem}"/></td></tr>
                    </c:forEach>
                  </table>
                </c:if>
                </div>
              <!-- end details -->
                </td>
            </tr>
          </table>
          </td>
      </tr>
</table>

    <script language="javascript">
      function showDetails( ) {
        document.getElementById("showDetailsLinkDiv").style.display = "none";
        document.getElementById("hideDetailsLinkDiv").style.display = "inline";
        document.getElementById("stackTraceDiv").style.display = "inline";
      }
      function hideDetails( ) {
        document.getElementById("showDetailsLinkDiv").style.display = "inline";
        document.getElementById("hideDetailsLinkDiv").style.display = "none";
        document.getElementById("stackTraceDiv").style.display = "none";
      }
    </script>

</div>
</body>
</html:html>
```

Create an error-page element for handling HTTP Status 500 errors in your *web.xml* file, specifying the location as the error page:

```
<error-page>
    <error-code>500</error-code>
    <location>/error.jsp</location>
</error-page>
```

For exceptions thrown from Struts Actions, create a global exception handler for exceptions of type java.lang.Exception in the *struts-config.xml* file with the path set to the error page:

```
<global-exceptions>
    <exception key="error.general"
            type="java.lang.Exception"
            path="/error.jsp"/>
    ...
</global-exceptions>
```

Discussion

Exception handling tends to be an afterthought. You're sitting there testing the path for your application when a 500 error pops up and your boss says "Ugh. That's ugly. I want the same page to come up no matter what the problem and don't make the details obvious, but the users need to be able to display the details so they can tell tech support what happened."

The JSP shown in Example 9-8 can be used for this because it is designed to handle any type of exception that can be thrown by the container. If the exception has a causing exception, the details can be shown for that exception as well. Figure 9-1 shows the display when a `NullPointerException` is thrown from an `Action`.

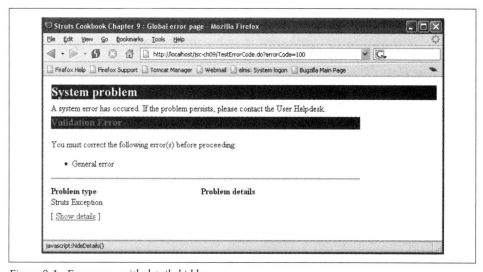

Figure 9-1. Error page with details hidden

Clicking "Show Details" reveals the stack trace, as shown in Figure 9-2.

When a `ServletException` containing a nested root cause is thrown by a servlet, the error page shows the cause details as well. Figure 9-3 shows the error page with the stack trace details shown.

If you scroll down the page in Figure 9-3, you will see the stack trace for the causing exception, as shown in Figure 9-4.

To handle any situation, the error page determines what kind of exception has been thrown. The JSTL `c:choose` block contains the following logic:

```
<c:choose>
    <c:when test="${not empty pageContext.exception}">
        <c:set var="problemType">JSP Exception</c:set>
        <c:set var="appException" value="${pageContext.exception}"/>
        <c:set var="causeException" value="${appException.cause}"/>
```

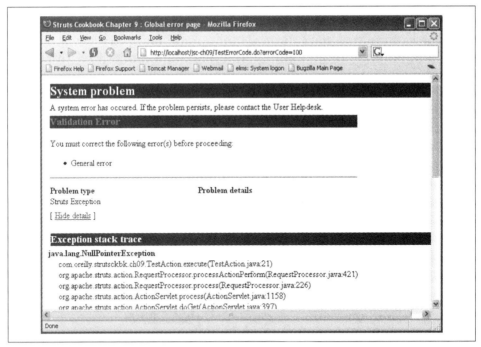

Figure 9-2. Error page with details shown

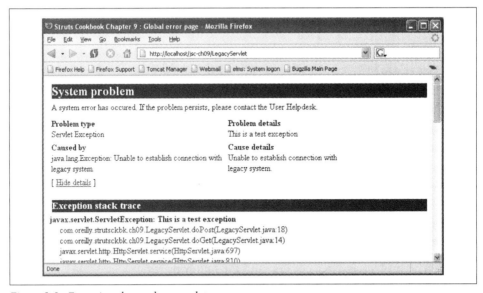

Figure 9-3. Exception thrown by a servlet

```
    </c:when>
    <c:when test="${not empty requestScope['javax.servlet.error.exception']}">
        <c:set var="problemType">Servlet Exception</c:set>
```

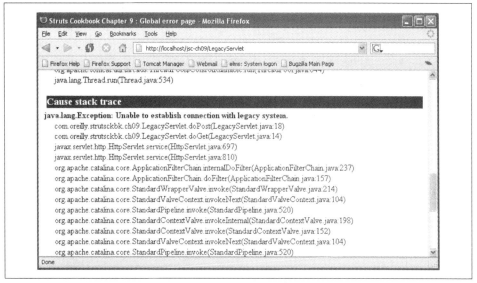

Figure 9-4. Stack trace of causing exception

```
            <c:set var="appException"
                value="${requestScope['javax.servlet.error.exception']}"/>
            <c:set var="causeException" value="${appException.rootCause}"/>
        </c:when>
        <c:when test="${not empty
                requestScope['org.apache.struts.action.EXCEPTION']}">
            <c:set var="problemType">Struts Exception</c:set>
            <c:set var="appException"
                value="${requestScope['org.apache.struts.action.EXCEPTION']}"/>
            <c:set var="causeException" value="${appException.cause}"/>
        </c:when>
        <c:otherwise>
            <c:set var="problemType">Unidentified Server Error</c:set>
        </c:otherwise>
    </c:choose>
```

This block determines if the error is a `JSPException`, `ServletException`, or an exception thrown by Struts. For each exception, the causing exception is retrieved.

 You get the causing exception for a `ServletException` using the `rootCause` property instead of the normal cause property.

The rest of the page displays the exception message and exception stack trace for the exception and its cause, if any. For exceptions thrown by Struts, the `html:errors` tag renders any error messages. JavaScript provides the magic for showing and hiding the exception details. The trick is to put the stack trace details in a `div` tag and then use a JavaScript function to toggle the CSS `display` style from `none` to `inline`.

The one common error this page doesn't handle is an HTTP Status 404 (Page Not Found) response. If you wanted to use this page for handling these errors, add an additional error-page element to the *web.xml*. However, you will probably want to handle this error differently, perhaps forwarding to the main menu page of your application or some other location.

This solution works well for intranet applications; for external applications, though, you will probably want to display less information for security purposes. One thing you can do is use this error page in development and testing and then replace it with a terser version when you deploy to production.

See Also

Recipe 9.1 shows you the details on configuring a global exception using Struts declarative exception handling. Recipe 9.6 shows alternatives to `html:errors` for displaying error messages. Recipe 13.5 shows you a JSP page that you can use specifically for debugging.

For other approaches to localizing exception messages, take a look at some guidelines from Sun's Java Blueprints at *http://java.sun.com/blueprints/guidelines/designing_enterprise_applications_2e/i18n/i18n8.html*.

Brian Goetz's excellent series on exception handling from *JavaWorld* is a must-read for any Java developer. He discusses the use of message catalogs for exception localization in Part 3 of the series. You can find the entire series at *http://www.javaworld.com/javaworld/jw-08-2001/jw-0803-exceptions.html*.

9.5 Reporting Errors and Messages from an Action

Problem

You want to display error messages to the user when things go wrong and success messages when things go right.

Solution

For Struts 1.1, use `ActionErrors` for reporting errors and `ActionMessages` for informational messages. For Struts 1.2, use `ActionMessages` for informational messages and errors.

Discussion

Struts gives you a least four classes and three custom tags for creating, storing, and displaying errors and messages. In Struts 1.1, the `ActionErrors` class is used to hold a collection of errors, represented by `ActionError` instances. Each `ActionError` consists

of a key to be looked up from the default MessageResources bundle and an optional
set of Objects (up to four) to be used as parameters for message substitution. The
Action class in Example 9-9 shows typical usage of ActionErrors.

Example 9-9. Creating ActionErrors from an Action

```
package com.oreilly.strutsckbk.ch09;

import javax.servlet.http.HttpServletRequest;
import javax.servlet.http.HttpServletResponse;

import org.apache.commons.beanutils.PropertyUtils;
import org.apache.struts.Globals;
import org.apache.struts.action.Action;
import org.apache.struts.action.ActionError;
import org.apache.struts.action.ActionErrors;
import org.apache.struts.action.ActionForm;
import org.apache.struts.action.ActionForward;
import org.apache.struts.action.ActionMapping;

public class RegistrationAction extends Action {

    public ActionForward execute(ActionMapping mapping,
                                 ActionForm form,
                                 HttpServletRequest request,
                                 HttpServletResponse response)
            throws Exception {

        ActionErrors errors = new ActionErrors();

        String username = (String) PropertyUtils.getSimpleProperty(
                                        form, "username");
        String password = (String) PropertyUtils.getSimpleProperty(
                                        form, "password");

        if (username.equals(password)) {
            ActionError error = new ActionError(
                    "error.register.sameAsPassword", username);
            // Use  Action Message with Struts 1.2
            //ActionMessage error = new ActionMessage(
            //      "error.register.sameAsPassword", username);
            errors.add("username", error);
        }

        if (!errors.isEmpty()) {
            saveErrors(request, errors);
            return mapping.getInputForward();
        }
        User user = new User();
        user.setUsername(username);
        user.setPassword(password);
```

Example 9-9. Creating ActionErrors from an Action (continued)

```
        SecurityService service = new SecurityService( );
        service.add(user);

        return mapping.findForward("success");
    }
}
```

If you need to create informational messages, use the `ActionMessages` and `ActionMessage` classes in a similar fashion, as shown in Example 9-10.

Example 9-10. Creating ActionMessages from an Action

```
package com.oreilly.strutsckbk.ch09;

import javax.servlet.http.HttpServletRequest;
import javax.servlet.http.HttpServletResponse;

import org.apache.commons.beanutils.PropertyUtils;
import org.apache.struts.action.Action;
import org.apache.struts.action.ActionForm;
import org.apache.struts.action.ActionForward;
import org.apache.struts.action.ActionMapping;
import org.apache.struts.action.ActionMessage;
import org.apache.struts.action.ActionMessages;

public class LoginAction extends Action {

    public ActionForward execute(ActionMapping mapping,
                                 ActionForm form,
                                 HttpServletRequest request,
                                 HttpServletResponse response)
            throws Exception {

        ActionMessages messages = new ActionMessages( );

        String username = (String) PropertyUtils.getSimpleProperty(
                                            form, "username");
        String password = (String) PropertyUtils.getSimpleProperty(
                                            form, "password");
        SecurityService service = new SecurityService( );
        service.authenticate( username, password);

        User user = new User( );
        user.setUsername(username);
        request.getSession( ).setAttribute("user", user);

        ActionMessage message = new ActionMessage(
                "message.login.success", username);

        messages.add(ActionMessages.GLOBAL_MESSAGE, message);
```

Example 9-10. Creating ActionMessages from an Action (continued)

```
        if (!messages.isEmpty()) {
            saveMessages( request, messages );
        }

        return mapping.findForward("success");
    }
}
```

Though you'll find little difference in the APIs you use to create errors or messages, the approaches for rendering errors or messages can differ. You can display all errors on a JSP page this way:

```
<html:errors/>
```

You would think you could do the same thing with the html:messages tag, but the html:messages tag behaves differently than the html:errors tag. By default, the html: messages tag retrieves the values stored as errors—not messages—from the HttpServletRequest. You must explicitly set the message attribute to *true* to retrieve values stored as messages.

 The html:messages tag was originally created to display error messages without requiring that the message resources contain HTML. After ActionMessages were added to Struts, the html:messages tag was amended to support display of information messages in addition to error messages.

Unlike the html:errors tag, the html:messages tag is a looping tag, like logic: iterate. The tag iterates through ActionErrors, ActionMessages, or an array of strings. The required id attribute defines a page-scoped variable that contains the formatted message. You can use the bean:write or the JSTL c:out tag to display each message:

```
<html:messages message="true" id="msg">
    <c:out value="${msg}"/><br />
</html:messages>
```

Unlike the html:errors tag, the html:messages tag doesn't use a predefined header and footer for display. The presentation details are left to you. Recipe 9.6 shows you some ways to create custom presentation for your errors and messages.

What if you are using Struts 1.2? Well, the ActionError class has been deprecated in favor of ActionMessage in Struts 1.2. On the other hand, ActionErrors has *not* been deprecated; however, in most places you can use an ActionMessages object where you used to use ActionErrors.

To preserve the Struts core API, `ActionErrors` was not deprecated.

So, how do you identify errors versus messages? It depends on the attribute name that they are stored under in the request.

The `saveErrors()` method now accepts `ActionMessages` instead of `ActionErrors`; yet it stores the object in the request as errors using the key identified by the constant `org.apache.struts.Globals.ERROR_KEY`. The `saveMessages()` method accepts `ActionMessages`. It stores the object in the request using the key identified by the `org.apache.struts.Globals.MESSAGE_KEY` constant. The `html:errors` and `html:messages` tags are used in Struts 1.2 just like in Struts 1.1.

If you have ever needed to store messages HTTP session, you can use a new method, added in Struts 1.2, of the base `Action` class:

```
saveMessages(HttpSession session, ActionMessages messages);
```

This method was added to provide a workaround for message display when the rendering page is the result of a redirect instead of a forward. When the messages are saved in the servlet request, the JSP page that displays those messages must be the result of a forward; if the JSP were redirected to the messages would be lost. With the new `saveMessages()` method, messages are saved in the session and are therefore available whether the page is the result of a forward or a redirect.

 You can redirect instead of forward to the "success page" to prevent double-submission problems. See Recipe 7.9 for more details.

Now that the messages are saved in the session, what's to prevent them from showing up on a page where they shouldn't? The Struts developers anticipated this problem. The `ActionMessages` class provides the `isAccessed()` method to indicate if the messages have been displayed (accessed) or not. The `RequestProcessor`, in the new `processCachedMessages()` method, checks this value and removes any messages stored in the session that have been accessed. So, though you store the messages in the session, they will be cleaned on the next request after they have been displayed.

Here's how you would use the new `saveMessages` method in the `Action` shown in Example 9-10:

```
if (!messages.isEmpty()) {
    saveMessages( request.getSession(true), messages );
}
```

You can change the forward for the success page to a redirect:

```
<forward name="success" path="/login_success.jsp" redirect="true"/>
```

Your messages will still be available on the success page, and you don't have to worry about double postings.

See Also

Struts 1.2 introduced the ability to have session-scoped action messages. The Struts 1.2 release notes at *http://struts.apache.org/userGuide/release-notes.html* describe this feature.

You can use the `html:messages` tag to render errors or messages; see Recipe 9.6 for additional details on this and other related tags.

9.6   Formatting Error Messages

Problem

Your application requires a custom look and feel for error messages beyond the abilities of the `html:errors` tag.

Solution

Use the `logic:messagesPresent` and the `html:messages` tags to display the error messages in a custom format. The JSP fragment (*errors.inc.jsp*) shown in Example 9-11 can be included on any page that may need to display errors.

Example 9-11. Custom error display

```
<logic:messagesPresent>
<table border="1" bgcolor="orange" width="100%" align="center">
    <tr><td>
        <p>
            <img src="/images/icon-warning.gif" border="0"
              vspace="2" hspace="10" align="center">
            WARNING: <bean:message key="errors.heading"/>
        </p>
        <ul>
            <html:messages id="error">
                <li><bean:write name="error"/></li>
            </html:messages>
        </ul>
    </td></tr>
</table>
<p>
</logic:messagesPresent>
```

 The images used in the examples are included with the online source.

Discussion

Errors displayed using the JSP code in Example 9-11 result in a display similar to Figure 9-5.

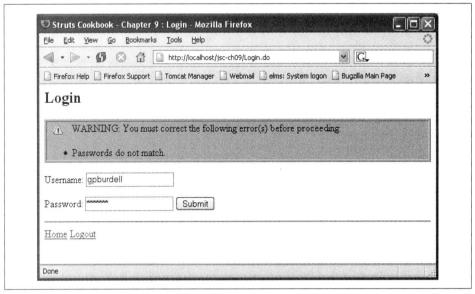

Figure 9-5. Custom formatted errors

Though the `html:errors` tag is a convenient way of displaying error messages, it's fairly restrictive in its formatting. By default, it displays all errors for a page, starting with a header markup, then each error message, and ending with footer markup.

 Using the `property` attribute, you can tell the `html:errors` tag to display error messages for a specific field. This ability is commonly used to display validation errors beside the invalid input field.

This tag relies on predefined messages in your `MessageResources` to control the look and feel of the display. These messages are shown in Table 9-1.

Table 9-1. html:errors formatting resources

Message key	Description	Sample value
errors.header	Markup rendered for the header	`<font color="red"> Validation Errors<ul>`
errors.prefix	Markup rendered before each error message	`<li>`
errors.suffix	Markup rendered after each error message	`</li>`
errors.footer	Markup rendered for the footer	`</ul></font><p />`

Though you can use these special message resources to format errors many ways, having HTML markup in a properties file spells trouble. After all, one of the goals of using an MVC framework such as Struts is to separate—not commingle—data and its presentation.

The Solution presents an approach where the entire markup for presentation is contained on the JSP page. First, the `logic:messagesPresent` tag is used to determine if any errors will display. This tag processes its tag body if it can find a scoped variable stored under the `org.apache.struts.Global.ERROR_KEY` key. The tag body contains an HTML table used for formatting. A warning icon and message are displayed. Then, the `html:messages` tag lists each error message:

```
<ul>
    <html:messages id="error">
        <li><bean:write name="error"/></li>
    </html:messages>
</ul>
```

The `html:messages` tag doesn't render the message; rather, it acts like the `logic:iterate` tag. It iterates over a set of errors, creating a page-scoped variable containing the error message with a name equal to the value of the `id` attribute. The error message can be rendered using the `bean:write` or `c:out` tags.

So what would you do if you needed to display different types of messages? Say you wanted to display validation errors as warnings, and exceptions as more severe problems. All you need to do is store the different messages in the request using attribute names of your own choosing. Start by creating a base `Action`, like the one shown in Example 9-12, which provides methods that save the different errors in the servlet request. If you are using a base `Action`, you can add the methods shown in Example 9-12 to your own class.

Example 9-12. Base Action for saving custom error types

```java
package com.oreilly.strutsckbk.ch09;

import javax.servlet.http.HttpServletRequest;

import org.apache.struts.action.Action;
import org.apache.struts.action.ActionMessages;

public class BaseAction extends Action {

    public static final String APP_WARNING_KEY = "APP_WARNING_KEY";
    public static final String APP_ERROR_KEY = "APP_ERROR_KEY";

    protected void saveAppWarnings(HttpServletRequest request,
                                   ActionMessages messages) {
        saveAppMessages(request, messages, APP_WARNING_KEY);
    }
```

Example 9-12. Base Action for saving custom error types (continued)

```
    protected void saveAppErrors(HttpServletRequest request,
                                 ActionMessages messages) {
        saveAppMessages(request, messages, APP_ERROR_KEY);
    }

    private void saveAppMessages(HttpServletRequest request,
                                 ActionMessages messages, String key) {
        // Remove any messages attribute if none are required
        if ((messages == null) || messages.isEmpty( )) {
            request.removeAttribute(key);
            return;
        }

        // Save the messages we need
        request.setAttribute(key, messages);
    }
}
```

Actions that subclass this base Action call these specialized methods to store the messages based on severity. The custom Action shown in Example 9-13 subclasses this base Action, calling the saveAppWarnings and saveAppErrors methods as needed.

Example 9-13. Custom error handling by an Action

```
package com.oreilly.strutsckbk.ch09;

import javax.servlet.http.HttpServletRequest;
import javax.servlet.http.HttpServletResponse;

import org.apache.commons.beanutils.PropertyUtils;
import org.apache.struts.action.ActionForm;
import org.apache.struts.action.ActionForward;
import org.apache.struts.action.ActionMapping;
import org.apache.struts.action.ActionMessage;
import org.apache.struts.action.ActionMessages;

public class ValidatingLoginAction extends BaseAction {

    public ActionForward execute(ActionMapping mapping,
                                 ActionForm form,
                                 HttpServletRequest request,
                                 HttpServletResponse response)
            throws Exception {

        ActionMessages appWarnings = form.validate(mapping, request);
        saveAppWarnings(request, appWarnings);

        String username = (String)
                PropertyUtils.getSimpleProperty(form, "username");
        String password = (String)
                PropertyUtils.getSimpleProperty(form, "password");
```

Example 9-13. Custom error handling by an Action (continued)

```
        ActionMessages appErrors = new ActionMessages( );

        try {
            SecurityService service = new SecurityService( );
            service.authenticate( username, password);
        }
        catch (PasswordMatchException e) {
            appErrors.add("password", new ActionMessage("error.password.match"));
        }

        saveAppErrors(request, appErrors);

        if (!appWarnings.isEmpty( ) || !appErrors.isEmpty( )) {
            return mapping.getInputForward( );
        }

        User user = new User( );
        user.setUsername(username);
        request.getSession( ).setAttribute("user", user);

        ActionMessages messages = new ActionMessages( );
        ActionMessage message = new ActionMessage("message.login.success",
                                                  username);

        messages.add(ActionMessages.GLOBAL_MESSAGE, message);

        if (!messages.isEmpty( )) {
            saveMessages( request.getSession(true), messages );
        }

        return mapping.findForward("success");
    }
}
```

If you look closely at the Action in Example 9-13, you'll see that it does something kind of strange: The ActionForm's validate method is called within the execute( ) method. Why would you do something like this? Well, remember from the requirements, you want to store validation errors as warnings; in other words, the errors should be stored under a custom request attribute name. The only way to accomplish this is for the Action to call the ActionForm's validate method. Since your Action controls the validation workflow, configure the corresponding action mapping in the *struts-config.xml* file so Struts doesn't call the ActionForm's validate method:

```
    <action    path="/ValidatingLogin"
               type="com.oreilly.strutsckbk.ch09.ValidatingLoginAction"
               scope="request"
               name="LoginForm"
             validate="false"
               input="/validating_login.jsp">
        <forward name="success" path="/login_success.jsp" redirect="true"/>
    </action>
```

Now that you've got the warnings and errors being stored under separate attribute names, you can create a common JSP fragment to display them. The JSP fragment (*errors2.inc.jsp*) shown in Example 9-14 uses the name attribute of the logic:messagesPresent tag and html:messages tag to indicate the type of error to process.

Example 9-14. JSP fragment for displaying custom errors

```
<logic:messagesPresent name="APP_ERROR_KEY">
    <table border="1" bgcolor="orange" width="100%" align="center"><tr><td>
    <p>
        <img src="/images/icon-alert.gif" border="0"
          vspace="2" hspace="10" align="center">
        <bean:message key="errors.heading"/>
    </p>
    <ul>
        <html:messages id="error" name="APP_ERROR_KEY">
            <li><bean:write name="error"/></li>
        </html:messages>
    </ul>
</td></tr></table>
<p>
</logic:messagesPresent>
<logic:messagesPresent name="APP_WARNING_KEY">
    <table border="1" bgcolor="yellow" width="100%" align="center"><tr><td>
    <p>
        <img src="/images/icon-warning.gif" border="0"
          vspace="2" hspace="10" align="center">
        <bean:message key="warnings.heading"/>
    </p>
    <ul>
        <html:messages id="error" name="APP_WARNING_KEY">
            <li><bean:write name="error"/></li>
        </html:messages>
    </ul>
</td></tr></table>
<p>
</logic:messagesPresent>
```

Now, when the errors are displayed, you'll see a page like the one shown in Figure 9-6.

If you're new to web development, this last example may seem a bit extreme, but it demonstrates the flexibility afforded by Struts. If you don't like the way Struts handles errors, then you can do it yourself. As long as you utilize the Struts APIs, you'll find that the Struts tags can cope with most customizations in an intelligent and logical way.

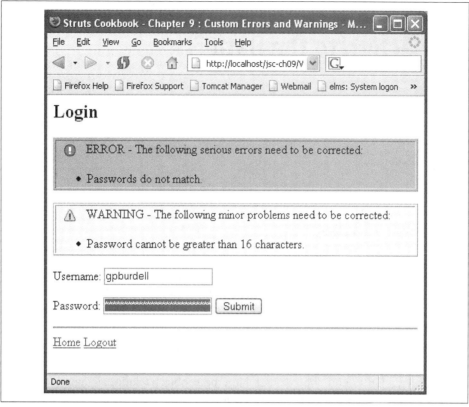

Figure 9-6. Display of different error types

See Also

Ted Husted discusses custom error formatting in his invaluable set of Struts Tips. The specific tip (#17) can be found at *http://husted.com/struts/tips/017.html*.

Rick Reumann, a frequent poster to the *struts-user* mailing list and all-around good guy, prefers to call the ActionForm's validate method as he explains in the archived posting at *http://marc.theaimsgroup.com/?l=struts-user&m=109242668231755&w=2*.

If you are using declarative exception handling, you can use a similar approach for storing the exception error message by creating a custom exception handler. Custom exception handlers are discussed in Recipe 9.2.

## CHAPTER 10

Connecting to the Data

10.0 Introduction

You often hear Struts referred to as a *model-view-controller* (MVC) framework for web applications. Struts *can* help you build web applications that separate the data (model) from the presentation (view); however, Struts doesn't provide a framework for the model. Rather, it supports custom Actions which broker the *interaction* between the view and model.

This chapter contains several recipes that offer different approaches to interacting with your application's model. You will find solutions related to accessing relational data by using JDBC and the popular Hibernate object/relational mapping framework. This chapter shows you ways to create pluggable interfaces for your business services. Finally, this chapter demonstrates some techniques for working with XML-based data stored in flat files.

10.1 Accessing JDBC Data Sources from an Action

Problem

You want to access a data source directly from a Struts Action.

Solution

Don't do it! Only access the data source from within your application's model.

Discussion

Though Struts is referred to as an MVC framework for web applications, Struts doesn't attempt to provide the model of that paradigm. Struts provides only the bridge between the view and the model, Struts Actions. An Action shouldn't access the database; an `Action` shouldn't need to know how the data is stored and accessed. Instead, an `Action` acts as a thin façade to your business services, marshalling data from the view to the model and back. The following FAQ from the Struts web site puts it quite succinctly:

> Ideally, all the database access code should be encapsulated behind the business API classes, so Struts doesn't know what persistence layer you are using (or even if there is a persistence layer). It passes a key or search String and gets back a bean or collection of beans. This lets you use the same business API classes in other environments, and lets you run unit tests against your business API outside of Struts or a HTTP environment.

While Struts does support the `data-source` element for configuring JDBC data sources, the Struts release notes state that this element may not be supported in the future. According to the Struts documentation, you should use the `data-source` element when you need to pass a `javax.sql.DataSource` to a legacy API. This results in a dependency between the `Action` and the persistence layer as illustrated in Figure 10-1.

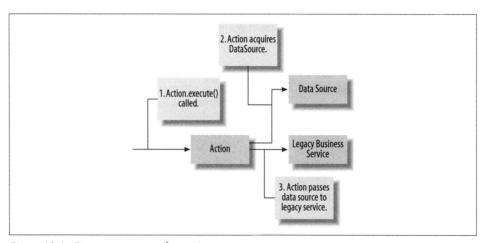

Figure 10-1. Data source access by an Action

A better approach in this situation is to create a façade around the legacy API. The façade provides a data-independent implementation of the legacy API. Internally, the façade is responsible for acquiring the required data source and delegating calls to the legacy service, passing the data source as needed. Your `Actions` can interact with the façade without needing to be bound to the persistence details. This (better) model is shown in Figure 10-2.

The façade-based architecture results in a more flexible system that can adapt from low-level changes to legacy systems without requiring you to rewrite your `Actions`.

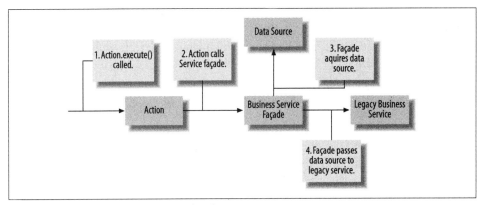

Figure 10-2. Data source by a service façade

See Also

The Struts FAQ on database-related issues can be found at *http://struts.apache.org/faqs/database.html*. For more information on accessing databases, see *Java Database Best Practices* by George Reese (O'Reilly).

10.2 Displaying Relational Data

Problem

You want to display data from a relational database, but you don't know the structure of the data.

Solution

Use the RowSetDynaClass class (org.apache.commons.beanutils.RowSetDynaClass) provided by the Jakarta Commons BeanUtils project.

 The JAR files for BeanUtils are included with the Struts distribution so no additional download is needed.

Start by creating a data access object, like the one shown in Example 10-1, which performs the database query and returns a BeanUtils RowSetDynaClass created from a JDBC result set.

Example 10-1. RowSetDynaClass-based data access object

```
package com.oreilly.strutsckbk.ch05;

import java.sql.Connection;
import java.sql.ResultSet;
```

Example 10-1. RowSetDynaClass-based data access object (continued)

```java
import java.sql.Statement;
import java.sql.DriverManager;

import org.apache.commons.beanutils.RowSetDynaClass;

public class UserDao {

    public RowSetDynaClass getUsersRowSet( ) throws Exception {
        Connection conn = null;
        Statement stmt = null;
        ResultSet rs = null;
        RowSetDynaClass rowSet = null;
        try {
            conn = getConnection( );
            stmt = conn.createStatement( );
            rs = stmt.executeQuery("select * from users");
            rowSet = new RowSetDynaClass(rs);
        }
        finally {
            if (conn != null) conn.close( );
        }
        return rowSet;
    }

    private Connection getConnection( ) throws Exception {
        Class.forName("com.mysql.jdbc.Driver");
        return DriverManager.getConnection("jdbc:mysql://localhost/test");
    }

}
```

Create an Action that retrieves the RowSetDynaClass from the data access object and stores it in the servlet request. The Action shown in Example 10-2 retrieves a row set from the data access object of Example 10-1.

Example 10-2. Retrieving a RowSetDynaClass from an Action

```java
package com.oreilly.strutsckbk.ch05;

import javax.servlet.http.HttpServletRequest;
import javax.servlet.http.HttpServletResponse;

import org.apache.commons.beanutils.RowSetDynaClass;
import org.apache.struts.action.Action;
import org.apache.struts.action.ActionForm;
import org.apache.struts.action.ActionForward;
import org.apache.struts.action.ActionMapping;

public class ViewUsersAction extends Action {

    public ActionForward execute(ActionMapping mapping,
                                 ActionForm form,
```

Example 10-2. Retrieving a RowSetDynaClass from an Action (continued)

```
                                HttpServletRequest request,
                                HttpServletResponse response)
                    throws Exception {
        UserDao dao = new UserDao( );
        RowSetDynaClass rowSet = dao.getUsersRowSet( );
        request.setAttribute("rowSet", rowSet);
        return mapping.findForward("success");
    }
}
```

Then create a JSP page, such as the one shown in Example 10-3, that iterates through the RowSetDynaClass stored in the request, first retrieving the column names, and then the data itself.

Example 10-3. JSP page that renders a RowSetDynaClass

```
<%@ page contentType="text/html;charset=UTF-8" language="java" %>
<%@ page import="org.apache.commons.beanutils.*" %>
<%@ taglib uri="http://jakarta.apache.org/struts/tags-bean" prefix="bean" %>
<%@ taglib uri="http://jakarta.apache.org/struts/tags-logic" prefix="logic" %>
<html>
<head>
  <title>Struts Cookbook - Chapter 5 : Viewing Row Sets</title>
</head>
<body>
  <h2>Viewing Row Sets</h2>
  <bean:define id="cols" name="rowSet" property="dynaProperties"/>
  <table border="2">
    <tr>
      <logic:iterate id="col" name="cols">
        <th><bean:write name="col" property="name"/></th>
      </logic:iterate>
    </tr>
    <logic:iterate id="row" name="rowSet" property="rows">
      <tr>
        <logic:iterate id="col" name="cols">
          <td>
            <bean:write name="row" property="<%=((DynaProperty)col).getName( )%>"/>
          </td>
        </logic:iterate>
      </tr>
    </logic:iterate>
  </table>
</body>
</html>
```

Of course, you tie the Action to the JSP using an action element in the *struts-config.xml*:

```
    <action   path="/ViewUsers"
              type="com.oreilly.strutsckbk.ch05.ViewUsersAction">
        <forward name="success" path="/view_users.jsp"/>
    </action>
```

Discussion

A sizeable percentage of web applications use a relational database for storing data. In an architecture that emphasizes separation of concerns, controller actions interact with the model through business objects, data transfer objects, and service-oriented interfaces. But sometimes it makes more sense to provide direct views of data in the database.

The RowSetDynaClass provides an effective mechanism for accessing and retrieving data from JDBC result sets. This class, provided in the Jakarta Commons BeanUtils package, maps a JDBC result set—rows and columns retrieved from a relational database—to a JavaBean which can be accessed on a JSP page.

Figure 10-3 shows the results of executing the "select * from users" query from Example 10-1 against a MySQL test database.

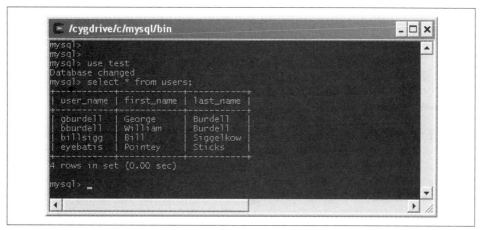

Figure 10-3. Query results from MySQL

You construct a RowSetDynaClass by passing the JDBC ResultSet to the RowSetDynaClass's constructor. Because the data is copied, you can safely close the ResultSet and JDBC Connection without losing data. The RowSetDynaClass includes the data and contains the name and type of each column. In Example 10-3, the dynaProperties array property is used to render the table column headers. Then, the rowSet property is used to access a List of DynaBeans. Each DynaBean represents a row. Each field of the row is retrieved by name from each DynaBean.

Figure 10-4 shows the generated page for the */ViewUsers* action.

See Also

The API documentation for the BeanUtils packages is the best source of additional information for the RowSetDynaClass. The BeanUtils API can be found at *http://jakarta.apache.org/commons/beanutils/*.

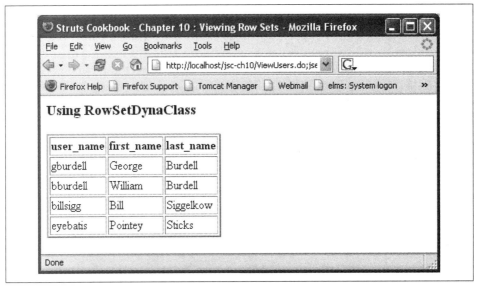

Figure 10-4. JSP displaying data from a RowSetDynaClass

You can consult the chapter on BeanUtils in the *Jakarta Commons Cookbook* by Tim O'Brien (O'Reilly).

If you're familiar with JSTL, you can use the SQL tags instead of the `RowSetDynaClass` to display relational data However, you need to be judicious in using these tags since you will be coupling your application's view to the model. You can find a tutorial on the JSTL SQL tag library at *http://java.sun.com/webservices/docs/1.0/tutorial/doc/ JSTL8.html#63722*.

10.3   Mapping SQL Data to Java Objects

Problem

You want to map SQL statements to Java objects without having to employ a full-blown object-relational mapping framework.

Solution

Use iBATIS SQL maps.

Discussion

There is a middle-ground in Java database access, a shadowy land that lies between straight JDBC and full-blown ORM, a place known as the iBATIS zone. *iBATIS* (pronounced "eye-bay-tis"), created by Clinton Begin, provides an elegant framework for mapping SQL statements and results to Java objects. It offers the simplicity and control of straight JDBC, yet it supports data mapping, caching, and transactions, features usually available from complex object-relational mapping tools. This recipe introduces you to the core feature of iBATIS: SQL maps. It doesn't delve into the full-functionality of iBATIS; you can find additional reference documentation and tutorials online at *http://www.ibatis.com*.

SQL maps allow you to specify how Java objects map to the inputs and outputs of an SQL statement. The inputs traditionally take the form of parameters bound to an SQL where clause. SQL maps let you map object properties to statement parameters. For output, SQL maps let you specify a Java object that maps to the result set returned by an SQL statement.

You can use iBATIS to access and display the data used in Recipe 10.2. Start by downloading iBATIS from *http://www.ibatis.com*. For this example, iBATIS Version 2.0.7 was used. Extract the distribution into a directory such as */ibatis-2.0.7*. Copy the *ibatis-sqlmap-2.jar* and *ibatis-common-2.jar* files to your *WEB-INF/lib* folder.

Next, you create the configuration files that specify how you connect to your database. iBATIS, by default, searches for its configuration files in the application's class path. This example stores these files in the application's top-level *src* directory; when the application is compiled, the configuration files are copied to the *WEB-INF/classes* directory.

iBATIS reads database connection settings from a properties file. Example 10-4 shows the *sqlMapConfig.properties* used to connect to a MySQL database.

Example 10-4. iBATIS database configuration properties

```
driver=com.mysql.jdbc.Driver
url=jdbc:mysql://localhost/test
username=gpburdell
password=matech
```

iBATIS reads and uses these properties in its XML configuration file. Example 10-5 shows the *sqlMapConfig.xml* used in this recipe.

Example 10-5. iBATIS SQL map configuration file

```
<?xml version="1.0" encoding="UTF-8"?>
<!DOCTYPE sqlMapConfig
  PUBLIC "-//iBATIS.com/DTD SQL Map Config 2.0//EN"
  "http://www.ibatis.com/dtd/sql-map-config-2.dtd">
<sqlMapConfig>
    <properties resource="sqlMapConfig.properties"/>
    <transactionManager type="JDBC">
        <dataSource type="SIMPLE">
            <property name="JDBC.Driver" value="${driver}"/>
            <property name="JDBC.ConnectionURL" value="${url}"/>
            <property name="JDBC.Username" value="${username}"/>
            <property name="JDBC.Password" value="${password}"/>
        </dataSource>
```

Example 10-5. iBATIS SQL map configuration file (continued)

```
    </transactionManager>
    <sqlMap resource="UserSqlMap.xml"/>
</sqlMapConfig>
```

The properties element makes the configuration properties of Example 10-4 available as variables (${*propertyName*}) that can be used throughout the rest of the XML configuration file. The `sqlMap` element references an SQL Map configuration file for use by this application. Typically, you'll have one SQL map file for each table.

For this example, you want to map the results of selecting all rows from the *users* table into a collection of objects. Figure 10-5 shows the structure of the *users* table.

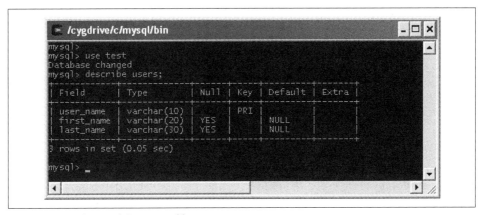

Figure 10-5. Schema of the users table

Example 10-6 shows the *UserSqlMap.xml* file that enables this mapping.

Example 10-6. iBATIS SQL map for the users table

```
<?xml version="1.0" encoding="UTF-8"?>
<!DOCTYPE sqlMap
  PUBLIC "-//iBATIS.com/DTD SQL Map 2.0//EN"
  "http://www.ibatis.com/dtd/sql-map-2.dtd">
<sqlMap namespace="UserSqlMap">
    <select id="getAllUsers" resultClass="com.oreilly.strutsckbk.ch10.User">
        SELECT user_name  as username,
               first_name as firstName,
               last_name  as lastName
          FROM users
    </select>
</sqlMap>
```

The select element defines how a select SQL select statement, contained in the element's body, maps to a Java class. When the query is executed, iBATIS will return a collection of Java objects of the type specified by the `resultClass` attribute.

Example 10-7 shows the User object. By using the "*column* as *name*" syntax in the query, you automatically map a column to JavaBean property.

Example 10-7. Plain old User object

```
package com.oreilly.strutsckbk.ch10;

public class User {
    public String getUsername( ) {
        return username;
    }
    public void setUsername(String username) {
        this.username = username;
    }

    public String getPassword( ) {
        return password;
    }
    public void setPassword(String password) {
        this.password = password;
    }
    public String getFirstName( ) {
        return firstName;
    }
    public void setFirstName(String firstName) {
        this.firstName = firstName;
    }
    public String getLastName( ) {
        return lastName;
    }
    public void setLastName(String lastName) {
        this.lastName = lastName;
    }
    private String username;
    private String password;
    private String firstName;
    private String lastName;
}
```

Now you need to create the data access object that retrieves the collection of users. Example 10-8 shows the action used in this recipe that uses the SQL Maps API to execute the query and map the results.

Example 10-8. Data access object that utilizes iBATIS

```
package com.oreilly.strutsckbk.ch10;

import java.io.Reader;
import java.sql.SQLException;
import java.util.List;

import com.ibatis.common.resources.Resources;
import com.ibatis.sqlmap.client.SqlMapClient;
import com.ibatis.sqlmap.client.SqlMapClientBuilder;
```

Example 10-8. Data access object that utilizes iBATIS (continued)

```java
public class MyUserDao {

    private static final SqlMapClient sqlMapClient;

    static {
        try {
            Reader reader = Resources.getResourceAsReader("sqlMapConfig.xml");
            sqlMapClient = SqlMapClientBuilder.buildSqlMapClient(reader);
        } catch (Exception e) {
            e.printStackTrace( );
            throw new RuntimeException("Unable to create iBATIS sql map client.",
                                       e);
        }
    }

    public List getAllUsers( ) throws SQLException {
        return sqlMapClient.queryForList("getAllUsers", null);
    }
}
```

This data access object provides a getAllUsers( ) method to retrieve the results returned by the "getAllUsers" SQL map statement shown in Example 10-6. The SqlMapClient serves as a façade over the iBATIS API. This object is thread-safe; you can define and initialize it in a static block and use it throughout your action.

Example 10-9 shows the data access object which utilizes the iBATIS API.

Example 10-9. Simple action that calls the DAO

```java
package com.oreilly.strutsckbk.ch10;

import java.util.List;

import javax.servlet.http.HttpServletRequest;
import javax.servlet.http.HttpServletResponse;

import org.apache.struts.action.Action;
import org.apache.struts.action.ActionForm;
import org.apache.struts.action.ActionForward;
import org.apache.struts.action.ActionMapping;

public class ViewMyUsersAction extends Action {

    public ActionForward execute(ActionMapping mapping,
                                 ActionForm form,
                                 HttpServletRequest request,
                                 HttpServletResponse response) throws Exception {
        MyUserDao dao = new MyUserDao( );
        List users = dao.getAllUsers( );
        request.setAttribute("users", users);
        return mapping.findForward("success");
    }
}
```

The actual JSP page to render the users object is shown in Example 10-10. Unlike the solution for Recipe 10.2, the object used on the page is a well-known custom business object. You access its properties using run-of-the-mill Struts bean:write or JSTL c:out tags.

Example 10-10. Iterating through the list of users

```
<%@ page contentType="text/html;charset=UTF-8" language="java" %>
<%@ taglib uri="http://struts.apache.org/tags-bean" prefix="bean" %>
<%@ taglib uri="http://struts.apache.org/tags-logic" prefix="logic" %>
<html>
<head>
  <title>Struts Cookbook - Chapter 10 : Using iBATIS</title>
</head>
<body>
  <h3>Using iBATIS</h3>
  <table border="2">
    <tr>
      <th>Username</th>
      <th>First Name</th>
      <th>Last Name</th>
    </tr>
    <logic:iterate id="user" name="users">
      <tr>
        <td>
          <bean:write name="user" property="username"/>
        </td>
        <td>
          <bean:write name="user" property="firstName"/>
        </td>
        <td>
          <bean:write name="user" property="lastName"/>
        </td>
      </tr>
    </logic:iterate>
  </table>
</body>
</html>
```

This results in a display like that shown in Figure 10-6.

This recipe hints at the capabilities of iBATIS SQL maps. If your application needs some means of mapping objects to data and back, you should consider iBATIS. It may be exactly what you were looking for.

See Also

Documentation, examples, and tutorials for iBATIS can be found at *http://www. ibatis.com*. You will also find the iBATIS data access object (DAO) framework. This framework is highly extensible yet provides a simple means of getting started with iBATIS. This DAO layer can even be used against non-iBATIS mapped data.

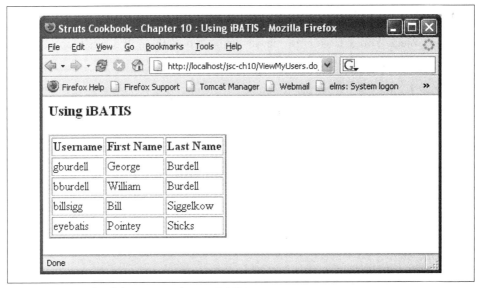

Figure 10-6. Rendered data retrieved using iBATIS

10.4   Integrating Struts with Hibernate

Problem

You want to use Hibernate for object/relational mapping in your Struts application.

Solution

Use a servlet filter such as the `Persistence` class shown in Example 10-11.

Example 10-11. Servlet filter for Hibernate sessions

```
package com.jadecove.util;

import java.io.*;
import javax.servlet.*;
import net.sf.hibernate.*;
import net.sf.hibernate.cfg.Configuration;

/**
 * Filter which manages a ThreadLocal hibernate session.  Obtain the session
 * by calling Persistance.getSession().
 */
public class Persistence implements Filter {

    /**
     * Holds the current hibernate session, if one has been created.
     */
    protected static ThreadLocal hibernateHolder = new ThreadLocal();
```

Example 10-11. Servlet filter for Hibernate sessions (continued)

```java
    protected static SessionFactory factory;

    public void init(FilterConfig filterConfig) throws ServletException {
        // Initialize hibernate
        try {
            doInit( );
        }
        catch (HibernateException ex) {
            throw new ServletException(ex);
        }
    }

    /**
     * This method should only be called when this class is used directly -
     * that is, when using this class outside of the servlet container.
     * @throws HibernateException
     */
    public static void doInit( ) throws HibernateException {
        factory = new Configuration().configure().buildSessionFactory( );
    }

    public void doFilter(ServletRequest request,
                         ServletResponse response,
                         FilterChain chain)
                throws IOException, ServletException {
        if (hibernateHolder.get( ) != null)
            throw new IllegalStateException(
                "A session is already associated with this thread!  "
                + "Someone must have called getSession( ) outside of the context "
                + "of a servlet request.");

        try {
            chain.doFilter(request, response);
        }
        finally {
            Session sess = (Session)hibernateHolder.get( );
            if (sess != null) {
                hibernateHolder.set(null);

                try {
                    sess.close( );
                }
                catch (HibernateException ex) {
                    throw new ServletException(ex);
                }
            }
        }
    }

    /**
     * ONLY ever call this method from within the context of a servlet request
     * (specifically, one that has been associated with this filter).  If you
```

Example 10-11. Servlet filter for Hibernate sessions (continued)

```
 * want a Hibernate session at some other time, call getSessionFactory()
 * and open/close the session yourself.
 *
 * @return an appropriate Session object
 */
public static Session getSession() throws HibernateException {
    Session sess = (Session)hibernateHolder.get();

    if (sess == null) {
        sess = factory.openSession();
        hibernateHolder.set(sess);
    }
    return sess;
}

/**
 * @return the hibernate session factory
 */
public static SessionFactory getSessionFactory() {
  return factory;
}

/**
 * This is a simple method to reduce the amount of code that needs
 * to be written every time hibernate is used.
 */
public static void rollback(net.sf.hibernate.Transaction tx) {
    if (tx != null) {
        try {
            tx.rollback();
        }
        catch (HibernateException ex) {
            // Probably don't need to do anything - this is likely being
            // called because of another exception, and we don't want to
            // mask it with yet another exception.
        }
    }
}

public void destroy() {
    // Nothing necessary
}
}
```

Declare the filter in your *web.xml* file with a filter mapping configured for all URLs that need access to persistent data. Here the filter mapping is set to all URLs:

```
<filter>
    <filter-name>PersistenceFilter</filter-name>
    <filter-class>com.jadecove.util.Persistence</filter-class>
</filter>
```

```
<filter-mapping>
    <filter-name>PersistenceFilter</filter-name>
    <url-pattern>/*</url-pattern>
</filter-mapping>
```

You get a session from the filter by calling the static getSession( ) method. Here's an example method that you can use in your own DAOs:

```
protected Session getSession( ) throws PersistenceException {
    Session session = null;
    try {
        session = Persistence.getSession( );
    } catch (HibernateException e) {
        log.error("Exception accessing persistence session");
        throw new PersistenceException(
            "Exception accessing persistence session", e);
    }
    return session;
}
```

Discussion

If you haven't heard of Hibernate, then you've obviously been sleeping in a cave. Hibernate is one of the most popular object/relational mapping frameworks in use today. It can be used to provide transparent persistence for Java objects, populating and storing object properties using data stored in a relational database.

The Persistence filter shown in Example 10-11 provides a Hibernate session for every servlet request that goes through the filter. It uses a ThreadLocal variable to hold the Hibernate session (see the sidebar "Thread Local Variables Explained"). Each HTTP request is a separate thread; therefore, each request has its own Hibernate session. The Hibernate session is automatically closed when the request is complete—that is, immediately before the HTTP response is sent. The finally block in the doFilter( ) method closes the Hibernate session and sets the value for the session in the ThreadLocal variable to null.

Thread Local Variables Explained

If you look at the filter in Example 10-11, it may appear that only on Hibernate session will be for the application because the session is held in a static ThreadLocal variable. While it's true that there will be only one ThreadLocal variable, that variable will hold multiple object instances, Hibernate sessions in this case. When an object is added to a ThreadLocal variable via the ThreadLocal.set( ) method, that object is implicitly associated with the current thread. In that sense, a ThreadLocal object is like a hash-table entry. The implicit entry key is the current thread, and the entry value, accessible via the ThreadLocal.get( ) method, is the Hibernate session.

A class that needs to load or store persistent data gets a Hibernate session by calling the static `Persistence.getSession( )` method.

Hibernate can defer the loading of specific object properties from the database. The database won't be accessed until that property's accessor method is explicitly called. This feature is known as *lazy-loading*. Since Hibernate persists a graph of objects, lazy-loading can allow you to retrieve a complex object without necessarily paying the performance price of retrieving all the data from the database. The one caveat to this feature is that a lazy-loaded property can only be retrieved if that object is associated with an open Hibernate session.

Without using the `Persistence` filter, a Hibernate session would have to remain open if you needed to lazy-load a property on a JSP page. However, it is dangerous to leave a Hibernate session—essentially a database connection—open between user requests. If you close the Hibernate session before forwarding to a JSP page, attempting to access a lazy-loaded property will fail because an open Hibernate session isn't available. The `Persistence` filter solves this problem. Because the Hibernate session is opened by a filter; the session remains open until the request is complete. JSP pages and other web resources can successfully read persistent object properties, even if they are lazy-loaded.

For unit testing, the `Persistence` filter can be used outside of the application server. In this case, you use the `Persistence` class to initialize Hibernate and retrieve a Hibernate session factory. Example 10-12 shows an abstract JUnit test base class that uses the `Persistence` class.

Example 10-12. Abstract persistence base test case

```
package com.jadecove.facet;

import junit.framework.TestCase;
import net.sf.hibernate.Session;

import com.jadecove.util.Persistence;

public abstract class PersistenceTestCase extends TestCase {

    public PersistenceTestCase(String name) {
        super(name);
    }

    protected void setUp( ) throws Exception {
        super.setUp( );
        Persistence.doInit( );
        openSession( );
        doSetUp( );
    }

    /**
     * Override this method to provide test-specific set-up
```

Example 10-12. Abstract persistence base test case (continued)

```
     */
    protected void doSetUp( ) throws Exception {
    }

    /**
     * Override this method to provide test-specific tear-down
     */
    protected void doTearDown( ) throws Exception {
    }

    protected void tearDown( ) throws Exception {
        super.tearDown( );
        session.close( );
        doTearDown( );
    }

    protected void openSession( ) throws Exception {
        session = Persistence.getSessionFactory().openSession( );
    }

    protected void closeSession( ) throws Exception {
        session.close( );
    }
    protected Session session;

}
```

See Also

The Persistence filter of the Solution is based on a recommended practice presented on the Hibernate web site. The relevant page can be found at *http://www.hibernate. org/43.html.*

If you were to search the Internet for "Struts Hibernate" you'd probably come upon the HibernatePlugin for Struts. This class can be used as a Hibernate session factory; however, it doesn't have the advantages afforded by the Persistence filter. This class can also be found on the Hibernate web site at *http://www.hibernate.org/105.html.*

10.5   Decoupling Your Application from External Services

Problem

You want to decouple your Struts application from a specific implementation of an external business service.

Solution

Create an interface that provides an API for the business service. Then use a ServiceFactory class like the one shown in Example 10-13 to provide access to the service.

Example 10-13. Service factory

```
package com.oreilly.strutsckbk.ch10;

import org.apache.commons.logging.Log;
import org.apache.commons.logging.LogFactory;

public class ServiceFactory {

    private static Log log = LogFactory.getLog(ServiceFactory.class);

    public SecurityService createSecurityService( ) {
        SecurityService service = null;
        try {
            service = (SecurityService)
                Class.forName(securityServiceImpl).newInstance( );
        } catch (Exception e) {
            log.error(
                "Unable to create SecurityService for impl:"+
                    securityServiceImpl);
        }
        return service;
    }

    protected void setSecurityServiceImpl(String securityServiceImpl) {
        this.securityServiceImpl = securityServiceImpl;
    }
    private String securityServiceImpl;
}
```

You can use a Struts PlugIn, like the one shown in Example 10-14, to bind a service implementation to the interface, and store a reference to the service in the servlet context.

Example 10-14. Service factory plug-in

```
package com.oreilly.strutsckbk.ch10;

import javax.servlet.ServletException;

import org.apache.struts.action.ActionServlet;
import org.apache.struts.action.PlugIn;
import org.apache.struts.config.ModuleConfig;

public class ServiceFactoryPlugin implements PlugIn {
```

Example 10-14. Service factory plug-in (continued)

```
    public void init(ActionServlet servlet, ModuleConfig config) throws ServletException {
        ServiceFactory factory = new ServiceFactory( );
        factory.setSecurityServiceImpl(securityService);
        servlet.getServletContext( ).setAttribute("APP_SERVICE_FACTORY", factory);
    }

    public void destroy( ) {
    }

    public void setSecurityService(String securityService) {
        this.securityService = securityService;
    }
    private String securityService;
}
```

Discussion

In corporate environments, it's more likely that a web application will be used as a private intranet application than as a public site on the World Wide Web. These internal applications commonly interface to existing corporate software-based services. These services could be Java-based applications, Enterprise JavaBeans, or web services to name a few. Your web application will have little control of the interface to the legacy system; likewise, you're likely to receive little notice when the interface changes. You can mitigate these risks by decoupling your application from the underlying service using the approach shown in the Solution. Using the Solution, you can easily replace the interface to the implementation with a simplified implementation for testing and development.

Suppose your corporation provides a security service that authenticates existing users and allows the addition of new users. The current service is based on a legacy in-house developed application, but future plans are to move to a system based on Lightweight Directory Access Protocol (LDAP). Your Struts application that will interface to this system needs to be able to support the current and future implementations of the security service.

You can apply techniques in the Solution to this problem. The first thing you will want to do is define an interface for this service like the one shown in Example 10-15.

Example 10-15. Security service interface

```
package com.oreilly.strutsckbk.ch10;

public interface SecurityService {

    public void authenticate(String username,
                             String password)
```

Example 10-15. Security service interface (continued)

```
        throws UnknownUserException, PasswordMatchException;

    public void add(User user) throws DuplicateUsernameException;
}
```

For development and testing purposes, you can create an implementation of the
SecurityService, like that shown in Example 10-16, that uses an in-memory Map of
user data.

Example 10-16. In-memory security service implementation

```
package com.oreilly.strutsckbk.ch10;

import java.util.HashMap;
import java.util.Map;

public class MemorySecurityService implements SecurityService {

    public void authenticate(String username,
                             String password)
            throws UnknownUserException, PasswordMatchException {
        if (users.get(username) == null) {
            throw new UnknownUserException();
        } else if (!users.get(username).equals(password)) {
            throw new PasswordMatchException();
        }
        return;
    }

    public void add(User user) throws DuplicateUsernameException {
        if (users.containsKey(user.getUsername()))
            throw new DuplicateUsernameException();
        users.put(user.getUsername(),user.getPassword());
    }

    private static Map users;
    static {
        users = new HashMap();
        users.put("gpburdell","gotech");
        users.put("fflintstone","yabbadabbado");
        users.put("mpython","nopuftas");
    }
}
```

Now you can use a ServiceFactory (Example 10-13) that knows how to create a
new SecurityService given the name of a class that implements the SecurityService
interface.

A Struts Plug-In (Example 10-14) can be used to create, configure, and store an
instance of the ServiceFactory in the servlet context. The plug-in is configured in the

struts-config.xml to create instances of the SecurityService interface using the specified implementation:

```
<plug-in className="com.oreilly.strutsckbk.ch10.ServiceFactoryPlugin">
    <set-property property="securityService"
                    value="com.oreilly.strutsckbk.ch10.MemorySecurityService"/>
</plug-in>
```

It's a good idea to create a BaseAction (Example 10-17) that accesses the servlet context to retrieve the service factory and returns an implementation of the service interface.

Example 10-17. Base action that provides a security service

```
package com.oreilly.strutsckbk.ch10;

import javax.servlet.ServletContext;
import javax.servlet.http.HttpServletRequest;

import org.apache.struts.action.Action;

public class BaseAction extends Action {

    public SecurityService getSecurityService(HttpServletRequest request) {
        ServletContext ctx = request.getSession(true).getServletContext();
        ServiceFactory factory = (ServiceFactory)
            ctx.getAttribute("APP_SERVICE_FACTORY");
        return factory.createSecurityService();
    }
}
```

As you add more types of services, you can add corresponding methods to the ServiceFactory and ServiceFactoryPlugin. Alternatively, the ServiceFactory and ServiceFactoryPlugin could be made to return any type of service by some agreed on name. Regardless of your preferred approach, this *Service Locator* pattern yields code that is more flexible and easier to test than more tightly coupled systems.

See Also

Struts plug-ins are discussed in Recipe 2.1. The Spring Framework takes pluggability like this to the nth degree. Recipe 10.6 shows you how to integrate an existing Struts application with the Spring Framework.

The Service Locator pattern is considered a Core J2EE Pattern. A page that documents this and other related patterns can be found at *http://www.corej2eepatterns.com/ Patterns2ndEd/ServiceLocator.htm*.

Martin Fowler compares the Service Locator pattern to the Inversion of Control/Dependency Injection pattern in his must-read article at *http://www.martinfowler.com/articles/ injection.html*.

10.6   Integrating Spring with Struts

Problem

You've heard about the Spring framework and want to use it with your Struts application.

Solution

There is no better way of learning than by doing. This recipe shows you how to apply Spring to the *struts-example* web application.

Discussion

There are many ways to use Spring. The Solution shown here uses Spring for two main purposes:

- To configure portions of the model
- To inject model dependencies into Struts Actions

 Spring is an active project. You may find that APIs, filenames, and XML schemas have changed since this book was published; however, the basic process should be about the same.

Here's what you need to do:

1. Download the Spring framework from *http://www.springframework.org*. At the time of this writing, Version 1.1 had just been released.

2. Download the Struts 1.2.4 source distribution.

3. Copy the Struts libraries, *struts-example* classes, *struts-example* web resources, and *struts-example* configuration files into a web application directory structure.

4. Copy the *spring.jar* file from the downloaded Spring framework into the web-application's *WEB-INF/lib* folder.

Now that you've got these mundane preliminaries out of the way, you can get to the gist of Spring. The first thing you are going to do is change the MemoryDatabase used by the *struts-example* to be managed and loaded by Spring instead of by a Struts plug-in.

In the *struts-example*, the MemoryDatabasePlugIn loads and opens the MemoryUserDatabase. To use Spring instead of this plug-in, you need to make a minor change to the MemoryUserDatabase source. Change the open( ) method to read the input file from the classpath instead of the filesystem. This makes the solution easier to deploy. Here's the revised open( ) method with the two modified lines shown in bold.

```java
public void open( ) throws Exception {

    InputStream fis = null;
    BufferedInputStream bis = null;

    try {

        // Acquire an input stream to our database file
        if (log.isDebugEnabled( )) {
            log.debug("Loading database from '" + pathname + "'");
        }
        fis = this.getClass( ).getResourceAsStream(pathname);
        bis = new BufferedInputStream(fis);

        // Construct a digester to use for parsing
        Digester digester = new Digester( );
        digester.push(this);
        digester.setValidating(false);
        digester.addFactoryCreate
            ("database/user",
             new MemoryUserCreationFactory(this));
        digester.addFactoryCreate
            ("database/user/subscription",
             new MemorySubscriptionCreationFactory( ));

        // Parse the input stream to initialize our database
        digester.parse(bis);
        bis.close( );
        bis = null;
        fis = null;
    } catch (Exception e) {
        log.error("Loading database from '" + pathname + "':", e);
        throw e;
    } finally {
        if (bis != null) {
            try {
                bis.close( );
            } catch (Throwable t) {
                ;
            }
            bis = null;
            fis = null;
        }
    }
}
```

This change enables the MemoryUserDatabase to require the MemoryDatabasePlugin no longer. With this revised version of the MemoryUserDatabase, all you have to do is relocate the *database.xml* file from the *WEB-INF* directory to the web application's *classes* folder. Move *database.xml* to the subdirectory of *WEB-INF/classes* that contains the

MemoryUserDatabase.class file (*WEB-INF/classes/org/apache/struts/webapp/example/memory*).

Change the MemoryUserDatabase to be managed by Spring instead of the plug-in. Remove the MemoryDatabasePlugIn configuration from the *struts-config.xml*; it's no longer needed. Create the *applicationContext-struts.xml* file in the *WEB-INF* folder as shown in Example 10-18.

Example 10-18. Spring configuration for the MemoryUserDatabase

```
<?xml version="1.0" encoding="UTF-8" ?>
<!DOCTYPE beans PUBLIC "-//SPRING//DTD BEAN//EN" "http://www.springframework.org/dtd/
spring-beans.dtd">

<beans>
    <bean   id="userDatabase"
            class="org.apache.struts.webapp.example.memory.MemoryUserDatabase"
            init-method="open"
            destroy-method="close">
        <property name="pathname">
            <value>database.xml</value>
        </property>
    </bean>
</beans>
```

This *spring-beans* configuration file is the heart of Spring. The first bean element, shown in Example 10-18, configures the MemoryUserDatabase. The nested property element specifies a dependency that will be injected after the MemoryUserDatabase class is constructed. In this case, the pathname property is set to the path of the XML file containing the list of users for the *struts-example* application. After Spring instantiates the class (using its default constructor), property values are set based on the nested property elements. The init-method and destroy-method attributes allow you to control the lifecycle of the class. The init-method attribute specifies the name of a method that will be called once property values have been set. The method, named by the destroy-method attribute, will be called when the object is evicted from Spring's application context.

For Spring to work, it has to load the XML files that it will use to create the managed bean objects. In addition, each created object must be stored in Spring's application context. For Struts applications, Spring comes with a Struts plug-in that performs these tasks. Here's the plug-in element used for this Solution:

```
<plug-in className="org.springframework.web.struts.ContextLoaderPlugIn">
    <set-property property="contextConfigLocation"
                  value="/WEB-INF/applicationContext-struts.xml"/>
</plug-in>
```

Like other plug-ins, the ContextLoaderPlugIn can be passed through a comma-separated list of configuration files. For the Solution, only a single configuration file is used, the XML file shown in Example 10-18.

Recall that the MemoryDatabasePlugin instantiated and opened the MemoryUserDatabase, storing the created instance in the servlet context under a well-known key value. Since you are no longer using the plug-in, you can change how the Actions acquire a reference to the MemoryUserDatabase.

The "Spring-way" of doing this is to let Spring control the creation of the Actions. In a non-Spring Struts application, Actions are created by the RequestProcessor. When the RequestProcessor receives a request for a given path, it determines your corresponding action configuration, instantiates the specified Action class, and calls Action.execute( ). So, how do you let Spring control the creation of the Actions instead of the RequestProcessor?

The answer is the DelegatingActionProxy. This class, originally created as part of the original Struts Spring Plug-in effort led by Don Brown, is a general-purpose Action that proxies requests to custom Actions. The proxy action determines your custom Action associated with a request by matching the action path with a bean name in Spring's configuration file. At runtime, Spring instantiates your custom Action and injects any required dependencies.

The Actions provided in the *struts-example* extend from a BaseAction that provides a helper method for acquiring the UserDatabase:

```
protected UserDatabase getUserDatabase(HttpServletRequest request) {
    return (UserDatabase) servlet.getServletContext( ).getAttribute(
        Constants.DATABASE_KEY);
}
```

This method retrieves the UserDatabase from the servlet context, placed there by the MemoryDatabasePlugin. This is the kind of dependency that Spring was made to handle. Since the UserDatabase is a Spring-managed object, you can replace this method, which requires the servlet request, with a common property getter method. The getter method returns the UserDatabase from an instance variable of the the BaseAction. You will create a setter method that sets the value of that instance variable.

 Hold the phone! Did I say create an instance variable in a Struts Action? Doesn't this violate thread safety (see Recipe 6.4)? If you use the DelegatingActionProxy shown here, you don't need to worry about thread safety for the Actions. Spring will create a new Action instance *for every request*; alleviating thread-safety concerns.

Spring calls the setter method when an Action instance is created. Subclasses of the BaseAction call the getter method to retrieve the UserDatabase. Each Action that needs the UserDatabase is configured with this dependency via a Spring configuration file. The complete *applicationContext-struts.xml* file with the new entries for each Action is shown in Example 10-19.

Example 10-19. Spring configuration including Actions

```
<?xml version="1.0" encoding="UTF-8" ?>
<!DOCTYPE beans PUBLIC "-//SPRING//DTD BEAN//EN" "http://www.springframework.org/dtd/
spring-beans.dtd">

<beans>

    <bean  id="userDatabase"
          class="org.apache.struts.webapp.example.memory.MemoryUserDatabase"
          init-method="open"
          destroy-method="close">
        <property name="pathname">
            <value>database.xml</value>
        </property>
    </bean>

    <bean name="/Welcome"
         class="org.apache.struts.webapp.example.WelcomeAction">
        <property name="userDatabase">
            <ref bean="userDatabase"/>
        </property>
    </bean>

    <bean name="/SaveSubscription"
         class="org.apache.struts.webapp.example.SaveSubscriptionAction">
        <property name="userDatabase">
            <ref bean="userDatabase"/>
        </property>
    </bean>

    <bean name="/SaveRegistration"
         class="org.apache.struts.webapp.example.SaveRegistrationAction">
        <property name="userDatabase">
            <ref bean="userDatabase"/>
        </property>
    </bean>

    <bean name="/SubmitLogon"
         class="org.apache.struts.webapp.example.LogonAction">
        <property name="userDatabase">
            <ref bean="userDatabase"/>
        </property>
    </bean>

</beans>
```

The last step is to change the action elements in the *struts-config.xml* file to use the
DelegatingActionProxy instead of the Actions directly. For example, here's the new
action mapping for the /SubmitLogon path. The only thing that changed was the type
attribute, which refers to the Spring-provided DelegatingActionProxy:

```
<action  path="/SubmitLogon"
         type="org.springframework.web.struts.DelegatingActionProxy"
```

```
        name="LogonForm"
        scope="request"
        input="logon">
    <exception key="expired.password"
            type="org.apache.struts.webapp.example.ExpiredPasswordException"
            path="/ExpiredPassword.do"/>
</action>
```

Once you understand how Spring works, it makes programming easier. In fact, it's probably harder to convert existing code to use Spring than writing new code. When you write new Actions and business services, you won't need to worry about breaking out dependencies like you had to do with the UserDatabase in this recipe. Most of your objects will be plain-old-Java-objects (POJOs) that won't have any hardcoded dependencies on other objects. You wire your objects together in your *spring-beans.xml* file, and you're ready.

See Also

The original web site for the Struts Spring plug-in can be found at *http://struts. sourceforge.net/struts-spring/*. For the latest on the Spring framework, including its built-in support for Struts, go to *http://www.springframework.org*.

10.7   Loading XML Data into Your Application

Problem

You want an easy way to load XML data into application-scoped objects when your application starts up.

Solution

Use the DigestingPlugIn provided in Struts 1.2.

First, decide on the class that will represent the data. If the data will be used in drop-down lists, a convenient option is to use use the Struts-provided LabelValueBean (org.apache.struts.util.LabelValueBean). Next, create the XML-formatted datafile. The *struts-example* includes a file called *server-types.xml* that represents types of electronic mail server types:

```
<lv-beans>
    <lv-bean label="IMAP Protocol" value="imap" />
    <lv-bean label="POP3 Protocol" value="pop3" />
</lv-beans>
```

Create the rules file that controls how the Digester will parse the data into objects. The *lvb-digester-rules.xml* file shown in Example 10-20, from the *struts-example*, specifies the parsing rules to create an ArrayList of LabelValueBeans from the *server-types.xml* file.

Example 10-20. Label value bean Digester rules

```
<digester-rules>
    <object-create-rule pattern="lv-beans"
                        classname="java.util.ArrayList"/>
    <pattern value="lv-beans/lv-bean">
        <object-create-rule classname="org.apache.struts.util.LabelValueBean" />
        <set-properties-rule />
        <set-next-rule methodname="add" />
    </pattern>
</digester-rules>
```

Finally, add a plug-in declaration to your *struts-config.xml* for each file to be parsed and loaded:

```
<plug-in className="org.apache.struts.plugins.DigestingPlugIn">
    <set-property property="key"
                  value="serverTypes"/>
    <set-property property="configPath"
                  value="/WEB-INF/server-types.xml"/>
    <set-property property="digesterPath"
                  value="/WEB-INF/lvb-digester-rules.xml"/>
</plug-in>
```

You can now access the data from an Action or JSP page. The DigestingPlugIn stores the data as a servlet context attribute where the attribute name is the value of the key property.

Discussion

The DigestingPlugIn, a new feature of Struts 1.2, provides an easy way to load static, XML-formatted lookup data into the servlet context. The *struts-example* application, included with the Struts 1.2 source distribution, uses this plug-in. The examples shown in the Solution are taken from the *struts-example*. If the data you are loading will be used in drop-down lists, you can store the data as a List of LabelValueBeans. In fact, you can use the *lvb-digester-rules.xml* shown in Example 10-20 to load any set of XML data that conforms to the following format:

```
<lv-beans>
    <lv-bean label="Foo"
             value="foo" />
    <lv-bean label="Bar"
             value="bar" />
    <lv-bean label="Baz"
             value="baz" />
</lv-beans>
```

But you are by no means limited to this format. Using custom Digester rules, you can translate any XML file into an object representation. For example, suppose that you wanted to keep a list of Canadian provinces, including province capitals and date established as an application-scoped object. The object that you want to hold data about each province in is shown in Example 10-21.

Example 10-21. Value object for a province

```
package com.oreilly.strutsckbk.ch10;

public class Province {

    public String getCapital( ) {
        return capital;
    }
    public void setCapital(String capital) {
        this.capital = capital;
    }
    public int getEstablished( ) {
        return established;
    }
    public void setEstablished(int established) {
        this.established = established;
    }
    public String getName( ) {
        return name;
    }
    public void setName(String name) {
        this.name = name;
    }
    private String name;
    private String capital;
    private int established;
}
```

The XML file, *WEB-INF/canadian-provinces.xml*, containing the data to load is shown in Example 10-22.

Example 10-22. XML InfoSet of Canadian provinces

```
<provinces>
    <province name="Alberta" capital="Edmonton"
            founded="1905"/>
    <province name="British Columbia" capital="Victoria"
            founded="1871"/>
    <province name="Manitoba" capital="Winnipeg"
            founded="1870"/>
    <province name="New Brunswick" capital="Fredericton"
            founded="1867"/>
    <province name="Newfoundland and Labrador" capital="St. John's"
            founded="1949"/>
    <province name="Nova Scotia" capital="Halifax"
            founded="1867"/>
    <province name="Ontario" capital="Toronto"
            founded="1867"/>
```

Example 10-22. XML InfoSet of Canadian provinces (continued)

```
    <province name="Prince Edward Island" capital="Charlottetown"
          founded="1873"/>
    <province name="Quebec" capital="Quebec City"
          founded="1867"/>
    <province name="Saskatchewan" capital="Regina"
          founded="1905"/>
</provinces>
```

You create the Digester rules file that will parse the XML data into objects. The
WEB-INF/province-digester-rules.xml file is shown in Example 10-23.

Example 10-23. Digester rules for parsing province list

```
<digester-rules>
    <object-create-rule pattern="provinces"
                        classname="java.util.ArrayList"/>
    <pattern value="provinces/province">
        <object-create-rule
                classname="com.oreilly.strutsckbk.ch10.Province" />
        <set-properties-rule>
            <alias attr-name="founded" prop-name="established"/>
        </set-properties-rule>
        <set-next-rule methodname="add" />
    </pattern>
</digester-rules>
```

First, the object-create-rule element tells the Digester the type of object to create
when it encounters a certain pattern. In this case, when the Digester encounters the
provinces element, it creates an ArrayList. The next pattern specifies nested province
elements. For each of these, the Digester creates an instance of the Province class.

The Digester uses the values of XML attributes to set object property values. The
set-properties-rule element defines how XML attributes map to object properties.
Unless specified, the Digester maps attributes to properties based on name. If you
have an XML attribute with a different name than its corresponding object property,
the alias element explicitly defines the mapping. In Example 10-23, all of the
attribute names of the province element match the property names of the Province
class (except for the founded attribute, which maps to the established property).

You configure the DigestingPlugIn by setting properties that define the servlet context key for the created object, the location of the XML datafile, and the location of
the Digester rules file. Table 10-1 shows the properties you can set on the
DigestingPlugIn.

Table 10-1. DigestingPlugIn configuration properties

key	The name of the servlet context attribute that the created object will be stored under.
configSource	Indicates how the `configPath` is interpreted. Accepted values are:
	`classpath` The `configPath` is relative to the classpath and will be resolved by the web application's `ClassLoader`. Practically, this means the file will be stored under the *WEB-INF/classes* directory.
	`file` The `configPath` is relative to the filesystem, typically meaning that the path will be relative to the directory from with the application server was run. If you are running Tomcat, for example, the path will be relative to *${CATALINA_HOME}/bin*.
	`servlet` The `configPath` is relative to the servlet context. This source can be used when loading the data from a URL. In practice, this allows the file to be collocated with the other configuration files stored in the *WEB-INF* directory.
	The value defaults to `servlet` if not specified.
configPath	Path to the datafile to be loaded. This value is resolved based on the setting for the `configSource` element.
digesterSource	Indicates how the `digesterPath` is interpreted. Accepted values are:
	`classpath` The `digesterPath` is relative to the classpath and will be resolved by the web application's `ClassLoader`. Practically, this means the file will be stored under the *WEB-INF/classes* directory.
	`file` The `digesterPath` is relative to the filesystem, typically meaning the path will be relative to the directory from with the application server was run. If you are running Tomcat, for example, the path will be relative to *${CATALINA_HOME}/bin*.
	`servlet` The `digesterPath` is relative to the servlet context. This source can be used when loading the data from a URL. In practice, this allows the file to be collocated with the other configuration files stored in the *WEB-INF* directory.
	The value defaults to `servlet` if not specified.
digesterPath	Path to the XML datafile containing the Digester rules. This value is resolved based on the setting for the `digesterSource` element.

The loaded data can be accessed from the application-scope. For example, the `html:optionsCollection` tag can be used to set the label and value for a drop-down as shown in this snippet from the *subscription.jsp* file of the *struts-example*:

```
<html:select property="type">
    <html:options collection="serverTypes" property="value"
            labelProperty="label"/>
</html:select>
```

See Also

Recipe 10.8 demonstrates how to use the Digester to refresh application-scoped data on demand.

The JavaDocs for the `DigestingPlugIn` can be found at *http://struts.apache.org/api/org/apache/struts/plugins/DigestingPlugIn.html*.

The homepage for the Digester can be found at *http://jakarta.apache.org/commons/digester/*.

O'Reilly's ONJava.com has a good article called "Learning and Using Jakarta Digester" by Phillip K. Janert, Ph.D. at *http://www.onjava.com/pub/a/onjava/2002/10/23/digester.html*.

10.8   Refreshing Application Data

Problem

You want the ability to refresh application-scoped objects cached in the servlet context.

Solution

Provide an interface, such as the one shown in Example 10-24, which indicates if an object can be refreshed.

Example 10-24. Interface used to refresh cached objects

```
package com.oreilly.strutsckbk.ch10;

/**
 * An object that can be refreshed from its original source.
 */
public interface Refreshable {

    public void refresh( ) throws CacheException;

}
```

Create an `Action`, such as the one shown in Example 10-25, which refreshes objects in the servlet context. Alternatively, you could create a base `Action` that provides a protected method for refreshing a named object. This may be necessary to avoid chaining to the `ContextRefreshAction` whenever you need to refresh data.

Example 10-25. Context refresh action

```
package com.oreilly.strutsckbk.ch10;

import java.util.Enumeration;

import javax.servlet.ServletContext;
import javax.servlet.http.HttpServletRequest;
import javax.servlet.http.HttpServletResponse;

import org.apache.struts.action.Action;
import org.apache.struts.action.ActionForm;
```

Example 10-25. Context refresh action (continued)

```java
import org.apache.struts.action.ActionForward;
import org.apache.struts.action.ActionMapping;

public class ContextRefreshAction extends Action {

    public ActionForward execute(ActionMapping mapping, ActionForm form,
            HttpServletRequest request, HttpServletResponse response)
            throws Exception {
        String name = request.getParameter("name");
        ServletContext ctx = servlet.getServletContext();
        if (name != null && !"".equals(name)) {
            refreshObject(name, ctx);
        }
        else {
            Enumeration names = ctx.getAttributeNames();
            while (names.hasMoreElements()) {
                name = (String) names.nextElement();
                refreshObject(name, ctx);
            }
        }
        return mapping.findForward("success");
    }

    private void refreshObject(String name, ServletContext ctx)
            throws CacheException {
        Object obj = ctx.getAttribute(name);
        if (obj != null && obj instanceof Refreshable) {
            ((Refreshable) obj).refresh();
        }
    }
}
```

 Action chaining should be avoided in a Struts application. For an explanation, see the sidebar "Avoid Chaining Actions" in Chapter 6.

You can define an action in your *struts-config.xml* file for the ContextRefreshAction:

```xml
<action   path="/ContextRefresh"
          type="com.oreilly.strutsckbk.ch10.ContextRefreshAction">
    <forward name="success" path="/index.jsp"/>
</action>
```

Discussion

The Solution shows a flexible approach for refreshing application-scoped data. The Refreshable interface indicates if an object can be refreshed and provides a method that implementers use to reload cached data.

You need to use the Solution if the data in question isn't cached by some other mechanism. Data backed by a database or persistence layer is probably cached. For these data, it's better to access the data and not worry about caching.

For data not backed by persistence layer—for example, a flat file of Java properties or XML-formatted information—it's common to store those data in the servlet context. The data can be retrieved via the Servlet API or JSP tags. Data can be loaded into the servlet context using a ServletContextListener (Recipe 7.1) or a Struts PlugIn (Recipe 2.1). If the data seldom changes and you don't mind periodic application restarts, then bouncing the application will reload the data from its original source.

On the other hand, if the data may change more frequently and you don't want to restart the application, then you can use a mechanism such as the one shown in the Solution. To illustrate how this interface would be used, you can apply the Solution to the data loaded by the DigestingPlugIn shown in Recipe 10.7.

The basic approach is to provide a class that knows how to refresh itself using the Digester. First, create the RefreshableList abstract base class shown in Example 10-26.

Example 10-26. Abstract refreshable list

```
package com.oreilly.strutsckbk.ch10;

import java.util.*;

public abstract class RefreshableList implements Refreshable, List {
    public void add(int arg0, Object arg1) {
        backingList.add(arg0, arg1);
    }
    public boolean add(Object arg0) {
        return backingList.add(arg0);
    }
    public boolean addAll(Collection arg0) {
        return backingList.addAll(arg0);
    }
    public boolean addAll(int arg0, Collection arg1) {
        return backingList.addAll(arg0, arg1);
    }
    public void clear( ) {
        backingList.clear( );
    }
    public boolean contains(Object arg0) {
        return backingList.contains(arg0);
    }
    public boolean containsAll(Collection arg0) {
        return backingList.containsAll(arg0);
    }
    public Object get(int arg0) {
        return backingList.get(arg0);
```

Example 10-26. Abstract refreshable list (continued)

```
    }
    public int indexOf(Object arg0) {
        return backingList.indexOf(arg0);
    }
    public boolean isEmpty( ) {
        return backingList.isEmpty( );
    }
    public Iterator iterator( ) {
        return backingList.iterator( );
    }
    public int lastIndexOf(Object arg0) {
        return backingList.lastIndexOf(arg0);
    }
    public ListIterator listIterator( ) {
        return backingList.listIterator( );
    }
    public ListIterator listIterator(int arg0) {
        return backingList.listIterator(arg0);
    }
    public Object remove(int arg0) {
        return backingList.remove(arg0);
    }
    public boolean remove(Object arg0) {
        return backingList.remove(arg0);
    }
    public boolean removeAll(Collection arg0) {
        return backingList.removeAll(arg0);
    }
    public boolean retainAll(Collection arg0) {
        return backingList.retainAll(arg0);
    }
    public Object set(int arg0, Object arg1) {
        return backingList.set(arg0, arg1);
    }
    public int size( ) {
        return backingList.size( );
    }
    public List subList(int arg0, int arg1) {
        return backingList.subList(arg0, arg1);
    }
    public Object[] toArray( ) {
        return backingList.toArray( );
    }
    public Object[] toArray(Object[] arg0) {
        return backingList.toArray(arg0);
    }
    protected List backingList;
}
```

This class decorates the List interface with the Refreshable interface. The only abstract method is refresh( ). You can extend this class to provide different ways of refreshing list contents. An implementation that uses the Digester is shown in Example 10-27.

Example 10-27. Using the Digester to refresh a list

```java
package com.oreilly.strutsckbk.ch10;

import java.net.URL;
import java.util.List;

import org.apache.commons.digester.Digester;
import org.apache.commons.digester.xmlrules.DigesterLoader;
import org.apache.commons.logging.Log;
import org.apache.commons.logging.LogFactory;

public class DigestedList extends RefreshableList {

    private static Log log = LogFactory.getLog(DigestedList.class);

    public DigestedList(List list, URL sourceUrl, URL rulesUrl) {
        this.sourceUrl = sourceUrl;
        this.rulesUrl = rulesUrl;
        this.backingList = list;
    }

    public synchronized void refresh() throws CacheException {
        Digester digester = DigesterLoader.createDigester(rulesUrl);
        try {
            List list = (List) digester.parse(sourceUrl.openStream());
            if (list != null)
                backingList = list;
            else {
                log.error("Returned list was null due to unknown error");
                throw new CacheException("Backing list was null.");
            }
        } catch (Exception e) {
            log.error("Unable to redigest list.", e);
            throw new CacheException("Unable to redigest list.");
        }
    }

    private URL sourceUrl;
    private URL rulesUrl;
}
```

This class maintains instance variables for the original URL of the data source file and the URL of the Digester rules used to parse the source file. In the refresh( ) method, an instance of a Digester is created. The data in the source file is parsed, and the results are cast into a java.util.List. If the returned data is null or any other exception occurs, a CacheException is thrown.

Now that you have the classes that implement the Refreshable interface, you need to create a mechanism for loading the data on the application startup. The DigestingListPlugIn in Example 10-28 extends the DigestingPlugIn for the purpose of creating refreshable lists and storing them in the servlet context. It overrides storeGeneratedObject( )to provide this functionality.

Example 10-28. Plug-in for reloading a Digester-based refreshable list

```
package com.oreilly.strutsckbk.ch10;

import java.io.IOException;
import java.net.URL;
import java.util.List;

import org.apache.commons.logging.Log;
import org.apache.commons.logging.LogFactory;
import org.apache.struts.plugins.DigestingPlugIn;

public class DigestingListPlugin extends DigestingPlugIn {

    private static Log log = LogFactory.getLog(DigestingPlugIn.class);

    public DigestingListPlugin( ) {
    }

    protected void storeGeneratedObject(Object obj) {
        if (!(obj instanceof List))
            throw new IllegalArgumentException(
                "Digested object must be a list but is:"+obj);
        List list = (List) obj;
        URL sourceUrl =  null;
        URL rulesUrl =  null;
        try {
            sourceUrl = getConfigURL(configPath, configSource);
            rulesUrl = getConfigURL(digesterPath, digesterSource);
            DigestedList digestedList = new DigestedList(list,
                                                 sourceUrl,
                                                 rulesUrl );
            servlet.getServletContext( ).setAttribute(key, digestedList);
        } catch (IOException e) {
            log.error("Unable to create URL.", e);
        }
    }
}
```

You configure a DigestingListPlugIn plug-in in the *struts-config.xml* file like the DigestingPlugIn:

```
<plug-in className="com.oreilly.strutsckbk.ch10.DigestingListPlugIn">
    <set-property property="key"
                   value="serverTypes"/>
    <set-property property="configSource"
                   value="servlet"/>
```

```
<set-property property="configPath"
              value="/WEB-INF/server-types.xml"/>
<set-property property="digesterPath"
              value="/WEB-INF/lvb-digester-rules.xml"/>
</plug-in>
```

To see the refreshable lists in action, you need to modify the data source. You can modify the file using a text editor, the hard part is finding the file. The DigestingListPlugIn, like the DigestingPlugIn (Recipe 10.7), uses the configSource property to treat the data source file (identified by the configPath property) as relative to the classpath (classpath), the filesystem (file), or the web application context (servlet). The default value is servlet. If you were to deploy the Solution to Tomcat 5, you would find the file located at *$CATALINA_HOME/webapps/jsc-ch10/WEB-INF/server-types.xml*. Once you modify the file, you can use your browser to post a request to a URL that triggers the ContextRefreshAction:

```
http://localhost/jsc-ch10/ContextRefresh.do
```

If you wanted only to refresh a specific object, you can specify it by name:

```
http://localhost/jsc-ch10/ContextRefresh.do?name=serverTypes
```

Now that you've got a generic mechanism for refreshing data, you can extend this mechanism for reloading property files, comma-separated value files, and other types.

See Also

The subject of caching data comes up often on the struts-user mailing list. If you search the archives for caching, you will find a number of threads related to this topic.

The DigestingPlugIn is specifically discussed in Recipe 10.7.

## CHAPTER 11

Security

11.0 Introduction

Security is one of those aspects of development that often gets relegated to the end of the programming process. It seems like customers expect security features can be bolted on to an application. What makes things worse is you can implement security in many ways. When it comes to building security into an application, determine the requirements before you start coding. Additionally, it can be tempting to let technology drive requirements. Some technologies are flexible and let you get away with this, but when it comes to security, this is not the case. Choosing one security approach or technology over another without understanding what the user wants and needs can leave you scrambling at the end of the development cycle. You don't want to be recoding your entire security layer before your application goes into production.

Security features center around two basic concepts: authentication and authorization. Users authenticate to the system to prove they are who they say they are. Authorization allows or disallows access to certain application features. Authentication requirements are usually specific and concrete:

> Anybody can access the welcome page of the application. But if a users attempt to access any other page they will have to log in with a username and password.

Authorization needs tend to be broad and vague. In many cases, authorization rules can be complex, particularly if the authorization requirements are based on hierarchical or matrix-style organizations:

> Users can only look at the data they own. The user's manager can look at any information for users that work for him. Administrators can look at anybody's data but can only modify the data if approved by a manager.

Before you start coding to meet these requirements, ensure you understand what the various approaches to security can and cannot do. Security mechanisms for J2EE and Java-based applications fall into two broad categories: container-managed security and application-managed security. Container-managed security is specified as part of the J2EE and Servlet specifications. Any spec-compliant application server—such as

Tomcat, JBoss, Weblogic, or Websphere—supports container-managed security. Since Tomcat isn't an EJB container, it supports container-managed security as specified in the Servlet specification. Full-blown J2EE containers will support container-managed security for EJB applications and web applications.

Many think container-managed security is too restrictive. It's somewhat ironic that using container-managed security can lead to portability issues. The reason is that each container implements container-managed security in different ways. For example, each container has its own way of configuring security realms. A security realm provides data to the container used to authenticate and authorize users. This data could come from a database, an LDAP server, a flat file, or some other storage repository. If you use container-managed security, you'll have to make changes to your application's configuration if you want to deploy the application on a different application server. Several recipes related to setting up container-managed security are presented in this chapter.

With application-managed security, you're responsible for developing the security features of your specifications. You'll have to write more code; however, you won't have to compromise on the requirements. Many applications manage their own security requirements for this reason alone. Servlet filters, available on containers that support the Servlet 2.3 specification, provide a great vehicle for implementing application-managed security. This chapter provides many recipes focused on application-managed security. These recipes range from the use of base Actions to full-blown custom filters for authentication and authorization.

SecurityFilter is an open source servlet filter that provides the convenience and features of container-managed security yet allows the flexibility of application-managed security. This chapter includes a recipe that shows you how to use this powerful tool.

The Solutions and code samples in this chapter provide examples that demonstrate various approaches to security. As you look at the Recipes in this chapter, keep in mind that Security is rarely something a single solution can cover. Instead, you may want to employ a combination of solutions to fulfill your requirements.

11.1   Securing Actions Using a Base Action

Problem

You need to ensure that users are logged in before they can access certain actions.

Solution

Create a base Action, like the one shown in Example 11-1, which implements the security policy.

Example 11-1. Enforcing authentication with a base action

```
package com.oreilly.strutsckbk.ch11;

import javax.servlet.http.HttpServletRequest;
import javax.servlet.http.HttpServletResponse;
import javax.servlet.http.HttpSession;

import org.apache.struts.action.Action;
import org.apache.struts.action.ActionForm;
import org.apache.struts.action.ActionForward;
import org.apache.struts.action.ActionMapping;
import org.apache.struts.webapp.example.Constants;
import org.apache.struts.webapp.example.User;

public abstract class SecureAction extends Action {

    // final so cannot be overridden
    public final ActionForward execute(ActionMapping mapping,
                            ActionForm form,
                            HttpServletRequest request,
                            HttpServletResponse response)
        throws Exception {
      HttpSession session = request.getSession( );
      User user = (User) session.getAttribute(Constants.USER_KEY);

      // send back to the logon page if no user
      if (user == null) return (mapping.findForward("logon"));

      return doExecute(mapping, form, request, response, user);
    }

    public abstract ActionForward doExecute(ActionMapping mapping,
                            ActionForm form,
                            HttpServletRequest request,
                            HttpServletResponse response,
                            User user) throws Exception;
}
```

Concrete Actions that require this policy extend the base SecureAction, shown in
Example 11-2.

Example 11-2. SecureAction source code

```
package com.oreilly.strutsckbk.ch11;

import javax.servlet.http.HttpServletRequest;
import javax.servlet.http.HttpServletResponse;

import org.apache.struts.action.ActionForm;
import org.apache.struts.action.ActionForward;
import org.apache.struts.action.ActionMapping;
import org.apache.struts.webapp.example.User;
```

Example 11-2. SecureAction source code (continued)

```
public class TestSecureAction extends SecureAction {

    public ActionForward doExecute(ActionMapping mapping, ActionForm form,
            HttpServletRequest request, HttpServletResponse response, User user)
            throws Exception {
        // do real work here

        return mapping.findForward("success");
    }
}
```

Discussion

The base SecureAction is an abstract class that wraps the execute( ) method with the security policy. In the Solution, the policy is simple. The User object is retrieved from the HttpSession; if this object is not found, then the user must not be logged in; control is forwarded to "logon." Otherwise, the abstract doExecute( ) method is called. In addition to the standard execute( ) arguments, the User object is passed through. Your concrete subclasses then implement doExecute( ) instead of execute( ).

Enforcing security through a base SecureAction is an understandable approach. However, this solution requires that every concrete Action must subclass SecureAction. If you are using the DispatchAction or other Struts built-in Actions, you'll need to create your own subclasses for these that perform the security checks.

In a team environment, you'll need to ensure all developers abide by these rules. More importantly, the base Action approach only provides security for HTTP requests that go through your base Action. It doesn't provide any security for directly accessed JSPs, static HTML pages, and other resources accessed outside of Struts or through a different Action. If you ensure all requests go through your base Action, then this may not be an issue; however, many applications are not written in such a way.

See Also

The Base Action technique is discussed in *Programming Jakarta Struts* by Chuck Cavaness (O'Reilly).

The Struts JavaDoc for the Action class can be found at *http://struts.apache.org/api/ org/apache/struts/action/Action.html*.

11.2 Checking for User Login on Any Struts Request

Problem

You want to be able to check if a user is logged in for any request made to an action in your *struts-config.xml* file, but you don't want to have to subclass a custom base Action class.

Solution

Create a custom request processor, overriding the processPreprocess( ) or the processActionPerform( ) method. The custom request processor shown in Example 11-3 retrieves the user object from the HTTP session. If this object is null, an HTTP error response of 403 (Forbidden) is returned.

Example 11-3. Overriding the processPreprocess() method

```
package org.apache.struts.action;

import java.io.IOException;

import javax.servlet.http.HttpServletRequest;
import javax.servlet.http.HttpServletResponse;
import javax.servlet.http.HttpSession;

import org.apache.struts.webapp.example.Constants;
import org.apache.struts.webapp.example.User;

public class CustomRequestProcessor1 extends RequestProcessor {

    protected boolean processPreprocess(HttpServletRequest request,
            HttpServletResponse response) {
        HttpSession session = request.getSession( );
        User user = (User) session.getAttribute(Constants.USER_KEY);
        if (user == null) {
            try {
                response.sendError(403, "User not logged in");
            } catch (IOException e) {
                log.error("Unable to send response");
            }
            return false;
        }

        return true;
    }
}
```

If you need to use the Struts objects passed to an Action's execute( ) method, such as the ActionForm and ActionMapping, override the processActionPerform( ) method as shown in Example 11-4. In this example, if the user object is null, control is forwarded to the logon Struts forward; otherwise, the base RequestProcessor. processActionPerform( ) method is called to continue normal processing.

Example 11-4. Overriding the processActionPerform() method

```
package org.apache.struts.action;

import java.io.IOException;

import javax.servlet.ServletException;
import javax.servlet.http.HttpServletRequest;
import javax.servlet.http.HttpServletResponse;
import javax.servlet.http.HttpSession;

import org.apache.struts.webapp.example.Constants;
import org.apache.struts.webapp.example.User;

public class CustomRequestProcessor2 extends RequestProcessor {

    protected ActionForward processActionPerform(HttpServletRequest request,
            HttpServletResponse response, Action action, ActionForm form,
            ActionMapping mapping) throws IOException, ServletException {
        HttpSession session = request.getSession( );
        User user = (User) session.getAttribute(Constants.USER_KEY);
        if (user == null) {
            return mapping.findForward("logon");
        } else {
            return super.processActionPerform(request, response, action, form,
                    mapping);
        }
    }
}
```

You deploy the custom request processor using the controller element in the *struts-config.xml* file:

```
<controller type="com.oreilly.strutsckbk.ch11.CustomRequestProcessor1" />
```

Discussion

The Solutions shown in this recipe allow you to enforce a security policy across any requests handled by Struts without having to create and extend a special base Action. The first approach (Example 11-3) overrides the processPreprocess( ) method of the Struts RequestProcessor. This method is a general-purpose preprocessing method. The implementation in the base RequestProcessor is a no-op. You return true from this method to continue normal processing. If you return false, the RequestProcessor assumes that the response has been written and it aborts normal processing. In Example 11-3, the method checks for a user object in the session. If one is found, the method returns true; otherwise, the method sends the HTTP error code of 403 (Forbidden).

The second approach overrides the processActionPerform( ) method. Like the first approach, the user object is retrieved from the HTTP session. Unlike the first approach, however, Struts API objects are available. If the user object isn't found, you call the findForward( ) method on the ActionMapping to forward to "logon." Otherwise, you call the super.processActionPerform( ) method where the base RequestProcessor calls action.execute( ) and handles any thrown exception:

```
protected ActionForward processActionPerform(HttpServletRequest request,
                       HttpServletResponse response,
                       Action action,
                       ActionForm form,
                       ActionMapping mapping)
        throws IOException, ServletException {

    try {
        return (action.execute(mapping, form, request, response));
    } catch (Exception e) {
        return (processException(request, response,
                                 e, form, mapping));
    }
}
```

The two approaches shown here apply the security policy to all Actions. If needed, you can customize the Solution so the login check is selectively applied. In the first approach, which overrides processPreprocess( ), you could look for a special request parameter or attribute that indicates if the login check is required. In the second approach, you could employ a custom ActionMapping containing a property indicating if the action was secured or not.

 Some Struts applications require a custom RequestProcessor. Tiles applications, for example, use the TilesRequestProcessor. To implement this Solution, you'll need to extend the custom RequestProcessor currently used instead of the base Struts RequestProcessor.

See Also

Like using a base Action, directly accessed JSPs and static HTML pages aren't secured by the Solution. These resources can be selectively secured using a custom JSP tag as shown in Recipe 11.3.

The Struts RequestProcessor also processes roles. You can override the processRoles( ) method to achieve custom handling, as shown in Recipe 11.4. You can learn about additional RequestProcessor methods in the Struts User's Guide "Controller" section at *http://struts.apache.org/userGuide/building_controller.html*.

Custom action mappings are discussed in Recipe 2.8.

11.3   Securing a JSP Page

Problem

You want to ensure users can access a JSP page only if they are logged in.

Solution

Use a custom JSP tag, like the checkLogon tag from the Struts Mail Reader example application, on pages that require users to be logged in. The checkLogon tag is shown in Example 11-5.

Example 11-5. Struts-example check logon tag

```
package org.apache.struts.webapp.example;

import java.io.IOException;

import javax.servlet.ServletException;
import javax.servlet.http.HttpSession;
import javax.servlet.jsp.JspException;
import javax.servlet.jsp.tagext.TagSupport;
import org.apache.struts.config.ModuleConfig;

/**
 * Check for a valid User logged on in the current session.  If there is no
 * such user, forward control to the logon page.
 *
 * @author Craig R. McClanahan
 * @author Marius Barduta
 * @version $Revision: 1.3 $ $Date: 2004/11/18 13:28:00 $
 */

public final class CheckLogonTag extends TagSupport {

    // ------------------------------------------------ Instance Variables

    /**
     * The key of the session-scope bean we look for.
     */
    private String name = Constants.USER_KEY;

    /**
     * The page to which we should forward for the user to log on.
     */
    private String page = "/logon.jsp";

    // -------------------------------------------------------- Properties

    /**
     * Return the bean name.
     */
```

Example 11-5. Struts-example check logon tag (continued)

```java
public String getName( ) {
    return (this.name);
}

/**
 * Set the bean name.
 *
 * @param name The new bean name
 */
public void setName(String name) {
    this.name = name;
}

/**
 * Return the forward page.
 */
public String getPage( ) {
    return (this.page);
}

/**
 * Set the forward page.
 *
 * @param page The new forward page
 */
public void setPage(String page) {
    this.page = page;
}

// ----------- Public Methods -----------------

/**
 * Defer our checking until the end of this tag is encountered.
 *
 * @exception JspException if a JSP exception has occurred
 */
public int doStartTag( ) throws JspException {
    return (SKIP_BODY);
}

/**
 * Perform our logged-in user check by looking for the existence of
 * a session scope bean under the specified name.  If this bean is not
 * present, control is forwarded to the specified logon page.
 *
 * @exception JspException if a JSP exception has occurred
 */
public int doEndTag( ) throws JspException {

    // Is there a valid user logged on?
    boolean valid = false;
    HttpSession session = pageContext.getSession( );
```

Example 11-5. Struts-example check logon tag (continued)

```
        if ((session != null) && (session.getAttribute(name) != null)) {
            valid = true;
        }

        // Forward control based on the results
        if (valid) {
            return (EVAL_PAGE);
        } else {
            ModuleConfig config =
                (ModuleConfig) pageContext.getServletContext( ).getAttribute(
                    org.apache.struts.Globals.MODULE_KEY);

            try {
                pageContext.forward(config.getPrefix( ) + page);
            } catch (ServletException e) {
                throw new JspException(e.toString( ));
            } catch (IOException e) {
                throw new JspException(e.toString( ));
            }
            return (SKIP_PAGE);
        }
    }

    /**
     * Release any acquired resources.
     */
    public void release( ) {
        super.release( );
        this.name = Constants.USER_KEY;
        this.page = "/logon.jsp";
    }
}
```

Include the tag at the start of a page that requires users to be logged in. Example 11-6 lists the *mainMenu.jsp* taken from the Struts Mail Reader example application.

Example 11-6. Using the checkLogon tag on a JSP page

```
<%@ page contentType="text/html;charset=UTF-8" language="java" %>
<%@ taglib uri="/tags/app" prefix="app" %>
<%@ taglib uri="/tags/struts-bean" prefix="bean" %>
<%@ taglib uri="/tags/struts-html" prefix="html" %>
<%-- Check if the user is logged in and redirect to logon if not --%>
<app:checkLogon/>
<html>
<head>
<title><bean:message key="mainMenu.title"/></title>
<link rel="stylesheet" type="text/css" href="base.css" />
</head>
<h3><bean:message key="mainMenu.heading"/> <bean:write name="user" property="fullName" />
</h3>
<ul>
```

Example 11-6. Using the checkLogon tag on a JSP page (continued)

```
<li><html:link action="/EditRegistration?action=Edit"><bean:message key="mainMenu.
registration"/></html:link></li>
<li><html:link forward="logoff"><bean:message key="mainMenu.logoff"/></html:link></li>
</ul>
</body>
</html>
```

Discussion

If you use directly accessed JSP pages, you will need a mechanism to secure those pages. With a custom JSP tag, you can create the logic in one place and reuse the functionality throughout your application. The checkLogon tag, shown in Example 11-5 and applied in Example 11-6, attempts to retrieve an object from the HTTP session stored under a certain name. The name property defaults to the value defined by Constants.USER_KEY. If the object isn't found, the tag forwards to a module-relative page specified by the page property. This value defaults to */logon.jsp*.

You can use this tag in your own applications even if you store the user under a different name in the session and you want to forward to a different page. In the following snippet, the user object is stored under the name user. If the object cannot be found, the tag redirects to the Register action:

```
...
<%-- Check if there's a user and redirect to registration if not --%>
<app:checkLogon name="user" page="/Register.do"/>
...
```

Like using a base Action, this custom JSP tag only protects JSP pages on which it is included. It does *not* provide security for actions, static HTML pages, or other web resources.

> If you implement a static HTML page as a JSP page, you can secure the page using the checkLogon tag.

See Also

Recipe 11.1 shows you how to secure Actions in the same way that the Solution secures JSP pages.

Recipe 11.6 shows a more comprehensive mechanism, applicable to any web resource, for checking that a user is logged in.

11.4 Restricting Actions by Role

Problem

You want to allow a user to access an action if that user has a specific role.

Solution

Use the roles attribute of the action element to specify the roles that are permitted to use the action:

```
<!-- Display all users -->
<action    path="/ViewUsers"
        forward="/view_users.jsp"
          roles="manager,sysadmin"
/>
```

Discussion

Struts actions, configured via the action element in the *struts-config.xml* file, can be restricted to certain roles using the roles attribute. This attribute accepts a comma-separated list of role names. When a request is received for the action, the RequestProcessor.processRoles( ) method checks that the user has at least one of the roles specified. If the user doesn't have one of the roles, the HTTP 403 error (Forbidden) is sent; otherwise, processing continues normally. Here is the processRoles( ) method from the Struts RequestProcessor:

```
protected boolean processRoles( HttpServletRequest request,
                                HttpServletResponse response,
                                ActionMapping mapping )
        throws IOException, ServletException {

    // Is this action protected by role requirements?
    String roles[] = mapping.getRoleNames( );
    if ((roles == null) || (roles.length < 1)) {
        return (true);
    }

    // Check the current user against the list of required roles
    for (int i = 0; i < roles.length; i++) {
        if ( request.isUserInRole(roles[i]) ) {
            if (log.isDebugEnabled( )) {
                log.debug(" User '" + request.getRemoteUser( ) +
                    "' has role '" + roles[i] + "', granting access");
            }
            return (true);
        }
    }

    // The current user is not authorized for this action
    if (log.isDebugEnabled( )) {
```

```
            log.debug(" User '" + request.getRemoteUser( ) +
                "' does not have any required role, denying access");
        }

        response.sendError(
            HttpServletResponse.SC_FORBIDDEN,
            getInternal().getMessage("notAuthorized", mapping.getPath( )));

        return (false);

    }
```

The Struts RequestProcessor determines if a user has a role using the HttpServletRequest.isUserInRole( ) method. This method can only be used if you are using container-managed security (or if you use a Solution such as the one in Recipe 11.10). For application-managed security, you can create your own custom RequestProcessor that overrides the processRoles method.

In Example 11-7, the processRoles( ) method retrieves a User object from the HTTP session. Then, the hasRole( ) method is called on this object to determine if the user has at least one of the required roles.

Example 11-7. Custom role-handling RequestProcessor

```
package com.oreilly.strutsckbk.ch11;

import java.io.IOException;
import javax.servlet.ServletException;
import javax.servlet.http.*;
import org.apache.struts.action.*;
import org.apache.struts.webapp.example.User;

public class RoleRequestProcessor extends RequestProcessor {
    protected boolean processRoles( HttpServletRequest request,
                                    HttpServletResponse response,
                                    ActionMapping mapping )
        throws IOException, ServletException
    {
        // Is this action protected by role requirements? If not, return true.
        String roles[] = mapping.getRoleNames( );
        if ((roles == null) || (roles.length < 1)) {
            return true;
        }

        // Check the current user against the list of required roles
        HttpSession session = request.getSession( );
        User user = (User) session.getAttribute("user");
        if (user == null) {
            return false;
        }
        for (int i = 0; i < roles.length; i++) {
```

Example 11-7. Custom role-handling RequestProcessor (continued)

```
        if (user.hasRole(roles[i])) {
            return (true);
        }
    }

    // The user does not have one of the roles; send an error
    response.sendError( HttpServletResponse.SC_BAD_REQUEST,
                        getInternal( ).getMessage("notAuthorized",
                        mapping.getPath( )));
        return (false);
    }
}
```

This custom request processor is deployed using the `controller` element in the *struts-config.xml* file:

```
<controller processorClass="com.oreilly.strutsckbk.ch11.RoleRequestProcessor"/>
```

The customization, shown in Example 11-7, used to code the `processRoles( )` method to perform checks can be as complex as you want. You have complete access to the servlet request and response, servlet context, HTTP session, and the `ActionMapping`.

 Since container-managed security typically supports a simple flat role structure, using application-managed security along with a custom request processor allows you to handle more complex hierarchical schemes. Because you have access to the servlet response, you can redirect a user to a different URL if that user doesn't pass the security test.

See Also

You can learn about additional `RequestProcessor` methods in the Struts User's Guide "Controller" section at *http://struts.apache.org/userGuide/building_controller.html*.

If you want to implement container-managed security for your application, see Recipe 11.9.

11.5 Implementing "Remember Me" Logins

Problem

You want to provide a "remember me" feature so a user's username and password are prefilled on the logon form if that user has logged on before.

Solution

In your Action that logs a user in, create persistent cookies containing the user's base-64 encoded username and password. The private saveCookies() and removeCookies() methods shown in Example 11-8 manipulate the cookies as needed.

Example 11-8. An Action that stores or removes cookies

```
package com.oreilly.strutsckbk.ch11;

import javax.servlet.http.Cookie;
import javax.servlet.http.HttpServletRequest;
import javax.servlet.http.HttpServletResponse;
import javax.servlet.http.HttpSession;

import org.apache.commons.beanutils.PropertyUtils;
import org.apache.struts.action.Action;
import org.apache.struts.action.ActionErrors;
import org.apache.struts.action.ActionForm;
import org.apache.struts.action.ActionForward;
import org.apache.struts.action.ActionMapping;

import com.oreilly.servlet.Base64Encoder;

public final class MyLogonAction extends Action {

    public ActionForward execute( ActionMapping mapping,
                                  ActionForm form,
                                  HttpServletRequest request,
                                  HttpServletResponse response)
        throws Exception {

        HttpSession session = request.getSession( );

        ActionErrors errors = new ActionErrors( );

        String username = (String) PropertyUtils.getSimpleProperty(form, "username");
        String password = (String) PropertyUtils.getSimpleProperty(form, "password");
        boolean rememberMe = ((Boolean) PropertyUtils.getSimpleProperty(form,
                                    "rememberMe")).booleanValue( );

        // Call your security service here
        //SecurityService.authenticate(username, password);

        if (rememberMe) {
            saveCookies(response, username, password);
        } else {
            removeCookies(response);
        }

        session.setAttribute("username", username);

        return mapping.findForward("success");
    }
```

Example 11-8. An Action that stores or removes cookies (continued)

```
    private void saveCookies(HttpServletResponse response, String username, String
password) {
        Cookie usernameCookie = new Cookie("StrutsCookbookUsername",
                                    Base64Encoder.encode(username));
        usernameCookie.setMaxAge(60 * 60 * 24 * 30); // 30 day expiration
        response.addCookie(usernameCookie);
        Cookie passwordCookie = new Cookie("StrutsCookbookPassword",
                                    Base64Encoder.encode(password));
        passwordCookie.setMaxAge(60 * 60 * 24 * 30); // 30 day expiration
        response.addCookie(passwordCookie);
    }
    private void removeCookies(HttpServletResponse response) {
        // expire the username cookie by setting maxAge to 0
        // (actual cookie value is irrelevant)
        Cookie unameCookie = new Cookie("StrutsCookbookUsername", "expired");
        unameCookie.setMaxAge(0);
        response.addCookie(unameCookie);

        // expire the password cookie by setting maxAge to 0
        // (actual cookie value is irrelevant)
        Cookie pwdCookie = new Cookie("StrutsCookbookPassword", "expired");
        pwdCookie.setMaxAge(0);
        response.addCookie(pwdCookie);
    }
}
```

When a user goes to the logon page, fill the username and password fields with values from the cookie, decoded from base-64, using the Struts bean:cookie tag, as shown in Example 11-9.

Example 11-9. Setting logon form field values from cookies

```
<%@ page contentType="text/html;charset=UTF-8" language="java" %>
<%@ page import="com.oreilly.servlet.*" %>
<%@ taglib uri="/tags/struts-bean" prefix="bean" %>
<%@ taglib uri="/tags/struts-html" prefix="html" %>

<html>
<head>
<title>Struts Cookbook - Cookie Logon</title>
</head>
<body>
<html:errors/>

<html:form action="/SubmitCookieLogon" focus="username">
  <bean:cookie id="uname" name="StrutsCookbookUsername" value=""/>
  <bean:cookie id="pword" name="StrutsCookbookPassword" value=""/>
  <table border="0" width="100%">

  <tr>
    <th align="right">
      <bean:message key="prompt.username"/>:
```

Example 11-9. Setting logon form field values from cookies (continued)

```
      </th>
      <td align="left">
        <html:text property="username" size="16" maxlength="18"
            value="<%=Base64Decoder.decode(uname.getValue( ))%>"/>
      </td>
  </tr>

  <tr>
    <th align="right">
      <bean:message key="prompt.password" bundle="alternate"/>:
    </th>
    <td align="left">
      <html:password property="password" size="16" maxlength="18"
                     redisplay="false"
value="<%=Base64Decoder.decode(pword.getValue( ))%>"/>
    </td>
  </tr>

  <tr>
    <th align="right">
      <bean:message key="prompt.rememberMe"/>:
    </th>
    <td align="left">
      <html:checkbox property="rememberMe"/>
    </td>
  </tr>

  <tr>
    <td align="right">
      <html:submit property="Submit" value="Submit"/>
    </td>
    <td align="left">
      <html:reset/>
    </td>
  </tr>

</table>

</html:form>

</body>
</html>
```

Discussion

A *cookie* consists of a name-value data pair that can be sent to a client's browser and then read back again at a later time. Browsers provide security for cookies so a cookie can only be read by the server that originally created it. Cookies must have an expiration period.

Though cookies are in widespread use and are supported by modern browsers, they do pose a privacy risk. Most browsers allow the user to disable them. You can design your web application to use cookies to improve the user experience, but you shouldn't require users to use cookies.

The logon Action of Example 11-8 retrieves the username and password from the logon form. This form includes the true/false property rememberme, which indicates if the users want their login credentials remembered. If users want to be remembered, they check the checkbox for the rememberme property. In the MyLogonAction—if rememberme is true—the cookies are created and saved in the response. If rememberme is false, the cookies for username and password have their maxAge set to 0, effectively removing them from the response.

The bean:cookie tags used in Example 11-9 retrieve the cookie values from the request and store them in scripting variables. These tags specify the empty string ("") as the default value in case cookies are disabled. The initial values for the login form fields are set to the values from the scripting variables.

The Solution shown here does *not* address cookie security issues. For a production system, the data sent in the cookies should be encrypted. A simple encryption scheme, such as MD5 or a variant of the Secure Hash Algorithm (SHA), can be used to encrypt the cookie value when it is created. Since the server creates the cookie and is the only party that can legitimately use the data, it can encrypt and decrypt the data using the algorithm of its own choosing. Alternatively, you can send the cookies only over HTTPS, thereby providing encryption/decryption at the transport level.

See Also

You can use cookies to log in a user automatically; in other words, if users have a cookie(s) with valid credentials for the web application they don't have to submit the login form at all. The automatic login approach is shown in Recipe 11.7.

Recipe 11.10 shows how to use the open source SecurityFilter software to implement "remember me" functionality. Its implementation includes support for cookie encryption and other settings.

Java Servlet Programming by Jason Hunter (O'Reilly) covers servlet development from top to bottom, including the Cookie APIs. The Base64 encoder and decoder used in this recipe are part of the companion com.oreilly.servlet classes available from *http://www.servlets.com/cos/*.

The foundation of Java server-side cookie handling is the Servlet Specification and API, available for download from *http://java.sun.com/products/servlet/download.html*.

The JavaBoutique has a nice tutorial on server-side cookie handling found at *http://javaboutique.internet.com/tutorials/JSP/part09/*. Alexander Prohorenko has written a good article on cookie security issues for O'Reilly's ONLamp.com site at *http://www.onlamp.com/pub/a/security/2004/04/01/cookie_vulnerabilities.html*.

11.6 Ensuring Security Across Your Entire Application

Problem

You need to verify the user is logged in and authenticated when a request is received for any URL path of your web application.

Solution

Use an authentication servlet filter, such as the one in Example 11-10, which checks for a User object in the session.

Example 11-10. A servlet filter that checks if the user is logged in

```
package com.oreilly.strutsckbk.ch11.ams;

import java.io.IOException;

import javax.servlet.Filter;
import javax.servlet.FilterChain;
import javax.servlet.FilterConfig;
import javax.servlet.ServletException;
import javax.servlet.ServletRequest;
import javax.servlet.ServletResponse;
import javax.servlet.http.HttpServletRequest;
import javax.servlet.http.HttpServletResponse;
import javax.servlet.http.HttpSession;

public class AuthenticationFilter implements Filter {

    private String onFailure = "logon.jsp";
    private FilterConfig filterConfig;

    public void init(FilterConfig filterConfig) throws ServletException {
        this.filterConfig = filterConfig;
        onFailure = filterConfig.getInitParameter("onFailure");
    }

    public void doFilter(ServletRequest request,
                         ServletResponse response,
                         FilterChain chain)
                throws IOException, ServletException {
        HttpServletRequest req = (HttpServletRequest) request;
        HttpServletResponse res = (HttpServletResponse) response;
```

Example 11-10. A servlet filter that checks if the user is logged in (continued)

```
        // if the requested page is the onFailure page continue
        // down the chain to avoid an infinite redirect loop
        if (req.getServletPath( ).equals(onFailure)) {
            chain.doFilter(request, response);
            return;
        }

        HttpSession session = req.getSession( ); // get the session or create it
        User user = (User) session.getAttribute("user");
        if (user == null) {
            // redirect to the login page
            res.sendRedirect(req.getContextPath( )+onFailure);
        }
        else {
            chain.doFilter(request, response);
        }
    }

    public void destroy( ) {
    }
}
```

 This filter assumes that a separate Action authenticates the user and creates the User object.

Discussion

Servlet filters provide a convenient way to apply across-the-board processing of a servlet request. Servlet filters were introduced in the Servlet 2.3 specification. Most all containers support Servlet 2.3, so you can probably use them in your application. The filter looks for a User object from the HttpSession. If the object is found, then processing continues normally. If the object isn't found, then a redirect to the page specified by the onFailure initialization parameter is sent in the response.

You create a filter by implementing the Filter interface, declare the filter in your *web.xml* file, and map URLs to it using URL patterns (see the sidebar "Understanding URL Patterns"). In Example 11-11, the filter is declared by the filter element. The init-param element specifies the context-relative path of the URL to redirect if authentication fails.

Example 11-11. Filter declaration and mapping (partial)

```
<filter>
    <filter-name>AuthenticationFilter</filter-name>
    <filter-class>
        com.oreilly.strutsckbk.ch11.ams.AuthenticationFilter
    </filter-class>
```

Example 11-11. Filter declaration and mapping (partial) (continued)

```
    <init-param>
        <param-name>onFailure</param-name>
        <param-value>/logon.jsp</param-value>
    </init-param>
</filter>

<filter-mapping>
    <filter-name>AuthenticationFilter</filter-name>
    <url-pattern>/reg/*</url-pattern>
</filter-mapping>
```

The value of the url-pattern in the filter-mapping determines the URLs to be filtered. In this case, the filter mapping indicates users must be logged in before they can access a URL that matches the url-pattern */reg/**. URLs that match this pattern include */reg/Main.do*, */reg/viewReg.jsp*, */reg/help.html*, and */reg/sub/viewSub.jsp*.

Understanding URL Patterns

URL patterns, known as URL mappings, are dictated by the Java Servlet specification. The types of patterns you can use aren't as broad as you might think. Four patterns are searched in the following order:

Explicit mappings
> A complete context-relative path; no wildcards are used, for example, */add.jsp* or */admin/remove.do*.

Path prefix mappings
> Contains a / followed by a path prefix and then /*. This pattern can be used to specify an entire sub-branch of your web application—for example, */admin/** or */search/company/**.

Extension mappings
> A *. followed by an extension. This mapping can be used to specify all files of a certain type (e.g., **.jsp* or **.do*).

Default mapping
> Use a slash followed by an asterisk (/*) to match all URLs for a web application.

As you can tell, these patterns can be inflexible. You can't, for example, specify a pattern of */add.**. For security-related filters, locating URLs requiring authentication in a separate subfolder(s) allows you to use path-prefix mapping. Otherwise, you would have to add an explicit mapping to the *web.xml* each time you added a protected action or JSP.

See Also

Recipe 11.7 shows a servlet filter that authenticates using cookies. Recipe 11.8 presents a servlet filter that can be used for authorization.

Recipe 11.10 shows how to use the open source SecurityFilter software for providing functionality similar to the filter presented in this recipe.

Java Servlet Programming by Jason Hunter (O'Reilly) covers servlet filters in-depth. Sun's Java site has a good article on the essentials of servlet filters. It can be found at *http://java.sun.com/products/servlet/Filters.html*.

11.7   Allowing a User to Log in Automatically

Problem

You want to allow users to be logged in automatically if they have valid credentials stored in a cookie(s).

Solution

Use a servlet filter, such as the one shown in Example 11-12, that looks for cookies containing the user's credentials. The credentials are used to authenticate the user. If the authentication succeeds, the user is automatically logged in; otherwise, the user will be prompted to login.

Example 11-12. Cookie authentication filter for automatic login

```
package com.oreilly.strutsckbk.ch11;

import java.io.IOException;

import javax.servlet.Filter;
import javax.servlet.FilterChain;
import javax.servlet.FilterConfig;
import javax.servlet.ServletException;
import javax.servlet.ServletRequest;
import javax.servlet.ServletResponse;
import javax.servlet.http.Cookie;
import javax.servlet.http.HttpServletRequest;
import javax.servlet.http.HttpServletResponse;
import javax.servlet.http.HttpSession;

import org.apache.commons.logging.Log;
import org.apache.commons.logging.LogFactory;

/**
 * Filter which handles application authentication.  The filter implements
 * the following policy:
 * <ol>
```

Example 11-12. Cookie authentication filter for automatic login (continued)

```
 * <li>If the username is in the session the filter exits;
 * <li>If not, the authentication cookies are looked for;
 * <li>If found, the authentication is attempted
 * <li>If authentication is successful, the username is stored in the session
 * <li>Otherwise, the cookies are invalid and subsequently removed from the response
 * </ol>
 *
 * @author Bill Siggelkow
 */
public class AutomaticLoginFilter implements Filter {

    private String onFailure = "logon.jsp";

    public void init(FilterConfig filterConfig) throws ServletException {
        this.filterConfig = filterConfig;
        onFailure = filterConfig.getInitParameter("onFailure");
    }

    public void doFilter(ServletRequest request, ServletResponse response, FilterChain
chain)
                throws IOException, ServletException {
        HttpServletRequest req = (HttpServletRequest) request;
        HttpServletResponse res = (HttpServletResponse) response;

        String contextPath = req.getContextPath( );
        // if the requested page is the onFailure page continue
        // down the chain to avoid an infinite redirect loop
        if (req.getServletPath( ).equals(onFailure)) {
            chain.doFilter(request, response);
            return;
        }

        HttpSession session = req.getSession( ); // get the session or create it
        String username = (String) session.getAttribute("username");
        if (log.isDebugEnabled( )) log.debug("User in session:"+username);

        // if user is null get credentials from cookie; otherwise continue
        if (username == null) {
            boolean authentic = false;
            username = findCookie(req, "StrutsCookbookUsername");
            String password = findCookie(req, "StrutsCookbookPassword");
            if (username != null && password != null) {
                try {
                    if (log.isDebugEnabled( )) log.debug("Checking authentication");
                    // Call your security service here
                    //SecurityService.authenticate(username, password);
                    session.setAttribute("username", username);
                    authentic = true;
                }
                catch (Exception e) {
                    log.error("Unexpected authentication failure.", e);
```

```
                    clearCookie(res, "StrutsCookbookUsername");
                    clearCookie(res, "StrutsCookbookPassword");
                }
            }

            // if not authentic redirect to the logon page
            if (!authentic) {
                //redirect to the onFailure page, alternatively we could send
                //an HTTP error code such as 403 (Forbidden)
                res.sendRedirect(contextPath+onFailure);
                //abort filter instead of chaining
                return;
            }
        }
        if (log.isDebugEnabled( )) log.debug("Continuing filter chain ...");
        chain.doFilter(request, response);
    }

    public void destroy( ) {
        // Nothing necessary
    }

    private String findCookie(HttpServletRequest request, String cookieName) {
        Cookie[] cookies = request.getCookies( );
        String value = null;
        if (cookies != null) {
            for (int i=0; i<cookies.length; i++) {
                if (cookies[i].getName( ).equals(cookieName)) {
                    value = cookies[i].getValue( );
                }
            }
        }
        return value;
    }

    private void clearCookie(HttpServletResponse response, String cookieName) {
        // the cookie value does not matter
        Cookie cookie = new Cookie(cookieName, "expired");

        // setting maxAge to 0 effectively removes the cookie
        cookie.setMaxAge(0);
        response.addCookie(cookie);
    }

    private FilterConfig filterConfig;
    private static final Log log = LogFactory.getLog(AutomaticLoginFilter.class);
}
```

Discussion

This Solution assumes that cookies for the username and password have been stored
in the request; this filter does *not* store the cookies.

For that functionality, you need to use an Action such as the one shown in Recipe 11.5.

You map the servlet filter shown in the Solution to any application URLs requiring user authentication. If users aren't authenticated, they should be redirected to the page specified by the onFailure initialization parameter (defaults to logon.jsp). You describe the filter's configuration using the filter and filter-mapping elements in the *web.xml* file, as shown in Example 11-13.

Example 11-13. Filter deployment settings (partial)

```
<filter>
    <filter-name>AutomaticLoginFilter</filter-name>
    <filter-class>
        com.oreilly.strutsckbk.ch11.AutomaticLoginFilter
    </filter-class>
    <init-param>
        <param-name>onFailure</param-name>
        <param-value>/my_logon.jsp</param-value>
    </init-param>
</filter>

<filter-mapping>
    <filter-name>AutomaticLoginFilter</filter-name>
    <url-pattern>/reg/*</url-pattern>
</filter-mapping>

<filter-mapping>
    <filter-name>AutomaticLoginFilter</filter-name>
    <url-pattern>/admin/menu.do</url-pattern>
</filter-mapping>
```

When a request is received, the servlet filter attempts to retrieve specific cookie values for the username and password. If the values aren't present, control will be redirected to the onFailure page. If the cookies are present, the username and password will be verified using a SecurityService. If authentic, the request is passed to the next filter in the chain, effectively allowing the request to proceed as normal. If not authentic, the cookie values themselves are invalid and not legitimate. The cookies are removed and control is redirected to the onFailure page.

From a developer's perspective, one of the more interesting aspects of this filter is the following bit of code:

```
if (req.getServletPath( ).equals(onFailure)) {
    chain.doFilter(request, response);
    return;
}
```

When this filter was first written (by yours truly), this block was omitted. The filter was mapped to all application URLs (/) and the application was deployed. When an attempt was made to access to any part of the application, a browser message was displayed indicating too many redirects had been attempted. What happened was that when the filter redirected to the logon page, the request was routed back through the filter, essentially creating an HTTP infinite loop. To fix this problem, the code block was added to skip the authentication check if the request path is the same as the onFailure path.

See Also

Recipe 11.10 shows how to use the open source SecurityFilter software for providing similar functionality as the filter presented in this recipe.

Java Servlet Programming by Jason Hunter (O'Reilly) covers Servlet development in-depth, including filters and the cookie-related APIs.

11.8 Limiting Access for Specific URLs by Role

Problem

You need to verify the user is authorized to access selected URLs based on the user's security role and profile.

Solution

Use a servlet filter such as the one shown in Example 11-14.

Example 11-14. Authorization filter

```
package com.oreilly.strutsckbk.ch11.ams;

import java.io.IOException;

import javax.servlet.Filter;
import javax.servlet.FilterChain;
import javax.servlet.FilterConfig;
import javax.servlet.ServletException;
import javax.servlet.ServletRequest;
import javax.servlet.ServletResponse;
import javax.servlet.http.HttpServletRequest;
import javax.servlet.http.HttpServletResponse;
import javax.servlet.http.HttpSession;

import org.apache.struts.Globals;
import org.apache.struts.action.ActionErrors;
import org.apache.struts.action.ActionMessage;

public class AuthorizationFilter implements Filter {
    public void init(FilterConfig filterConfig) throws ServletException {
```

Example 11-14. Authorization filter (continued)

```
        String roles = filterConfig.getInitParameter("roles");
        if (roles == null || "".equals(roles)) {
            roleNames = new String[0];
        } else {
            roles.trim( );
            // use the new split method of JDK 1.4
            roleNames = roles.split("\\s*,\\s*");
        }
        onFailure = filterConfig.getInitParameter("onFailure");
        if (onFailure == null || "".equals(onFailure)) {
            onFailure = "/index.jsp";
        }
    }

    public void doFilter(ServletRequest request, ServletResponse response,
            FilterChain chain) throws IOException, ServletException {
        HttpServletRequest req = (HttpServletRequest) request;
        HttpServletResponse res = (HttpServletResponse) response;

        HttpSession session = req.getSession( );
        User user = (User) session.getAttribute("user");
        ActionErrors errors = new ActionErrors( );
        if (user != null) {
            boolean hasRole = false;
            for (int i = 0; i < roleNames.length; i++) {
                if (user.hasRole(roleNames[i])) {
                    hasRole = true;
                    break;
                }
            }
            if (!hasRole) {
                errors.add(ActionErrors.GLOBAL_MESSAGE, new ActionMessage(
                        "error.authorization.required"));
            }
        }
        if (errors.isEmpty( )) {
            chain.doFilter(request, response);
        } else {
            req.setAttribute(Globals.ERROR_KEY, errors);
            req.getRequestDispatcher(onFailure).forward(req, res);
        }
    }

    public void destroy( ) {
    }

    private String[] roleNames;

    private String onFailure;
}
```

Discussion

Servlet filters, introduced as part of the Servlet 2.3 specification, provide for custom request and response processing that can be applied across any (and all) web resources. Filters can alter a request before it arrives at its destination and, likewise, can modify the response after it leaves a destination. Filters can be applied to static HTML pages, JSP pages, Struts actions, essentially any resource that you can specify with a URL.

You can use a filter to prohibit or allow access to resources based on any user information. Container-managed security (Recipe 11.9) provides a limited form of this capability, known as role-based access control. With a filter, you can implement role-based access control or any other security policy desired. The Solution shows an example usage that implements custom role-based authorization. This filter performs a similar security check as the custom RoleRequestProcessor of Example 11-14.

Initialization parameters specify the required roles and the page to forward to if the authorization check fails. For each combination of roles and mapped URLs, you can deploy a separate instance of the filter class. Each instance, specified by the filter element, can have its own set of initialization parameters and filter mappings. Example 11-15, taken from the *web.xml* file, shows a deployment that uses two instances of the same authorization filter.

Example 11-15. Deploying two instances of the authorization filter (partial)

```
<filter>
    <filter-name>adminAuthFilter</filter-name>
    <filter-class>
        com.oreilly.strutsckbk.ch11.ams.AuthorizationFilter
    </filter-class>
    <init-param>
        <param-name>roles</param-name>
        <param-value>admin</param-value>
    </init-param>
    <init-param>
        <param-name>onFailure</param-name>
        <param-value>/index.jsp</param-value>
    </init-param>
</filter>

<filter>
    <filter-name>managerAuthFilter</filter-name>
    <filter-class>
        com.oreilly.strutsckbk.ch11.ams.AuthorizationFilter
    </filter-class>
    <init-param>
        <param-name>roles</param-name>
        <param-value>manager,asstManager</param-value>
    </init-param>
    <init-param>
```

Example 11-15. Deploying two instances of the authorization filter (partial) (continued)

```
            <param-name>onFailure</param-name>
            <param-value>/index.jsp</param-value>
        </init-param>
    </filter>

    <filter-mapping>
        <filter-name>adminAuthFilter</filter-name>
        <url-pattern>/admin/*</url-pattern>
    </filter-mapping>

    <filter-mapping>
        <filter-name> managerAuthFilter </filter-name>
        <url-pattern>/mgr/*</url-pattern>
    </filter-mapping>

    <filter-mapping>
        <filter-name> managerAuthFilter </filter-name>
        <url-pattern>/usr/*</url-pattern>
    </filter-mapping>
```

Unlike other filters in this chapter, the authorization filter of Example 11-14 truly integrates with Struts. If a user doesn't have a required role, then a set of `ActionErrors` are created and stored as a request attribute. Though the filter only has access to the request and response, it integrates with Struts based on knowing how Struts stores the `ActionErrors` in the request. Unlike `Actions`, filters don't have access to Struts helper methods for accessing objects, like `ActionErrors`, that may be stored in the servlet request or session. To get around this, you can retrieve Struts objects. By using the constants defined in the `org.apache.struts.Globals` class, you can protect your code from future changes to Struts internals.

See Also

For a complete application-managed security solution, you will want to implement an authentication mechanism. Recipe 11.6 presents a servlet filter that can be used for this purpose. To enforce authentication prior to authorization, list the authentication filter before the authorization filter in the `filter-mapping` declarations.

Recipe 11.10 shows how to use the open source SecurityFilter software for providing similar functionality as the filter presented in this recipe.

Java Servlet Programming by Jason Hunter (O'Reilly) covers servlet filters in-depth. Sun's Java site has a good article on the essentials of servlet filters. It can be found at *http://java.sun.com/products/servlet/Filters.html*.

11.9   Letting the Container Manage Security

Problem

You want to let the container manage security for your Struts application instead of you having to write all the Java code to support log in (authentication) and access checks (authorization).

Solution

Use container-managed security, as defined by the Java Servlet Specification.

Discussion

A servlet container or J2EE application server can manage security for web applications. Container-managed security provides three main features:

Authentication
>   You can specify to the container how users are to be authenticated using a login configuration. You indicate if you want the browser to prompt for the username and password, or if you want to use your own custom login page.

Authorization
>   You can establish security constraints that allow users with certain roles access to specific URLs of the application. If users attempt to access a page to which they aren't authorized, they will be prompted to login using the login configuration.

Secure transport
>   You can specify which URLs should be accessed using a secure protocol. In practical terms, you indicate which pages can be accessed with the HTTPS protocol (HTTP over Secure Socket Layer).

You configure container-managed security using special XML elements in your *web.xml*, as shown in Example 11-16.

Example 11-16. Configuring container-managed security in web.xml

```
<?xml version="1.0" encoding="ISO-8859-1"?>

<!DOCTYPE web-app PUBLIC
    "-//Sun Microsystems, Inc.//DTD Web Application 2.3//EN"
    "http://java.sun.com/dtd/web-app_2_3.dtd">

<web-app>
    <display-name>Struts Cookbook - Chapter 11 : CMS</display-name>

    <!-- Action Servlet Configuration -->
    <servlet>
        <servlet-name>action</servlet-name>
```

```
        <servlet-class>org.apache.struts.action.ActionServlet</servlet-class>
        <init-param>
            <param-name>config</param-name>
            <param-value>/WEB-INF/struts-config.xml</param-value>
        </init-param>
        <load-on-startup>1</load-on-startup>
    </servlet>

    <!-- Action Servlet Mapping -->
    <servlet-mapping>
        <servlet-name>action</servlet-name>
        <url-pattern>*.do</url-pattern>
    </servlet-mapping>

    <!-- The Welcome File List -->
    <welcome-file-list>
        <welcome-file>index.jsp</welcome-file>
    </welcome-file-list>

    <!-- Container-managed security configuration -->
    <security-constraint>
        <!-- At least one web-resource collection -->
        <web-resource-collection>
          <web-resource-name>RegPages</web-resource-name>
          <description>Registered user pages</description>
          <url-pattern>/reg/*</url-pattern>
        </web-resource-collection>
        <auth-constraint>
            <!-- Zero or more role-names -->
            <role-name>jscUser</role-name>
        </auth-constraint>
    </security-constraint>

    <security-constraint>
        <web-resource-collection>
            <web-resource-name>AdminPages</web-resource-name>
            <description>Administrative pages</description>
            <url-pattern>/admin/*</url-pattern>
        </web-resource-collection>
        <auth-constraint>
            <role-name>jscAdmin</role-name>
        </auth-constraint>
        <!-- Switch to HTTPS for the admin pages -->
        <user-data-constraint>
            <transport-guarantee>CONFIDENTIAL</transport-guarantee>
        </user-data-constraint>
    </security-constraint>

    <login-config>
        <auth-method>FORM</auth-method>
        <realm-name>StrutsCookbookCh11</realm-name>
        <form-login-config>
```

```
            <form-login-page>/cma_logon.jsp</form-login-page>
            <form-error-page>/cma_logon_error.jsp</form-error-page>
        </form-login-config>
    </login-config>

    <security-role>
        <description>Registered User</description>
        <role-name>jscUser</role-name>
    </security-role>

    <security-role>
        <description>Administrators</description>
        <role-name>jscAdmin</role-name>
    </security-role>

</web-app>
```

Authentication and authorization

You use the security-constraint element to apply constraints to one or more web resource collections—i.e., a set of URLs. URL patterns (see the sidebar "Understanding URL Patterns") identify the URLs that comprise each collection. The auth-constraint element identifies the user roles, specified using role-name elements, which can access a constrained URL. If users attempt to access a constrained URL, they must log in based on settings in the login-config element.

The login-config element indicates the authentication to be performed and where the user information can be found. A web application can have one login configuration. The auth-method nested element indicates the type of authentication and accepts the values detailed in Table 11-1.

Table 11-1. J2EE login configuration types

Authentication method	Description
BASIC	The browser pops up a dialog allowing the user to enter a username and password. The username and password are Base-64 encoded and sent to the server.
FORM	Allows for a custom form to be specified. The form must contain a j_username field for the username and j_password field for the password. The form must submit to j_security_check. The username and password are Base-64 encoded.
DIGEST	Just like BASIC authentication, except that the username and password are encrypted into a message digest value. All browsers may not support this configuration.
CLIENT-CERT	The client is required to provide a digital certificate for authentication. This is the most secure configuration and is the most costly; certificates for production use must be purchased from a Certificate Authority.

The majority of applications employing container-managed security use BASIC or FORM-based authentication. With FORM-based authentication, the form-login-page element specifies an HTML or JSP page that users use to submit their authentication credentials. That page, like the one shown in Example 11-17, must submit to the form action named j_security_check and have form fields named j_username and j_password.

Example 11-17. Form-based authentication login page

```
<%@ page contentType="text/html;charset=UTF-8" language="java" %>
<%@ taglib uri="http://struts.apache.org/tags-bean" prefix="bean" %>

<html>
<head>
<title><bean:message key="logon.cma.title"/></title>
</head>

<body>
<form action="j_security_check">
    <table border="0" width="100%">
        <tr>
            <th align="right">
                <bean:message key="prompt.username"/>:
            </th>
            <td align="left">
                <input type="text" name="j_username" size="16" maxlength="18">
            </td>
        </tr>

        <tr>
            <th align="right">
                <bean:message key="prompt.password"/>:
            </th>
            <td align="left">
                <input type="password" name="j_password" size="16" maxlength="18">
            </td>
        </tr>

        <tr>
            <td align="right">
                <input type="submit" value="Submit">
            </td>
            <td align="left">
                <input type="reset">
            </td>
        </tr>
    </table>
</form>
</body>
</html>
```

In addition to specifying the login, the login configuration may also specify a *security realm*. A security realm is essentially the store from which a web application retrieves and verifies user credentials. In addition, a realm provides a mechanism for specifying the roles users may have.

The user data for authentication comes from the security realm. The security realm serves as a reference to container-specific security storage. Realms can be based, for example, on property files, XML files, a relational database, or an LDAP-server. Some containers, such as JBoss, provide a mapping between a realm and a Java Authentication and Authorization Service (JAAS) implementation. The mechanism for associating the logical realm named in the *web.xml* to the concrete realm varies by container.

If you are experimenting with container-managed security and using Tomcat, you can use Tomcat's *UserDatabase* realm. In a default configuration, Tomcat supports this realm across all deployed applications. The realm uses usernames, passwords, roles, and role assignments specified in the *conf/tomcat-users.xml* file. A sample file is shown in Example 11-18.

Example 11-18. Sample Tomcat users file

```
<?xml version='1.0' encoding='utf-8'?>
<tomcat-users>
  <role rolename="jscUser"/>
  <role rolename="tomcat"/>
  <role rolename="role1"/>
  <role rolename="manager"/>
  <role rolename="jscAdmin"/>
  <role rolename="admin"/>
  <user username="bsiggelkow" password="crazybill" roles="jscUser,jscAdmin"/>
  <user username="tomcat" password="tomcat" roles="tomcat"/>
  <user username="role1" password="tomcat" roles="role1"/>
  <user username="both" password="tomcat" roles="tomcat,role1"/>
  <user username="gpburdell" password="gotech" roles="jscUser"/>
  <user username="admin" password="admin" roles="admin,manager"/>
</tomcat-users>
```

When users attempt to access an authorization-constrained URL, they will be challenged to enter authentication credentials. If you are using FORM-based authentication, the form-login-page will be displayed. Once the user has been authenticated, your web application can glean useful user data from the HTTP request. The HttpServletRequest provides three particular methods enabled when using container-managed security: getUserPrincipal( ); getRemoteUser( ), which returns user identity information, such as the username; and isUserInRole( ), which determines if a user has a specified role. These methods can be used in your Action classes to perform such things as the following:

- Loading the user's profile and storing it in the session
- Rendering a specific response or redirect to a certain URL based on the user's role
- Allowing role-based access to Actions as configured in the *struts-config.xml* file
- Hiding or displaying presentation components (links, buttons, menus, etc.) based on a user's role (using the logic:present and logic:notPresent tags)

A drawback to the challenge/response authentication model of container-managed security is that users must attempt access to a constrained URL to log in. This behavior can make it difficult for a user to log in proactively. A common trick to permit proactive logins is to create a link on an unsecured page to an authorization-constrained JSP page. Because the JSP page is secured, the user will be forced to log in. The secured JSP page then redirects back to the original unsecured page using the logic: redirect Struts tag:

```
<%@ taglib uri="http://struts.apache.org/tags-logic.tld" prefix="logic" %>
<logic:redirect page="/index.jsp"/>
```

Many web applications place the login form on every publicly accessible page, usually near the top of the page on the left or right. With container-managed security, however, this technique can't easily be employed. The container itself can only reference the login form specified in the login-config. This limitation forces the chicanery required to emulate a proactive login.

There is no easy workaround for this problem. If you need this capability, as many applications do, use application-managed security. To get the best of both worlds, consider using the Solution shown in Recipe 11.10.

Secure transport

Container-managed security allows you to force portions of your applications to run under the Secure Socket Layer (SSL) transport, using HTTP over SSL (HTTPS). The example *web.xml* file (Example 11-16) configures the AdminPages to effectively run under the HTTPS:

```
<security-constraint>
    <web-resource-collection>
        <web-resource-name>AdminPages</web-resource-name>
        <description>Administrative pages</description>
        <url-pattern>/admin/*</url-pattern>
    </web-resource-collection>
    <auth-constraint>
        <role-name>jscAdmin</role-name>
    </auth-constraint>
    <!-- Switch to HTTPS for the admin pages -->
    <user-data-constraint>
        <transport-guarantee>CONFIDENTIAL</transport-guarantee>
    </user-data-constraint>
</security-constraint>
```

The transport-guarantee element accepts values of NONE, INTEGRAL, and CONFIDENTIAL. Specifying either of the latter two values requires requests to the URLs to use the HTTPS protocol over a secured port (typically port 443 or 8443). The value of NONE indicates no particular transport security is required.

Specifying a transport-guarantee of NONE won't make the container switch from the secured protocol (https) to the unsecured protocol (http). Unless you specify http on a request, the application will continue to use https. If you need to switch protocols, consider using the Solution shown in Recipe 11.11.

Most application servers and servlet containers accept the HTTPS protocol. However, you may need to configure the container.

See Also

Container-managed security is convenient and easy to configure, but it can make your application inflexible to changing security requirements and less portable between application servers. Recipe 11.10 provides a Solution that mitigates these problems.

Enabling a servlet container to support https varies by application server. Tomcat provides a simple *how-to* for this. For Tomcat 5.0, the relevant documentation can be found at *http://jakarta.apache.org/tomcat/tomcat-5.0-doc/ssl-howto.html*.

If you need finer-grained control of transport security than can be provided by container-managed security, consider using the Solution shown in Recipe 11.11.

11.10 Mixing Application-Managed and Container-Managed Security

Problem

You want the convenience of container-managed security, yet need a custom mechanism for implementing your security policies.

Solution

Use the SecurityFilter (*http://securityfilter.sourceforge.net*) custom servlet filter and associated classes.

Discussion

Container-managed security, as shown in Recipe 11.9, has some advantages:

- When users attempt to access a protected URL, the container automatically prompts them to logon. Once authenticated, they are forwarded to the originally requested URL.

- The user identity can be determined using the getUserPrincipal( ) or getRemoteUser( ) methods of the HttpServletRequest. These methods can determine if a user is logged in.

- You can determine if a user has a specific role using the isUserInRole(*roleName*) method of the HttpServletRequest. Struts leverages this feature to provide role-constrained actions via the roles attribute. Struts provides for role-specific page generation using the logic:present role="*roleNames*" custom JSP tag.

Container-managed security has drawbacks, such as portability. With container-managed security, the implementation is split between your web application and the application server. You usually must configure container-specific resources to specify the repository, known as a *security realm,* from which the container acquires the user's credentials and roles. Container-managed security will *only* prompt users to login if they attempt access of a protected URL. Users *cannot* log in by going to a known page and entering their username and password. This restriction makes it difficult, for example, to include a login form on every page.

The SecurityFilter servlet filter and related classes provide a hybrid of container-managed security and application-managed security that solves most of these problems. SecurityFilter permits implementation of a custom security policy yet allows programmatic access to user identity and role information via the standard HttpServletRequest methods. You configure the SecurityFilter through an XML file. The format of this file is near identical to the security-constraint elements used for container-managed security in the *web.xml*. Example 11-19 shows a sample *security-filter-config.xml* file. This example is similar to the *web.xml* for container-managed security shown in Recipe 11.9.

Example 11-19. Configuration for SecurityFilter

```
<?xml version="1.0" encoding="ISO-8859-1"?>

<!DOCTYPE securityfilter-config PUBLIC
    "-//SecurityFilter.org//DTD Security Filter Configuration 2.0//EN"
    "http://www.securityfilter.org/dtd/securityfilter-config_2_0.dtd">

<securityfilter-config>

    <security-constraint>
        <web-resource-collection>
          <web-resource-name>RegPages</web-resource-name>
          <description>Registered user pages</description>
          <url-pattern>/reg/*</url-pattern>
        </web-resource-collection>
        <auth-constraint>
            <role-name>jscUser</role-name>
        </auth-constraint>
    </security-constraint>

    <security-constraint>
       <web-resource-collection>
          <web-resource-name>AdminPages</web-resource-name>
          <url-pattern>/admin/*</url-pattern>
       </web-resource-collection>
       <auth-constraint>
          <role-name>jscAdmin</role-name>
       </auth-constraint>
    </security-constraint>
```

Example 11-19. Configuration for SecurityFilter (continued)

```
    <!-- Use this login-config to test BASIC authentication -->
    <!--
    <login-config>
        <auth-method>BASIC</auth-method>
        <realm-name>StrutsCookbookCh11</realm-name>
    </login-config>
    -->
    <login-config>
        <auth-method>FORM</auth-method>
        <realm-name>StrutsCookbookCh11</realm-name>
        <form-login-config>
            <form-login-page>/sf_logon.jsp</form-login-page>
            <form-error-page>/sf_logon_error.jsp</form-error-page>
            <form-default-page>/Welcome.do</form-default-page>
        </form-login-config>
    </login-config>

    <security-role>
        <description>Regular Users</description>
        <role-name>jscUser</role-name>
    </security-role>

    <security-role>
        <description>Administrators</description>
        <role-name>jscAdmin</role-name>
    </security-role>

    <realm className="com.oreilly.strutsckbk.ch11.sf.MemorySecurityRealm"/>

</securityfilter-config>
```

Like container-managed security, with SecurityFilter you can specify allowed roles
for URLs using the security-constraint element. SecurityFilter supports BASIC and
FORM-based authentication. Unlike container-managed security, SecurityFilter
allows for a user to perform an "unsolicited" login. That is, the user can log in without having to attempt access to a protected URL. In this scenario, once logged in, the
user will be forwarded to the page specified in the form-default-page element. The
logon page that you specify for the form-login-page element follows the same convention as container-managed security. The logon form, *sf_logon.jsp*, shown in
Example 11-20, submits the j_username and j_password fields to j_security_check.

Example 11-20. SecurityFilter logon page

```
<%@ page contentType="text/html;charset=UTF-8" language="java" %>
<%@ taglib uri="http://struts.apache.org/tags-bean" prefix="bean" %>

<html>
<head>
<title>Security Filter : Logon Page</title>
</head>
```

Example 11-20. SecurityFilter logon page (continued)

```
<body>
<form method="POST" action="j_security_check">
    <table border="0" width="100%">
        <tr>
            <th align="right">
                <bean:message key="prompt.username"/>:
            </th>
            <td align="left">
                <input type="text" name="j_username" size="16" maxlength="18">
            </td>
        </tr>

        <tr>
            <th align="right">
                <bean:message key="prompt.password"/>:
            </th>
            <td align="left">
                <input type="password" name="j_password" size="16" maxlength="18">
            </td>
        </tr>

        <tr>
            <td align="right">
                <input type="submit" value="Submit">
            </td>
            <td align="left">
                <input type="reset">
            </td>
        </tr>
    </table>
</form>
</body>
</html>
```

With container-managed security, you have to separate the security realm configuration and code from the rest of the web application. The configuration is usually part of a container-specific XML file, and the code usually needs to be placed in a separate JAR file or in the server's classpath. With SecurityFilter, however, you include the configuration and code for your realm with your web application. It all gets bundled together in the same WAR file. Your custom realm must implement the SecurityRealmInterface interface (shown in Example 11-21). SecurityFilter is licensed under the SecurityFilter Software License, derived from and compatible with the Apache Software License. (For brevity, the license has been excluded in this example.)

Example 11-21. SecurityFilter realm interface

```
package org.securityfilter.realm;
import java.security.Principal;
```

Example 11-21. SecurityFilter realm interface (continued)

```java
public interface SecurityRealmInterface {

    /**
     * Authenticate a user.
     *
     * @param username a username
     * @param password a plain text password, as entered by the user
     *
     * @return a Principal object representing the user if successful, false otherwise
     */
    public Principal authenticate(String username, String password);

    /**
     * Test for role membership.
     *
     * Use Principal.getName( ) to get the username from the principal object.
     *
     * @param principal Principal object representing a user
     * @param rolename name of a role to test for membership
     *
     * @return true if the user is in the role, false otherwise
     */
    public boolean isUserInRole(Principal principal, String rolename);
}
```

If you want to work with only usernames and passwords and don't need to create Principals, you can extend the SimpleSecurityRealmBase class. The custom MemorySecurityRealm, shown in Example 11-22, extends this class and implements the booleanAuthenticate( ) and isUserInRole( ) methods by delegating to a custom security service.

Example 11-22. Extending the SimpleSecurityRealmBase

```java
package com.oreilly.strutsckbk.ch11.sf;

import org.securityfilter.realm.SimpleSecurityRealmBase;

public class MemorySecurityRealm extends SimpleSecurityRealmBase {

    private SecurityService serviceImpl = new SecurityServiceImpl( );

    public boolean booleanAuthenticate(String username, String password) {
        try {
            User user = serviceImpl.authenticate(username, password);
            if (user != null) return true;
        } catch (SecurityException e) {
            e.printStackTrace( );
        }
        return false;
    }
```

Example 11-22. Extending the SimpleSecurityRealmBase (continued)

```
    public boolean isUserInRole(String username, String role) {
        User user = serviceImpl.findUser(username);
        return user == null ? false : user.hasRole(role);
    }
}
```

The realm is configured and deployed in the *securityfilter-config.xml* file:

```
    <realm className="com.oreilly.strutsckbk.ch11.sf.MemorySecurityRealm"/>
```

Optionally, you can declaratively set properties on a custom realm using the realm-param element:

```
    <realm className="fully.qualified.classname.of.SecurityRealm">
        <realm-param name="propertyName" value="propertyValue" />
    </realm>
```

You describe the deployment of the actual SecurityFilter servlet filter in the *web.xml* file as shown in Example 11-23.

Example 11-23. Declaring SecurityFilter in the deployment descriptor

```
<?xml version="1.0" encoding="ISO-8859-1"?>

<!DOCTYPE web-app PUBLIC
    "-//Sun Microsystems, Inc.//DTD Web Application 2.3//EN"
    "http://java.sun.com/dtd/web-app_2_3.dtd">

<web-app>

    <display-name>Struts Cookbook - Chapter 11 : SecurityFilter</display-name>

    <!-- Security Filter -->
    <filter>
        <filter-name>Security Filter</filter-name>
        <filter-class>org.securityfilter.filter.SecurityFilter</filter-class>
        <init-param>
            <param-name>config</param-name>
            <param-value>/WEB-INF/securityfilter-config.xml</param-value>
            <description>Configuration file location (this is the default value)</
description>
        </init-param>
        <init-param>
            <param-name>validate</param-name>
            <param-value>true</param-value>
            <description>Validate config file if set to true</description>
        </init-param>
    </filter>

    <!-- map all requests to the SecurityFilter -->
    <filter-mapping>
        <filter-name>Security Filter</filter-name>
        <url-pattern>/*</url-pattern>
    </filter-mapping>
```

Example 11-23. Declaring SecurityFilter in the deployment descriptor (continued)

```
    <!-- Action Servlet Configuration -->
    <servlet>
        <servlet-name>action</servlet-name>
        <servlet-class>org.apache.struts.action.ActionServlet</servlet-class>
        <init-param>
            <param-name>config</param-name>
            <param-value>/WEB-INF/struts-config.xml</param-value>
        </init-param>
        <load-on-startup>1</load-on-startup>
    </servlet>

    <!-- Action Servlet Mapping -->
    <servlet-mapping>
        <servlet-name>action</servlet-name>
        <url-pattern>*.do</url-pattern>
    </servlet-mapping>

    <!-- The Welcome File List -->
    <welcome-file-list>
        <welcome-file>index.jsp</welcome-file>
    </welcome-file-list>

</web-app>
```

It's best to map all requests to the filter. Let the *securityfilter-config.xml* file set the security constraints for specific URLs.

SecurityFilter provides support for automatic logins using cookies. This gives you a similar capability to the custom solution shown in Recipe 11.7. Furthermore, you can configure all the details about the cookies, such as expiration and encryption, in the *securityfilter-config.xml* file, as shown in Example 11-24.

Example 11-24. Configuring the "remember me" cookie

```
<form-login-config>
    <!--Logon page must contain a checkbox for j_rememberme -->
    <form-login-page>/sf_logon.jsp</form-login-page>
    <form-error-page>/sf_logon_error.jsp</form-error-page>
    <form-default-page>/Welcome.do</form-default-page>
    <!-- remember-me config -->
    <remember-me
className="org.securityfilter.authenticator.persistent.DefaultPersistentLoginManager">
        <!-- optional settings for default persistent login manager -->
        <remember-me-param name="cookieLife" value="15"/>
        <remember-me-param name="protection" value="all"/>
        <remember-me-param name="useIP" value="true"/>
        <remember-me-param name="encryptionAlgorithm" value="DES"/>
        <remember-me-param name="encryptionMode" value="ECB"/>
        <remember-me-param name="encryptionPadding" value="PKCS5Padding"/>
        <!-- encryption keys; customize for each application -->
        <!-- NOTE: these kys must be speciied AFTER other encryption settings -->
```

Example 11-24. Configuring the "remember me" cookie (continued)

```
        <remember-me-param name="validationKey"
value="34738290248940248975489573489 0347"/>
        <remember-me-param name="encryptionKey"
value="3478923470284902374878462406 73842"/>
    </remember-me>
</form-login-config>
```

You enable the "remember me" capability by adding a checkbox to your logon form with the name of j_rememberme. Here's what you would add to the logon page shown in Example 11-20:

```
<tr>
    <th align="right">Remember me:</th>
    <td align="left">
        <input type="checkbox" name="j_rememberme" value="true">
    </td>
</tr>
```

The behavior you get with the SecurityFilter will look and feel like container-managed security. If users attempt to access a protected page, they will be prompted to log in. Of course, if they use the "remember me" feature, they can automatically log in. They can log in without having to attempt access to a protected page. Once authenticated, control is forwarded to the form-default-page.

Using SecurityFilter, you can use the getUserPrincipal( ), getRemoteUser( ), and isUserInRole( ) methods of the HttpServletRequest as if you were using full-blown container-managed security. Struts support for roles—the roles attribute of the action element and the roles attribute of the logic:present tag—will work as intended.

See Also

The SecurityFilter project's home page can be found at *http://securityfilter. sourceforge.net*. SecurityFilter provides a framework for authentication and authorization using a servlet filter. To understand how filters work for these purposes, take a look at Recipes 11.6 and 11.8.

Recipe 11.9 discusses the use of container-managed security.

11.11 Configuring Actions to Require SSL

Problem

You want to control if HTTPS is required on a page-by-page basis.

Solution

Use the SSLEXT Struts extension.

Discussion

The Struts SSL Extension (SSLEXT), an open source Struts plug-in, enables you to indicate if an action requires the secure (https) protocol. Steve Ditlinger created and maintains this project (with others), hosted at *http://sslext.sourceforge.net*.

SSLEXT enables fine-grained secure protocol control by providing:

- The ability to specify in the *struts-config.xml* file if an action should require a secure protocol. This feature essentially allows your application to switch actions and JSP pages from http to https.

- Extensions of the Struts JSP tags that generate URLs that include the https protocol.

The SSLEXT distribution consists of a plug-in class for initialization (SecurePlugIn), a custom request processor (SecureRequestProcessor), and a custom action mapping class (SecureActionMapping).

 If you have been using custom RequestProcessor or ActionMapping classes and you want to use SSLEXT, you will need to change these classes to extend the corresponding classes provided by SSLEXT.

For JSP pages, SSLEXT provides custom extensions of Struts tags for generating protocol-specific URLs. A custom JSP allows you to indicate if a JSP page requires https. SSLEXT depends on the Java Secure Socket Extension (JSSE). JSSE is included with JDK 1.4 or later. If you're using an older JDK, you can download JSSE from Sun's Java site. Finally, you'll need to enable SSL for your application server. For Tomcat, this can be found in the *Tomcat SSL How-To* documentation.

SSLEXT works by intercepting the request in its SecureRequestProcessor. If the request is directed toward an action that is marked as secure, the SecureRequestProcessor will generate a redirect. The redirect will change the protocol to https and the port to a secure port (e.g., 443 or 8443). Switching protocols sounds simple; however, a request in a Struts application usually contains request attributes, and these attributes are lost on a redirect. SSLEXT solves this problem by temporarily storing the request attributes in the session.

You can download the SSLEXT distribution from the project web site. SSLEXT doesn't include a lot of documentation, but it comes with sample applications that demonstrate its use and features. If all your requests go through Struts actions, you can apply SSLEXT without modifying any Java code or JSP pages. Here's how you would apply SSLEXT to a Struts application:

1. Copy the *sslext.jar* file into your application's *WEB-INF/lib* folder.

2. If you need to use the custom JSP tags, copy the *sslext.tld* file into the *WEB-INF/ lib* folder.

Make the following changes to the *struts-config.xml* file:

1. Add the `type` attribute to the `action-mappings` element to specify the custom secure action mapping class:

```
<action-mappings type="org.apache.struts.config.SecureActionConfig">
```

2. Add the `controller` element for the secure request processor:

```
<controller processorClass="org.apache.struts.action.SecureRequestProcessor" />
```

3. Add the plug-in declaration to load the SSLEXT code:

```
<plug-in className="org.apache.struts.action.SecurePlugIn">
    <set-property property="httpPort" value="80"/>
    <set-property property="httpsPort" value="443"/>
    <set-property property="enable" value="true"/>
    <set-property property="addSession" value="true"/>
</plug-in>
```

4. Set the secure property to `true` for any action you want to be accessed using `https`:

```
<action    path="/reg/Main"
           type="com.oreilly.strutsckbk.ch11.ssl.MainMenuAction">
    <!-- Force this action to run secured -->
    <set-property property="secure" value="true"/>
    <forward name="success" path="/reg/main.jsp"/>
</action>
```

5. Set the secure property to `false` for any action that you only want to run under an unsecured protocol (`http`):

```
<action    path="/Welcome"
           type="com.oreilly.strutsckbk.ch11.ssl.WelcomeAction">
    <!-- Force this action to run unsecured -->
    <set-property property="secure" value="false"/>
    <forward name="success" path="/welcome.jsp"/>
</action>
```

If you have accessible JSP pages you want to specify as secured (or unsecured), use the SSLEXT pageScheme custom JSP tag:

```
<%@ taglib uri="http://www.ebuilt.com/taglib" prefix="sslext"%>
<sslext:pageScheme secure="true"/>
```

Now rebuild and deploy the application. When you click on a link to a secured action, the protocol will switch to `https` and the port to the secure port (e.g., 8443 or 443). If you go to an action marked as unsecured, the protocol and port should switch back to `http` and the port to the standard port (e.g., 8080 or 80). If you access an action without a specified value for the secure property or the value is set to `any`, then the protocol won't switch when you access the action. If you're under `http`, the protocol will remain `http`; if you're under `https`, the protocol will remain `https`.

Be careful if you switch from a secured to unsecured protocol (https to http). Critical user-specific data, such as the current session ID, can be snooped by a hacker. The hacker could use this data to hijack the session and imposter the user. Here is a good rule to follow: *Once you switch to https, stay in https.*

You can use SSLEXT alongside container-managed security mechanisms for specifying secure transport. The container-managed security approach works well when you want to secure entire portions of your application:

```
<security-constraint>
    <web-resource-collection>
        <web-resource-name>AdminPages</web-resource-name>
        <description>Administrative pages</description>
        <url-pattern>/admin/*</url-pattern>
    </web-resource-collection>
    <auth-constraint>
        <role-name>jscAdmin</role-name>
    </auth-constraint>
    <!-- Switch to HTTPS for the admin pages -->
    <user-data-constraint>
        <transport-guarantee>CONFIDENTIAL</transport-guarantee>
    </user-data-constraint>
</security-constraint>
```

You can then use SSLEXT for fine-grained control of the protocol at the action level.

See Also

Enabling an application server to support https varies. Tomcat provides a how-to for this. For Tomcat 5.0, the relevant documentation can be found at *http://jakarta.apache.org/tomcat/tomcat-5.0-doc/ssl-howto.html*.

SSLEXT is hosted on SourceForge at *http://sslext.sourceforge.net*.

Craig McClanahan presents a good argument against switching back to http from https. His comments can be found in a *struts-user* mailing list thread archived at *http://www.mail-archive.com/struts-user@jakarta.apache.org/msg81889.html*.

Recipe 11.9 shows how you can specify the protocol in the *web.xml* file. This approach, presented as part of the J2EE tutorial, can be found at *http://java.sun.com/j2ee/1.4/docs/tutorial/doc/Security4.html*.

11.12 Limiting the Size of Uploaded Files

Problem

You want to limit the size of a file to be uploaded to your application.

Solution

In the *struts-config.xml* file, set the maxFileSize attribute on the controller element to the maximum accepted size (in bytes) for an uploaded file. In this example, a single uploaded file must be smaller than 700 KB:

```
<controller maxFileSize="700K"/>
```

Discussion

Whether intended or not, users may attempt to upload excessively large files to your web application. In most cases, the user accidentally picked the wrong file; however, a malicious user could be attempting to bring down your application. You can restrict uploads to a maximum file size using the maxFileSize attribute on the controller element in your *struts-config.xml* file. The value for this attribute is expressed as an integer value optionally followed by a "K," "M," or "G," interpreted as kilobytes, megabytes or gigabytes, respectively. If you specify the integer value with no units indicated, the value will be interpreted as bytes.

If you attempt to upload a file larger than the acceptable maximum, the FormFile property of the ActionForm will be null. You can handle this condition in your Action that processes the upload, as shown in Example 11-25.

Example 11-25. Handling null FormFile property (partial)

```
public ActionForward execute(ActionMapping mapping,
                             ActionForm form,
                             HttpServletRequest request,
                             HttpServletResponse response) throws Exception {

    // Get the form file property from the form
    UploadForm uploadForm = (UploadForm) form;
    FormFile content = uploadForm.getContent( );

    if (content == null) {
        ActionMessage msg = new ActionMessage("error.maxFileSize.exceeded");
        ActionMessages errors = new ActionMessages( );
        errors.add(ActionMessages.GLOBAL_MESSAGE, msg);
        saveErrors(request, errors);
        return mapping.getInputForward( );
    }

    // continue processing upload ...
```

If you don't specify the maxFileSize attribute, the default maximum will be 250 MB (250M). If you want a size different size than this, you must specify it (as shown in the Solution).

The controller element supports a related attribute with the name of memFileSize. This attribute specifies the maximum amount of memory that will be used to hold an uploaded file. If a file is larger than this amount, it will be written to some external storage, typically the filesystem. The value for the attribute is specified using the same notation as the `maxFileSize` attribute. The default memory file size is 256 KB. Here, the maximum file size is set to 5 MB, and the maximum amount held in memory is set to 500 KB:

```
<controller maxFileSize="5M" memFileSize="500K"/>
```

The `memFileSize` property sets the size threshold which determines at what point an uploaded file will be written to disk or cached in memory. The default value for this setting is 10,240 bytes (`10K`). Some containers are configured to allow limited or no ability for writing to disk from within a web application. If your container has this restriction, you may need to adjust this setting to a value greater than the largest expected file size.

See Also

Recipe 7.10 shows you how to allow users to upload files to your application.

The Struts User's Guide discusses controller configuration. The relevant section can be found at *http://struts.apache.org/userGuide/configuration.html#controller_config*.

Beneath the covers, Struts use the Jakarta Commons FileUpload package. Complete documentation and source for this package can be found at *http://jakarta.apache.org/commons/fileupload*.

## CHAPTER 12

Internationalization

12.0 Introduction

Struts has long been known as a good framework for constructing applications that can be used across multiple languages and geographies. The basis for Struts internationalization (i18n) support is Java. Java's features for internationalization and localization are quite mature, having been around since Java 1.1. At the heart of Struts i18n support is the `java.util.Locale` object. This object is used throughout Struts to identify a client user's language and country.

You can use Struts to adapt an application to a specific locale using the following features:

- `MessageResources` bundles (e.g., properties files) that provide localized messages, prompts, and data formats
- Creation of locales based on the user's browser settings
- Formatting of dates and numbers using locale-specific patterns
- Retrieval of locale-specific images
- Ability to specify an appropriate HTTP response character-encoding

Like Struts, JSTL provides tags for localizing data. The JSTL tags are, in many cases, more robust and easier to use than the Struts tags. Thankfully, you don't have to choose one or the other (see Recipe 12.2). The recipes in this chapter give you options for using Struts or JSTL where appropriate.

12.1 Detecting Browser Language Settings

Problem

Your web application needs to support the language settings of the client's browser.

Solution

If you are using the default settings of Struts, you don't have to do anything; the browser's locale will be automatically detected.

Discussion

When a request is routed through the Struts RequestProcessor, the processLocale( ) method is called. Example 12-1 shows the implementation of this method in the RequestProcessor from Struts 1.2.

Example 12-1. How the RequestProcessor sets the locale

```
/**
 * <p>Automatically select a <code>Locale</code> for the current user, if requested.
 * <strong>NOTE</strong> - configuring Locale selection will trigger
 * the creation of a new <code>HttpSession</code> if necessary.</p>
 *
 * @param request The servlet request we are processing
 * @param response The servlet response we are creating
 */
protected void processLocale(HttpServletRequest request,
                            HttpServletResponse response) {

    // Are we configured to select the Locale automatically?
    if (!moduleConfig.getControllerConfig().getLocale()) {
        return;
    }

    // Has a Locale already been selected?
    HttpSession session = request.getSession();
    if (session.getAttribute(Globals.LOCALE_KEY) != null) {
        return;
    }

    // Use the Locale returned by the servlet container (if any)
    Locale locale = request.getLocale();
    if (locale != null) {
        if (log.isDebugEnabled()) {
            log.debug(" Setting user locale '" + locale + "'");
        }
        session.setAttribute(Globals.LOCALE_KEY, locale);
    }

}
```

The method first checks if the controller is configured to set the locale automatically. If you don't want the controller to set the locale (which results in the creation of an HttpSession), set the controller's locale attribute to false in the *struts-config.xml* file.

```
<controller locale="false"/>
```

You need to ensure the browser renders your generated HTML appropriately for the user's language. The HTML html tag supports the lang attribute whose value represents the language generally used within the document. Here's how it would look if the page consisted primarily of text written in Russian:

```
<html lang="ru">
```

The value of the lang attribute should be set to an ISO-639 standard two-character language code. These codes are essentially the same language codes used by the Java Locale. You can indicate a language dialect by adding a subcode name; the subcode equates to the two-character country code of a Locale. For the lang attribute, separate the language code from the subcode with a hyphen; not an underscore (_) as used by Locale. You would indicate U.S. English as "en-US" and French Canadian as "fr-CA."

Struts can automatically generate an appropriate lang attribute for you. In Struts 1.1, set the locale attribute of the html:html tag to true to create the lang attribute.

```
<%@ page contentType="text/html;charset=UTF-8" language="java" %>
<%@ taglib uri="http://jakarta.apache.org/struts/tags-html" prefix="html" %>

<html:html locale="true">
```

The html:html tag uses the same heuristic to resolve the current locale as the processLocale( ) method shown in Example 12-1. The difference is that the tag allows you to process the locale on an as-needed basis, whereas the processLocale( ) method fires on every request unless explicitly disabled.

The html:html tag first looks for a Locale in the session; if one is found, it uses it. Otherwise, the tag looks for the language from the HttpServletRequest. The servlet request returns a Locale based on the Accept-Language HTTP header. If this header value is not set, then the server's default Locale is returned. The html:html tag stores the Locale in the session, creating the session if it didn't exist.

Some web applications are written not to use HttpSessions. With Struts 1.1, it was impossible to use the locale attribute of the html:html tag without creating an HttpSession. This problem has been resolved in Struts 1.2. The locale attribute of the html:html tag has been replaced with the lang attribute. Setting the lang attribute to true will render an html tag with the lang attribute set to the appropriate language but won't create an HttpSession:

```
<%@ page contentType="text/html;charset=UTF-8" language="java" %>
<%@ taglib uri="http://struts.apache.org/tags-html" prefix="html" %>

<html:html lang="true">
```

See Also

The Struts User's Guide includes a section on internationalization that covers this and other related topics. The relevant section can be found at *http://struts.apache.org/ userGuide/building_view.html#i18n*.

Sun's Java Tutorial has a trail on internationalization at *http://java.sun.com/docs/ books/tutorial/i18n/*.

Information on HTML's support for internationalization, such as the lang attribute of the html tag, can be found in *HTML and XHTML: The Definitive Guide* by Chuck Musciano and Bill Kennedy (O'Reilly).

12.2 Sharing Message Resources with JSTL

Problem

You want the JSTL formatting tags (fmt) tags to use the same MessageResources properties file used by Struts.

Solution

Set the value of the JSTL localization context parameter to your Struts MessageResources file, as shown in the partial *web.xml* file of Example 12-2.

Example 12-2. Setting the JSTL localization context

```
<?xml version="1.0" encoding="ISO-8859-1"?>
<!DOCTYPE web-app PUBLIC
    "-//Sun Microsystems, Inc.//DTD Web Application 2.3//EN"
    "http://java.sun.com/dtd/web-app_2_3.dtd">

<web-app>
    <context-param>
        <param-name>javax.servlet.jsp.jstl.fmt.localizationContext</param-name>
        <param-value>path.to.MessageResources</param-value>
    </context-param>
...
```

Discussion

The JSP Standard Tag Library (JSTL) provides powerful tags for support of internationalization. The JSTL formatting tag library, referred to as the fmt tags, support many of the same internationalization features provided by the Struts tags and a lot more. You can configure JSTL to use the same MessageResources file you use in your Struts application. The JSTL tags rely on a default resource bundle of properties. You define this default resource bundle for your JSTL tags with a web application context parameter.

Set the param-name to `javax.servlet.jsp.jstl.fmt.localizationContext` and the param-value to the same value as the parameter of the `message-resources` element in your *struts-config.xml* file.

If you use an alternate `MessageResources` file in your Struts applications, you can refer to those properties with the JSTL tags. You use the `fmt:bundle` or `fmt:setBundle` tag to specify the alternate properties file. The properties file must be on your classpath. Suppose your alternate resource bundle was defined in your *struts-config.xml* as follows:

```
<message-resources key="alt"
    parameter="AlternateResources">
</message-resources>
```

You would display a message from this properties file with a Struts tag like this:

```
<bean:message bundle="alt" key="msg.hello" arg0="Bill"/>
```

To do the same with JSTL, you need to make the message resources available to the `fmt:message` tag with the `fmt:setBundle` tag. The `fmt:setBundle` tag establishes the resource bundle used on the remainder of the JSP page.

```
<fmt:setBundle basename="AlternateResources">
<fmt:message key="msg.hello">
    <fmt:param value="Bill"/>
</fmt:message>
```

Alternatively, you can nest the `fmt:message` tag within the `fmt:bundle` tag. The specified bundle only applies to the nested tags.

```
<fmt:bundle basename="AlternateResources">
    <fmt:message key="msg.hello">
        <fmt:param value="Bill"/>
    </fmt:message>
</fmt:bundle>
```

See Also

JavaServer Pages by Hans Bergsten (O'Reilly) covers JSTL in great detail and is an invaluable source. Sun provides an excellent tutorial on JSTL that can be found at *http://java.sun.com/tutorials/jstl*.

You may want to read the JSTL specification. This well-written document provides a lot of insight to help you understand how and why JSTL works the way it does. This document and other related information can be downloaded from *http://java.sun.com/products/jsp/jstl/*.

12.3   Using an Application-Wide Locale

Problem

You want your web application to use the same locale settings for all users, regardless of their browser's language setting. You also want the JSTL tags to honor this application-wide locale.

Solution

Use a servlet Filter to set the Locale to the desired value (see Example 12-3). The Filter ensures that the Locale is set for all web requests, and not just those handled by Struts.

Example 12-3. Using a servlet filter to set the locale

```
package com.oreilly.strutsckbk.ch12;

import java.io.IOException;
import java.util.Locale;

import javax.servlet.Filter;
import javax.servlet.FilterChain;
import javax.servlet.FilterConfig;
import javax.servlet.ServletException;
import javax.servlet.ServletRequest;
import javax.servlet.ServletResponse;
import javax.servlet.http.HttpServletRequest;
import javax.servlet.http.HttpServletResponse;
import javax.servlet.http.HttpSession;
import javax.servlet.jsp.jstl.core.Config;

import org.apache.struts.Globals;

public class LocaleFilter implements Filter {

    // the locale code used to create the locale (e.g. en_US)
    private String localeCode;

    // indicates if the locale should always be set;
    // even if there is currently one in the session
    private boolean ignore = false;

    public void init(FilterConfig filterConfig) throws ServletException {
        this.filterConfig = filterConfig;
        localeCode = filterConfig.getInitParameter("locale");
        override = Boolean.valueOf(filterConfig.getInitParameter("ignore")).booleanValue(
);
    }

    public void doFilter(ServletRequest request, ServletResponse response, FilterChain
chain)
                throws IOException, ServletException {
```

Example 12-3. Using a servlet filter to set the locale (continued)

```
        HttpServletRequest req = (HttpServletRequest) request;
        HttpServletResponse res = (HttpServletResponse) response;

        // create the session if needed
        HttpSession session = req.getSession( );

        Locale currentLocale = (Locale) session.getAttribute(Globals.LOCALE_KEY);
        if (currentLocale == null || ignore) {
            // create the new locale
            Locale locale = new Locale(localeCode);

            // reset the Struts locale
            session.setAttribute(Globals.LOCALE_KEY, locale);

            // reset the JSTL locale
            Config.set(session, Config.FMT_LOCALE, locale);
        }
        chain.doFilter(request, response);
    }

    public void destroy( ) {
        // Nothing necessary
    }

    private FilterConfig filterConfig;
}
```

Declare the filter in your *web.xml*, as shown in Example 12-4.

Example 12-4. Locale filter configuration (partial)

```
<?xml version="1.0" encoding="ISO-8859-1"?>
<!DOCTYPE web-app PUBLIC
    "-//Sun Microsystems, Inc.//DTD Web Application 2.3//EN"
    "http://java.sun.com/dtd/web-app_2_3.dtd">

<web-app>
    <display-name>Struts Cookbook - Chapter 12 Examples</display-name>
    <context-param>
        <param-name>javax.servlet.jsp.jstl.fmt.localizationContext</param-name>
        <param-value>ApplicationResources</param-value>
    </context-param>

    <filter>
        <filter-name>LocaleFilter</filter-name>
        <filter-class>
            com.oreilly.strutsckbk.ch12.LocaleFilter
        </filter-class>
        <!-- Language and country -->
        <init-param>
            <param-name>locale</param-name>
            <param-value>en_US</param-value>
```

Example 12-4. Locale filter configuration (partial) (continued)

```
        </init-param>
        <!-- True to set locale even if already set in session -->
        <init-param>
            <param-name>ignore</param-name>
            <param-value>true</param-value>
        </init-param>
    </filter>

    <filter-mapping>
        <filter-name>LocaleFilter</filter-name>
        <url-pattern>/*</url-pattern>
    </filter-mapping>
...
```

Discussion

Usually, you want the user's Locale to reflect the browser's settings, as shown in Recipe 12.1. Some applications, however, need the opposite behavior. You want the application to reflect the same language and country regardless of how the client's browser, or the server's operating system, is configured. The servlet filter shown in the Solution provides this ability. The filter accepts two initialization parameters. The locale parameter defines the Locale to use by specifying a locale code (e.g., en_US) as its value. To use this filter, you must turn off locale processing in the Struts RequestProcessor using the controller element in the *struts-config.xml* file:

```
<controller locale="false"/>
```

The second parameter, the ignore parameter, indicates if the filter should ignore any Locale in session, always setting the locale even if one is present. You can set this value to false if you want to define a default locale but still allow a user to select and use a new locale (see Recipe 12.4).

Filters provide an excellent way to apply across-the-board behavior. Though you could override the processLocale method in a custom RequestProcessor, it would only affect requests to Struts actions. The Solution shown here will set the default locale for web requests to Struts actions, JSPs, and static HTML pages.

See Also

Servlet filters are a new addition to the Servlet API, being added in Version 2.3. *Java Servlet Programming* by Jason Hunter (O'Reilly) covers servlet filters in-depth.

Sun's Java site has a good article on the essentials of servlet filters found at *http://java.sun.com/products/servlet/Filters.html*.

12.4 Changing Locale on the Fly

Problem

You want to allow a user to choose the language and country to be used by the web application for his session.

Solution

Use my `ChangeLocaleAction`, based on the Struts built-in `LocaleAction`, as shown in Example 12-5.

Example 12-5. Struts action for changing the current locale

```
package com.oreilly.strutsckbk.ch12;

import java.util.Locale;

import javax.servlet.http.HttpServletRequest;
import javax.servlet.http.HttpServletResponse;
import javax.servlet.http.HttpSession;
import javax.servlet.jsp.jstl.core.Config;

import org.apache.commons.beanutils.PropertyUtils;
import org.apache.commons.logging.Log;
import org.apache.commons.logging.LogFactory;
import org.apache.struts.Globals;
import org.apache.struts.action.Action;
import org.apache.struts.action.ActionForm;
import org.apache.struts.action.ActionForward;
import org.apache.struts.action.ActionMapping;


/**
 * Implementation of <strong>Action</strong> that changes the user's
 * @link(java.util.Locale and forwards to a page, based on request level
 * parameters that are set  (language, country, variant, &amp; page).
 * Also changes the JSTL locale.
 */
public final class ChangeLocaleAction extends Action {

    private static final String SUCCESS = "success";

    /**
     * Commons Logging instance.
     */
    private Log log = LogFactory.getFactory().getInstance(this.getClass().getName());

    /**
     * <p>
     * Change the user's @link(java.util.Locale) based on @link(ActionForm)
     * properties.
```

Example 12-5. Struts action for changing the current locale (continued)

```
 *  </p>
 *  <p>
 *  This <code>Action</code> looks for <code>language</code> and
 *  <code>country</code> and <code>variant</code> properties on the given
 *  form, constructs an appropriate Locale object, and sets it as the Struts
 *  Locale for this user's session as well as the JSTL locale.
 *  Any <code>ActionForm, including a @link(DynaActionForm), may be used.
 *  </p>
 *  <p>
 *  If a <code>page</code> property is also provided, then after
 *  setting the Locale, control is forwarded to that URI path.
 *  Otherwise, control is forwarded to "success".
 *  </p>
 *
 *  @param mapping The ActionMapping used to select this instance
 *  @param form The optional ActionForm bean for this request (if any)
 *  @param request The HTTP request we are processing
 *  @param response The HTTP response we are creating
 *
 *  @return Action to forward to
 *  @exception java.lang.Exception if an input/output error or servlet exception occurs
 */
public ActionForward execute(ActionMapping mapping,
            ActionForm form,
            HttpServletRequest request,
            HttpServletResponse response)
throws Exception {

    // Extract attributes we will need
    HttpSession session = request.getSession();
    Locale locale = getLocale(request);

    String language = null;
    String country = null;
    String variant = null;
    String page = null;

    try {
        language = (String) PropertyUtils.getSimpleProperty(form, "language");
        country = (String) PropertyUtils.getSimpleProperty(form, "country");
        variant = (String) PropertyUtils.getSimpleProperty(form, "variant");
        page = (String) PropertyUtils.getSimpleProperty(form, "page");
    } catch (Exception e) {
        log.error(e.getMessage(), e);
    }

    boolean isLanguage = language != null && language.length() > 0;
    boolean isCountry  = country != null && country.length() > 0;
    boolean isVariant  = variant != null && variant.length() > 0;

    if ( isLanguage && isCountry && isVariant ) {
        locale = new java.util.Locale(language, country, variant);
```

Example 12-5. Struts action for changing the current locale (continued)

```
        } else if ( isLanguage && isCountry ) {
            locale = new java.util.Locale(language, country);
        } else if ( isLanguage ) {
            locale = new java.util.Locale(language, "");
        }

        // reset the Struts locale
        session.setAttribute(Globals.LOCALE_KEY, locale);

        // reset the JSTL locale
        Config.set(session, Config.FMT_LOCALE, locale);

        if (null==page || "".equals(page))
            return mapping.findForward(SUCCESS);
        else
            return new ActionForward(page);
    }
}
```

Discussion

The ChangeLocaleAction is based on the Struts 1.2 LocaleAction. This action provides the same capabilities at the Struts LocaleAction, and it supports a locale *variant*. Variants aren't defined by an ISO standard like language and country codes but are supported by Java and can give you additional means of organizing your localized messages. Even more importantly, the ChangeLocaleAction updates the Locale used by JSTL as well as the Struts Locale:

```
// reset the Struts locale
session.setAttribute(Globals.LOCALE_KEY, locale);

// reset the JSTL locale
Config.set(session, Config.FMT_LOCALE, locale);
```

The Struts LocaleAction doesn't do this because it would be dependent on the JSTL APIs. But if you're using Struts and JSTL's internationalization capabilities, you will want to update the Locale for both.

Similar to the LocaleAction, the ChangeLocaleAction reads the language, country, and variant codes from properties on an ActionForm. It creates a Locale using these values and stores this Locale in the session. The action returns an ActionForward using the path specified by the page property or found under the name "success."

To use the ChangeLocaleAction, you'll need to create an ActionForm containing the required properties. You can extend ActionForm, or you can use a DynaActionForm specified in your *struts-config.xml* file:

```
<form-bean name="LocaleForm" type="org.apache.struts.action.DynaActionForm">
    <form-property name="language" type="java.lang.String"/>
    <form-property name="country" type="java.lang.String"/>
    <form-property name="variant" type="java.lang.String"/>
```

```
        <form-property name="page" type="java.lang.String"/>
    </form-bean>
```

Then declare an action in the *struts-config.xml* file that uses this ActionForm and the ChangeLocaleAction:

```
<action path="/ChangeLocale"
        name="LocaleForm"
        scope="request"
        type="com.oreilly.strutsckbk.ch12.ChangeLocaleAction"/>
```

Here's a set of links using this action that allow the user to change languages between English, Russian, and U.S. English (Southeastern variant):

```
<html:link action="/ChangeLocale?language=en">
  English
</html:link><br />
<html:link action="/ChangeLocale?language=ru">
  Russian
</html:link><br />
<html:link action="/ChangeLocale? language=en&country=US&variant=SE">
  Southeastern U.S. English
</html:link><br />
```

Here's an HTML form that allows a user to change the current language. Once changed the request will be forwarded to the /Welcome.do page.

```
<%@ page contentType="text/html;charset=UTF-8" language="java" %>
<%@ taglib uri="http://struts.apache.org/tags-bean" prefix="bean" %>
<%@ taglib uri="http://struts.apache.org/tags-html" prefix="html" %>

<html:html lang="true">
<head>
  <title>Change language</title>
</head>
<body>
<html:form action="/ChangeLocale">
    <html:select property="language">
        <html:option value="en">English</html:option>
        <html:option value="fr">French</html:option>
        <html:option value="ru">Russian</html:option>
    </html:select>
    <html:hidden property="page" value="/Welcome.do"/>
    <html:submit/>
</html:form>
</body>
</html:html>
```

If you're using Struts 1.2 and you're not using JSTL or locale variants, then it doesn't matter if you use the Struts LocaleAction or my ChangeLocaleAction. However, if you aren't using Struts 1.2 or you're using JSTL, then my ChangeLocaleAction will work best.

See Also

The API for the LocaleAction can be found at *http://struts.apache.org/api/org/apache/struts/actions/LocaleAction.html*.

If you're using Struts and JSTL together, you can share the resource bundles using the Solution in Recipe 12.2.

12.5 Creating Localized Messages from an Action

Problem

You need to create a localized message from within an Action.

Solution

```
MessageResources resources = getResources(request);
Locale locale = getLocale(request);
String msg1 = resources.getMessage(locale, "message.success"));
String msg2 = resources.getMessage(locale, "msg.hello", "Bill"));
```

Discussion

Application messages for information and errors are typically created using the ActionMessage and ActionError classes. These messages are saved in the request using the saveMessages( ) and saveErrors( ) methods.

The ActionError class has been deprecated in Struts 1.2. The ActionMessage class should be used instead.

But you can retrieve localized text messages in the Action itself. You may need the message in the Action because you are logging this information or you need to pass the message to some other service. The Solution shows how you can get a localized message in an Action. The MessageResources and current Locale are retrieved using the getResources( ) and getLocale( ) methods of the base Action class. MessageResources provides a number of variations of the getMessage( ) method. There are three basic pieces of information you can pass:

locale
    The requested message Locale or null for the system default Locale

key
    The message key to look up

args
    An array of replacement parameters for placeholders in the message

You can retrieve messages from an alternate `MessageResources` set. Suppose you've declared your alternate set in the *struts-config.xml* file:

```
<message-resources key="alt"
    parameter="AlternateResources">
</message-resources>
```

The getResources( ) method takes an optional parameter specifying the name of the `MessageResources` bundle, identified by the key attribute of the message-resources element:

```
MessageResources resources = getResources(request, "alt");
```

If you only have access to the servlet request, you can create messages but you have to get the `Locale` and `MessageResources` through different means. To get the `Locale`, use the RequestUtils class in the org.apache.struts.util package:

```
Locale locale = RequestUtils.getUserLocale(request, null);
```

The default set of `MessageResources` can be retrieved using:

```
MessageResources resources =
    (MessageResources) request.getAttribute(Globals.MESSAGES_KEY));
```

You can use one of the `MessageResources.getMessage( )` methods to retrieve the message.

You can retrieve an alternate set of `MessageResources`, but the code is more involved because modules are taken into account. Take a look at the source for the `Action` class if you're interested.

See Also

The JavaDocs for the Struts `Action` class (*http://struts.apache.org/api/org/apache/struts/action/Action.html*) provide details on the convenience methods used in this recipe.

12.6   Displaying Locale-Specific Text

Problem

Your Struts application needs to display correctly formatted text—particularly numbers, dates, and messages—based on a user's locale.

Solution

From the Struts *bean* tag library, use the following:

```
<%-- Format a number --%>
<bean:write name="beanName"
        property="numericProperty"
          format="number pattern"/>
```

```
<%-- Format a date --%>
<bean:write name="beanName"
        property="dateProperty"
          format="date pattern"/>

<%-- Format a message with parameters --%>
<bean:message key="message.key"
              argn="replacement value"/>
```

From the JSTL *fmt* tag library, use the following:

```
<%-- Format a number --%>
<fmt:formatNumber value="${beanName.numericProperty}"
                  pattern="number pattern"/>

<%-- Format a date --%>
<fmt:formatDate value="${beanName.dateProperty}"
                pattern="date pattern"/>

<%-- Format a message with parameters --%>
<fmt:message key="message.key">
    <fmt:param value="replacement value"/>
</fmt:message>
```

Discussion

Struts provides the generic bean:write tag to output text formatted for a specific locale and bean:message to render localized messages. If you're using JSTL, you can use the tags of the fmt tag library.

Using the Struts bean tags

This bean:write tag renders a value specified by the standard Struts name and property attributes. This tag can format dates and numbers before outputting the value using the pattern specified by the format attribute. The format pattern will be applied if the value is a java.lang.Number or java.util.Date object. Numbers are formatted using the java.text.DecimalFormat class and dates with the java.text.SimpleDateFormat class.

The bean:write tag accounts for the current locale when formatting by using a locale-specific instance of the formatter class. For example, suppose you are outputting a numeric value:

```
<bean:write name="order" property="amount" format="#,##0.00"/>
```

With the locale set to English ("en") and the amount to 13995.78, the following text is rendered:

```
13,995.78
```

With the locale set to Russian ("ru"), the number is formatted for that locale. Like other European languages, Russian uses a space for the grouping separator and a comma (,) for the decimal separator.

```
13 995,78
```

You can use the formatKey attribute of the bean:write tag to refer to a pattern stored in your message resources bundle. For numbers, the pattern retrieved from the bundle will be applied as a *localized pattern*; in other words, the pattern is expected to be written for that specific locale.

> If you use the formatKey attribute of the bean:write tag, be aware of a known issue (Apache Bugzilla ticket #27636): you must specify a value for the key in *all* of your resource bundles that may use it. Because the pattern is applied as a localized pattern, a nonlocalized pattern retrieved from a fallback resource bundle can result in meaningless output. Date patterns are not applied as localized patterns and are not affected by this issue.

For the pattern used in the previous example, you would store a name/value pair in *ApplicationResources_en.properties* like the following:

```
format.amount = #,##0.00
```

In the properties file localized for Russian (*ApplicationResources_ru.properties*), you would have:

```
format.amount = # ##0,00
```

This formatKey attribute proves more useful when working with dates. Say you wanted to generate dates such as Sep 14, 2004 for English and 14 __ 2004 for Russian. In your English properties file, you would have the following:

```
format.date=MMM dd, yyyy
```

In the Russian properties file, you would use the following:

```
format.date=dd MMM yyyy
```

You could use one bean:write tag to render the date in the appropriate format using the following:

```
<bean:write name="order" property="datePlaced" formatKey="format.date"/>
```

For messages, use the bean:message tag. Suppose you want to render an order confirmation message on a "success" page. The message should display the quantity of items ordered, the part number, and the total cost. Here's one way you could specify the message in your base resource bundle (*ApplicationResources.properties*):

```
msg.confirm.order=You ordered {0} of part {1} at a total cost of ${2}.
```

On a JSP page, the bean:message tag retrieves the message by key. The arg*n* attributes contain the substitution values. Unless you are using the Struts-EL version of the bean tags or a JSP 2.0 container, you must resort to scriptlet for the substitution arguments:

```
<!-- Create a scripting variable -->
<bean:define id="theOrder" name="order"  type="com.oreilly.strutsckbk.ch12.Order"/>
<!-- Render the message -->
```

```
<bean:message key="msg.confirm.order"
            arg0="<%=theOrder.getQuantity().toString()%>"
            arg1="<%=theOrder.getPartNumber().toString()%>"
            arg2="<%=theOrder.getAmount().toString()%>"
/>
```

To display the message for a different locale, like Spanish, you only need to place the translated message into that locale's resource bundle (*ApplicationResources_es.properties*):

```
msg.confirm.order = Usted ordeno {0} unidades de parte {1} resultando en un costo
total de ${2}.
```

The bean:message tag formats the message using the java.text.MessageFormat class. This class even allows you to format the replacement values themselves using a special notation. Check the JavaDocs for this class (online at *http://java.sun.com/j2se/1.4.2/docs/api/java/text/MessageFormat.html*) if you are using this mechanism.

Using the JSTL format tags

The JSTL formatting tags provide similar capabilities as the Struts tags. The JSTL *fmt* tag library provides two primary tags for localizing data. The fmt:formatNumber tag formats numeric values. You can specify a specific pattern, or you can specify characteristics such as the minimum and maximum digits. If you are migrating from using bean:write and were using the format attribute to specify a pattern, you can use that same pattern with JSTL:

```
<fmt:formatNumber value="${order.amount}" pattern="#,##0.00"/>
```

If you were using the bean:write's formatKey attribute, the corresponding pattern can only be used if it localized the server's default locale. Unlike the bean:write tag, JSTL number formatting tags don't expect the pattern to be localized.

For formatting dates and times, use the fmt:formatDate tag. Like the fmt:formatNumber tag, you can specify a pattern or formatting characteristics, such as a date style. If you were using bean:write's formatKey attribute to use a pattern from a resource bundle, you can achieve the same affect with JSTL.

```
<fmt:message key="format.date" var="dateFmt"/>
<fmt:formatDate value="${order.datePlaced}" pattern="${dateFmt}"/>
```

Like the bean:message tag, JSTL's fmt:message tag builds and localizes messages from a resource bundle. The fmt:param tag substitutes a value for a message parameter placeholder.

```
<fmt:message key="msg.confirm.order">
    <fmt:param value="${order.quantity}"/>
    <fmt:param value="${order.partNumber}"/>
    <fmt:param value="${order.amount}"/>
<fmt:message key="msg.confirm.order">
```

All in all, JSTL tags tend to be less verbose and cleaner than the corresponding Struts tags. More importantly, the power of the JSTL expression language (EL) alleviates the need for request-time expressions and scriptlet.

See Also

Check out the Struts User's Guide for more details. The documentation for the *bean* tag library can be found at *http://struts.apache.org/userGuide/struts-bean.html*.

For a good source on the JSTL tags, check out *Java Server Pages* by Hans Bergsten (O'Reilly).

Struts issues are tracked using Bugzilla. You can browse the issues at *http://issues. apache.org/bugzilla*.

12.7   Displaying Locale-Specific Images

Problem

Your Struts application needs to show a graphic image specific to a user's locale.

Solution

Create a property in the locale's resource bundle specifying the path to the image source file. Here's an example from a Spanish locale properties file (*ApplicationResouces_es. properties*) file:

```
# spanish language properties
img.source.yes=images/es/yes.gif
```

Use the html:img tag with the srcKey or pageKey attribute set to the property key:

```
<html:img border="0" srcKey="img.source.yes"/>
```

Discussion

Most production web applications use images extensively. Images are frequently used, in place of text, for buttons and links. In many cases, images are used to create "fancy" buttons, as shown in Figure 12-1.

If the user speaks Spanish, Figure 12-1 must be modified since the text message needs to be translated to Spanish and the "yes" button should be changed to "sì." The text can be localized using the bean:message or fmt:message tag (Recipe 12.6). For the button images, you can use the html:img to retrieve a locale-specific image and generate an appropriate HTML img element. The html:img tag supports two attributes, srcKey and pageKey, which allow you to specify a key, to be looked up from a resource bundle. The bundle's value dictates the path to the file. The path will be retrieved from the default Struts MessageResources bundle for the current locale. If srcKey is specified, the resultant value is used "as is" for the image location;

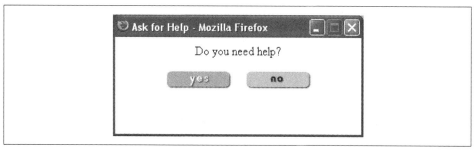

Figure 12-1. Using images for buttons

if pageKey is used, the resultant value is treated as a module-relative path to the image.

The JSP page (*need_help.jsp*) shown in Example 12-6 generates the HTML pop-up window in Figure 12-1.

Example 12-6. Using html:img to display localized images

```
<%@ page contentType="text/html;charset=UTF-8" language="java" %>
<%@ taglib uri="http://struts.apache.org/tags-bean" prefix="bean" %>
<%@ taglib uri="http://struts.apache.org/tags-html" prefix="html" %>

<html:html lang="true">
<head>
  <title>Ask for Help</title>
</head>
<body>
    <p align="center">
        <bean:message key="prompt.help"/>
    </p>
    <p align="center">
        <a href="javascript:close( )">
            <html:img border="0" srcKey="img.yes.src" titleKey="img.yes.title"/>
        </a>
         
        <a href="javascript:close( )">
            <html:img border="0" srcKey="img.no.src" titleKey="img.no.title"/>
        </a>
    </p>
</body>
</html:html>
```

The titleKey specifies the key to the text to be used for the title attribute of the generated img tag. Most modern browsers display the title when the mouse hovers over the image. The html:img tag supports the altKey attribute to retrieve localized text for the img tag's alt attribute (displayed when the image isn't available).

For the JSP of Example 12-6, here are the resource bundle properties from *ApplicationResources.properties* (default locale):

```
prompt.help=Do you need help?
img.yes.src=images/yes.gif
img.yes.title=Yes
img.no.src=images/no.gif
img.no.title=No
```

Here are those same properties from *ApplicationResources_es.properties* (Spanish locale):

```
prompt.help=Necesita ayuda?
img.yes.src=images/es/yes.gif
img.yes.title=Si
img.no.src=images/es/no.gif
img.no.title=No
```

When the users set their language to Spanish, the JSP of Example 12-6 generates the pop up shown in Figure 12-2.

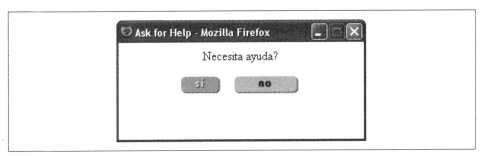

Figure 12-2. Localized text and images

The text and images are retrieved from the bundle for the current locale. The images are retrieved from a locale-specific directory. You can organize your images however you wish, but if you have many localized images, placing them under a folder that's named using the language code, like *images/es*, works quite well.

See Also

The documentation on the html:img tag provides details on all of the supported attributes. The documentation for this and other Struts tags can be accessed at *http://struts.apache.org/userGuide/struts-html.html*.

12.8   Supporting Character Sets

Problem

Your Struts application needs to display characters from any language correctly.

Solution

Use Tomcat's SetCharacterEncoding filter shown in Example 12-7.

Example 12-7. Using a filter to set the character encoding

```
/*
 * Copyright 2004 The Apache Software Foundation
 *
 * Licensed under the Apache License, Version 2.0 (the "License");
 * you may not use this file except in compliance with the License.
 * You may obtain a copy of the License at
 *
 *     http://www.apache.org/licenses/LICENSE-2.0
 *
 * Unless required by applicable law or agreed to in writing, software
 * distributed under the License is distributed on an "AS IS" BASIS,
 * WITHOUT WARRANTIES OR CONDITIONS OF ANY KIND, either express or implied.
 * See the License for the specific language governing permissions and
 * limitations under the License.
 */

package filters;

import java.io.IOException;
import javax.servlet.Filter;
import javax.servlet.FilterChain;
import javax.servlet.FilterConfig;
import javax.servlet.ServletException;
import javax.servlet.ServletRequest;
import javax.servlet.ServletResponse;
import javax.servlet.UnavailableException;


/**
 * <p>Example filter that sets the character encoding to be used in parsing the
 * incoming request, either unconditionally or only if the client did not
 * specify a character encoding.  Configuration of this filter is based on
 * the following initialization parameters:</p>
 * <ul>
 * <li><strong>encoding</strong> - The character encoding to be configured
 *     for this request, either conditionally or unconditionally based on
 *     the <code>ignore</code> initialization parameter.  This parameter
 *     is required, so there is no default.</li>
 * <li><strong>ignore</strong> - If set to "true", any character encoding
 *     specified by the client is ignored, and the value returned by the
 *     <code>selectEncoding()</code> method is set.  If set to "false,
 *     <code>selectEncoding()</code> is called <strong>only</strong> if the
 *     client has not already specified an encoding.  By default, this
 *     parameter is set to "true".</li>
 * </ul>
 *
 * <p>Although this filter can be used unchanged, it is also easy to
 * subclass it and make the <code>selectEncoding()</code> method more
```

Example 12-7. Using a filter to set the character encoding (continued)

```
 * intelligent about what encoding to choose, based on characteristics of
 * the incoming request (such as the values of the <code>Accept-Language</code>
 * and <code>User-Agent</code> headers, or a value stashed in the current
 * user's session.</p>
 *
 * @author Craig McClanahan
 * @version $Revision: 1.3 $ $Date: 2004/11/18 13:28:09 $
 */
public class SetCharacterEncodingFilter implements Filter {

    // ------------------------------------------------------ Instance Variables

    /**
     * The default character encoding to set for requests that pass through
     * this filter.
     */
    protected String encoding = null;

    /**
     * The filter configuration object we are associated with.  If this value
     * is null, this filter instance is not currently configured.
     */
    protected FilterConfig filterConfig = null;

    /**
     * Should a character encoding specified by the client be ignored?
     */
    protected boolean ignore = true;

    // --------------------------------------------------------- Public Methods

    /**
     * Take this filter out of service.
     */
    public void destroy() {
        this.encoding = null;
        this.filterConfig = null;
    }

    /**
     * Select and set (if specified) the character encoding to be used to
     * interpret request parameters for this request.
     *
     * @param request The servlet request we are processing
     * @param result The servlet response we are creating
     * @param chain The filter chain we are processing
     *
     * @exception IOException if an input/output error occurs
     * @exception ServletException if a servlet error occurs
     */
```

Example 12-7. Using a filter to set the character encoding (continued)

```java
public void doFilter(ServletRequest request, ServletResponse response,
                     FilterChain chain)
    throws IOException, ServletException {

    // Conditionally select and set the character encoding to be used
    if (ignore || (request.getCharacterEncoding( ) == null)) {
        String encoding = selectEncoding(request);
        if (encoding != null)
            request.setCharacterEncoding(encoding);
    }

    // Pass control on to the next filter
    chain.doFilter(request, response);
}

/**
 * Place this filter into service.
 *
 * @param filterConfig The filter configuration object
 */
public void init(FilterConfig filterConfig) throws ServletException {
    this.filterConfig = filterConfig;
    this.encoding = filterConfig.getInitParameter("encoding");
    String value = filterConfig.getInitParameter("ignore");
    if (value == null)
        this.ignore = true;
    else if (value.equalsIgnoreCase("true"))
        this.ignore = true;
    else if (value.equalsIgnoreCase("yes"))
        this.ignore = true;
    else
        this.ignore = false;
}

// ------------------------------------------------------ Protected Methods

/**
 * Select an appropriate character encoding to be used, based on the
 * characteristics of the current request and/or filter initialization
 * parameters.  If no character encoding should be set, return
 * <code>null</code>.
 * <p>
 * The default implementation unconditionally returns the value configured
 * by the <strong>encoding</strong> initialization parameter for this
 * filter.
 *
 * @param request The servlet request we are processing
 */
protected String selectEncoding(ServletRequest request) {
    return (this.encoding);
}
}
```

Then declare the filter in your *web.xml* file, setting filter to use "UTF-8" and mapping the filter to all URLs:

```
<filter>
    <filter-name>SetCharacterEncodingFilter</filter-name>
    <filter-class>
        filters.SetCharacterEncodingFilter
    </filter-class>
    <init-param>
        <param-name>encoding</param-name>
        <param-value>UTF-8</param-value>
     </init-param>
    <init-param>
        <param-name>ignore</param-name>
        <param-value>true</param-value>
     </init-param>
</filter>

<filter-mapping>
    <filter-name>SetCharacterEncodingFilter</filter-name>
    <url-pattern>/*</url-pattern>
</filter-mapping>
```

Discussion

You can ensure your application will accept any character encoding using a filter. The Tomcat distribution includes an example servlet filter that sets the servlet request character encoding to any desired value. Specifying an encoding of UTF-8, a well-supported *charset* of Unicode, ensures all character sets can be handled.

For web applications, character encoding problems typically occur with forms. The user inputs text on a form using non-Western characters, such as in Russian (Cyrllic) as shown in Figure 12-3, and submits the form.

Figure 12-3. Form fields containing Russian (Cyrillic) characters

But when the input data is displayed on a successive page, the characters appear as gibberish as in Figure 12-4. When the server received the data, it didn't know how to translate the byte sequence into the correct Cyrillic characters.

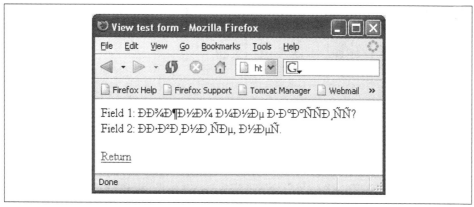

Figure 12-4. Incorrectly encoded characters

However, if you use the `SetCharacterEncoding` filter, configured to set the character encoding to UTF-8, the page will display correctly, as in Figure 12-5.

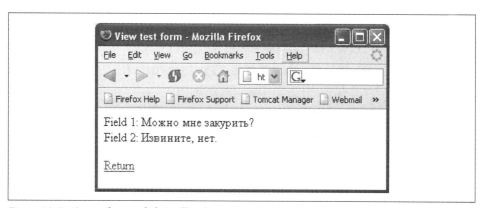

Figure 12-5. Correctly encoded Cyrillic characters

Browser and operating system support for non-Western character encodings varies by vendor and version. Most modern browsers allow you to set the default character encoding to UTF-8. Likewise, most operating systems allow you to input text using non-Western characters. It can be a challenge to keep it all straight, but for your application, this servlet filter solution eliminates a lot of the frustration.

See Also

I18nGurus.com (The Open Internationalization Resources Directory) has a boatload of information internationalization topics. The links on using character sets and character encoding can be found at *http://www.i18ngurus.com/docs/984813247.html*.

12.9   Localizing Look and Feel

Problem

You want your HTML pages to have a different style depending on the user's locale.

Solution

Use a combination of a global Cascading Style Sheet (CSS) and a locale-specific style sheet. The paths for the style sheets are stored as resource bundle properties. Because style sheets are merged, you only need to override those locale-specific styles that are different than the global styles.

Using Struts tags

```
<style>
    <!--
        <bean:define id="globalStyle">
            <bean:message key="css.global"/>
        </bean:define>
        @import url(<html:rewrite page="<%=globalStyle%>"/>);

        <bean:define id="localStyle">
            <bean:message key="css.local"/>
        </bean:define>
        @import url(<html:rewrite page="<%=localStyle%>"/>);
    -->
</style>
```

Using JSTL tags

```
<style>
    <!--
    <fmt:message key="css.global" var="globalStyle"/>
    @import url(<c:url value="${globalStyle}"/>)

    <fmt:message key="css.local" var="localStyle"/>
    @import url(<c:url value="${localStyle}"/>)
    -->
</style>
```

Discussion

Style sheets can be chosen and applied based on locale in the same manner that images are retrieved as shown in Recipe 12.7. You can use the Struts tags or the JSTL tags. Use `bean:message` or `fmt:message` to retrieve a context-relative style sheet path. For example, you would configure paths for a global and locale-specific style sheet in your base resource bundle (*ApplicationResources.properties*):

```
css.global=/styles/global.css
css.local=/styles/local.css
```

The locale-specific file, */styles/local.css*, needs to be defined but doesn't need to contain any text. It's specified in the base resource bundle as a fallback value in case a locale-specific style sheet isn't defined. To define the locale-specific style sheet, specify a property in that locale's resource bundle for the style sheet. Here are the properties, for example, for a style sheet with styles and colors specific to Spanish from the *ApplicationResources_es.properties* file:

```
css.local=/styles/es/local.css
```

As with organizing locale-specific images, using directory names that correspond to locales is a good way to organize your style sheets.

See Also

CSS have advanced significantly in recent years. Check out *Cascading Style Sheets: The Definitive Guide* by Eric Meyer (O'Reilly) for complete details.

## CHAPTER 13

Testing and Debugging

13.0 Introduction

You can write the coolest Struts applications in the world, but if you don't know how to test them, or you can't seem to debug them, you might as well not have written them in the first place. Testing and debugging web applications can be a frustrating experience. If you test your application by deploying it to your application server and "banging on it," then the recipes in this chapter will provide some techniques that are worth learning. If your only approach to debugging involves sticking `System.out.println( )` in places where you *think* the problem might be, then you'll definitely want to check out some of these solutions.

The key to debugging an application is visibility; the more information you have about the internal workings of the application, the easier it can be to pinpoint the problem. The chapter has solutions that show you how to monitor what your application is doing. This first half of this chapter presents some solutions related to logging and debugging that will help you understand what's going on inside your application.

The heart of testing and debugging is the *unit test*. A unit test verifies that a specific portion of your application does what it is supposed to do. Java developers commonly think of the "unit" as a Java class. But the unit can be anything as long as it can be identified by discrete boundaries and isolated from code external to the unit. This chapter has two recipes that show you how to unit test your Struts actions.

In "traditional" software testing, the tester ensures that the application functions as the user expects. You can apply the concepts of unit testing to functional testing by considering a scenario as the "unit." Use cases such as "Login," "New User Registration," or "Place an Order" to drive your unit tests. These functional unit tests are as valid as the low-level tests, though these tests can be more difficult to isolate from outside effects. If you follow the best practices of web application design—using the Model-View-Controller (MVC) design pattern supported by Struts—your most important unit tests will be testing your application's model and business services.

Struts-specific tests should comprise a small portion of your application's entire unit test suite.

Without a doubt, the JUnit (*http://www.junit.org*) framework, developed by Erich Gamma and Kent Beck, provides an elegant, extensible framework that has become the *de facto* standard for Java unit testing. JUnit provides the base test class, TestCase, that you extend to create your specific unit test. You write test methods that exercise the unit under test and verify the unit behaves as expected for different inputs.

JUnit provides the test harness for running your tests. JUnit treats any method in your test class that begins with the word "test" as a method to run; your test methods will have names like testSearchByName( ), testSuccess( ), etc. JUnit runs your test by instantiating your test class and calling these test methods. Within each test method, you exercise the class under test and verify the results using assertion methods defined in the TestCase base class. An *assertion* expresses a Boolean (true/false) relationship. For example, you may assert that a value returned from a method is not null, or that the returned value has a specific value. If an assertion fails, that particular test method will fail. You can run your tests using command-line and graphical test runners included with JUnit. Many popular Java development environments, such as Eclipse and IDEA, come with built-in JUnit test runners. You can also run your tests as part of your application's Ant build script.

The second half of this chapter shows you some recipes that make it easier to write unit tests for your Struts application. The solutions make use of a number of excellent open source extensions to JUnit such as StrutsTestCase, Cactus, and JWebUnit.

13.1   Deploying an Application Automatically

Problem

You want to be able to test and retest your web application in Tomcat without having to redeploy the application whenever a change is made to a Java class or JSP page.

Solution

Use the development directories of your application as the actual directories that the application server uses for the deployed application. For Tomcat, you would create a Context element immediately before the </Host> end tag in the *conf/server.xml* file (under your *CATALINA_HOME* top-level directory).

```
<Host...>
   ...
   <Context path="/struts-cookbook"
         docBase="/path/to/myapp/web"
      reloadable="true"/>
</Host>
```

Discussion

This recipe is not particular to Struts but is applicable to any J2EE-based web applications. However, the Solution is particular to Tomcat. If you aren't using Tomcat, your application server most likely uses a similar mechanism. If you use the Solution, you won't have to deploy your application when changes are made; your application will always be deployed.

The docBase attribute specifies a file path to your deployment directory. If you're using Windows, you'll need to include the drive letter on the path as shown here:

```
docBase="c:/Documents and Settings/My App/web"
```

The structure of this directory must match the structure of a valid J2EE web application. Its contents would look something like this:

```
/index.html
/welcome.jsp
/feedback.jsp
/images/banner.gif
/WEB-INF/web.xml
/WEB-INF/struts-config.xml
/WEB-INF/classes/ApplicationResources.properties
/WEB-INF/classes/com/foo/MyBar.class
/WEB-INF/classes/...
/WEB-INF/lib/struts.jar
/WEB-INF/lib/...
```

By setting reloadable="true" Tomcat will monitor the *WEB-INF/classes* and *WEB-INF/lib* directories of your application. When changes occur in either of these directories, Tomcat will restart your application and the changes will get picked up. Setting reloadable to true will negatively impact performance and should only be used in development. If you're making JSP changes, you don't have to set reloadable to true. Tomcat detects changes to JSPs automatically, translating and recompiling on the fly. However, if you change configuration files, such as the *struts-config.xml*, *web.xml*, and *validation.xml*, you'll need to restart the web application manually as these files are read on application initialization.

This deployment approach increases your productivity by reducing the code-compile-test cycle time. However, the Solution depends on the platform—both the application server and the operating system—and is not viable for production and QA deployments. Therefore, your application should include a platform-independent build script. Ant (*http://ant.apache.org*) provides an excellent framework for these scripts.

See Also

Recipe 1.7 shows you how to define a repeatable process for the compile-deploy cycle.

Recipe 13.4 describes how to enable remote debugging of a web application running in a different JVM.

You can find additional details on configuring Tomcat at *http://jakarta.apache.org/tomcat*.

13.2   Configuring Struts Logging

Problem

You need to set the severity level and details of the log messages generated by internal Struts components.

Solution

Configure Struts logging to use Log4J as its logging implementation:

1. Download the *Log4J* jar file from *http://jakarta.apache.org/log4j*.
2. Copy the jar file to your application's *WEB-INF/lib* folder.
3. Set the log level and log destination (referred to as an *appender*) for all Struts packages (org.apache.struts), as shown in Example 13-1 (*log4j.properties*). Place this file in your application's *WEB-INF/classes* folder.

Example 13-1. Configuring Log4J for Struts packages

```
# The output information consists of relative time, log level, thread
# name, logger name, nested diagnostic context and the message in that
# order.
# For the general syntax of property based configuration files see the
# documentation of org.apache.log4j.PropertyConfigurator.

log4j.rootLogger=WARN,Console
log4j.logger.org.apache.struts=DEBUG,Console,File

log4j.appender.Console=org.apache.log4j.ConsoleAppender
log4j.appender.Console.layout=org.apache.log4j.PatternLayout
log4j.appender.Console.layout.ConversionPattern=%d [%t] %-5p %c - %m%n

# File is set to be a FileAppender which outputs to struts-debug.log
log4j.appender.File=org.apache.log4j.FileAppender
log4j.appender.File.file=struts-log.log

# File uses PatternLayout.
log4j.appender.File.layout=org.apache.log4j.PatternLayout

# The conversion pattern uses format specifiers. You might want to
# change the pattern an watch the output format change.
log4j.appender.File.layout.ConversionPattern=%d [%t] %-5p %c - %m%n
```

4. Configure Commons Logging to use Log4J in the *commons-logging.properties* file shown in Example 13-2. Save this file in your *WEB-INF/classes* directory.

Example 13-2. Configuring the Commons Logging factory

```
# Set the commons logging factory to the Log4J implementation

org.apache.commons.logging.LogFactory=org.apache.commons.logging.impl.Log4jFactory
```

Discussion

If your application is misbehaving, the first thing to do is check the log files. If Struts is recording informational messages, then you will need to adjust the logging so you can see more detail. Struts records log messages using the Jakarta Commons Logging API. This API acts as a lightweight, generic façade around several popular Java logging packages. Most users employ the Log4J (*http://jakarta.apache.org/log4j*) or JDK 1.4 Logging as the logging implementation. Many developers prefer Log4J even if they are using JDK 1.3. Log4J is more mature and feature-rich than JDK 1.4 Logging and is easily configured.

Log4J reads its settings from a configuration file, *log4j.properties*. Classes write logging messages using a *logger*. In most cases, the logger name matches the fully qualified class name. For each logger, you can set the logging level and the destination of the log messages, known as an *appender*. With Log4J, you can set the log level and the appenders with one property. For example, you could configure the Struts `RequestProcessor` to log debug messages to the console with this property:

```
log4j.logger.org.apache.struts.action.RequestProcessor=DEBUG,Console
```

Loggers are hierarchical; therefore, you can set the logging level for all Struts classes like this:

```
log4j.logger.org.apache.struts=DEBUG,Console,File
```

Log4J supports the concept of a default logger, known as the root logger. The root logger is configured like this:

```
log4j.rootLogger=WARN,Console
```

If a `log4j.logger` property isn't set for a specific logger, the log messages will be written based on the root logger settings. In Example 13-1, the default logging level is set to WARN. Period messages that are warnings, or have a higher severity such as ERROR or FATAL, will be logged, and the messages will be written to the `Console` appender.

Appenders are configured using a `log4j.appender` property. The console and file appenders shown in Example 13-1 will work on any system. For more details on configuring appenders, see the Log4J documentation at *http://logging.apache.org/log4j*.

Figure 13-1 shows a sample of logging output when the Solution is applied to the *struts-example*.

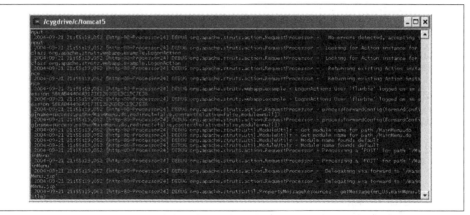

Figure 13-1. Debug level logging messages

The information displayed in each log message is based on the layout properties specified for the appender. In the Solution, a series of format specifiers are used:

```
log4j.appender.Console.layout.ConversionPattern=%d [%t] %-5p %c - %m%n
```

These format specifiers result in the display of the date (%d), thread (%t), priority (%-5p), class name (%c), log message (%m), and a carriage return (%n). For a complete list of all supported format specifiers, see the documentation for the Log4J PatternLayout class.

See Also

For additional details on configuring Struts logging, check the Struts User's Guide at *http://struts.apache.org/userGuide/configuration.html#config_logging*.

You can find information on Commons Logging at *http://jakarta.apache.org/commons/logging*. For more information on Log4J, point your browser to *http://logging.apache.org/log4j*.

13.3   Adding Logging to Your Own Classes

Problem

You want to log messages of varying severity from your own classes.

Solution

Use Commons Logging within your own classes, as shown in Example 13-3.

Example 13-3. Using Commons Logging in a custom class

```
package com.fooware.barapp;

import org.apache.commons.logging.Log;
import org.apache.commons.logging.LogFactory;

public class MyClazz {

    private static Log log = LogFactory.getLog(MyClazz.class);

    public void doSomething( ) {
        log.debug("About to do something.");
        try {
            //call something that throws an exception
        } catch (Exception e) {
            log.error("An exception occured doing something.", e);
        }
        log.info("Successfully did something.");
    }
}
```

Discussion

Any critical application should use logging of some kind. Relying on System.out.
println( ) limits logging flexibility and can significantly downgrade application performance. You can roll your own logging mechanism, as many shops have done, or
you can take advantage of frameworks and APIs such as Log4J and Commons Logging that make logging easy.

The Solution uses the Commons Logging API. Messages are logged to a logging category. If you use the class name as the category, you can control logging at the class
level. In addition, you can use the package name as a hierarchy. The Commons Logging API supports the following logging levels in increasing order of severity:

1. Trace
2. Debug
3. Info
4. Warn
5. Error
6. Fatal

Using Commons Logging gives you the flexibility of choosing a logging implementation as desired. If you were using Log4J, you would configure logging for your package or classes as was done for the Struts packages in Recipe 13.2. Example 13-4
shows the *log4j.properties* file that enables console logging of errors and warnings for
the class in the Solution.

Example 13-4. Log4J configuration for a custom class

```
log4j.rootLogger=ERROR,Console
log4j.logger.com.foo.bar.MyClazz=WARN,Console
#
# The output information consists of relative time, log level, thread
# name, logger name, nested diagnostic context and the message in that
# order.
log4j.appender.Console=org.apache.log4j.ConsoleAppender
log4j.appender.Console.layout=org.apache.log4j.PatternLayout
log4j.appender.Console.layout.ConversionPattern=%d [%t] %-5p %c - %m%n
```

See Also

You can find information on Commons Logging at *http://jakarta.apache.org/commons/logging*. For more information on Log4J, point your browser to *http://logging.apache.org/log4j*.

13.4   Enabling Remote Debugging

Problem

You want to debug your Struts application running on a remote server.

Solution

Configure the JVM running your application server to use the Java Platform Debugger Architecture (JPDA). You will need to add the following options to the java command that starts your application server.

JDK 1.3

```
-classic
-Xdebug
-Xnoagent
-Djava.compiler=NONE
-Xrunjdwp:transport=dt_socket,address=8787,server=y,suspend=y
```

JDK 1.4

```
-Xdebug
-Xrunjdwp:transport=dt_socket,address=8787,server=y,suspend=y
```

You can use any IDE or tool that supports JPDA debugging such as Eclipse, IntelliJ IDEA, and JSWAT.

Discussion

The JPDA has made debugging Java applications much easier: You can use any debugging tool you want independently of the application being debugged. JPDA allows you to debug a Java application running in a separate JVM on a remote server on your network. Your local JVM, running the debugger, connects to the remote JVM across the network using the host name and a known port. In the Solution, the address specifies the port.

This approach works well when the two computers are the same—for example, your desktop machine. JPDA permits you to have two JVMs—one for your IDE or debugger and one for the application server—that can work together. You no longer have to run the application server and your IDE all within the same process.

If you're using Tomcat as your application server, debugging is easier. Tomcat's startup scripts include the JPDA options shown in the Solution. By default, Tomcat reserves port 8000 for the JPDA port. Figure 13-2 shows how to start Tomcat, on a Linux/Unix machine, using the *catalina.sh* shell script.

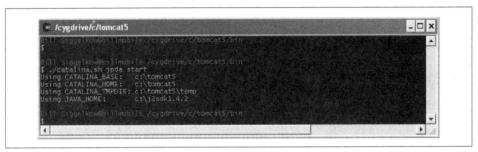

Figure 13-2. Starting Tomcat in debug mode (Linux/Unix)

For Win32 machines, the *catalina.bat* startup script configures JPDA to use shared memory instead of TCP/IP sockets for the transport mechanism. The use of shared memory is only supported by Win32, and most IDEs don't support connecting using this transport; you're better sticking with the socket approach. If you're using a Tomcat on a Win32 machine, you have two main options: You can use the Cygwin Unix emulator and execute the *catalina.sh* shell script, or you can modify the *catalina.bat* file to use sockets. Change the variables for the transport and address as follows:

```
...
rem set JPDA_TRANSPORT=dt_shmem
set JPDA_TRANSPORT=dt_socket
...
rem set JPDA_ADDRESS=jdbconn
set JPDA_ADDRESS=8000
...
```

Of course, you can change the JPDA_ADDRESS to any available port you like and execute the *catalina.bat* file to start Tomcat in debug mode. Figure 13-3 shows the results.

Figure 13-3. Starting Tomcat in debug mode (Win32)

Once the application server is started, you connect to the server's JVM using your debugger. You only need to specify the host name and port for the remote JVM. As an example, here's how you would configure Eclipse IDE for debugging. You start by selecting Run → Debug… from the Eclipse menus. Figure 13-4 shows the window displayed for creating a new debug run configuration.

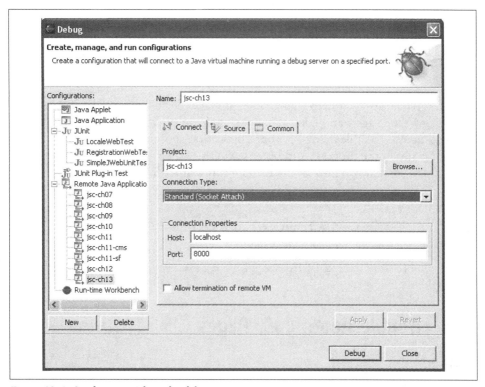

Figure 13-4. Configuring Eclipse for debugging

Clicking the Debug button will attach to the remote JVM. Figure 13-5 shows the Eclipse Debug perspective; here, the breakpoint has been set within the Struts RequestProcessor.

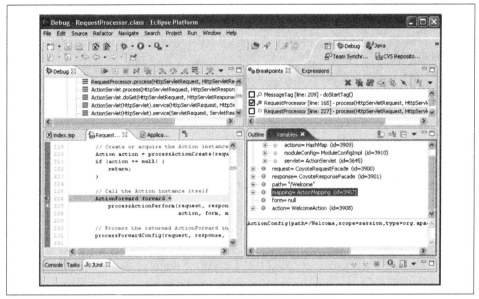

Figure 13-5. Eclipse debug perspective

The latest IDEs have made debugging easier. If you debug using System.out.println( ) calls, logging messages, and educated guessing, learn how to use a debugger. It will save you hours, you'll learn about your application's internals, and you'll probably have some fun in the process. And because you have free access to the Struts source code, you can step down into the Struts framework if needed.

See Also

JSWAT, a standalone, JPDA-compliant, open source debugger can be downloaded from *http://www.bluemarsh.com/java/jswat/*.

To learn more about using JPDA, see *http://java.sun.com/j2se/1.4.2/docs/guide/jpda/conninv.html*.

13.5   Troubleshooting JSP Pages

Problem

You want to see a dump of the names and values of servlet request and HTTP session attributes and for a particular JSP page so you can troubleshoot rendering problems.

Solution

Include the *debug.jsp* file shown on the JSP page (see Example 13-5).

Example 13-5. JSP dump of request, session, and context data

```
<hr width="3px">
Debug Information:<br>
<table border="1" width="50%" class="debug">
    <tr>
        <th colspan="3" style="background:orange">
            <b>Request Parameters</b>
        </th>
    </tr>
    <c:forEach items="${paramValues}" var="parameter">
        <tr>
            <td><c:out value="${parameter.key}"/></td>
            <td colspan="2">
                <c:forEach var="value" items="${parameter.value}">
                    <textarea rows="2" cols="50">
                        <c:out value="${value}"/>
                    </textarea>
                </c:forEach>
            </td>
        </tr>
    </c:forEach>

    <tr>
        <th colspan="3" style="background:orange">
            <b>Header Values</b>
        </th>
    </tr>
    <c:forEach items="${header}" var="h">
        <tr>
            <td><c:out value="${h.key}"/></td>
            <td colspan="2">
                <textarea rows="2" cols="50">
                    <c:out value="${h.value}"/>
                </textarea>
            </td>
        </tr>
    </c:forEach>

    <tr>
        <th colspan="3" style="background:orange">
            <b>Initialization Parameters</b>
        </th>
    </tr>
    <c:forEach items="${initParam}" var="parameter">
        <tr>
            <td><c:out value="${parameter.key}"/></td>
            <td colspan="2">
                <textarea rows="2" cols="50">
                    <c:out value="${parameter.value}"/>
```

Example 13-5. JSP dump of request, session, and context data (continued)

```
                </textarea>
            </td>
        </tr>
    </c:forEach>

    <tr>
        <th colspan="3" style="background:orange">
            <b>Cookies</b>
        </th>
    </tr>
    <c:forEach items="${cookie}" var="mapEntry">
        <tr>
            <td rowspan="8"><c:out value="${mapEntry.key}"/></td>
            <td align="right">Name:</td>
            <td><c:out value="${mapEntry.value.name}"/></td>
        </tr>
        <tr>
            <td align="right">Value:</td>
            <td><c:out value="${mapEntry.value.value}"/></td>
        </tr>
        <tr>
            <td align="right">Domain:</td>
            <td><c:out value="${mapEntry.value.domain}"/></td>
        </tr>
        <tr>
            <td align="right">Max Age:</td>
            <td><c:out value="${mapEntry.value.maxAge}"/></td>
        </tr>
        <tr>
            <td align="right">Path:</td>
            <td><c:out value="${mapEntry.value.path}"/></td>
        </tr>
        <tr>
            <td align="right">Secure:</td>
            <td><c:out value="${mapEntry.value.secure}"/></td>
        </tr>
        <tr>
            <td align="right">Version:</td>
            <td><c:out value="${mapEntry.value.version}"/></td>
        </tr>
        <tr>
            <td align="right">Comment:</td>
            <td><c:out value="${mapEntry.value.comment}"/></td>
        </tr>
    </c:forEach>

    <tr>
        <th colspan="3" style="background:orange">
            <b>Page Scope Attributes</b>
        </th>
    </tr>
    <c:forEach items="${pageScope}" var="itm">
```

Example 13-5. JSP dump of request, session, and context data (continued)

```
        <c:if test="${itm.key != 'javax.servlet.jsp.jspResponse'}">
            <tr>
                <td><c:out value="${itm.key}"/></td>
                <td colspan="2">
                    <textarea rows="2" cols="50">
                        <c:out value="${itm.value}"/>
                    </textarea>
                </td>
            </tr>
        </c:if>
    </c:forEach>

    <tr>
        <th colspan="3" style="background:orange">
            <b>Request Scope Attributes</b>
        </th>
    </tr>
    <c:forEach items="${requestScope}" var="itm">
        <tr>
            <td><c:out value="${itm.key}"/></td>
            <td colspan="2">
                <textarea rows="2" cols="50">
                    <c:out value="${itm.value}"/>
                </textarea>
            </td>
        </tr>
    </c:forEach>

    <tr>
        <th colspan="3" style="background:orange">
            <b>Session Scoped Attributes</b>
        </th>
    </tr>
    <c:forEach items="${sessionScope}" var="itm">
      <tr>
        <td><c:out value="${itm.key}"/></td>
        <td colspan="2">
            <textarea rows="2" cols="50">
                <c:out value="${itm.value}"/>
            </textarea>
        </td>
      </tr>
    </c:forEach>

    <tr>
        <th colspan="3" style="background:orange">
            <b>Application Scope Attributes</b>
        </th>
    </tr>
    <c:forEach items="${applicationScope}" var="itm">
      <tr>
        <td><c:out value="${itm.key}"/></td>
```

Example 13-5. JSP dump of request, session, and context data (continued)

```
        <td colspan="2">
            <c:choose>
                <c:when test="${itm.key eq 'org.apache.struts.action.PLUG_INS'}">
                    <c:forEach items="${itm.value}" var="subitm">
                        <textarea rows="2" cols="50">
                            <c:out value="${subitm}"/>
                        </textarea>
                    </c:forEach>
                </c:when>
                <c:otherwise>
                    <textarea rows="2" cols="50">
                        <c:out value="${itm.value}"/>
                    </textarea>
                </c:otherwise>
            </c:choose>
        </td>
    </tr>
    </c:forEach>
</table>
```

Discussion

During development, JSP pages commonly show incorrect data, to render halfway, or to throw an exception. Developers troubleshoot these problems by commenting out portions of the page that appear to be causing the problem, and then entering scriptlet to display the values of request and session attributes used on the page. This is the equivalent of commenting out troublesome Java code and adding System.out.println( ) statements.

This solution doesn't replace this arcane approach but makes it easier to apply. You have to comment out the failing portion of the page, but you can use the JSP fragment in Example 13-5 to eliminate the handcoded scriptlet. This reusable JSP fragment, derived from work by James Mitchell, displays request headers, scoped attributes, and other Struts-specific information to help you debug your problem. You can include the fragment anywhere on the page though, typically, it would be placed near the bottom of the page using the include directive:

```
...
<!-- Debug Data -->
<%@ include file="debug.jsp" %>
<!-- End Debug Data -->
</body>
</html:html>
```

The *debug.jsp* displays the following data:

- Request parameter values
- Request header values
- Application initialization parameters

- Cookies
- Page-scope attributes
- Request-scope attributes
- Session-scope attributes
- Application-scope attributes

You can modify *debug.jsp* to display custom attributes that you may use in your application. Figure 13-6 shows a sample of the displayed information when *debug.jsp* is included at the bottom of the *Registration.jsp* file from the *struts-example* web application.

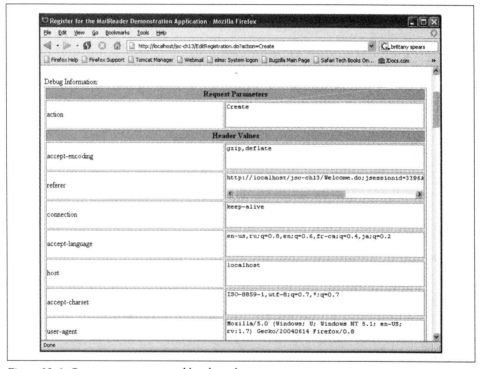

Figure 13-6. Request parameters and header values

The *debug.jsp* page displays detailed information about cookies, as shown in Figure 13-7.

The *debug.jsp* page fragment should only be used in development; leaving this information displayed in production will make you look silly and will open a major security hole.

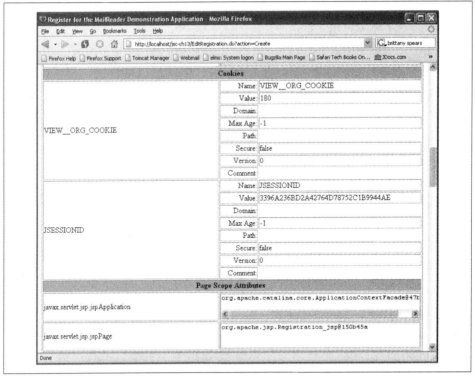

Figure 13-7. Cookie details and page-scoped attributes

See Also

The *debug.jsp* page uses JSTL. You can use JSTL tags in your own application using the Solution shown in Recipe 3.1.

13.6   Testing Your Actions with Mock Objects

Problem

You want to unit test your Struts actions without running the application on an application server.

Solution

Use the *StrutsTestCase* framework to create a unit test, extending the StrutsTestCase MockStrutsTestCase base class, which verifies that your action does what it's supposed to do.

Discussion

The StrutsTestCase framework (*http://strutstestcase.sourceforge.net*), a JUnit extension, specifically targets the testing of Struts actions. You can download StrutsTestCase from *http://strutstestcase.sourceforge.net*. If you are coding to the Servlet 2.2 specification, download the binary for 2.2, *strutstest212_1.1-2.2.zip*; for Servlet 2.3 or later, download *strutstest212_1.1-2.3.zip*. You should also download the source code for StrutsTestCase; when you need to use a debugger, you can step into the StrutsTestCase code. Unzip the binary and source zip files into a directory.

Copy the *strutstest-2.1.2.jar* to a location on your application's classpath. Separate your test source code, classes, and libraries from the rest of your application code. You should create a *test* directory for the application that contains the following:

- A *src* folder your test source code
- A *classes* folder to compile the test source into
- A *lib* folder containing test-specific JAR files such as the StrutsTestCase Jar

When testing, place the *test/classes* directory and the JAR files in your *test/lib* directory on your classpath. When you build the actual distribution for your application (for example, the WAR file), you can easily exclude the *test* directory. Without a separate *test* directory, it's much more cumbersome to separate test code from production code.

 StrutsTestCase uses your application's *struts-config.xml* file and *web.xml* file for performing the test, as well as verifying results. So StrutsTestCase can find these files, you must place the directory that contains your *WEB-INF* directory on your classpath.

With StrutsTestCase, you can create tests that run standalone outside of the servlet container. StrutsTestCase simulates the servlet container using mock objects that represent the servlet-related managed objects such as the `HttpServletRequest`, `HttpServletResponse`, `HttpSession`, and `ServletContext`. This approach runs tests easier and faster and allows you to make your test immune to side effects of the servlet container and other external objects. Your test focuses exclusively on the `Action` being tested.

The Struts MailReader example application provides a good basis for demonstration. Say you wanted to create a test for the `LogonAction` shown in Example 13-6.

Example 13-6. Struts example (MailReader) LogonAction

```
package org.apache.struts.webapp.example;

import javax.servlet.http.HttpServletRequest;
import javax.servlet.http.HttpServletResponse;
import javax.servlet.http.HttpSession;
```

Example 13-6. Struts example (MailReader) LogonAction (continued)

```
import org.apache.commons.beanutils.PropertyUtils;
import org.apache.struts.action.ActionForm;
import org.apache.struts.action.ActionForward;
import org.apache.struts.action.ActionMapping;
import org.apache.struts.action.ActionMessage;
import org.apache.struts.action.ActionMessages;

public final class LogonAction extends BaseAction {

    /**
     * Name of username field ["username"].
     */
    static String USERNAME = "username";

    /**
     * Name of password field ["password"].
     */
    static String PASSWORD = "password";

    // -------------------------------------------------- Protected Methods

    /**
     * <p>Confirm user credentials. Post any errors and return User object
     * (or null).</p>
     *
     * @param database Database in which to look up the user
     * @param username Username specified on the logon form
     * @param password Password specified on the logon form
     * @param errors ActionMessages queue to passback errors
     *
     * @return Validated User object or null
     * @throws ExpiredPasswordException to be handled by Struts exception
     * processor via the action-mapping
     */
    User getUser(UserDatabase database, String username,
                        String password, ActionMessages errors)
        throws ExpiredPasswordException {

        User user = null;
        if (database == null){
            errors.add(
                ActionMessages.GLOBAL_MESSAGE,
                new ActionMessage("error.database.missing"));
        }
        else {
            user = database.findUser(username);
            if ((user != null) && !user.getPassword().equals(password)) {
                user = null;
            }
            if (user == null) {
                errors.add(
```

Example 13-6. Struts example (MailReader) LogonAction (continued)

```
                ActionMessages.GLOBAL_MESSAGE,
                new ActionMessage("error.password.mismatch"));
        }
    }

    return user;

}


/**
 * <p>Store User object in client session.
 * If user object is null, any existing user object is removed.</p>
 *
 * @param request The request we are processing
 * @param user The user object returned from the database
 */
void SaveUser(HttpServletRequest request, User user) {

    HttpSession session = request.getSession();
    session.setAttribute(Constants.USER_KEY, user);
    if (log.isDebugEnabled()) {
        log.debug(
            "LogonAction: User '"
                + user.getUsername()
                + "' logged on in session "
                + session.getId());
    }

}

// --------------------------------------------------------- Public Methods

/**
 * Use "username" and "password" fields from ActionForm to retrieve a User
 * object from the database. If credentials are not valid, or database
 * has disappeared, post error messages and forward to input.
 *
 * @param mapping The ActionMapping used to select this instance
 * @param form The optional ActionForm bean for this request (if any)
 * @param request The HTTP request we are processing
 * @param response The HTTP response we are creating
 *
 * @exception Exception if the application business logic throws
 *   an exception
 */
public ActionForward execute(
    ActionMapping mapping,
    ActionForm form,
    HttpServletRequest request,
    HttpServletResponse response)
    throws Exception {
```

Example 13-6. Struts example (MailReader) LogonAction (continued)

```
        // Local variables
        UserDatabase database = getUserDatabase(request);
        String username = (String) PropertyUtils.getSimpleProperty(form,
                USERNAME);
        String password = (String) PropertyUtils.getSimpleProperty(form,
                PASSWORD);
        ActionMessages errors = new ActionMessages( );

        // Retrieve user
        User user = getUser(database,username,password,errors);

        // Report back any errors, and exit if any
        if (!errors.isEmpty( )) {
            this.saveErrors(request, errors);
            return (mapping.getInputForward( ));
        }

        // Save (or clear) user object
        SaveUser(request,user);

        // Otherwise, return "success"
        return (findSuccess(mapping));

    }

}
```

This Action is used by the /SubmitLogon action defined in the *struts-config.xml* file:

```
    <!-- Process a user logon -->
    <action    path="/SubmitLogon"
               type="org.apache.struts.webapp.example.LogonAction"
               name="LogonForm"
               scope="request"
               input="logon">
        <exception
               key="expired.password"
               type="org.apache.struts.webapp.example.ExpiredPasswordException"
               path="/ExpiredPassword.do"/>
    </action>
```

Now, you can create a test to verify that the LogonAction performs as expected. Example 13-7 presents a unit test that verifies the following:

- If a valid username and password are entered, the correct User object is added to the session and control is forwarded to the "success" page.

- If an invalid username and password are entered, an ActionError with the key of "error.password.mismatch" is generated and control is forwarded to the "logon" page.

Example 13-7. Unit test for the LogonAction

```
package com.oreilly.strutsckbk.ch13;

import org.apache.struts.webapp.example.Constants;
import org.apache.struts.webapp.example.User;

import servletunit.struts.MockStrutsTestCase;

public class SubmitLogonActionTest extends MockStrutsTestCase {

    private static final String ACTION_PATH = "/SubmitLogon";

    public SubmitLogonActionTest (String theName) {
        super(theName);
    }

    public void testValidUserLogon() throws Exception {
        addRequestParameter("username", "user");
        addRequestParameter("password", "pass");

        setRequestPathInfo(ACTION_PATH);
        actionPerform();

        verifyNoActionErrors();

        User user = (User) getSession().getAttribute(Constants.USER_KEY);
        assertNotNull("User", user);
        assertEquals("Username", "user", user.getUsername());

        verifyForward("success");
    }

    public void testInvalidUserLogon() throws Exception {
        addRequestParameter("username", "junk");
        addRequestParameter("password", "bond");

        setRequestPathInfo(ACTION_PATH);
        actionPerform();

        verifyActionErrors(new String[] {"error.password.mismatch"});

        verifyForward("logon");
    }
}
```

Each test adds request parameters corresponding to the username and password. The ACTION_PATH constant contains the URL of the action being tested. The actionPerform( ) method processes the request through the mock container. Upon completion of this method, you can check that the Action did what you expected. Because the MockStrutsTestCase extends the JUnit TestCase class, your unit test has full access to all of the assertion methods that JUnit provides. On top of that, Struts-TestCase adds additional methods for verifying Struts-specific behavior:

verify[No]ActionErrors
Checks that specific errors were generated or that none were generated

verify[No]ActionMessages
Checks that a specific set of action messages, identified by key, were sent or that none were sent

verifyForward
Checks that the Action forwarded to a specific ActionForward identified by logical name

verifyForwardPath
Checks that the Action forwarded to a specific URL

verifyInputForward
Checks that the controller forwarded to the path identified by the action mappings input attribute

verifyTilesForward
Checks that the controller forwarded to a specified logical forward name from the Struts configuration and a Tiles definition name from the Tiles configuration

verifyInputTilesForward
Checks that the controller forwarded to the defined input of a specified Tiles definition

My initial coding of the SubmitLogonActionTest used verifyInputForward( ), instead of verifyForward("logon"), to check that control was forwarded back to the appropriate page when invalid data was submitted. Unexpectedly, the verifyInputForward( ) assertion failed with the following message:

```
junit.framework.AssertionFailedError: was expecting '/logon' but received '/Logon.do'
```

It took a second to realize that the *struts-example* configures the controller to treat the input attribute value as a local or global forward instead of a module-relative path:

```
<controller pagePattern="$M$P" inputForward="true"/>
```

Unfortunately, verifyInputForward( ) expects the value of the input attribute on the action element to be a module-relative path. Changing verifyInputForward( ) to verifyForward("logon") resolved the issue and the test passed.

You'll find another wrinkle in testing the Struts MailReader example that's worth exploring. Suppose you wanted to test an action related to the application's registration features. These actions are declared in the *struts-config-registration.xml* file, and not the standard *struts-config.xml* file. When you use an alternate configuration file like this, you have to tell StrutsTestCase to use it. The setConfigFile( ) method gives you this ability:

```
setConfigFile(java.lang.String pathname);
setConfigFile(java.lang.String moduleName,java.lang.String pathname);
```

Use the first variation to specify the location of the nonstandard Struts configuration file if you aren't using modules; for the default module, use the second variation to specify the nonstandard Struts configuration file for a specific module.

Your test's setUp( ) method is the logical place to call this method. You can put other common code, required to initialize every test, in the setUp( ) method as well.

 If you choose to override the setUp( ) method, you must call super.setUp( ). This base method performs some important initialization routines, and StrutsTestCase will not work if it isn't called.

Example 13-8 shows a test case for the EditRegistrationAction.

Example 13-8. A test using an alternate Struts configuration file

```
package com.oreilly.strutsckbk.ch13;

import org.apache.struts.Globals;
import servletunit.struts.MockStrutsTestCase;

public class EditRegistrationActionTest extends MockStrutsTestCase {

    private static final String ACTION_PATH = "/EditRegistration";

    public EditRegistrationActionTest (String theName) {
        super(theName);
    }

    public void setUp( ) throws Exception {
        super.setUp( );
        setConfigFile("/WEB-INF/struts-config-registration.xml");
        setRequestPathInfo(ACTION_PATH);
    }

    public void testCreateRegistration( ) throws Exception {
        addRequestParameter("action", "Create");

        actionPerform( );

        String token = (String) getRequest( ).getAttribute(
                            Globals.TRANSACTION_TOKEN_KEY);
        assertNotNull(token, "Token was not saved");

        verifyForward("success");
    }
}
```

This test shows how you can verify that attributes are stored, as expected, in the request. In this case, the EditRegistrationAction is supposed to store a Struts transaction token in the request.

See Also

StrutsTestCase provides two base classes for creating Action unit tests. MockStrutsTestCase is used for creating tests that can be run outside of a servlet container. The other base class, CactusStrutsTestCase, can be used for testing actions running in a live container using the Cactus (*http://jakarta.apache.org/cactus*) test framework. Recipe 13.7 shows this approach.

If you need to verify the actual HTML generated by an Action or JSP, you can use *HttpUnit* (*http://httpunit.sourceforge.net*). *HttpUnit* provides an object-oriented Java API that allows you to inspect the returned HTTP response.

13.7   Testing Your Actions in the Container

Problem

You want to unit test an action as it's running within your application server.

Solution

Use StrutsTestCase to create a test that can be run using the Cactus integration testing framework.

Discussion

Recipe 13.6 shows you how to test an action independently from the servlet container using StrutsTestCase (*http://strutstestcase.sourceforge.net*). You can use StrutsTestCase, in conjunction with the Cactus testing framework (*http://jakarta.apache.org/cactus*), to test Struts actions running in the servlet container. This type of testing is referred to as *integration unit testing*.

Integration unit testing isn't unit testing in the pure sense. Unit tests isolate the unit from outside dependencies. This makes it easier to identify the cause of errors when a test fails. However, an integrated unit test may give you a more realistic view than a non-integrated test. If you are planning on deploying your application to different application servers (or different versions of the same application server), then you'll find integration unit testing to be invaluable.

Cactus was developed to provide these types of unit tests. It was originally developed to test Enterprise JavaBeans but is equally up to the task of testing servlets, servlet filters, and JSPs. In fact, Cactus can be used to test any type of behavior that relies on a J2EE/Servlet container. However, these tests come at a cost of increased complexity and slower test performance. Using StrutsTestCase, Cactus-executed action tests are easy to write, but configuration and deployment can be complex. If you are running your unit tests frequently as part of your build process, you'll find that the build script takes more time to run. The reason Cactus tests take longer is that Cactus starts your application server every time it runs its suite of tests. A good option is to run Cactus tests periodically, such as on nightly automated builds.

Unit Testing—Where Do I Start?

If you are just starting out with unit testing, knowing where to begin can be difficult. Your manager or team lead might tell you to unit test everything, but in practical terms you need to start where you have the best chance of seeing real benefits. Here are some guidelines to help you decide what type of testing to use and when:

Using plain old JUnit, concentrate on unit tests for the model, first. Your domain model classes hold the majority of your business logic. When something goes wrong, it's likely to be here.

Use the StrutsTestCase with mock objects to test your Action classes. Tests using mock objects can be run faster and don't require a servlet container.

Use Cactus testing for those classes that rely on container-provided services. For example, if you are using JNDI or testing behavior based on container-managed security, you should use Cactus.

If you're unsure about when to use a mock object test versus an in-container test, the Cactus site (*http://jakarta.apache.org/cactus*) includes an even-handed comparison of these two approaches.

Start by downloading and extracting the StrutsTestCase and Cactus binary distributions. Each of these packages provides separates distributions for a Servlet 2.3 (or later) container or Servlet 2.2 container. For Cactus, these versions are identified by the J2EE version as 1.3 or 1.2.

Copy the *strutstest.jar* file and all the JAR files from Cactus's *lib* directory to the *WEB-INF/lib* directory of your web application. Cactus uses a servlet to redirect HTTP requests to your test class. You'll need to declare this servlet in your application's *web.xml* file. Before the `ActionServlet` declaration, add this servlet declaration:

```
<!-- Cactus Servlet Redirector -->
<servlet>
    <servlet-name>
        ServletRedirector
    </servlet-name>
    <servlet-class>
        org.apache.cactus.server.ServletTestRedirector
    </servlet-class>
</servlet>
```

Before the `ActionServlet` servlet mapping, add this servlet mapping:

```
<!-- Cactus Servlet Redirector mapping -->
<servlet-mapping>
    <servlet-name>ServletRedirector</servlet-name>
```

```
        <url-pattern>/ServletRedirector</url-pattern>
    </servlet-mapping>
```

It's time to write the test using StrutsTestCase. StrutsTestCase provides two base classes for creating tests: `MockStrutsTestCase` and `CactusStrutsTestCase`. Figure 13-8 shows how the StrutsTestCase, Cactus, and JUnit base classes relate to each other.

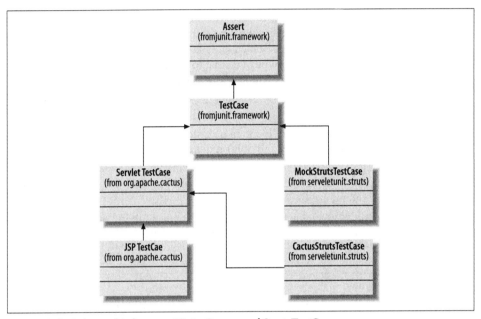

Figure 13-8. Relationship between JUnit, Cactus, and StrutsTestCase

You extend the `MockStrutsTestCase` (see Example 13-7) to create a standalone unit test for an `Action`. You can change a mock test into an in-container test by changing it to inherit from `CactusStrutsTestCase` instead of `MockStrutsTestCase`. Example 13-9 shows a Cactus test, identical to the excerpt in Example 13-7 of the parent class, that tests the `LogonAction` of the Struts MailReader example application.

Example 13-9. Cactus test for the Struts example LogonAction

```
package com.oreilly.strutsckbk.ch13;

import org.apache.struts.webapp.example.Constants;
import org.apache.struts.webapp.example.User;

import servletunit.struts.CactusStrutsTestCase;

public class SubmitLogonActionCactusTest extends CactusStrutsTestCase {
```

Example 13-9. Cactus test for the Struts example LogonAction (continued)

```
    private static final String ACTION_PATH = "/SubmitLogon";

    public SubmitLogonActionCactusTest(String testName) {
        super(testName);
    }

    public void testValidUserLogon( ) throws Exception {
        addRequestParameter("username", "user");
        addRequestParameter("password", "pass");

        setRequestPathInfo(ACTION_PATH);
        actionPerform( );

        verifyNoActionErrors( );

        User user = (User) getSession( ).getAttribute(Constants.USER_KEY);
        assertNotNull("User", user);
        assertEquals("Username", "user", user.getUsername( ));

        verifyForward("success");
    }

    public void testInvalidUserLogon( ) throws Exception {
        addRequestParameter("username", "junk");
        addRequestParameter("password", "bond");

        setRequestPathInfo(ACTION_PATH);
        actionPerform( );

        verifyActionErrors(new String[] {"error.password.mismatch"});

        verifyForward("logon");
    }

}
```

The CactusStrutsTestCase provides the same verification methods available with the MockStrutsTestCase. See Recipe 13.6 for a detailed explanation of these methods.

To run the test, you have to build and deploy your application and run your application server. You can run your test using any JUnit test runner. Cactus executes your test using a client Java virtual machine (the JUnit test runner's JVM) and a server Java virtual machine (the application server's JVM).

Before running your test, you have to tell Cactus how to find your application from the client side. You will need to create a file named *cactus.properties* and save it on your classpath. Example 13-10 shows the *cactus.properties* file used in this recipe.

Example 13-10. Client-side Cactus configuration file

```
# Configuration file for Cactus.

# Each project using Cactus need to have such a file put in the client side
# CLASSPATH (Meaning the directory containgin this file should be in the client
# side CLASSPATH, not the file itself of course ... :) )

# Defines the URLs that will be used by Cactus to call it's redirectors
# (Servlet and JSP). You need to specify in these URLs the webapp context
# that you use for your application.

cactus.contextURL = http://localhost/jsc-ch13
cactus.servletRedirectorName = ServletRedirector
cactus.enableLogging=true
```

Like any kind of unit testing, it's pretty boring (but satisfying) when the test passes. Interesting things happen when the test fails. For a Cactus test, though it's executed from the client side, you get the failure information and stack trace from the server side. Figure 13-9 shows the results when the test was changed to send an invalid username for the testValidUserLogon( ) method.

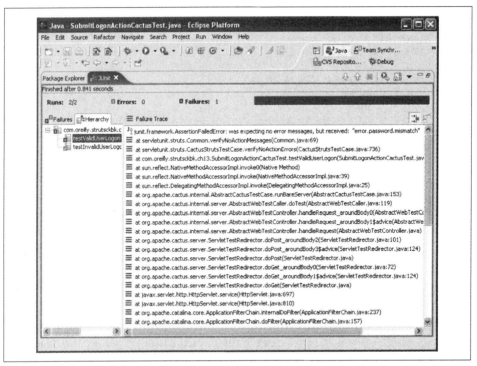

Figure 13-9. Stack trace of a failed Cactus unit test

See Also

Lu Jian has written an interesting article, "Unit Test Your Struts Application," for *ONJava*. This article delves into the use of aspect-oriented programming for testing Struts applications. It can be found at *http://www.onjava.com/pub/a/onjava/2004/09/22/test-struts.html*.

The StrutsTestCase web site, *http://strutstestcase.sourceforge.net*, has an active forum for posting questions and getting answers.

Cactus can be used in many different ways and a complete treatment is beyond the scope of this recipe. In addition to Struts actions, you can use Cactus to test servlets, servlet filters, JSP pages, and custom JSP tags. Cactus works best when it's integrated in your Ant build process. You can find complete details on the Cactus web site (*http://jakarta.apache.org/cactus*).

13.8 Testing Application Functionality

Problem

You want to verify that your application, deployed and running on an application server, does what it's supposed to do for a specific use case or scenario.

Solution

Use the *JWebUnit* acceptance testing framework.

Discussion

JWebUnit, an extension of the JUnit testing framework, leverages JUnit and Http-Unit for web application acceptance testing. JUnit provides the test harness and basic assertion methods, and HttpUnit (*http://httpunit.sourceforge.net*) provides a mechanism for programmatically sending requests and reading responses from a web application. JWebUnit exercises a running web application by programmatically sending requests, clicking links, filling out and submitting forms, and inspecting the response.

To get started with JWebUnit, download it from the project site, *http://jwebunit.sourceforge.net*. The source distribution includes everything you need; the JWebUnit Jar file, dependent Jar files, documentation, and the JWebUnit source code. Create a *test* directory structure in your application's project directory like that shown in Figure 13-10. You will need to copy the Jar files included with JWebUnit to your *test/lib* directory.

The easiest way to create a new JWebUnit test class is to subclass net.sourceforge.jwebunit.WebTestCase.

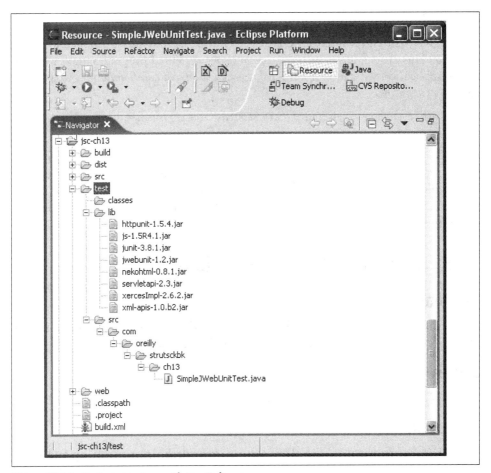

Figure 13-10. Project structure with "test" directory

If you have been using your own extension of the JUnit TestCase and cannot subclass WebTestCase, you can delegate calls to the net. sourceforge.jwebunit.WebTester class. The source for the WebTestCase class shows how this is done.

Example 13-11 shows a simple test case verifying that the *jsc-ch13* web application is up and running.

Example 13-11. Simple JWebUnit test case

```
package com.oreilly.strutsckbk.ch13;

import net.sourceforge.jwebunit.TestContext;
import net.sourceforge.jwebunit.WebTestCase;
```

Example 13-11. Simple JWebUnit test case (continued)

```java
public class SimpleWebTest extends WebTestCase {
    public SimpleWebTest(String name) {
        super(name);
    }

    public void setUp() throws Exception {
        TestContext testContext = getTestContext();
        testContext.setBaseUrl("http://localhost/jsc-ch13");
        // Use the message resources properties file
        testContext.setResourceBundleName(
            "org.apache.struts.webapp.example.ApplicationResources"
        );
    }

    public void testAppAvailable() {
        beginAt("/index.jsp");
        // use the title text from the testContext resource bundle
        assertTitleEqualsKey("index.title");
    }
}
```

You can run this test using any of the JUnit test runners. Like any other JUnit test, a successful test run is rather boring to look at; it's more interesting to look at a failed test. Figure 13-11 shows the results from Eclipse's JUnit test runner when the SimpleWebTest of Example 13-11 fails because the application server isn't running.

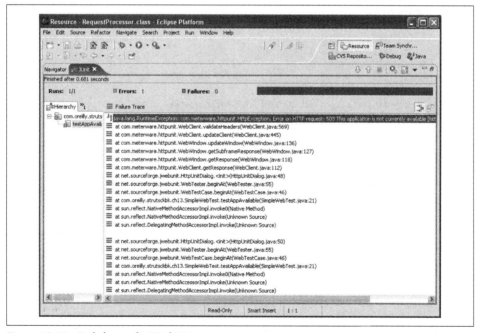

Figure 13-11. Failed run of a JWebUnit test case

Every JWebUnit test has a test context. This context, typically configured in the setUp( ) method, contains information applicable to the test case such as the base URL. In Example 13-11 this value was set to the web application's context:

```
testContext.setBaseUrl("http://localhost/jsc-ch13");
```

You can use JWebUnit to test the internationalization features of your web application. The test context allows you to specify the resource bundle for your localized text as well as the locale being tested. JWebUnit looks up properties from the resource bundle using that locale. The locale that you set in the test context is only used on the client side to look up resource bundle properties. To mimic the browser's locale settings, you must set the Accept-Language header to the locale being tested. The Struts MailReader can be localized for Russian. Example 13-12 tests this localization by verifying that the response title has the correct value.

Example 13-12. Using JWebUnit to test internationalization

```
package com.oreilly.strutsckbk.ch13;

import java.util.Locale;

import net.sourceforge.jwebunit.TestContext;
import net.sourceforge.jwebunit.WebTestCase;

public class LocaleWebTest extends WebTestCase {

    public LocaleWebTest(String name) {
        super(name);
    }

    public void setUp( ) throws Exception {
        testContext = getTestContext( );
        testContext.setBaseUrl("http://localhost/jsc-ch13");
        testContext.setResourceBundleName(
            "org.apache.struts.webapp.example.ApplicationResources"
        );
    }

    public void testRussian( ) {
        testContext.setLocale(new Locale("ru"));
        testContext.getWebClient( ).setHeaderField("Accept-Language","ru");
        beginAt("/index.jsp");
        assertTitleEqualsKey("index.title");
    }

    private TestContext testContext;
}
```

Want more you say? JWebUnit shines at testing application scenarios and use cases. Say you wanted to verify the registration process of the Struts MailReader. The following simple case illustrates this process:

1. The users browse to the application's welcome page.

2. The users click the "Register" link.

3. The registration form is displayed.

4. The users fill out the registration form with their full name, username, password, and email information.

5. The users submit the form.

6. The main menu page is displayed with a heading message personalized for the users.

You can create a JWebUnit test case that implements this use case, as shown in Example 13-13.

Example 13-13. Testing user registration

```
package com.oreilly.strutsckbk.ch13;

import com.meterware.httpunit.HttpUnitOptions;

import net.sourceforge.jwebunit.TestContext;
import net.sourceforge.jwebunit.WebTestCase;

public class RegistrationWebTest extends WebTestCase {
    public RegistrationWebTest(String name) {
        super(name);
    }

    public void setUp() throws Exception {
        // disable JavaScript handling
        HttpUnitOptions.setScriptingEnabled(false);
        TestContext testContext = getTestContext();
        testContext.setBaseUrl("http://localhost/jsc-ch13");
        testContext.setResourceBundleName("org.apache.struts.webapp.example.
ApplicationResources");
    }

    public void testRegistration() {
        // start at the welcome page
        beginAt("/index.jsp");

        // find the registration link and click it
        String regLinkText = getMessage("index.registration");
        clickLinkWithText(regLinkText);

        // check that the registration form is displayed
        assertFormElementPresent("username");
```

Example 13-13. Testing user registration (continued)

```
        // use the current time as part of the username for repeatability
        long ts = System.currentTimeMillis( );

        // fill out the form
        setFormElement("username","t"+ts);
        setFormElement("password","gotech");
        setFormElement("password2","gotech");
        String fullName = "George P. Burdell";
        setFormElement("fullName", fullName);
        setFormElement("fromAddress","gpburdell@matech.com");
        setFormElement("replyToAddress","gpburdell@matech.com");

        // submit the form
        submit( );

        // check that the main menu is displayed with the name included
        assertTextPresent(getMessage("mainMenu.heading")+' '+fullName);
    }

    public void tearDown( ) {
        // logoff to clean up the session
        gotoPage("/Logoff.do");
    }
}
```

This test shows off the power of JWebUnit and, though hidden from view, HttpUnit. For complete details, download JWebUnit and give it a try!

See Also

Other tools provide similar functionality as JWebUnit. Canoo WebTest (*http://www.canoo.com*) uses an Ant-like XML file to describe a test scenario. If your test writers aren't comfortable with Java, then take a look at this excellent open source tool.

## CHAPTER 14

Tiles and Other Presentation Approaches

14.0 Introduction

Struts is primarily intended to provide the controller for web applications. Some developers immediately associate Struts with the Struts JSP tags, but any Struts enthusiast will tell you that the Struts controller framework and API, not the tags, comprise the heart of the framework. You can limit, augment, and even replace your use of the Struts view-rendering features and still gain many of the advantages afforded by Struts.

The first half of this chapter focuses on Tiles. This framework, distributed and integrated with Struts, provides a robust approach for reusing pages and page layouts across your application. If you've never used Tiles, you'll find recipes to get you started along with some more advanced uses of Tiles. The second half of this chapter takes a step back and shows you how to use new ways of generating HTML within the context of a Struts application.

The topics in this chapter, particularly the latter half, are broader in scope than most of the recipes in this book. Entire books have been written about some of these technologies, such as Java ServerFaces and XSLT, and it would be impossible to cover them completely in a single chapter, let alone a single recipe. The recipes here will help you get started using these technologies and will give you some insight and understanding on the technology and its application.

14.1 Reusing a Common Page Layout with Tiles

Problem

You want to define a common layout for your application and use that layout throughout your application without having to cut and paste HTML everywhere.

Solution

Use Tiles with your Struts application.

Discussion

Tiles has been distributed with Struts since the Struts 1.1 release. Prior to that, it was available as a separate add-on known as *Components*. Tiles allows you to create page component definitions that can be reused throughout your application.

The first step in using Tiles is to understand your needs. What are the common elements and what are the elements that change on every page? Is the layout the same across your application? If not, would your application be more usable if it did have a common layout?

To understand how to apply Tiles, this recipe walks you through its application for a simple web site. Say you want to apply a common page layout, such as the one in Figure 14-1, to every page of your application.

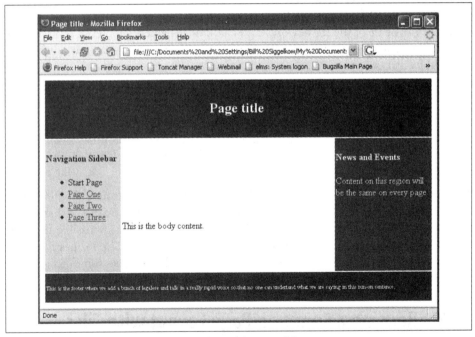

Figure 14-1. Typical page layout with header, sidebars, and footer

Moving from left to right and top to bottom, you pull the page apart into its component pieces described in Table 14-1.

Table 14-1. Components of a page layout

Component name	Description	Page position
Title	Text, specific to the body content, displayed in the browser title as well as the header	Browser title bar and within the header
Header	Contains the page title as header text	Top, from left to right margin
Navigation Bar	Contains a set of links for pages that you can display as the body content	Left sidebar
Body Content	Primary content of the page, varies for every page	Centered below the header and between the sidebars
News Sidebar	News and events; this content will be the same on every page	Right sidebar
Footer	Contains legalese and related information, displayed in a smaller font	Bottom, from left to right margin

You can think of the entire page as a single component that contains these components laid out in a particular fashion. You can define this set of components in a Tiles definition file (*tiles-defs.xml*), as shown in Example 14-1.

Example 14-1. Tiles definitions file

```
<?xml version="1.0" encoding="ISO-8859-1" ?>

<!DOCTYPE tiles-definitions PUBLIC
     "-//Apache Software Foundation//DTD Tiles Configuration 1.1//EN"
     "http://jakarta.apache.org/struts/dtds/tiles-config_1_1.dtd">

<tiles-definitions>
    <definition name="mainLayoutDef" path="/layouts/mainLayout.jsp">
        <put name="title" value="Struts Cookbook - Chapter 14 : Tiles"/>
        <put name="header" value="/common/header.jsp"/>
        <put name="navbar" value="/common/navbar2.jsp"/>
        <put name="body"   type="string"/>
        <put name="news"   value="/common/news.html"/>
        <put name="footer" value="/common/footer.jsp"/>
    </definition>
</tiles-definitions>
```

The path attribute of the definition element specifies the location of the JSP page that lays out the components. Each put element defines a page component, and the value attribute specifies the contents of that component.

If you have prototyped the layout using an HTML or JSP page, you can transform it into a Tiles layout page. Example 14-2 (*sample.html*) shows the static source HTML from Figure 14-1.

Example 14-2. Prototype HTML layout page

```
<html>
<head>
```

Example 14-2. Prototype HTML layout page (continued)

```
    <title>Page title</title>
</head>
<body bgcolor="white">
    <table border="0" width="100%">
        <tr>
            <td align="center" colspan="3" height="100" bgcolor="darkblue">
                <h2><font color="white">Page title</font></h2>
            </td>
        </tr>
        <tr height="300">
            <td width="20%" valign="top" bgcolor="gold">
                <p></p><h4>Navigation Sidebar</h4>
                <ul>
                    <li>Start Page</li>
                    <li><a href="page1.jsp">Page One</a></li>
                    <li><a href="page2.jsp">Page Two</a></li>
                    <li><a href="page3.jsp">Page Three</a></li>
                </ul>
            </td>
            <td width="55%" bgcolor="white">This is the body content.</td>
            <td width="25%" bgcolor="blue" valign="top">
                <span style="color:white">
                    <h4>News and Events</h4>
                    <p>Content on this region will be the same on every page.</p>
                </span>
            </td>
        </tr>
        <tr><td colspan="3" height="50" bgcolor="darkblue">
                <font color="white" size="-2">
                    This is the footer where we add a bunch of legalese and
                    talk in a really rapid voice so that no one can undertand
                    what we are saying in this run-on sentence.
                </font>
            </td>
        </tr>
    </table>
</body>
</html>
```

To convert this page for Tiles, you use the Tiles JSP tags. The `tiles:insert` tag serves as a placeholder for a component named in a Tiles definition. Example 14-3 (*main-Layout.jsp*) shows the results of converting the static page in Example 14-2. Though not required, it helps organize your application if you save your layout pages in a separate directory of your application. Conventionally, these common layout JSPs are stored in the *web/layouts* directory.

Example 14-3. Laying out Tiles components in a reusable JSP

```
<%@ taglib uri="http://struts.apache.org/tags-bean" prefix="bean" %>
<%@ taglib uri="http://struts.apache.org/tags-html" prefix="html" %>
<%@ taglib uri="http://struts.apache.org/tags-logic" prefix="logic" %>
<%@ taglib uri="http://struts.apache.org/tags-tiles" prefix="tiles" %>
```

Example 14-3. Laying out Tiles components in a reusable JSP (continued)

```
<html:html lang="true">
<head>
  <title><tiles:getAsString name="title"/></title>
  <html:base/>
</head>
<body bgcolor="white">
    <table border="0" width="100%">
        <tr>
            <td align="center" colspan="3" height="100" bgcolor="darkblue">
                <tiles:insert attribute="header">
                    <tiles:put name="title" beanName="title" beanScope="tile"/>
                </tiles:insert>
            </td>
        </tr>
        <tr height="300">
            <td width="20%" valign="top" bgcolor="gold">
                <tiles:insert attribute="navbar"/>
            </td>
            <td width="55%" bgcolor="white">
                <tiles:insert attribute="body"/>
            </td>
            <td width="25%" bgcolor="blue" valign="top">
                <tiles:insert attribute="news"/>
            </td>
        </tr>
        <tr>
            <td align="center" colspan="3" height="50" bgcolor="darkblue">
                <tiles:insert attribute="footer"/>
            </td>
        </tr>
    </table>
</body>
</html:html>
```

You can create a JSP page, as shown in Example 14-4 (*view_start_page.jsp*), that renders the definition using the layout.

Example 14-4. Rendering a Tiles definition in a JSP page

```
<%@ taglib uri="http://struts.apache.org/tags-tiles" prefix="tiles" %>
<tiles:insert definition="mainLayoutDef">
    <tiles:put name="title" type="string" value="Start Page"/>
    <tiles:put name="body" value="/pages/pageStart.jsp"/>
</tiles:insert>
```

Here's another JSP page (*view_page_one.jsp*) that uses the same definition:

```
<%@ taglib uri="http://struts.apache.org/tags-tiles" prefix="tiles" %>
<tiles:insert definition="mainLayoutDef">
    <tiles:put name="title" type="string" value="Page One"/>
    <tiles:put name="body" value="/pages/pageOne.jsp"/>
</tiles:insert>
```

With Tiles, you reduce the amount of HTML that you have to cut and paste. More importantly, when you need to modify the layout for all pages, you only have to make the change in one place. If you wanted to swap the position of the sidebars, you could make the change in the layout JSP page and all the Tiles that use the corresponding definition would reflect the new layout.

Tiles ships with Struts so no installation is required. To enable Tiles for your application, do the following:

1. Place your Tiles definition file (*tiles-defs.xml*) in your */WEB-INF* directory.

2. Add the Tiles plug-in to your *struts-config.xml* file, setting the *definitions-config* property appropriately:

```
<plug-in className="org.apache.struts.tiles.TilesPlugin" >
    <!-- Path to XML definition file -->
    <set-property property="definitions-config"
                  value="/WEB-INF/tiles-defs.xml" />
</plug-in>
```

See Also

The Struts User's Guide includes a section called "Page Composition with Tiles" available at *http://struts.apache.org/userGuide/building_view.html#Tiles*.

Struts ships with a sample Tiles web application, *tiles-documentation.war*. This application includes the Tiles documentation and highlights the power of Tiles for complex portal-style applications.

Recipe 14.2 shows you how to create definitions by extending a base definition. Instead of using a JSP to render a Tiles definition, such as the one shown in Example 14-4, you can use the technique shown in Recipe 14.3.

Cedric Dumoulin, the creator of Tiles, has a number of resources, papers, and sample code for Tiles. You can find these materials on his Tiles portal site at *http://www.lifl.fr/~dumoulin/tiles/*.

14.2   Extending Tile Definitions

Problem

You want to create a new Tiles definition that reuses a similar one.

Solution

When you define a new definition in your Tiles definition file (*tiles-def.xml*), you can specify a definition to extend using the extends="*definitionName*" attribute. The new definition inherits attributes of the extended definition and can override attribute values. (See Example 14-5.)

Example 14-5. Extending a new definition from a base definition

```xml
<?xml version="1.0" encoding="ISO-8859-1" ?>

<!DOCTYPE tiles-definitions PUBLIC
      "-//Apache Software Foundation//DTD Tiles Configuration 1.1//EN"
      "http://jakarta.apache.org/struts/dtds/tiles-config_1_1.dtd">

<tiles-definitions>
    <!-- A base Tile -->
    <definition name="mainLayoutDef2" path="/layouts/mainLayout.jsp">
        <put name="title" value="Struts Cookbook - Chapter 14 : Tiles"/>
        <put name="header" value="/common/header.jsp"/>
        <put name="navbar" value="/common/navbar2.jsp"/>
        <put name="body"   type="string"/>
        <put name="news"   value="/common/news.html"/>
        <put name="footer" value="/common/footer.jsp"/>
    </definition>

    <!-- Extensions of the base mainLayoutDef2 tile -->
    <definition name=".start" extends="mainLayoutDef2">
        <put name="title" value="Start Page"/>
        <put name="body"  value="/pages/pageStart.jsp"/>
    </definition>

    <definition name=".pageOne" extends="mainLayoutDef2">
        <put name="title" value=" Page One"/>
        <put name="body"  value="/pages/pageOne.jsp"/>
        <put name="news"  value="/pages/pageOneNews.jsp"/>
    </definition>
<tiles-definitions>
```

Discussion

With Tiles, you can base a Tile definition on the definition of another Tile. The new definition, which extends the base definition, inherits the attributes of the base definition and overrides attributes as needed. When using Tiles, developers commonly use the approach shown in the Solution. The `mainLayoutDef2` definition defines the basic layout to be used across the application. In object-oriented terms, you can think of the base definition as an abstract class. The `.start` and `.pageOne` definitions extend `mainLayoutDef2`. These definitions are like concrete subclasses of the abstract base class.

The `.start` definition overrides two attributes: `title` and `body`. The overridden `title` specifies title text appropriate for the Start page. The body attribute in the base `mainLayoutDef2` does not specify a value; think of it as an abstract property. The `.start` definition overrides the body attribute by specifying a concrete value, a JSP page. The `.pageOne` definition, which extends the `mainLayoutDef2` definition, overrides the news attribute and sets the `title` and body.

To create a page that uses the new definition, you insert the definition using the tiles:
insert JSP tag as shown by Example 14-6 (*startPage.jsp*).

Example 14-6. JSP that references a definition extension

```
<%@ taglib uri="http://struts.apache.org/tags-tiles" prefix="tiles" %>
<tiles:insert definition=".start"/>
```

See Also

You can bypass the trivial JSP page used in Example 14-6 by forwarding directly to a
definition, as shown in Recipe 14.3.

14.3   Displaying Tiles Using a Struts Forward

Problem

You don't like having to write and maintain minimal JSP pages that insert a Tiles
definition.

Solution

Use action forwards in your *struts-config.xml* file that specify the definition name for
the path attribute on the forward element. The TilesRequestProcessor, deployed
behind the scenes by the TilePlugin, will forward to the definition as if it were
inserted by a JSP.

Assuming Tiles definitions are in your *tiles-defs.xml* file named .someTilesDef and
.anotherTilesDef, you can create actions such as the following in your *struts-config.
xml* file:

```
<action path="/doStartPage"
    forward=".someTilesDef"/>

<action path="/doPageOne"
        type="com.foo.SomeAction">
    <forward name="success" path=".anotherTilesDef"/>
</action>
```

Discussion

If you've read over the first couple of Tiles recipes, you'll notice that once a definition
is created, its trivial to write JSP code to render the page. Tiles uses a custom request
processor to eliminate the need for these trivial pages. The TilesPlugin installs the
TilesRequestProcessor when the plug-in initializes. The TilesRequestProcessor provides special handling that allows you to use a Tiles definition as the target path for a
Struts forward. When the TileRequestProcessor processes the forward, if the forward
path matches a Tiles definition name, it loads the definition, creates and initializes the

Tile's context attributes, and inserts the corresponding definition. If the path doesn't match a definition, the `TilesRequestProcessor` lets the base `RequestProcessor` handle the request.

Using this approach you can elminate almost all direct references to JSPs in your *struts-config.xml* file. You will end up with many actions and definitions; for each action, you eliminate one JSP file that you would have had to maintain. Instead of *n* JSP pages, you will have *n* actions mappings in your *struts-config.xml* file.

Local and global forwards can use this technique. The common convention is to specify definition names using a dot (".") separator instead of a slash ("/").

See Also

For more information, check out the JavaDocs for the `TilesRequestProcessor`. These are included with Struts, or you can find this documentation at *http://struts.apache.org/ api/org/apache/struts/tiles/TilesRequestProcessor.html*.

14.4   Creating Tabbed Panes

Problem

You want your pages to display as tabbed folders.

Solution

Use the Tiles Tabbed Layout. Example 14-7 shows the JSP page (*tabsLayout.jsp*) that lays out components in a tabbed fashion.

Example 14-7. Tiles tabbed layout

```
<%@ taglib uri="http://struts.apache.org/tags-bean" prefix="bean" %>
<%@ taglib uri="http://struts.apache.org/tags-logic" prefix="logic" %>
<%@ taglib uri="http://struts.apache.org/tags-tiles" prefix="tiles" %>

<%--
  Tabs Layout .
  This layout allows to render several tiles in a tabs fashion.
  @param tabList A list of available tabs. We use MenuItem to carry data (name, body,
icon, ...)
  @param selectedIndex Index of default selected tab
  @param parameterName Name of parameter carrying selected info in http request.
--%>

<%--
Use tiles attributes, and declare them as page java variable.
These attribute must be passed to the tile.
--%>
```

Example 14-7. Tiles tabbed layout (continued)

```
<tiles:useAttribute name="parameterName" classname="java.lang.String" />
<tiles:useAttribute id="selectedIndexStr" name="selectedIndex" ignore="true"
classname="java.lang.String" />
<tiles:useAttribute name="tabList" classname="java.util.List" />
<%
  String selectedColor="#98ABC7";
  String notSelectedColor="#C0C0C0";

  int index = 0; // Loop index
  int selectedIndex = 0;
    // Check if selected come from request parameter
  try {
    selectedIndex = Integer.parseInt(selectedIndexStr);
    selectedIndex = Integer.parseInt(request.getParameter( parameterName ));
    }
   catch( java.lang.NumberFormatException ex )
    { // do nothing
    }
  // Check selectedIndex bounds
  if( selectedIndex < 0 || selectedIndex >= tabList.size( ) ) selectedIndex = 0;
  String selectedBody = ((org.apache.struts.tiles.beans.MenuItem)tabList.
get(selectedIndex)).getLink( ); // Selected body

%>

<table border="0"  cellspacing="0" cellpadding="0">
  <%-- Draw tabs --%>
<tr>
  <td width="10"> </td>
  <td>
    <table border="0"  cellspacing="0" cellpadding="5">
      <tr>
<logic:iterate id="tab" name="tabList" type="org.apache.struts.tiles.beans.MenuItem" >
<% // compute href
  String href = request.getRequestURI( ) + "?"+parameterName + "=" + index;
    // Don't add request URI prefix , but let the client compute the original URL
    // This allows to use a Struts action as page URL, and perform a forward.
    // Bug reported by Don Peterkofsky
  //String href = "" + "?"+parameterName + "=" + index;
  String color = notSelectedColor;
  if( index == selectedIndex )
    {
    selectedBody = tab.getLink( );
    color = selectedColor;
    } // enf if
  index++;
%>
  <td bgcolor="<%=color%>">
  <a href="<%=href%>" ><%=tab.getValue( )%></a>
  </td>
  <td width="1" ></td>
```

Example 14-7. Tiles tabbed layout (continued)

```
</logic:iterate>
      </tr>
    </table>
  </td>
  <td width="10" > </td>
</tr>

<tr>
  <td height="5" bgcolor="<%=selectedColor%>" colspan="3" > </td>
</tr>

  <%-- Draw body --%>
<tr>
  <td width="10" bgcolor="<%=selectedColor%>"> </td>
  <td>
  <tiles:insert name="<%=selectedBody%>" flush="true" />
  </td>
  <td width="10" bgcolor="<%=selectedColor%>"> </td>
</tr>

<tr>
  <td height="5" bgcolor="<%=selectedColor%>" colspan="3" > </td>
</tr>

</table>
```

Create a definition in your *tiles-defs.xml* file that uses this layout such as the following:

```
<!-- Tiles used for Tabbed pane recipe -->
<definition name="example.tabs" path="/layouts/tabsLayout.jsp">
    <put name="selectedIndex" value="0"/>
    <put name="parameterName" value="selected"/>
    <putList name="tabList">
        <item value="Page One" link="/pages/pageOne.jsp"
            classtype="org.apache.struts.tiles.beans.SimpleMenuItem"/>
        <item value="Page Two" link="/pages/pageTwo.jsp"
            classtype="org.apache.struts.tiles.beans.SimpleMenuItem"/>
        <item value="Page Three" link="/pages/pageThree.jsp"
            classtype="org.apache.struts.tiles.beans.SimpleMenuItem"/>
    </putList>
</definition>
```

Finally, create a JSP page that inserts the definition:

```
<%@ taglib uri="http://struts.apache.org/tags-tiles" prefix="tiles" %>
<html>
    <head>
        <title>Tiles Tabbed Panes</title>
    </head>
    <body>
        <tiles:insert definition="example.tabs"/>
    </body>
</html>
```

Discussion

Tiles includes a tabbed layout that you can use and customize for your own user interfaces. This layout creates a page that will look something like Figure 14-2.

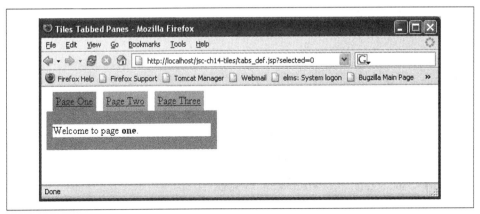

Figure 14-2. Using Tiles for tabbed panes

When you click on a link on a tab, the tab becomes highlighted and the content associated with that tab is displayed. Tiles uses the URL to determine the page to display as defined in the definition. For example, when you click on the "Page Two" tab, you will see the URL:

    http://localhost/jsc-ch14-tiles/tabs_def.jsp?selected=1

Tiles uses the selected request parameter to index into the items specified in the definition. As shown in Figure 14-3, this results in the display of the content from the /pages/pageTwo.jsp page.

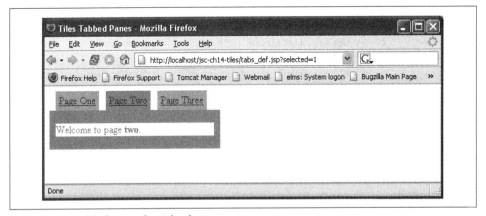

Figure 14-3. Tabbed pane after tab selection

You can see the power of Tiles when you combine different Tiles together. For example, you can combine the classic layout defined in mainLayoutDef2 with the tabbed layout using the definitions shown in Example 14-8. In this example, the example.tabs2 definition creates the list of tabs using the putList element. This element contains three item elements that define the tabs. Each item specifies a link attribute. The value of this attribute dictates the page to be displayed when you select the tab. Like most other Tiles definitions, the link attribute accepts a URL to a web resource or a definition name.

Example 14-8. Tiles definition for a tabbed layout

```
<?xml version="1.0" encoding="ISO-8859-1" ?>

<!DOCTYPE tiles-definitions PUBLIC
      "-//Apache Software Foundation//DTD Tiles Configuration 1.1//EN"
      "http://jakarta.apache.org/struts/dtds/tiles-config_1_1.dtd">

<tiles-definitions>
    <!-- Tiles used for Recipe 14.1, 14.2, and 14.3 -->
    <!-- A base Tile -->
    <definition name="mainLayoutDef2" path="/layouts/mainLayout.jsp">
        <put name="title" value="Struts Cookbook - Chapter 14 : Tiles"/>
        <put name="header" value="/common/header.jsp"/>
        <put name="navbar" value="/common/navbar2.jsp"/>
        <put name="body"   type="string"/>
        <put name="news"   value="/common/news.html"/>
        <put name="footer" value="/common/footer.jsp"/>
    </definition>

    <!-- Extensions of the base mainLayoutDef tile -->
    <definition name=".start" extends="mainLayoutDef2">
        <put name="title" value="Start Page"/>
        <put name="body"  value="/pages/pageStart.jsp"/>
    </definition>

    <definition name=".pageOne" extends="mainLayoutDef2">
        <put name="title" value=" Page One"/>
        <put name="body"  value="/pages/pageOne.jsp"/>
    </definition>

    <definition name=".pageTwo" extends="mainLayoutDef2">
        <put name="title" value="Page Two"/>
        <put name="body"  value="/pages/pageTwo.jsp"/>
    </definition>

    <definition name=".pageThree" extends="mainLayoutDef2">
        <put name="title" value="Page Three"/>
        <put name="body"  value="/pages/pageThree.jsp"/>
    </definition>

    <!-- Tabbed layout that uses nested components -->
    <definition name="example.tabs2" path="/layouts/tabsLayout.jsp">
```

Example 14-8. Tiles definition for a tabbed layout (continued)

```
        <put name="selectedIndex" value="0"/>
        <put name="parameterName" value="selected"/>
        <putList name="tabList">
            <item value="Page One" link=".pageOne"
                classtype="org.apache.struts.tiles.beans.SimpleMenuItem"/>
            <item value="Page Two" link=".pageTwo"
                classtype="org.apache.struts.tiles.beans.SimpleMenuItem"/>
            <item value="Page Three" link=".pageThree"
                classtype="org.apache.struts.tiles.beans.SimpleMenuItem"/>
        </putList>
    </definition>

</tiles-definitions>
```

Rendering the `examples.tabs2` Tiles definition results in a page such as the one in Figure 14-4.

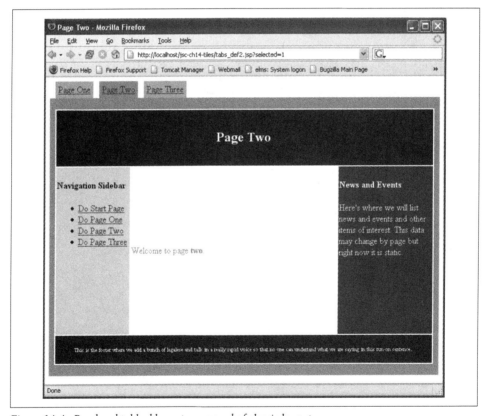

Figure 14-4. Rendered tabbed layout composed of classic layout

See Also

Tiles includes a nested tabbed layout that allows you to contain submenus on each tab. Tiles comes with several other useful layouts. You can see these layouts in action with the tiles-documentation sample application included with Struts. The source code for these layouts ships with the Struts source distribution.

14.5 Using Tiles for I18N

Problem

You want to customize a Tiles definition based upon the user's language and country.

Solution

Create a separate version of your Tiles definition file for the specific locale; appending the locale code to the file name. If you saved your Tiles definition file as *tiles-def.xml*, you would save the locale-specific definitions file for Spanish as *tiles-def_es.xml*.

Discussion

Developers commonly localize JSP pages in a Struts application using a localized *message resources* file and the bean:message tag. If you need to display a different page and you are using Tiles, you can set aside a Tiles definition for a specific locale by placing it in a locale-specific Tiles definition file. At runtime, Tiles searches for a matching definition by considering the definition name and the current locale. You indicate the locale that applies to the definition by appending the locale's language and country code to the file name, as you would for localizing a message resources properties file. For example, if your Tiles definitions are specified in *tiles-def.xml*, definitions specific to the Spanish language will be placed in *tiles-def_es.xml*. If you needed definitions specific for French-Canadians, you would store them in *tiles-def_fr_CA.xml*.

Example 14-9 shows the Tiles definition file, *tiles-def_es.xml*, that overrides the .pageOne definition from Example 14-5.

Example 14-9. Overriding a definition for a specific locale

```
<?xml version="1.0" encoding="ISO-8859-1" ?>

<!DOCTYPE tiles-definitions PUBLIC
        "-//Apache Software Foundation//DTD Tiles Configuration 1.1//EN"
        "http://jakarta.apache.org/struts/dtds/tiles-config_1_1.dtd">

<tiles-definitions>
    <definition name=".pageOne" extends="mainLayoutDef2">
        <put name="title" value=" Page One"/>
        <put name="body"  value="/pages/pageOneEs.jsp"/>
```

Example 14-9. Overriding a definition for a specific locale (continued)

```
    </definition>
</tiles-definitions>
```

This technique is useful for localizing the layout. For some locales, you may want to reorient the sidebars so the predominant sidebar is on the right instead of the left. Tiles localization solves this problem.

See Also

Development of an internationalized application takes planning and forethought. Chapter 12 addresses a number of problems that you may run into when localizing a Struts application.

14.6   Using Tiles in a Modular Application

Problem

You are using Struts modules, and you want to define module-specific Tiles definitions.

Solution

Create a separate Tiles definitions file for each module. Then, in each module's Struts configuration file, configure the TilesPlugin, as shown in Example 14-10, to use that module's definitions file and be module-aware.

Example 14-10. Configuring Tiles for a specific module

```
<plug-in className="org.apache.struts.tiles.TilesPlugin" >
    <!-- Path to XML definition file -->
    <set-property property="definitions-config"
                  value="/WEB-INF/tiles-defs-module1.xml" />
    <!-- Set Module-awareness to true -->
    <set-property property="moduleAware" value="true" />
</plug-in>
```

Discussion

Like configuration files for the Struts Validator, you can separate your Tiles definitions into multiple files. If you are using modules, you can create Tiles definitions, which can only be accessed from within a specific module, by declaring that definition file in the module's Struts configuration file. To ensure that Tiles handles module-relative paths when it processes requests, you must set the moduleAware property to true. By being module-aware when you forward to a definition, the definition name will be pulled from the definitions *for that module*. Definition names have to be unique within a module.

Suppose your application has two modules: the default module and an administration module. The *struts-config-admin.xml* file, shown in Example 14-11 configures the administration module.

Example 14-11. Struts configuration file for a module

```xml
<?xml version="1.0" encoding="ISO-8859-1" ?>

<!DOCTYPE struts-config PUBLIC
        "-//Apache Software Foundation//DTD Struts Configuration 1.2//EN"
        "http://jakarta.apache.org/struts/dtds/struts-config_1_2.dtd">

<struts-config>

    <action-mappings>
        <action
            path="/doStartPage"
            forward=".start"/>
    </action-mappings>

    <plug-in className="org.apache.struts.tiles.TilesPlugin" >
        <set-property property="definitions-config"
                        value="/WEB-INF/tiles-defs-admin.xml" />
        <set-property property="moduleAware" value="true" />
    </plug-in>

</struts-config>
```

You can specify the Tiles definitions used by the administration module in the *tiles-defs-admin.xml* file shown in Example 14-12.

Example 14-12. Module-specific Tiles definition file

```xml
<?xml version="1.0" encoding="ISO-8859-1" ?>

<!DOCTYPE tiles-definitions PUBLIC
        "-//Apache Software Foundation//DTD Tiles Configuration 1.1//EN"
        "http://jakarta.apache.org/struts/dtds/tiles-config_1_1.dtd">

<tiles-definitions>
    <definition name="adminLayout" path="/layouts/adminLayout.jsp">
        <put name="title" value="Struts Cookbook - Chapter 14 : Tiles"/>
        <put name="body"    type="string"/>
    </definition>

    <definition name=".start" extends="adminLayout">
        <put name="title" value="Admin Start Page"/>
        <put name="body"   value="/pages/adminMain.jsp"/>
    </definition>
</tiles-definitions>
```

The paths used in a Tiles definition file are treated as context-relative even if that definition is used for a specific module.

See Also

This topic has been discussed on the struts-user mailing list. One particular thread you may find helpful is archived at *http://marc.theaimsgroup.com/?l=struts-user&m=109579114312336&w=2*.

If you are unfamiliar with Struts modules, see Recipe 2.5.

14.7   Reusing a Common Page Layout with SiteMesh

Problem

You want render your application's pages using a common layout without having to change your JSP pages or your application's Struts configuration.

Solution

Use SiteMesh to wrap your application's pages with a common layout and other presentation features.

Discussion

SiteMesh (*http://www.opensymphony.com/sitemesh/*) is a web-page layout and decoration framework. It allows you to decorate the web pages of an existing application with a common layout. It provides similar features as Tiles but uses a completely different approach. When you use Tiles, you adopt the Tiles-way of doing things by constructing pages using Tiles custom JSP tags, creating definitions in a Tiles configuration file, and linking actions to Tiles using the TilesRequestProcessor. Tiles becomes a pervasive part of your web application.

SiteMesh takes a different approach. It uses a servlet filter to modify the HTTP responses generated by your application, with responses typically generated by JSP pages. SiteMesh amends the response based on settings in a configuration file.

Suppose you have a site with three web pages: a main page, and two secondary pages. The main page looks something like Figure 14-5.

The secondary pages referred to by the two hyperlinks are, like this page, simple. The *struts-config.xml* file for this application is shown in Example 14-13.

Figure 14-5. Page slated for decoration by SiteMesh

Example 14-13. Struts configuration for sample application

```
<!DOCTYPE struts-config PUBLIC
          "-//Apache Software Foundation//DTD Struts Configuration 1.2//EN"
          "http://jakarta.apache.org/struts/dtds/struts-config_1_2.dtd" >
<struts-config>

    <global-forwards>
        <forward name="main" path="/main.do"/>
    </global-forwards>

    <!--  Action Mapping Definitions  -->
    <action-mappings>
        <action path="/main"
                type="org.apache.struts.actions.ForwardAction"
                parameter="/WEB-INF/jsps/main.jsp"
        />
        <action path="/test"
                type="org.apache.struts.actions.ForwardAction"
                parameter="/WEB-INF/jsps/test.jsp"
        />
        <action path="/summary"
                type="org.apache.struts.actions.ForwardAction"
                parameter="/WEB-INF/jsps/summary.jsp"
        />
    </action-mappings>

    <!-- message resources -->
    <message-resources parameter="ApplicationResources"/>

</struts-config>
```

Now your boss comes along and tells you that the site needs to be revised. He wants a titled header across the top of the page, a sidebar with navigation links on the left, and a footer with legalese on the bottom. He also wants the summary page to be displayed in a pop-up window. There are three choices for implementing these changes:

- Add the new sections to the existing JSPs.
- Convert your application to use Tiles.
- Use SiteMesh to adorn the existing site with the new sections.

If your site has only three pages, then the first solution is the most cost effective. However, if your site has 300 pages, the first solution requires changing every page, and the second solution requires refactoring your entire application.

The third solution, using SiteMesh, can be your savior. To install SiteMesh and enable it for your web application, you need to do the following:

1. Download the SiteMesh full source ZIP file from *http://www.opensymphony.com/ sitemesh*. Version 2.2.1 was used for this recipe. Extract the ZIP file into a directory named something like */sitemesh*.

2. Copy all the JAR files from */sitemesh/lib* into your application's *WEB-INF/lib* directory.

3. Add the SiteMesh servlet filter and corresponding filter mapping shown in Example 14-14 to your application's *web.xml* file.

Example 14-14. SiteMesh servlet filter and mapping

```
<!-- Sitemesh Filter -->
<filter>
    <filter-name>sitemesh</filter-name>
    <filter-class>com.opensymphony.module.sitemesh.filter.PageFilter</filter-class>
</filter>

<!-- Sitemesh Filter Mapping -->
<filter-mapping>
    <filter-name>sitemesh</filter-name>
    <url-pattern>/*</url-pattern>
</filter-mapping>
```

4. Create the *decorators.xml* file shown in Example 14-15. Save this file to your application's *WEB-INF* directory.

Example 14-15. SiteMesh decorators configuration file

```
<decorators defaultdir="/decorators">
    <decorator name="main" page="mainDecorator.jsp">
        <pattern>*</pattern>
    </decorator>
    <decorator name="panel" page="panelDecorator.jsp"/>
    <decorator name="popup" page="popupDecorator.jsp"/>
</decorators>
```

You are ready to define the decorating content to be added to your existing JSPs. Create the *web/decorators* directory. This directory, similar to the *layouts* directory used in a Tiles-based application, contains your decorating JSP pages and stylesheet. Example 14-16 shows the *mainDecorator.jsp* page.

Example 14-16. Main decorator JSP page

```
<%@ taglib prefix="decorator" uri="http://www.opensymphony.com/sitemesh/decorator" %>
<%@ taglib prefix="page" uri="http://www.opensymphony.com/sitemesh/page" %>
<%@ taglib prefix="bean" uri="http://struts.apache.org/tags-bean" %>
<%@ taglib prefix="html" uri="http://struts.apache.org/tags-html" %>
<%@ taglib prefix="c" uri="http://java.sun.com/jsp/jstl/core" %>
<html>
    <head>
        <title>
            <decorator:title default="{ Unknown Page - shouldn't see this, since
                                        pages should define title }" />
        </title>
        <html:base/>
        <link href="decorators/main.css" rel="stylesheet" type="text/css">
        <%--pulls the header from the page we are decorating and inserts it here --%>
        <decorator:head />
    </head>

    <body>
        <table width="100%" height="100%">
            <tr>
                <td id="header" colspan="2">
                    <bean:message key="label.header" />
                </td>
            </tr>
            <tr>
                <td valign="top" width="20%">
                    <%-- grabs the navigation.jsp page and decorates with the
                        panel decorator and puts it here --%>
                    <page:applyDecorator page="/WEB-INF/jsps/navigation.jsp"
name="panel" />
                </td>
                <td>
                    <table width="100%" height="100%">
                        <tr>
                            <td id="pageTitle">
                                <div class="pageTitle">
                                    <%--pulls the title from the page we are decorating
                                        and inserts it here --%>
                                    <decorator:title />
                                </div>
                            </td>
                        </tr>
                        <tr>
                            <td valign="top" height="100%">
                                <%--pulls the body from the page we are decorating and
                                    inserts it here --%>
```

Example 14-16. Main decorator JSP page (continued)

```
                            <decorator:body />
                    </td>
                </tr>
            </table>
        </td>
    </tr>
    <tr>
        <td id="footer" colspan="2">
            <bean:message key="label.footer" />
        </td>
    </tr>
    </table>
    </body>
</html>
```

This decorator page references the "panel" decorator defined by the *panelDecorator.jsp* page shown in Example 14-17.

Example 14-17. Simple panel decorator

```
<%@ taglib prefix="decorator" uri="http://www.opensymphony.com/sitemesh/decorator" %>
<decorator:head />
<div class="panelDiv">
    <span class="panelTitle"><decorator:title default="Unknown panel" /></span>
    <br/>
        <%--inserts the body of whatever we are decorating here --%>
    <decorator:body />
</div>
```

Example 14-18 shows the decorator (*popupDecorator.jsp*) used for pop-up windows.

Example 14-18. Decorator for a pop-up window

```
<%@ taglib prefix="decorator" uri="http://www.opensymphony.com/sitemesh/decorator" %>
<html>
    <head>
        <title><decorator:title default="{ Unknown Page - shouldn't see this,
                                since pages should define title }" /></title>
        <link href="<%= request.getContextPath( ) %>/decorators/main.css"
                rel="stylesheet" type="text/css">
        <%--pulls the header from the page we are decorating and inserts it here --%>
        <decorator:head />
    </head>

    <body>
        <div class="popupDiv">
            <span class="popupTitle"><decorator:title
                            default="Unknown Title - shouldn't see this" /></span>
            <br/>
            <%--inserts the body of whatever we are decorating here --%>
            <decorator:body />
        </div>
```

Example 14-18. Decorator for a pop-up window (continued)

```
    </body>
</html>
```

Finally, Example 14-19 shows the *main.css* stylesheet, used by the main decorator,
you need to create.

Example 14-19. CSS stylesheet for the main decorator

```
body, td, p {
    font-family: verdana, arial, helvetica, sans-serif;
    font-size: 12px;
}
.panelDiv {
    border-color: black;
    border-width: 2;
    border-style: solid;
    padding: 4px;
    font-size: 12px;
    color: black;
    background: #COCOCO;
    height: 450px;
}
.panelTitle {
    font-size: 14px;
    font-weight: bold;
}
.popupDiv {
    font-family: verdana, arial, helvetica, sans-serif;
    font-size: 12px;
    background-color:yellow;
}
#pageTitle {
    background-color: #COCOCO;
    color: black;
    font-weight: bold;
    font-size: 14px;
    border-color: black;
    border-width: 1;
    border-style: solid;
    padding: 3px;
}
#header {
    padding: 5px;
    font-size: 16px;
    color: White;
    font-weight: bold;
    background-color: Navy;
    text-align: center;
    height: 75px;
}
#footer {
    border-color: navy;
```

Example 14-19. CSS stylesheet for the main decorator (continued)

```
    border-width: 2;
    border-style: solid;
    font-size: 10px;
    color: black;
    font-weight: bold;
    text-align: center;
    padding-top: 10px;
    background: white;
}
```

The only additional JSP page you need to create is for the sidebar navigation.
Example 14-20 (*navigation.jsp*) shows this JSP page.

Example 14-20. Sidebar navigation JSP page

```
<%@ taglib uri="http://struts.apache.org/tags-bean" prefix="bean" %>
<%@ taglib uri="http://java.sun.com/jsp/jstl/core"  prefix="c" %>
<html>
    <head>
        <title><bean:message key="title.navigation"/></title>
        <script>
            function popUp( url ) {
                var windowFeatures = "scrollbars=yes,resizable=yes,width=300,height=300";
                popUp = window.open(url,"popup",windowFeatures);
                popUp.focus( );
            }
        </script>
    </head>
    <body>
        <br/>
        <c:url var="url" value="/main.do"/>
        <a href="<c:out value='${url}'/>">Main Page</a>
        <br/><br/>
        <c:url var="url" value="/test.do"/>
        <a href="<c:out value='${url}'/>">Test Another Page</a>
        <br/><br/>
        <c:url var="url" value="/summary.do"/>
        <a href="<c:out value='${url}'/>">Summary Example</a>
        <br/><br/>
        <%-- Look at the ParameterDecoratorMapper definition in the sitemesh.xml,
        You will see how it takes a decorator parameter and can take a confirm
parameter --%>
        <c:url var="url" value="/summary.do">
            <c:param name="decorator" value="popup"/>
            <c:param name="confirm" value="true"/>
        </c:url>
        <a href="javascript:popUp( '<c:out value='${url}'/>' );">Summary As PopUp</a>
<br/><br/>
    </body>
</html>
```

After you've created these directories and files, your application's file structure should look something like Figure 14-6.

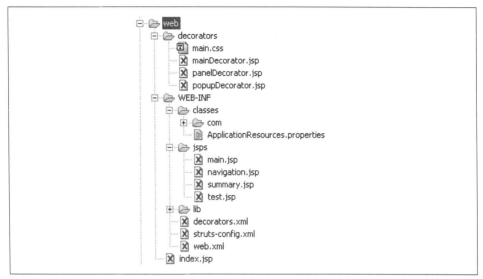

Figure 14-6. Directory structure of a Struts-SiteMesh application

Once you've got all of this in place, you can build and deploy your application. Figure 14-7 shows the main page now decorated by SiteMesh.

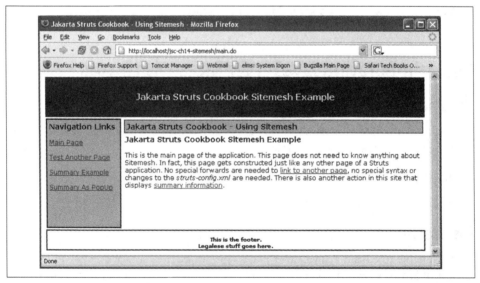

Figure 14-7. Struts-generated JSP decorated using SiteMesh

The pop-up window displayed when you click on the "Summary As PopUp" link is shown in Figure 14-8.

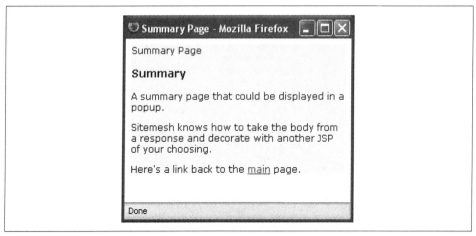

Figure 14-8. Pop-up browser window generated by SiteMesh

See Also

You'll find a good tutorial on using SiteMesh with Struts in one of Rick Reumann's "Struttin' with Struts" lessons at *http://www.reumann.net/struts/ lessons/sitemesh/rr_sitemesh_example.jsp*.

Will Iverson has written a good SiteMesh introduction available at *http://today.java.net/ pub/a/today/2004/03/11/sitemesh.html*.

14.8   Integrating JavaServer Faces with Struts

Problem

You want to migrate an existing Struts application to JavaServer Faces without having to rewrite the entire application.

Solution

Use the Struts-Faces integration library.

Discussion

It's reasonable to consider JavaServer Faces (JSF) to be the "son of Struts." In fact, the creator of Struts, Craig McClanahan, serves as co-lead for the JSF specification. Unlike Struts, JSF specifies a component model for the user interface of applications. Theoretically, that model can be rendered by any type of user interface, and not just a web-based interface. But in its current release, JSF targets web application development.

There are two implementations of JSF available. The reference implementation (RI) has been developed and is distributed by Sun. MyFaces, an open source Apache project, implements the JSF specification and adds additional components not contained in the reference implementation.

Struts-Faces, initially developed by Craig McClanahan, allows you to use JSF technology in a Struts application. Using this library, you can continue to use your actions and action forms as written, but you use the JSF custom tags instead of the Struts tags for the user interface. Struts-Faces allows you to migrate your existing Struts applications to JSF a page at a time.

This recipe will help you get started with Struts-Faces. It applies this technology to a three-page application having an index page, a login page, and a welcome page displayed upon login.

Struts-Faces is under active development. For the latest documentation and code, download the nightly build of Struts-Faces from *http://svn.apache.org/builds/struts/ nightly/struts-faces/*, extracting the archive into a directory on your system:

1. Copy the *struts-faces.jar* and *struts-faces.tld* from the struts-faces/lib directory to your *WEB-INF/lib* directory.

2. Download and extract Sun's JSF reference implementation from *http://java.sun. com/jsf*. At the time of this writing, Version 1.1 was the latest available.

3. Copy the *jsf-api.jar* and *jsf-impl.jar* from the *jsf-1.1/lib* directory to your *WEB-INF/lib* directory.

4. If your application doesn't use JSTL, copy the *jstl.jar* and *standard.jar* files from the *jakarta-struts-1.2.x/lib* directory to your *WEB-INF/lib* directory.

5. Add the servlet declaration and mapping for the JavaServer Faces servlet to your *web.xml* file. Set the load-on-startup value for the FacesServlet so it starts up before the Struts ActionServlet:

```
<!-- Faces Servlet Configuration -->
<servlet>
    <servlet-name>faces</servlet-name>
    <servlet-class>javax.faces.webapp.FacesServlet</servlet-class>
    <load-on-startup>1</load-on-startup>
</servlet>

<!-- Action Servlet Configuration -->
<servlet>
    <servlet-name>action</servlet-name>
    <servlet-class>org.apache.struts.action.ActionServlet</servlet-class>
    <init-param>
        <param-name>config</param-name>
        <param-value>/WEB-INF/struts-config.xml</param-value>
    </init-param>
    <load-on-startup>2</load-on-startup>
</servlet>
```

```
<!-- Servlet Mappings -->
<servlet-mapping>
    <servlet-name>faces</servlet-name>
    <url-pattern>*.faces</url-pattern>
</servlet-mapping>

<servlet-mapping>
    <servlet-name>action</servlet-name>
    <url-pattern>*.do</url-pattern>
</servlet-mapping>
```

The servlet mapping for the Faces servlet directs all requests with a .faces extension through the JSF FacesServlet for standard JSF processing. You will need to configure Struts to use a custom request processor for handling JSF integration. Example 14-21 shows the *struts-config.xml*, which specifies the controller declaration for the FacesRequestProcessor, that includes the action mappings for this example application.

Example 14-21. Struts configuration file that uses Struts-Faces

```
<?xml version="1.0" encoding="ISO-8859-1" ?>

<!DOCTYPE struts-config PUBLIC
        "-//Apache Software Foundation//DTD Struts Configuration 1.1//EN"
        "http://jakarta.apache.org/struts/dtds/struts-config_1_1.dtd">
<struts-config>
    <form-beans>
        <form-bean name="logonForm" type="org.apache.struts.action.DynaActionForm">
            <form-property name="username" type="java.lang.String"/>
            <form-property name="password" type="java.lang.String"/>
        </form-bean>
    </form-beans>

    <global-forwards>
        <forward name="welcome" path="/welcome.faces"/>
        <forward name="logon" path="/logon.faces"/>
        <forward name="home" path="/index.jsp" redirect="true"/>
    </global-forwards>


    <!-- ========== Action Mapping Definitions ============================== -->
    <action-mappings>
        <action    path="/Logon"
                   name="logonForm"
                 scope="request"
                   type="com.oreilly.strutsckbk.ch14.LogonAction">
            <forward name="success" path="welcome.faces"/>
        </action>
    </action-mappings>

    <controller>
        <set-property property="processorClass"
```

```
          value="org.apache.struts.faces.application.FacesRequestProcessor"/>
    </controller>

    <message-resources parameter="ApplicationResources"/>

</struts-config>
```

The first page of the application, shown in Example 14-22 (*index.jsp*), provides a link to the "logon" page. This conventional JSP page doesn't contain any JSF or Struts-Faces components.

Example 14-22. Regular Struts-based index page

```
<%@ page contentType="text/html;charset=UTF-8" language="java" %>
<%@ taglib prefix="c" uri="http://java.sun.com/jstl/core" %>
<%@ taglib prefix="html" uri="http://struts.apache.org/tags-html" %>

<html>
<head>
  <title>Struts Cookbook - Integrating Struts and JSF</title>
</head>
<body>
  <h2>Struts Cookbook - Integrating Struts and JSF</h2>
  <html:link forward="logon">Try out Struts and JSF</html:link>
</body>
</html>
```

The second page, *logon.jsp* shown in Example 14-23, contains the logon form submitted to the */Logon* action.

Example 14-23. Logon page using Struts-Faces components

```
<%@ page contentType="text/html;charset=UTF-8" language="java" %>
<%@ taglib prefix="f" uri="http://java.sun.com/jsf/core" %>
<%@ taglib prefix="h" uri="http://java.sun.com/jsf/html" %>
<%@ taglib prefix="s" uri="http://struts.apache.org/tags-faces" %>

<f:view>
<s:html locale="true">
<head>
  <title>Struts Cookbook - Integrating Struts and JSF</title>
</head>
<body>
  <p />
  <s:form id="logon" action="/Logon"
    focus="username" styleClass="form">
    <h:outputLabel for="username" styleClass="label" value="Username:"/>
    <h:inputText id="username" value="#{logonForm.username}"
          required="true" size="10"/> <p />
    <h:outputLabel for="password" styleClass="label" value="Password:"/>
```

Example 14-23. Logon page using Struts-Faces components (continued)

```
    <h:inputSecret id="password" value="#{logonForm.password}"
            required="true" size="10"/> <p />
    <h:commandButton id="submit" type="SUBMIT" value="Logon" />
  </s:form>
</body>
</s:html>
</f:view>
```

If you've never used JavaServer Faces, this page probably looks funky. The page starts conventionally and declares the `taglib` directives for the JSF *core* and *html* tag libraries, as well as the Struts-Faces tag library.

 To prevent collision with the JSTL *core* tag library, the `taglib` declaration for the JSF *core* tag library commonly uses "f" instead of "c" as the prefix. You can think of "f" as standing for "faces" or "framework."

On this page, the `f:view` tag contains the entire content of the view. All JSF pages must contain a `f:view` tag that encapsulates the custom JSF tags. The `s:form` tag, from the Struts-Faces library, creates an HTML form that can be submitted to a Struts action. The `h:outputLabel` tags display label text for input fields declared with the `h:inputText` tags. The `h:inputSecret` tag creates a password input field. The `h:commandButton` tag creates the form's submit button.

When this page was first written, yours truly inadvertently left off the `value` attribute for the `h:inputText` and `h:inputSecret` tags. As Struts developers, the best practice is to eschew specifying the `value` attribute for tags like `html:text` since the values are automatically retrieved from the form based on name. When this application was tested, data entered on the form wasn't populated to the action form. Because JavaServer Faces uses a different binding convention than Struts, you must explicitly bind each field to a form-bean property. Adding the `value` attributes to the form as shown solved the problem.

The Struts-Faces tags resemble the Struts *html* tag library. By design, Struts developers will find it easy to learn the Struts-Faces tags. The `s:form` tag, for example, closely matches the Struts `html:form` tag. However, with the `s:form` tag, you use the JSF *html* tags instead of the Struts *html* tags. Table 14-2 provides a complete list of tags included with Struts-Faces.

Table 14-2. Struts-Faces tags

Tag name	Description
base	Creates a `<base>` element, similar to the Struts `html:base` tag
commandLink	Creates a hyperlink that can be used to submit a form
errors	Displays accumulated action errors, similar to the Struts `html:errors` tag
form	Creates an HTML form that submits to a Struts action, similar to the Struts `html:form` tag

---

Table 14-2. Struts-Faces tags (continued)

Tag name	Description
html	Generates an `<html>` element with optional locale-sensitivity, similar to the Struts `html:html` tag
javascript	Generates the JavaScript for client-side validation using the Validator, similar to the Struts `html:javascript` tag
loadMessages	Loads messages resources into a map for access by JSF tags such as `h:outputText`
message	Displays a localized message, similar to the `bean:message` tag
stylesheet	Generates a link to a stylesheet
write	Renders a property value from a model object, similar to the `bean:write` tag

The `FacesRequestProcessor` processes the submitted logon form and executes the `LogonAction`. This action doesn't have to do anything special related to JSF. The Struts-Faces library integrates Struts and JSF so your action classes and action forms require no modification when using JSF. Example 14-24 shows the `LogonAction` for this application. A "real" action would authenticate the user.

Example 14-24. Action for logon

```
package com.oreilly.strutsckbk.ch14;
import javax.servlet.http.HttpServletRequest;
import javax.servlet.http.HttpServletResponse;

import org.apache.commons.beanutils.PropertyUtils;
import org.apache.struts.action.Action;
import org.apache.struts.action.ActionForm;
import org.apache.struts.action.ActionForward;
import org.apache.struts.action.ActionMapping;

public class LogonAction extends Action {
    public ActionForward execute(ActionMapping mapping, ActionForm form,
            HttpServletRequest request, HttpServletResponse response)
            throws Exception {
        String name = (String) PropertyUtils.getSimpleProperty(form, "username");
        User user = new User( );
        user.setUsername(name);
        request.getSession( ).setAttribute("user", user);
        return mapping.findForward("success");
    }
}
```

The application culminates by rendering a "welcome" page that includes text from the message resources bundle as well as the username entered on the preceding form. The *welcome.jsp* page, accessed through the *welcome.faces* path, is shown in Example 14-25.

Example 14-25. Rendering HTML with JSF and Struts-Faces tags

```
<%@ page contentType="text/html;charset=UTF-8" language="java" %>
<%@ taglib prefix="f" uri="http://java.sun.com/jsf/core" %>
```

Example 14-25. Rendering HTML with JSF and Struts-Faces tags (continued)

```
<%@ taglib prefix="h" uri="http://java.sun.com/jsf/html" %>
<%@ taglib prefix="s" uri="http://struts.apache.org/tags-faces" %>

<f:view>
<s:loadMessages var="messages"/>
<s:html locale="true">
<head>
  <title>Struts Cookbook - Integrating Struts and JSF</title>
</head>
<body>
  <h2>Struts Cookbook - Integrating Struts and JSF</h2>
  <h3><s:message key="index.welcome"/></h3>
  <h:outputText value="#{messages['msg.loggedIn']}"/>
  <b><h:outputText value="#{user.username}"/></b>.
</body>
</s:html>
</f:view>
```

At this point, you have a working application, which uses Struts and JSF together, that preserves your custom action classes and action forms and allows you to take advantage of the rich components afforded by JavaServer Faces.

See Also

For the latest documentation on Struts-Faces, consult the documentation included with the Struts-Faces nightly build. If you're unsure about using JSF or Struts, Craig McClanahan presents a fair assessment on his blog at *http://java.net/craigmcc*.

You'll find a good article on integrating Struts, JSF, and Tiles on IBM's Developer Works at *http://www-106.ibm.com/developerworks/java/library/j-integrate/*.

The source for information on JavaServer Faces, including the specification and the reference implementation, can be found at *http://java.sun.com/jsf*.

You can use Struts-Faces with any JSF compliant implementation. The MyFaces project (*http://incubator.apache.org/projects/myfaces.html*) implements the JSF specification and provides an alternative to the reference implementation.

You'll find the quick reference for the standard JSF tags at *http://www.horstmann.com/corejsf/jsf-tags.html* to be quite handy.

14.9 Integrating Struts and Velocity

Problem

You want to use a template engine for HTML page generation instead of JSPs in your Struts application.

Solution

Integrate the Velocity template engine into your Struts application, replacing your JSP pages with Velocity templates.

Discussion

The Velocity template engine (*http://jakarta.apache.org/velocity*) can create any kind of textual document by merging Java objects with a template. The template document contains special markup that Velocity parses and replaces with values from Java objects stored in a template context.

When you use Velocity with Struts, instead of forwarding to JSP pages, you forward to a Velocity template. The Velocity servlet services the request, processing the template through the Velocity template engine and returning the generated HTML as the response.

Here's an action, adapted from the Struts MailReader example, that forwards to a Velocity template to display the "Welcome" page:

```
<action    path="/WelcomeVel"
           type="org.apache.struts.webapp.example.WelcomeAction">
    <forward name="failure" path="/Error.jsp" />
    <forward name="success" path="/welcome.vm" />
</action>
```

To use Velocity with Struts, you'll need to download the Velocity distribution from *http://jakarta.apache.org/velocity*. You also need to download the VelocityTools from *http://jakarta.apache.org/velocity/tools/*. VelocityTools includes helper classes that allow you to reference Struts-managed objects such as the action form and message resources. From the Velocity distribution, copy the *velocity-1.4.jar* and the *velocity-dep-1.4.jar* from the Velocity distribution directory to your application's *WEB-INF/ lib* directory. For the VelocityTools */lib* directory, copy the *velocity-tools-1.1.jar*, *velocity-tools-generic-1.1.jar*, *velocity-tools-view-1.1.jar* to your application's *WEB-INF/lib* directory.

Next, declare the Velocity view servlet and servlet mapping in your *web.xml* file. Traditionally, the *.vm* extension is used for Velocity templates. Example 14-26 shows the portion of a *web.xml* file that configure the Velocity servlet.

Example 14-26. VelocityViewServlet declaration and mapping

```
<!-- Velocity View Servlet -->
<servlet>
    <servlet-name>velocity</servlet-name>
    <servlet-class>
        org.apache.velocity.tools.view.servlet.VelocityViewServlet
    </servlet-class>
```

Example 14-26. VelocityViewServlet declaration and mapping (continued)

```
    <init-param>
        <param-name>org.apache.velocity.toolbox</param-name>
        <param-value>/WEB-INF/toolbox.xml</param-value>
    </init-param>

    <init-param>
        <param-name>org.apache.velocity.properties</param-name>
        <param-value>/WEB-INF/velocity.properties</param-value>
    </init-param>

    <load-on-startup>2</load-on-startup>
</servlet>
...
<!-- Map *.vm files to Velocity -->
<servlet-mapping>
    <servlet-name>velocity</servlet-name>
    <url-pattern>*.vm</url-pattern>
</servlet-mapping>
```

Velocity has the notion of a toolbox containing tools you can use in your templates. A tool is essentially a Java class you can reference by name. The */WEB-INF/ toolbox.xml* file, shown in Example 14-27, declares the Struts tools available to your templates.

Example 14-27. Toolbox containing the Velocity-Struts tools

```
<?xml version="1.0"?>
<!--
  Copyright 2003-2004 The Apache Software Foundation.

  Licensed under the Apache License, Version 2.0 (the "License");
  you may not use this file except in compliance with the License.
  You may obtain a copy of the License at

      http://www.apache.org/licenses/LICENSE-2.0

  Unless required by applicable law or agreed to in writing, software
  distributed under the License is distributed on an "AS IS" BASIS,
  WITHOUT WARRANTIES OR CONDITIONS OF ANY KIND, either express or implied.
  See the License for the specific language governing permissions and
  limitations under the License.

  $Id: ch14,v 1.3 2004/11/18 13:28:26 jhawks Exp mhutchin $
-->
<toolbox>

    <tool>
        <key>math</key>
        <scope>application</scope>
        <class>org.apache.velocity.tools.generic.MathTool</class>
    </tool>
```

Example 14-27. Toolbox containing the Velocity-Struts tools (continued)

```
<tool>
    <key>link</key>
    <class>org.apache.velocity.tools.struts.StrutsLinkTool</class>
</tool>

<!-- ordinarily the SecureLinkTool would simply replace the StrutsLinkTool
     if SSL Ext. is in use - in that case the key would be 'link' but it's
     'slink' here to distinguish between the two. -->
<tool>
    <key>slink</key>
    <class>org.apache.velocity.tools.struts.SecureLinkTool</class>
</tool>

<tool>
    <key>text</key>
    <class>org.apache.velocity.tools.struts.MessageTool</class>
</tool>

<tool>
    <key>link</key>
    <scope>request</scope>
    <class>org.apache.velocity.tools.struts.StrutsLinkTool</class>
</tool>

<tool>
    <key>errors</key>
    <class>org.apache.velocity.tools.struts.ErrorsTool</class>
</tool>

<tool>
    <key>messages</key>
    <class>org.apache.velocity.tools.struts.ActionMessagesTool</class>
</tool>

<tool>
    <key>text</key>
    <scope>request</scope>
    <class>org.apache.velocity.tools.struts.MessageTool</class>
</tool>

<tool>
    <key>form</key>
    <class>org.apache.velocity.tools.struts.FormTool</class>
</tool>

<tool>
    <key>tiles</key>
    <class>org.apache.velocity.tools.struts.TilesTool</class>
</tool>

<tool>
    <key>validator</key>
```

Example 14-27. Toolbox containing the Velocity-Struts tools (continued)

```
        <class>org.apache.velocity.tools.struts.ValidatorTool</class>
    </tool>

</toolbox>
```

For each tool, the key element specifies the name that the tool can be referenced by within your Velocity template. The */WEB-INF/velocity.properties* contains general configuration information used by the Velocity view servlet. You can use these properties to control Velocity's log level and other settings.

```
#*
 * Copyright 2003 The Apache Software Foundation.
 *
 * Licensed under the Apache License, Version 2.0 (the "License");
 * you may not use this file except in compliance with the License.
 * You may obtain a copy of the License at
 *
 *     http://www.apache.org/licenses/LICENSE-2.0
 *
 * Unless required by applicable law or agreed to in writing, software
 * distributed under the License is distributed on an "AS IS" BASIS,
 * WITHOUT WARRANTIES OR CONDITIONS OF ANY KIND, either express or implied.
 * See the License for the specific language governing permissions and
 * limitations under the License.
 *
 * $Id: ch14,v 1.3 2004/11/18 13:28:26 jhawks Exp mhutchin $
 *#


#----------------------------------------------------------------------------
# These are the default properties for the
# Velocity Runtime. These values are used when
# Runtime.init( ) is called, and when Runtime.init(properties)
# fails to find the specified properties file.
#----------------------------------------------------------------------------


#----------------------------------------------------------------------------
# R U N T I M E   L O G
#----------------------------------------------------------------------------
# Velocity uses the Servlet APIs logging facilites.

#----------------------------------------------------------------------------
# This controls if Runtime.error(), info() and warn( ) messages include the
# whole stack trace. The last property controls whether invalid references
# are logged.
#----------------------------------------------------------------------------

runtime.log.error.stacktrace = false
runtime.log.warn.stacktrace = false
runtime.log.info.stacktrace = false
runtime.log.invalid.reference = true
```

```
#----------------------------------------------------------------------
# T E M P L A T E   E N C O D I N G
#----------------------------------------------------------------------

input.encoding=ISO-8859-1
output.encoding=ISO-8859-1


#----------------------------------------------------------------------
# F O R E A C H   P R O P E R T I E S
#----------------------------------------------------------------------
# These properties control how the counter is accessed in the #foreach
# directive. By default the reference $velocityCount will be available
# in the body of the #foreach directive. The default starting value
# for this reference is 1.
#----------------------------------------------------------------------

directive.foreach.counter.name = velocityCount
directive.foreach.counter.initial.value = 1


#----------------------------------------------------------------------
# I N C L U D E   P R O P E R T I E S
#----------------------------------------------------------------------
# These are the properties that governed the way #include'd content
# is governed.
#----------------------------------------------------------------------

directive.include.output.errormsg.start = <!-- include error :
directive.include.output.errormsg.end   =  see error log -->


#----------------------------------------------------------------------
# P A R S E   P R O P E R T I E S
#----------------------------------------------------------------------

directive.parse.max.depth = 10


#----------------------------------------------------------------------
# VELOCIMACRO PROPERTIES
#----------------------------------------------------------------------
# global : name of default global library.  It is expected to be in the regular
# template path.  You may remove it (either the file or this property) if
# you wish with no harm.
#----------------------------------------------------------------------
#dev-changes by Marino
webapp.resource.loader.cache = false
velocimacro.library.autoreload = true

velocimacro.library = /WEB-INF/VM_global_library.vm,/WEB-INF/Validator_library.vm
```

```
velocimacro.permissions.allow.inline = true
velocimacro.permissions.allow.inline.to.replace.global = false
velocimacro.permissions.allow.inline.local.scope = false

velocimacro.context.localscope = false


#----------------------------------------------------------------------------
# INTERPOLATION
#----------------------------------------------------------------------------
# turn off and on interpolation of references and directives in string
# literals.  ON by default :)
#----------------------------------------------------------------------------
runtime.interpolate.string.literals = true



#----------------------------------------------------------------------------
# RESOURCE MANAGEMENT
#----------------------------------------------------------------------------
# Allows alternative ResourceManager and ResourceCache implementations
# to be plugged in.
#----------------------------------------------------------------------------
resource.manager.class = org.apache.velocity.runtime.resource.ResourceManagerImpl
resource.manager.cache.class = org.apache.velocity.runtime.resource.ResourceCacheImp
```

Now, you create the Velocity template itself. Suppose you wanted to replace a JSP page with an equivalent Velocity template. Example 14-28 shows the *welcome.jsp* page from the Struts MailReader application.

Example 14-28. Welcome page from the Struts example application

```
<%@ page contentType="text/html;charset=UTF-8" language="java" %>
<%@ taglib uri="/tags/struts-bean" prefix="bean" %>
<%@ taglib uri="/tags/struts-html" prefix="html" %>

<html>
<head>
<title><bean:message key="index.title"/></title>
<link rel="stylesheet" type="text/css" href="base.css" />
</head>

<h3><bean:message key="index.heading"/></h3>
<ul>
<li><html:link action="/EditRegistration?action=Create"><bean:message key="index.
registration"/></html:link></li>
<li><html:link action="/Logon"><bean:message key="index.logon"/></html:link></li>
</ul>

<h3>Language Options</h3>
<ul>
<li><html:link action="/Locale?language=en">English</html:link></li>
<li><html:link action="/Locale?language=ja" useLocalEncoding="true">Japanese</html:link></
li>
```

Example 14-28. Welcome page from the Struts example application (continued)

```
<li><html:link action="/Locale?language=ru"
  useLocalEncoding="true">Russian</html:link></li>
</ul>

<hr />

<p><html:img bundle="alternate" pageKey="struts.logo.path" altKey="struts.logo.alt"/></p>

<p><html:link action="/Tour"><bean:message key="index.tour"/></html:link></p>

</body>
</html>
```

Example 14-29 shows this same page implemented as a Velocity template (*welcome.vm*).

Example 14-29. Welcome page implemented as a Velocity template

```
#*
 * These are comments and will be ignored by the Velocity engine.
 *#
<html>
<head>
<title>$text.get("index.title")</title>
<link rel="stylesheet" type="text/css" href="base.css" />
</head>

<h3>$text.get("index.heading")</h3>
<ul>
<li>
    <a href="$link.setAction('/EditRegistration').addQueryData('action','Create')">
        $text.get("index.registration")
    </a>
<li>
    <a href="$link.setAction('/Logon')">
        $text.get("index.logon")
    </a>
</ul>

<h3>Language Options</h3>
<ul>
<li><a href="$link.setAction('/Locale').addQueryData('language','en')">English</a></li>
<li><a href="$link.setAction('/Locale').addQueryData('language','ja')">Japanese</a></li>
<li><a href="$link.setAction('/Locale').addQueryData('language','ru')">Russian</a></li>
</ul>

<hr />

<p><a href="$link.setAction('/Tour')">$text.get("index.tour")</a></p>

</body>
</html>
```

When you build and deploy this modified Struts MailReader application, you'll see that this page looks and behaves exactly as it does when implemented as a JSP page, and no changes had to be made to any Struts actions or action forms.

See Also

The Velocity project site is located at *http://jakarta.apache.org/velocity*. From here, you can download Velocity and the VelocityTools used in this recipe. You'll also find several essays that compare Velocity to JSP and other page-generation technologies.

14.10 Integrating Struts and XSLT

Problem

You want to use XSL transformations for HTML page generation instead of JSP pages in your Struts application.

Solution

Use the STXX framework with Struts.

Discussion

The Struts for Transforming XML with XSL (STXX) framework was developed by Don Brown. (The STXX project site can be found at *http://stxx.sourceforge.net*.) STXX fits into Struts in a manner similar to Velocity. Instead of forwarding requests to JSP pages, your action forwards to a special URL that is processed by the StxxRequestProcessor. Based on request data, this custom request processor reads a configuration file to determine the corresponding XSLT stylesheet. The request processor then uses an XSLT transformation engine to transform the received XML data, using the XSLT stylesheet, into XHTML.

 XHTML is HTML that is well-formed, valid XML. XHTML is specified by the World Wide Web Consortium (W3C); details can be found at *http://www.w3.org/MarkUp/*.

To get started, download STXX from the project web site (*http://stxx.sourceforge.net*). This recipe was built using the full download of STXX Version 1.3. Extract the download to your system.

Copy the following JAR files to your application's *WEB-INF/lib* directory:

- *dist/stxx-1.3.jar*
- *libs/core/jdom.jar*
- *libs/xform/commons-jxpath-1.1.jar*
- *libs/xform/xmlform.jar*

The configuration of STXX is specified in the *stxx.properties* file. For this recipe, you can use this file without modification. From the STXX directory, copy *source/web/WEB-INF/classes/stxx.properties* to your application's *WEB-INF/classes* directory. STXX uses the concept of *pipelines* to chain transformations together. The *stxx-pipelines.xml* controls how the pipelines work. For this recipe, copy the *source/web/WEB-INF/stxx-pipelines.xml* file to your application's */WEB-INF* directory.

As shown in Example 14-30, add an initialization parameter specifying the location of the *stxx.properties* file to the Struts `ActionServlet` declaration in your *web.xml* file.

Example 14-30. Adding STXX to your application's web.xml

```
<!DOCTYPE web-app
    PUBLIC "-//Sun Microsystems, Inc.//DTD Web Application 2.2//EN"
    "http://java.sun.com/j2ee/dtds/web-app_2_2.dtd">

<web-app>
    <display-name>Struts Cookbook - Chapter 14 : STXX</display-name>

    <!-- Standard Action Servlet Configuration (with debugging) -->
    <servlet>
        <servlet-name>action</servlet-name>
        <servlet-class>org.apache.struts.action.ActionServlet</servlet-class>
        <init-param>
            <param-name>config</param-name>
            <param-value>/WEB-INF/struts-config.xml</param-value>
        </init-param>
        <init-param>
            <param-name>stxxInit</param-name>
            <param-value>/stxx.properties</param-value>
        </init-param>
        <load-on-startup>2</load-on-startup>
    </servlet>

    <!-- Standard Action Servlet Mapping -->
    <servlet-mapping>
        <servlet-name>action</servlet-name>
        <url-pattern>*.do</url-pattern>
    </servlet-mapping>

    <!-- The Usual Welcome File List -->
    <welcome-file-list>
        <welcome-file>index.jsp</welcome-file>
    </welcome-file-list>

</web-app>
```

You configure the integration between Struts and STXX in your Struts configuration file. Example 14-31 shows the *struts-config.xml* used for this sample application.

Example 14-31. Integrating Struts and STXX in a Struts configuration file

```xml
<?xml version="1.0" encoding="ISO-8859-1" ?>

<!DOCTYPE struts-config PUBLIC
        "-//Apache Software Foundation//DTD Struts Configuration 1.2//EN"
        "http://jakarta.apache.org/struts/dtds/struts-config_1_2.dtd">

<struts-config>

    <form-beans>
        <form-bean name="userForm" type="com.oroad.stxx.xform.JDOMForm"/>
    </form-beans>

    <global-exceptions>
    </global-exceptions>

    <global-forwards>
    </global-forwards>

    <action-mappings>
        <action    path="/viewUserList"
                 type="com.oreilly.strutsckbk.ch14.UserListAction">
            <forward name="success" path="simple/viewUserList.dox"/>
        </action>
        <action    path="/addUser"
                  name="userForm"
                 scope="request"
               forward="simple/addUser.dox"
        />
        <action    path="/saveUser"
                  type="com.oreilly.strutsckbk.ch14.SaveUserAction"
                  name="userForm"
                 scope="request">
            <forward name="success" path="/viewUserList.do"/>
        </action>
    </action-mappings>

    <message-resources parameter="ApplicationResources"
                         factory="com.oroad.stxx.util.PropertyMessageResourcesFactory"/>

    <plug-in className="com.oreilly.strutsckbk.ch14.DataLoadPlugIn"/>

    <plug-in className="com.oroad.stxx.plugin.StxxPlugin" >
        <set-property property="pipeline-config"
                         value="/WEB-INF/stxx-pipelines.xml" />
        <set-property property="xmlform-models"
                         value="/WEB-INF/xmlform-models.xml" />
        <set-property property="xmlform-schema"
                         value="" />
    </plug-in>

</struts-config>
```

In a STXX application, your action form holds XML data. STXX provides two specialized classes that wrap XML data in an `ActionForm`. The contained XML can be represented as a traditional DOM object using the `DOMForm` or as a JDOM object using `JDOMForm`. JDOM provides a more natural API than DOM, so the `JDOMForm` was used in this recipe.

```
<form-bean name="userForm" type="com.oroad.stxx.xform.JDOMForm"/>
```

This `form-bean` element references an XML model that describes the XML structure of the form data. The XML models for your application are defined in the *WEB-INF/ xmlform-models.xml* file. Example 14-32 shows the model, representing user information, used in this recipe.

Example 14-32. XML models used by STXX

```
<document>
  <model name="userForm">
    <user>
      <name>
          <firstname />
          <lastname />
      </name>
      <email />
    </user>
  </model>
</document>
```

A custom action in STXX performs the same functions as in a conventional Struts application: you retrieve data from the form, access the model, and forward to a destination. For STXX, the pattern can be specifically laid out as follows:

1. Retrieve the `ActionForm` and extract the form data as a DOM or JDOM object.
2. Access the business model to retrieve data.
3. Format the data into an XML in-memory representation.
4. Forward the request to a STXX transformation pipeline.

The actions defined in Example 14-31 represent a typical flow common to most web applications. The first action, */viewUserList*, displays data on a page. The second action, */addUser*, presents a form where a user can input data. The third action, */saveUser*, saves the data in the model and forwards back to the first action.

Here's the first action mapping:

```
<action    path="/viewUserList"
           type="com.oreilly.strutsckbk.ch14.UserListAction">
    <forward name="success" path="simple/viewUserList.dox"/>
</action>
```

The `UserListAction`, shown in Example 14-33, retrieves data stored in application-scope and builds a JDOM document from it. The action saves the document in the request and forwards to "success."

Example 14-33. Action that prepares an XML document

```
package com.oreilly.strutsckbk.ch14;

import java.util.Iterator;
import java.util.List;

import com.oroad.stxx.action.Action;

import javax.servlet.http.*;

import org.jdom.*;
import org.apache.struts.action.*;

public class UserListAction extends Action {
    public ActionForward execute(ActionMapping mapping,
                                ActionForm form,
                                HttpServletRequest request,
                                HttpServletResponse response)
            throws Exception {

        List usersList = (List) getServlet().getServletContext().getAttribute("users");

        //create a new XML document for this Action with the root
        //element of "userList"
        Document document =
        new Document(new Element("userList"));

        //add some data to the XML document so that the Action
        //will produce XML in the form
        Element users = new Element("users");

        for (Iterator k=usersList.iterator(); k.hasNext(); ) {
            Element user = new Element("user");
            Element name = new Element("name");
            User u = (User) k.next();
            name.addContent(new Element("firstname").setText(u.getFirstName()));
            name.addContent(new Element("lastname").setText(u.getLastName()));
            user.addContent(name);
            user.addContent(new Element("email").setText(u.getEmail()));

            // add the user
            users.addContent(user);
        }

        // add to the root element and save the document
        document.getRootElement().addContent(users);
        saveDocument(request, document);

        return mapping.findForward("success");
    }
}
```

The success forward specifies a path of *simple/viewUserList.dox*. The forward is processed by STXX and matched against patterns in the *stxx-pipelines.xml* file. In this example, the matching pattern defines a simple XML to XHTML transformation using an XSL stylesheet:

```
<pipeline match="simple/*.dox">
    <display-name>Simple XSLT</display-name>
    <description>Performs simple XSLT transformations</description>
    <transform type="html">
        <param name="path" value="/xsl/{1}.xsl" />
        <param name="render" value="server" />
    </transform>
</pipeline>
```

The first param element specifies the context-relative path to the XSL stylesheet. The value contains a substitution value retrieved from the wildcard-matched path.

 If the {1} notation looks familiar, that's because it's the same wildcard-matching approach shown in Recipe 7.8. Wildcard mappings, as well as the STXX pipeline approach, originated in the Apache Cocoon project.

In this case, the transformation uses the *xsl/viewUserList.xsl* stylesheet shown in Example 14-34.

Example 14-34. XSL stylesheet that renders the user list

```
<xsl:stylesheet version="1.0"
    xmlns:xsl="http://www.w3.org/1999/XSL/Transform">

<xsl:output method="html" />

<xsl:template match="/">
    <xsl:apply-templates select="stxx/userList"/>
</xsl:template>

<xsl:template match="userList">
    <html>
        <body>
            <table width="75%" border="1" align="center">
                <tr>
                    <td bgcolor="lightblue" align="center">
                        <a href="./xsl/viewUserList.xsl">View XSL</a>
                    </td>
                    <td bgcolor="lightblue" align="center">
                        <a href="./index.jsp">
                            <xsl:value-of
    select="/stxx/applicationResources/key[@name='link.index']"/>
                        </a>
                    </td>
                    <td bgcolor="lightblue" align="center">
                        <a href="./addUser.do">
```

Example 14-34. XSL stylesheet that renders the user list (continued)

```
                                <xsl:value-of
    select="/stxx/applicationResources/key[@name='link.add.user']"/>
                                </a>
                            </td>
                        </tr>
                        <xsl:apply-templates select="users"/>
                    </table>
                </body>
            </html>
        </xsl:template>

    <xsl:template match="users">
        <tr bgcolor="lightgrey">
            <td><b>First Name</b></td>
            <td><b>Last Name</b></td>
            <td><b>Email</b></td>
        </tr>
        <xsl:apply-templates select="user"/>
    </xsl:template>

    <xsl:template match="user">
        <tr>
            <td><xsl:value-of select="./name/firstname"/></td>
            <td><xsl:value-of select="./name/lastname"/></td>
            <td><xsl:value-of select="./email"/></td>
        </tr>
    </xsl:template>
</xsl:stylesheet>
```

Figure 14-9 shows the page that gets displayed when you access the */viewUserList* action.

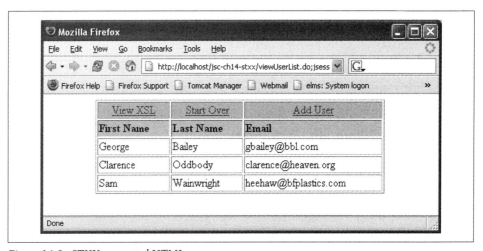

Figure 14-9. STXX-generated HTML page

Clicking the "Add User" link sends a request to the */addUser* action:

```
<action    path="/addUser"
           name="userForm"
          scope="request"
        forward="simple/addUser.dox"
/>
```

STXX processes this request through the *xsl/addUser.xsl* stylesheet shown in Example 14-35.

Example 14-35. XSL stylesheet that generates an HTML form

```
<xsl:stylesheet version="1.0" xmlns:xsl="http://www.w3.org/1999/XSL/Transform">
    <xsl:output method="html" />
    <xsl:template match="/">
        <html>
        <body>
            <form action="saveUser.do">
                <table width="75%" border="1" align="center">
                    <tr bgcolor="lightgrey">
                        <td colspan="2"><b>Add User</b>
                            <a href="./xsl/addUser.xsl"> (View XSL) </a>
                        </td>
                    </tr>
                    <tr>
                        <td><font color="red">*</font>First name:</td>
                        <td>
                            <input type="text" name="user/name/firstname"
                                    value="{stxx/form/userForm/user/name/firstname}"/>
                        </td>
                    </tr>
                    <tr>
                        <td><font color="red">*</font>Last name:</td>
                        <td>
                            <input type="text" name="user/name/lastname"
                                    value="{stxx/form/userForm/user/name/lastname}"/>
                        </td>
                    </tr>
                    <tr>
                        <td><font color="red">*</font>Email:</td>
                        <td>
                            <input type="text" name="user/email"
                                    value="{stxx/form/userForm/user/email}"/>
                        </td>
                    </tr>
                    <tr align="center">
                        <td colspan="2">
                            <input type="submit" value="Submit"/>
                        </td>
                    </tr>
                </table>
            </form>
        </body>
```

Example 14-35. XSL stylesheet that generates an HTML form (continued)

```
        </html>
    </xsl:template>
</xsl:stylesheet>
```

Unlike a conventional Struts application, STXX doesn't use the Commons BeanUtils classes to populate the `ActionForm`. Instead, it treats the `name` attribute as an XPath expression into the XML form model specified for the action form.

Figure 14-10 shows the rendered form for adding a user.

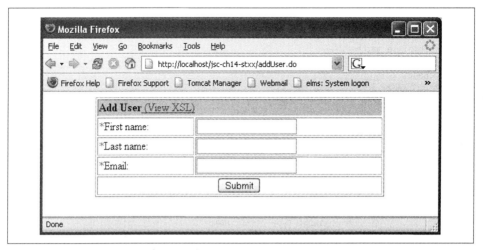

Figure 14-10. STXX-generated HTML form

The */saveUser* action receives and processes this form:

```
<action     path="/saveUser"
            type="com.oreilly.strutsckbk.ch14.SaveUserAction"
            name="userForm"
            scope="request">
    <forward name="success" path="/viewUserList.do"/>
</action>
```

The `SaveUserAction`, shown in Example 14-36, extracts the data from the JDOM-backed form and updates the model stored in the servlet context.

Example 14-36. Action that retrieves XML data from an action form

```
package com.oreilly.strutsckbk.ch14;

import java.util.List;

import javax.servlet.http.HttpServletRequest;
import javax.servlet.http.HttpServletResponse;
```

Example 14-36. Action that retrieves XML data from an action form (continued)

```
import org.apache.struts.action.ActionForm;
import org.apache.struts.action.ActionForward;
import org.apache.struts.action.ActionMapping;

import com.oroad.stxx.action.Action;
import com.oroad.stxx.xform.JDOMForm;

public class SaveUserAction extends Action {
    public ActionForward execute(ActionMapping mapping,
                                 ActionForm form,
                                 HttpServletRequest request,
                                 HttpServletResponse response)
            throws Exception {

        List usersList = (List) getServlet().getServletContext().getAttribute("users");
        JDOMForm jdomForm = (JDOMForm) form;
        String firstName = jdomForm.getValue("/user/name/firstname");
        String lastName  = jdomForm.getValue("/user/name/lastname");
        String email     = jdomForm.getValue("/user/email");
        usersList.add(new User(firstName, lastName, email));
        return mapping.findForward("success");
    }
}
```

The sample application shown in this recipe represents a fraction of the capabilities of STXX. STXX supports validation, XForms, SOAP, FOP, and Velocity just to name a few. If you have a site that relies heavily on XML-based data, and needs to render that data in a number of formats, STXX may be what you need.

See Also

The STXX project web site (*http://stxx.sourceforge.net*) has complete details on the full functionality of STXX.

The StrutsCX project (*http://it.cappuccinonet.com/strutscx*) is another popular Struts-XSL integration framework.

Index

We'd like to hear your suggestions for improving our indexes. Send email to *index@oreilly.com*.

HTML, tag characters *(continued)*
  parsers for error correction, 83
  rendering data containing, 81–83
html-el tags, 66
html:form tag, target attribute, 100
html:frame tag, 100
html:html tag, locale attribute, 379
html:image tag, 69
html:link tag, 97
  documentation web site, 98
  request parameters, adding, 98–99
  target attribute, 100
  URLs include module name, 41
html:multibox control, 90
html:rewrite tag, 97
  request parameters, adding, 98–99
  session token generation with disabled
    cookies, 203
  URLs include module name, 41
html:text tag, 66
HTTP
  GET method, 104
  over SSL (see HTTPS)
  POST method, 104
HTTPS (HTTP over SSL), 358, 363
  security requirements by individual
    page, 371–374
HttpSessionListener interface, 191

I

iBATIS framework
  API, 300
  data access object utilizing, 299
  SQL maps, 296–301
    configuration file, 297
    configuration properties, 297
    UserSqlMap.xml file, 298
images
  html:image tag, 69
  locale-specific, 394–396
  using Java, 115
indexed properties
  displaying in JSP pages, 58–61
  fields, creating for, 67
  forms, using on, 61–66
  JSTL c:forEach loop, 66–69
  nested simple property, setting, 65
  struts-user mailing list, 238
  validation error problems, 237
input validation, 217–256

interfaces
  HttpSessionAttributeListener, 193
  HttpSessionBindingListener, 195
  HttpSessionListener, 191
  ServletContextListener, 189
  wizard-style, 202
internationalization (see localization)
intRange validator, 236
introspection utilities of BeanUtils
    package, 152

J

Jakarta Commons
  BeanUtils package, 61
  FileUpload project, 214
Jakarta ORO project regular expression
    engine, 227
Jakarta Taglibs
  JSTL reference implementation, 55
  project web site, 37
Java objects
  comparing with BeanComparator, 125
  mapped to SQL statements, 296–301
  transparent persistence with Hibernate
    framework, 305
Java Platform Debugger Architecture (see
    JPDA)
JavaBeans
  accessing public static variables with, 37
  ActionForm class, 138
  data collection example, 128
  language choices example, 84
  weather-related data example, 109
  WebLink, 62
JavaScript
  business rules not in, 78
  calling function in HTML from Struts, 71
  complex data structures, populating, 71
  double-clicks, preventing, 210
  forms, submitting using example, 78
  generating dynamically, 70–71
  options
    changeOptions event handler,
      resetting, 72
    dynamically changing select, 72–77
    onchange event handler, changing set
      at runtime, 72
  URLs, generating, 97
  window.open( ) function, 97
JavaServer Faces (see JSF)

About the Author

Bill Siggelkow is an independent consultant specializing in software design, development, and technical training. Bill is an active member of the Atlanta Struts User Group (*http://www.struts-atlanta.org*) and frequently serves as a presenter for the group. With nearly 20 years of development experience, he has designed and developed systems for the manufacturing, energy-marketing, e-commerce, and financial-service industries.

Bill enjoys training and mentoring developers in the art of object-oriented programming and web development. He lives in Atlanta, Georgia, and has a degree in industrial engineering from Georgia Tech.

Colophon

Our look is the result of reader comments, our own experimentation, and feedback from distribution channels. Distinctive covers complement our distinctive approach to technical topics, breathing personality and life into potentially dry subjects.

The animal on the cover of *Jakarta Struts Cookbook* is a tragopan. Tragopans, or horned pheasants, are found along the Himalayas from Kashmir to central and southeastern China. Male tragopans are among the world's most spectacular birds because of their brilliant array of colors and spots, long crown feathers, and blue crests. In villages near the Great Himalayan National Park, the western tragopan has earned the local name Jujurana, or "the king of the birds." There, legend has it that when this pheasant was created, every bird in the universe donated a feather to give it color and unparalleled beauty. Female tragopans, on the other hand, are rather dull looking. Even breeders sometimes find it difficult to distinguish hens of one species from those of another.

Tragopans feed on insects, leaves, sprouts, and seeds, and are thought to be monogamous. Although incubation is done entirely by the female, the male may assist in tending the chicks. Most tragopans are good breeders in captivity, adapting well to various cold-weather climates and becoming quite tame.

There are five species of tragopans, four of which are in danger of extinction due to the destruction of their habitats. Unlike most fowl, tragopans live at very high elevations ranging from 925 to 3,650 meters. In the winter, they are typically found in the thickest parts of pine trees, but during mating season, they travel upward to the extreme limits of the forest. Finding a high branch, the male western tragopan establishes a territorial perch from which he calls at five-minute intervals. His call, which some have described as similar to that of a goose or young lamb, can be heard for more than a mile.

Matt Hutchinson was the production editor for *Jakarta Struts Cookbook*. GEX, Inc. provided production services. Darren Kelly, Mary Anne Weeks Mayo, and Claire Cloutier provided quality control.

Ellie Volckhausen designed the cover of this book, based on a series design by Edie Freedman. The cover image is a 19th-century engraving from the Dover Pictorial Archive. Emma Colby produced the cover layout with Adobe InDesign CS using Adobe's ITC Garamond font.

David Futato designed the interior layout, based on his own series design. This book was converted by Julie Hawks to FrameMaker 5.5.6 with a format conversion tool created by Erik Ray, Jason McIntosh, Neil Walls, and Mike Sierra that uses Perl and XML technologies. The text font is Linotype Birka; the heading font is Adobe Myriad Condensed; and the code font is LucasFont's TheSans Mono Condensed. The illustrations that appear in the book were produced by Robert Romano and Jessamyn Read using Macromedia FreeHand MX and Adobe Photoshop CS. The tip and warning icons were drawn by Christopher Bing. This colophon was written by Lydia Onofrei.

Better than e-books

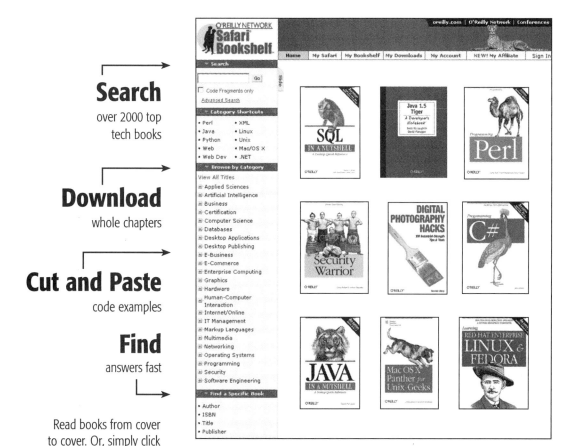

Search
over 2000 top
tech books

Download
whole chapters

Cut and Paste
code examples

Find
answers fast

Read books from cover
to cover. Or, simply click
to the page you need.

**Search Safari! The premier electronic reference
library for programmers and IT professionals**